Integrated Wealth Management

The New Direction for Portfolio Managers

Integrated Wealth Management

The New Direction for Portfolio Managers

Jean L.P. Brunel, CFA

Published by

Institutional Investor Books

a division of Euromoney Institutional Investor Plc

Published by
Euromoney Institutional Investor Plc
Nestor House
Playhouse Yard
London EC4V 5EX
United Kingdom

Telephone: +44 (0)20 7779 8544
E-mail: books@euromoneyplc.com
www.euromoneybooks.com

Copyright © 2002 Jean L.P. Brunel, CFA

Reprinted in 2003

ISBN 1 85564 923 3

Typeset by Julie Foster
Printed in England by Hobbs the Printers

To Debbie, Karen, Pierre, Thierry and Emmanuelle;

Work brings freedom
Freedom begets responsibility.

Contents

Contents

Acknowledgments

I express my gratitude to many individuals who have inspired or motivated me to go on with this project. The first person must be the late Nick Potter, formerly head of J.P. Morgan's Asset Management Group. Nick unfortunately passed away recently, before he knew that I was writing this book, but I nevertheless owe him a huge debt of gratitude. He was my mentor through my career at Morgan and gave me the opportunity to become the private bank's chief investment officer, without which I would probably never have gravitated toward the world of private asset management. Also, I would like to express my thanks to current and former clients, without whose prodding I might not have developed the insights I can now discuss, and whose names I cannot mention, in order to maintain the confidentiality that I know they all value. It also behooves me to thank all the authors whose work is referenced in the book. I have benefited a great deal from their insights, delivered either through these papers or in individual conversations. I would also like to thank colleagues and peers, at J.P. Morgan and U.S. Bank, too numerous to be mentioned here individually, whose suggestions and challenges have also helped me develop the ideas discussed in this book.

Paul Dow and Tom Plumb, former colleagues at U.S. Bank, as well as Pat Flavin, an old friend, colleague, and one-time boss at J.P. Morgan, encouraged me to write this book, arguing that there was a story to be told. Craig Ruff of the Association for Investment Management and Research saw the outline and pushed me to proceed, suggesting that the book would be a good compendium of the critical issues and potential solutions. So did a number of members of AIMR's Private Client Task Force, such as Leslie Kiefer, Bob Luck and Chris Kehoe, to name only a few. Gauri Goyal who, as the first publisher of the *Journal of Wealth Management*, hired me as its editor, also proved an important early supporter and helped me frame the issues in a way that was more likely to be of interest to my intended readership.

Jose Peris, also of U.S. Bank, played a determining part in the organization and the flow of the book, agreeing to review the initial drafts, and prodding me to offer principles and then examples. He was a critical help when I was trying to structure my thoughts. Mark Cirilli similarly provided much appreciated critical comments and ideas, which I am sure have made this book better than it would otherwise have been. Across the Atlantic, my Monegasque friend, Lotfi Maktouf, inspired me to move beyond a narrow U.S. focus, showing me the appeal of more sophisticated wealth management approaches to families residing around the Mediterranean basin.

I owe a debt of particular gratitude to Charlotte Beyer, the founder of the Institute for Private Investors, who agreed to write the foreword to the book. She was enough of a friend to tell me when I needed to rewrite it to make the book more reader-friendly. Liz Gray and Allison Adams, respectively my editor and the current publisher of the *Journal of Wealth Management*, also provided invaluable help and were both sterling examples of patience. Sara Hamilton and Mary-Jane Frederickson also deserve mention here, as they both patiently provided unique insights and perspectives.

Several close French friends, the Brouillots, Ferons, Lemiesles and Schebats, and our four children, none of whom is even involved in the world of investment management, also deserve sincere thanks. They had the patience to put up with me when, at home in Minnesota or vacationing in Florida or southern France, I spent countless hours at the keyboard of my laptop, rather than sharing precious time by the pool, in the garden or walking in the countryside. Finally, last but not least, my wife Debbie had to labor through a seemingly infinite number of drafts, and offer both the conceptual and the proofreading help without which, I suspect, the book would never have been completed.

Jean L.P. Brunel, CFA
January 2002

The author

Mr Brunel is the managing principal of Brunel Associates, a firm offering consulting services to ultra affluent individuals. He spent the bulk of his career in the asset management group of J.P. Morgan, where he worked in the United States and abroad from 1976 until his retirement in the spring of 1999. In 1990 he assumed the position of chief investment officer of J.P. Morgan's global private bank, where he focused on the issues of special concern to individual investors, such as tax-efficiency and downside risk protection. Prior to that, he served as an analyst in New York and Tokyo, head of research in Hong Kong, and head of investment management in Singapore and Melbourne. Upon retiring from J.P. Morgan he began consulting to wealthy individuals and institutions that serve them. He became the chief investment officer of Private Asset Management at U.S. Bancorp, a position he held until June 2001, when he left to found Brunel Associates. Jean is the editor of the *Journal of Wealth Management*, published by Institutional Investor Journals, and has participated in various taskforces for the Association for Investment Management and Research. A graduate of Ecole des Hautes Etudes Commerciales in France, Jean holds an MBA from the Kellogg Graduate School of Management at Northwestern University and is a Chartered Financial Analyst.

Foreword

Private investors confide in me because they know I have no axe to grind and no product to sell. As the founder of the Institute for Private Investors, I hear stories about private bankers, money managers, and stockbrokers. Some of these stories are filled with praise for a trusted advisor. Others are tales of disillusionment and disappointment. What determines whether the relationship is a success or a failure?

Perhaps an actual investor is the best person to hear from first. Here is an email this investor sent me in late 2000:

> As the economy shifts, I am seeing just how free our investment counsel is and has been to chart its own direction and set its own benchmarks in the name of taking our interest into account for decisions. How do I set up a strategy to define an appropriate asset mix that will make sense over time? How do I set a benchmark that makes sense for me and why? How do I measure performance among advisors? How do I define, measure and assess risk? How do I assess volatility for decision-making purposes as opposed to just understanding it? These are the questions my advisor has sought to ask and answer for me ... The more they do it, the more dependent I feel.

This investor should be the first in line to purchase *Integrated Wealth Management: The New Direction for Portfolio Managers*. Right behind him on line in the bookstore should be his advisor.

Integrated Wealth Management: The New Direction for Portfolio Managers is a book that explores uncharted territory and has been written by the right person just in time. The uncharted territory is wealth management. The author is Jean Brunel, the Lewis and Clark of wealth management. He has mapped the territory of asset allocation, tax efficiency, risk, and the myriad of investment choices with insight and clarity. Relying on Jean's impressive intellect and his intuitive understanding of human behavior, the private investor traveler can avoid perilous dead-end streets and stay off the rutted highways.

Until recently, few investment firms chose to focus on individual clients. Beginning in 1974, with the passage of the Employee Retirement and Income Safety Act (ERISA) by the U.S. Congress, pension plans were far more attractive as new clients for the rapidly expanding money management industry. When the Institute for Private Investors held its inaugural program in 1992, the concept of managing money with taxes in mind was unheard of. Back then, unlike most of his peers, Jean Brunel saw what was broken and needed fixing. Not content to offer pension plan advice to individual investors, Jean set out on a journey that encountered several unpleasant questions:

- Why do investment theories ignore taxes?
- Why do most portfolio managers prefer tax-exempt clients?
- Why do portfolio accounting statements measure returns but not risk?
- Why do private investors, especially entrepreneurs, overestimate their appetite for risk and then, too often, blame the money manager?

I first met Jean in the early 1990s. Even then his views were controversial. He was never one to 'run with the pack.' Throughout the 1990s, Jean was known for telling it like it is but shouldn't be. Now he is known for inventing the way it *could* be. His intellect is, as the teenagers say, 'awesome.' At the same time he is practical and pragmatic. Therein lies his charm. Could his being French have something to do with that? Just when you think that he's lost you in the theoretical underpinning of his views, Jean gives a concrete illustration that produces the 'Aha! So that's how it works!' Investors and advisors alike will find this book enlightening. The journey the reader is about to undertake carries with it significant rewards – both tangible and intangible. The more obvious and tangible reward is personal wealth managed far more successfully. The less obvious, intangible reward is to grasp, at long last, a sensible framework for informed wealth management decisions.

Happy reading!

Charlotte B. Beyer
Founder & CEO
Institute for Private Investors
New York, New York
January 2002

The foundations of the new paradigm

Introduction: changing the wealth management paradigm

This book is dedicated to a single, simple observation: *private wealth management requires a different paradigm*. Private wealth management is a new, discrete discipline and not just a variation on the traditional institutional investment management theme.[1] *The impact of taxation, and the interaction between investor psychology and the uncertainties of both capital markets and individual cash flow needs, mandate a new set of investment solutions*. Though these new processes can at times be remarkably similar to those employed by institutional investment managers, they are often radically different. In writing this book, my goal is not only to share the insights developed over the last dozen years, but, more importantly, to discuss the principles underpinning them.

Indeed, I strongly believe that we are in the middle of the second major revolution in the asset management industry and that much more change lies ahead. The first revolution came about when developments in modern portfolio theory interacted with the Employee Retirement and Income Safety Act (ERISA) enacted in the United States in 1974. Then, the traditional investment problem was redefined from a single-minded focus on return to a two-dimensional trade-off balancing return and risk. The second revolution relates to the 'discovery' that taxes matter and is facilitated by the Uniform Prudent Investor Act enacted in 1995, also in the United States, which prescribed a new 'total portfolio' approach in the management of assets held in trusts. This added a third dimension to the wealth management problem: tax efficiency.

The ability to recognize the need for change and the capacity to develop the appropriate response are the two most critical success factors. A book simply describing a few solutions, in effect patterned after the proverbial cookbook and thus full of recipes, would, in my view, fall substantially short of the mark.

This book is really intended for a global audience. Though it has a residual focus on investors in the United States, one of the countries where tax-efficient investing has moved furthest, I have tried to keep it as broad as possible, because I believe that the issues discussed here transcend borders. The fact that we need to adopt a different approach when dealing with individual investors is not a phenomenon solely applicable to the United States In fact, having had the pleasant opportunity to deal with individual investors residing in five continents, I can unequivocally state that there are numerous common features, which can be ignored only at your own peril. These include facets that are explained by behavioral finance, and elements that are specific to the institutional, regulatory and tax frameworks of each country.

The legal landscape does differ substantially from one place to the next. For instance, there will be ample opportunities to discuss the 'wash sale rules,' which prohibit U.S. investors who have taken a capital loss in a security from transacting in that security for 30 days on either side of the loss-generating trade. A Frenchman would not understand that, as he is allowed to do an *acheté-vendu* (roundtrip trade) without adverse tax consequences. Similarly, a U.S. investor might be surprised to learn that mutual funds often shelter European investors from the tax consequences associated with trades executed within the mutual fund. Most European countries, indeed, do not have an equivalent to the U.S. Investment Company Act of 1940, which requires that 90% of the taxable income realized within a registered investment company (the legal characterization of a U.S. mutual fund) be distributed to shareholders in the year in which they are generated.

For all of these individual differences, however, there are many similarities that beget similar broad principles; and these principles must then be customized to the specific local circumstances. In particular, of course, the fact that individuals do not tend to view investment problems through an asset-liability prism and often have to pay taxes – either on the returns earned in portfolios or when assets are gifted or bequeathed – is more or less universal.

The goal I have therefore set myself here is to provide insights that I hope will help investment advisors and individual investors to deal better with wealth management issues in their own jurisdictions. In addition, I would like to help investment advisors outside of the United States understand better the specific hoops through which U.S. individual investors must jump. This should help them serve and provide useful advice to what is increasingly becoming the largest part of the U.S. asset management market.

The need for a new paradigm

The need for a new paradigm did not suddenly appear. Rather, the idea germinated slowly as the stock answers to simple wealth management questions appeared increasingly inadequate or unsatisfying. Let me illustrate the point, which is neither simple nor obvious, from the discovery process that I followed. Somewhat paradoxically, my personal discovery process started while working with and for generally tax-exempt institutional investors. The world was relatively simple and the path had been well traveled. Through hard work and heartbreaking mistakes, many individuals had developed the processes we all used and lit the beacons to keep us operating safely. However, experience in applying these tried and true principles in Japan, Hong Kong, Singapore, and Australia made me realize that there was more to the issue than originally met the eye. That 14-year trek around the western end of the Pacific laid the foundations for a better understanding of the needs of individual investors.

Incorporating a subjective dimension into the process

East Asia proved to be a great teacher of behavioral finance. Puzzled by the reactions of the people with whom I worked, I learned the need to make substantial adjustments in order to be effective, and was ready to make them, initially thinking they were a function of cultural differences. Little did I know then that I was discovering one of the differences between individual and institutional needs, rather than just the cultures of the East or the West.

The first lesson was that I needed to incorporate a subjective dimension to a process often viewed strictly in quantitative and objective terms. In truth, the institutional world does require some measure of subjectivity, for instance in the 'agency risk' discussed by David F. Swensen.[2] He refers to the tendency that a fiduciary agent – someone who is responsible for the management of a portfolio – may have to overlay his or her own risk profile on that of the institution on whose behalf he or she is acting. In the past, I have dubbed this risk 'maverick risk' or 'scuba risk.' The former term refers to the degree to which a fiduciary is willing to risk his or her job by being very different from his or her peers in the industry. The latter, more facetiously, refers to the amount of time a fiduciary can spend 'under water.'

An example of 'agency risk' is provided by the manager of the pension fund of a large, government-owned company in South East Asia. Though he was responsible for a fund that covered young employees and should therefore have had a long-term focus, he was principally concerned by the fact that he needed to report to his political masters quarterly. There was a clear conflict between the long-term objectives of the fund and the short-term time horizon of the manager's supervisory structure. For quite a while, the fund had had much too conservative a strategic asset allocation, as the desire of the manager to keep his job was stronger than his commitment to the goals of the fund.

However, the world of the individual investor bears the full brunt of the fact that his or her goals are rarely absolute or straightforward. Rather, individuals respond to a number of stimuli and usually do not react in the ways that standard finance would predict. Different explanations were required. A short example illustrates the point.

The executive of a Singapore family office on whose behalf I was managing a portfolio looked at investment results in a way that seemed to make the manager look bad. He appeared to have a multiplicity of benchmarks, which kept changing according to circumstances. Initially, I thought that his behavior was deliberately meant to make me uncomfortable. After a while, I realized that his behavior was in fact dictated by a conflict in which he was himself caught. He knew that he needed a few objective benchmarks to judge his managers. At the same time, the owner of the wealth did not: in fact, he looked only at the best performing strategy in the most recent period. The executive's behavior was therefore reflecting the changing needs and wants of the owner of the wealth.

Though this example applied to a circumstance that had at least in part an institutional nature, it highlighted the fact that individuals can behave in decidedly different ways: the institutional framework was not sufficient to overwhelm the individual dimension. Watching the developments in behavioral finance in the last quarter century, I can see that they provide exceptionally rich insights for those who are willing to use them. They helped me realize that the traditional trade-off, exclusively expressed in terms of risk and return, is not sufficient.

The impact of taxes on portfolio optimality

The second lesson I learned was that taxes can make you accept a suboptimal strategy in one part of the portfolio for the sake of total portfolio optimality. Let me illustrate this with an example, also involving the Singapore family mentioned above.

The Chiang family had comparably modest financial investments, but massive real estate assets, with a very low tax cost. Singapore's tax laws were patterned after the British system and incorporated the concepts of 'investor' and 'trader.' Investors were not subject to capital gains taxes, while traders were. The critical feature of the code was that it was not possible to be an investor with a certain amount of assets and a trader with another amount – it was an 'all or nothing' proposition. Though the code was not absolutely specific, there were a number of relatively simple 'safe harbor' rules for the investor who did not want to be treated as a trader. Thus, the head of the family office was adamant that we had to abide by these 'investor' rules.

It made sense to adopt a suboptimal localized investment strategy, in this instance applied to the financial assets, in order to truly optimize the management of the family's overall wealth, including real estate assets. Being classified a trader because of activity in the financial portfolio would be debilitating for the Chiangs, as they looked at their assets in aggregate. We will find an echo of this story in one of the five principles of tax efficiency discussed later in the book: the need to focus on the whole portfolio.

The impact of taxes on portfolio management

The third lesson still deals with taxes: they have an insidious tendency of requiring numerous changes in the way a portfolio is managed. They require different day-to-day investment management and accounting processes, and can have an impact on the strategic asset allocation and portfolio structure. The change experienced in 1988 by Australian superannuation funds (the local term for pension funds) provides an excellent example.

In 1988, the investment returns of Australian superannuation funds became taxable, after having previously enjoyed tax-exempt status. Changes to the day-to-day investment and portfolio accounting processes immediately became necessary, because of the need to consider individual tax lots. In fact, the issue had considerably greater implications.

The Australian tax system provides relief from the double taxation of corporate dividends. Corporate dividends come with 'franking credits' (very similar to the French *avoir fiscal*), tax credits that can be used to meet the overall tax liability of the portfolio. This had two principal portfolio implications. The first was that tax-lot accounting made the day-to-day buy and sell decisions more complex, as we needed to evaluate the impact of capital gain realization on the attractiveness of any trade. The second was that we needed to consider the portfolio as a whole, rather than through the traditional building block process, focused on each asset class. Further, from a strategic asset allocation standpoint, it led us to raise the strategic exposure to equities, as they became relatively more attractive. Indeed, they provided both higher than expected after-tax returns on their own *and* the opportunity to shelter some of the interest income earned on bonds.

Formulating the new paradigm

We have seen that dealing with individual investors requires a paradigm change. The question is how to conceptualize and then make these changes. In my own circumstances, the process integrated the insights gleaned in East Asia and Australia with ideas subsequently acquired in the United States, Europe, and the Middle East. Again, it took time to place individual insights into an overall pattern of thinking, as I kept resisting, but I was driven inexorably toward it by clients and friends. The ultimate evolution of this thinking is the subject of this book.

The two principal differences between the institutional and individual asset management universes boil down to, first, the impact of taxation and, second, the interaction between investor psychology and uncertainty – the uncertainty associated with capital markets and individual cash flow needs. The new paradigm involves moving from investment management to the concept of wealth management. Though superficially almost innocuous, the changes this requires are very important. Taxes and behavioral finance change the process and its outcome. This makes individual and institutional asset management fundamentally different, and dooms to suboptimality, if not failure, anyone who tries simply to retrofit institutional solutions to private wealth management. The new paradigm introduces at least three important new issues: a focus on after-tax returns, time horizons, and performance assessment.

Focus on after-tax wealth accumulation

We will have many opportunities to look into after-tax wealth accumulation, rather than periodic pre-tax returns, as it is the most visible change for investment professionals. There is, however, an important and subtle point to be made from the outset: we need to look for *accumulation over time*, rather than *periodic returns*. Though one can certainly argue that accumulation over time is made up of a succession of short-term returns, the impact of compounding and seeking optimal tax efficiency through time requires a different thought process.

This in turn has two implications. First, we need to control overall portfolio volatility as it exerts a negative impact on compound returns. A simple example: you need a 25% return to get back to square one if your portfolio has incurred a 20% loss. Second, optimal tax efficiency through time may lead you to accept a suboptimal return or tax efficiency in a given period, because of the potential benefit that this could produce for the portfolio as a whole over time. For instance, imagine a situation where taking a loss exposes the portfolio to the risk of some short-term performance penalty, but gives you the opportunity to offset unrealized gains elsewhere in the portfolio. I will come back to this example in a moment, when I introduce the concept of simultaneous portfolio optimization.

A sharper look at time horizons

Individual circumstances do change over time, and actual outcomes have a way of differing from actuarial expectations. In an institutional context, managers have the benefit of being able to deal with large groups rather than individuals. For them, it is not only reasonable to assume that actuarial assumptions will hold true; it is in fact the sole practical approach. This allows pension funds to think in a disciplined manner and to be relatively clear about their investment horizons. Individuals, however, do experience change, some of it very real and some of it less so, but nevertheless still viewed as real and important. Being able to deal with that change and anticipate means of avoiding what can be called 'decision risk' must be made a fundamental part of the process. Thus, and paradoxically, though many individuals, particularly at the high end of the wealth scale, should most likely have extremely long, multigenerational investment horizons, they often have somewhat shorter performance horizons. I define 'performance horizon' as the time period over which investment decisions are assessed and investment strategy can be reconsidered.

A different way of measuring performance

The third new issue has to do with the way individuals measure performance. They typically do not take comfort in relative returns. This is the investment management equivalent of the 'money illusion,'[3] which holds that we are influenced by nominal as well as real monetary values in our economic lives. This sets individuals apart from institutional investors, who most often judge performance strictly relative to some market index and to a manager universe.

In my view, the attraction of institutional investors to relative returns reflects the way they tend to think of portfolio optimization. They typically operate in a sequential optimization mode: each investment problem is broken down into a number of individual decisions (asset classes, sub-asset classes or even specific manager mandates), which are made and subsequently assessed in their own discrete environments.

By contrast, individuals are required by tax considerations to live in a simultaneous optimization mode, and they are predisposed to do so because of their behavioral construct. Simultaneous optimization means that, when making any decision, they must consider the portfolio in as much of its totality as possible. This reflects the multiplicity of interactions among all the moving parts.

Take yourself back to the fourth quarter of 1998 and imagine that your portfolio holds only two asset classes: U.S. equities and emerging market equities. Here in 1998, it is virtually impossible to find a U.S. equity manager worth his or her salt who does not produce double-digit returns. Given the performance of U.S. equities in the previous three years, many of the tax-aware U.S. equity managers also feel constrained by substantial unrealized gains in their portfolios. These constraints may be preventing them from achieving their full potential. On the other hand, the crises in East Asia and Russia have made it virtually impossible to find an emerging market equity manager with a positive return. In addition, most of them have portfolios with significant unrealized losses due to the poor performance of their asset class for some time. Now, sequential portfolio optimization would tell you to look at your U.S. and emerging market equity managers individually, and judge them relative to their peers. Simultaneous portfolio optimization would have you look to the opportunity to take losses in your emerging market equity portfolio, *even if it penalizes its performance relative to its peers*. These losses could then be used to offset unrealized gains in the U.S. equity portfolio and make it more manageable.

Let us get back to the performance measurement issue. Simultaneous optimization makes individuals less sensitive to relative returns and more prone to seek absolute returns, because it eliminates the need, and the opportunity, to look at individual subsets of the portfolio and judge them relative to their narrowly defined universe. Note, however, that it would be a mistake to take the idea of absolute return to an extreme. Individuals often view returns in a loose, relative performance context, as most of them *will* understand some decline in the value of their portfolios when news headlines talk of substantial equity price declines.

Illustrating the new paradigm

Imagine two investors having both the same amount of money today, and broadly comparable *stated* goals and needs. In an institutional context, it would be reasonable to conclude that they would have broadly similar portfolios and that the levels of their wealth at some future point in time would be broadly similar. In an individual context, the situation is likely to be quite different: not only is it likely that their next portfolios will not be similar, but they will almost certainly further diverge over time. That their current portfolios are in fact probably different and that they both have different tax bases (or tax book values or costs) will likely prevent them holding similar investments in the immediate future. Further, rebalancing costs will interact with capital market dynamics to make it harder for their portfolios to converge over time. In fact, in normal circumstances, they will most likely diverge further. Finally, the ways in which each investor reacts, psychologically, to market developments will tend to introduce one further dimension to portfolio divergence over time.

The impact of having different starting portfolios

Even if our two investors have the same wealth today, they probably will not own exactly the same assets, or hold them with the same tax basis. Thus, there is probably no optimal portfolio common to both of them. We will discuss this further when we look into the pitfalls of a traditional efficient frontier analysis, as we uncover what I have come to call 'the cost of getting there.' The main insight here is simply that the optimality of a portfolio is highly dependent on the costs associated with moving from the existing to the optimal mix of assets and strategies, and with periodic rebalancing. Thus, because the starting and next immediate iterations of each portfolio are likely to differ, they will probably diverge further over time. This happens precisely because of the tax costs associated with portfolio rebalancing. Portfolio rebalancing costs will indeed make a transaction sensible in certain circumstances, but unattractive in others. Thus, actual portfolio outcomes are 'path dependent,' as the tax cost associated with any portfolio change is a major determinant of the final attractiveness of any investment decision.

It is interesting to take this idea one step further and consider an everyday consequence of it. Imagine that two investors who own the same security want to consider a switch from that security to some other investment. The attractiveness of the trade is critically dependent upon the friction cost associated with the sale of the security currently in the portfolio. Thus, the transaction may make sense if the unrealized capital gain is low and make no sense if it is high. This means that the two investors should not necessarily view the relative attractiveness of any investment in the same light, as they must consider, first, where they are, and, second, how much it will cost to trade. Consider the 'surprising' implication, which is well worth pondering given the tendency of the financial media to focus on individual investment ideas:

absolute individual stock recommendations make no sense unless you know what the actual trade would be for that recommendation to be implemented. Individual investors should be evaluating both sides of any trade (buy and sell), rather than simply one leg of the transaction. They need to think in total portfolio terms. The current composition of their portfolio will interact with the wide range of investment opportunities, making a few of these opportunities attractive and others unattractive. We will look into this issue further when we discuss principles of tax efficiency and introduce the notion that taxable investors must be concerned with two kinds of transactions: 'alpha generating' and 'alpha enabling,' while institutional or tax-oblivious investors need worry only about 'alpha generating' trades.

Introducing behavioral finance

The second and third major reasons why the portfolios of our two individuals will likely diverge over time are directly related to the fact that they are individuals. Behavioral finance helps[4] us analyze and understand these reasons.

An important first step is to pay due attention to the maxim 'investor, know thyself' – to which one should add 'advisor, know thy client.' Beyond the traditional and regulatory meanings of that admonition lies one of the most fertile and fascinating facets of private wealth management. A short definition of behavioral finance helps: it is the study of how psychology affects the way in which people behave when they make financial decisions. It differs from the other investment approach, standard finance, in that standard finance is based on 'expected utility theory' and can be described as a *prescriptive* model. It is prescriptive in the sense that it is built on assumptions of how people should behave. Behavioral finance is a *descriptive* model, aimed at identifying ways in which people are likely to behave, particularly when dealing with uncertainty. The critical distinction is thus drawn between how people *should behave* and how people *actually behave*. Behavioral finance comes into the private wealth management process through two different doors.

Discovering decision risk

First, behavioral finance introduces an important new notion, 'decision risk,' which I define as the risk of changing horses in mid-race. Practically, it is the risk of changing strategy at the worst possible moment, because you may have overestimated your ability to deal with the pain associated with that particular strategy. Note that this is different from what has been dubbed 'agency risk' or 'maverick risk' in the institutional world. Agency or maverick risk refers to the fact that the optimality of a portfolio might be in part driven by a desire not to be too different from everyone else. That risk, which is also part of the individual landscape, in fact tends to compound decision risk and thus makes the challenge even more complex. Indeed, individuals may not fully understand their ability to take on risk, or the risk actually associated with a given strategy. As a result, they may be influenced into a decision to go in certain directions, which, in fact, they should avoid, with inevitably adverse consequences later on. That influence may arise from their own biases or from what people around them do or suggest that they do. Thus, decision risk and the need to manage it impose on the investment advisor or sophisticated private investor a particularly important duty: to ensure that all risks are fully understood and that those risks are understood in the context of each investor's own psychological make-up.

These considerations have led me to the belief that individual investors travel on the road to optimality, but rarely move immediately to an optimal state, an idea that we will revisit when discussing the wealth management process. Individuals gain an understanding of the realities of capital markets, and of their comfort investing in them, only gradually and over time. As they are the products of their own experiences, they need to take the time to accumulate experience before jumping in with both feet. We will later see how important this insight is, as it influences both the nature of the investment strategy formulation process and the way in which that strategy is implemented. Let me, however, mention here one of the most important consequences: *continuing investment education is one of the critical needs of individual investors and one of the most important duties of their advisors.*

Dealing with uncertainty

Another important behavioral insight fundamentally alters the landscape. We operate in a world of uncertainty, and the interaction between that uncertainty and our psychological self is one of the principal elements in the investment process. Practically, the best we can do is to determine the probability of certain things happening. However, we should know that there is a good chance that our assessment will not be very good, because we do not have the luxury of dealing with a large number of independent events or with large groups.

Let me again use the institutional world to offer a contrast. Institutional investors tend to rely on an asset-liability analysis to formulate their investment policy, with two important implications.

First, it injects a measure of discipline into the process, as the investment problem relates to keeping some balance between the value of the portfolio and the liabilities that it is set to meet at some future point in time. That discipline reduces, but admittedly does not eliminate, the scope for emotional decisions.

Second, the principal source of uncertainty in the institutional world is usually found in the behavior of capital markets. Indeed, as institutions work with large groups, it is unlikely that an unusual event will completely change the nature of their problem. For instance, the early death or retirement of a few members of the group are unlikely to affect the size of the institution's liabilities in a material manner. Also, liabilities and their valuations in fact respond to many of the same sources of uncertainty, because of the asset-liability lens through which they look at the problem. For instance, the values of both assets and liabilities fluctuate in response to changes in interest rates. This is not true in the individual investment world.

The need to consider the full range of potential outcomes matters to both institutional investors and individual investors, but it is particularly relevant to individuals, because of their psychological make-up and the tools they use.

The first piece of the puzzle is of a psychological nature. In an article entitled 'Monte Carlo Analysis of the Impact of Portfolio Volatility on After-Tax Wealth,' Bernard McCabe demonstrates the importance of considering the full range of possible outcomes, rather than a simple mean expectation.[5] The insight is important as it focuses our attention on the concept of 'outcome,' which is so fundamental to the world of individual wealth management. It reflects the fact that individuals tend to look at investment results as they would look at still pictures, rather than movies. Behavioral finance indeed tells us that they value changes in states – do they have more or less money than when they last looked? – rather than total wealth levels relative to some goal or other. The relevance of this insight is clear after we have experienced a sharp market upswing: individuals may have a sense of loss during a normal market correction, although they may still have more money than they would have expected to have. (McCabe takes this further in a second article entitled 'Analytic Approximation of the Probability that a Portfolio Survives Forever.'[6])

The second piece of the puzzle reflects the fact that certain individual needs are *time-dependent*. Looking at the interaction between market volatility and the probability of achieving investment goals,[7] Darryl Meyers notes that the assumption that underpins most planning activity is essentially faulty. Markets do not follow a simple mean geometric compounding rule. Though return variations from one period to the next may have a negligible impact on certain strategies, they can dramatically affect situations in which assets are transferred between persons and entities. This reflects the fact that these transfers are scheduled to happen at some exact point in time, rather than on average over time.

In fact, Meyers's observations should be taken further and applied to circumstances where there is no fixed evaluation date, bringing us back to the world of investor psychology. Return variations may have a theoretically or financially negligible impact on certain strategies, *if they are allowed to run their course*. In reality, of course, the whole problem revolves around the fact that they may not be allowed to run their course, because individuals may not have the time or the patience to live through a full cycle.

Moving to the new paradigm

The lesson we learn from these three observations is that private portfolios must be considered individually, and that the process must reflect their own particular circumstances. These circumstances will reflect tax considerations or the interaction between investor psychology and the various sources of uncertainty, be they driven by markets or by investor needs. In 1997, I wrote an article entitled 'The Upside-Down World of Tax-Aware Investing.'[8] Then, I probably overemphasized the issue of taxes and failed to account fully for the psychological dimension. Nevertheless, thinking of the private wealth management world as an 'upside-down' world may well still be the appropriate analogy.

I prefer to start by thinking that things will be different, possibly very different, and be surprised that the difference is minor. The alternative is very dangerous. Indeed, thinking that things just involve small variations on the same theme is likely to expose me to the risk of trying to fit a square peg into a round hole. In the last two decades, our industry has been split between two equally poor extremes. One side has spent the bulk of the last 20 years displaying a clear tendency toward retrofitting institutional solutions to private wealth management problems. Though a few may occasionally have been successful following that approach, the lack of a truly appropriate solution has deprived many individual investors of the opportunity to have the right portfolio for their own circumstances. The other extreme faction in the industry simply eschewed all new approaches, effectively missing many of the important insights that could be gleaned from developments in modern portfolio theory. This has caused many individual investors to incur unnecessary risks, or to miss attractive new approaches or strategies.

The specific needs of private wealth management are increasingly appreciated. A task force formed under the aegis of the Association for Investment Management Research in 2000 determined, in early 2001, that there was a need for a specific continuing education program for chartered financial analysts. Yet we still have quite a way to go, as evidenced by the fact that there still exist portfolio managers who believe that there is no need to change their approach. In fact, they argue that a good investor can manage money on behalf of a multitude of clienteles, without making much more than a few modest modifications to their investment processes. I even recently heard a portfolio manager emphatically state that: 'tax efficiency is a fad.' Yet we are in the middle of a major investment management revolution, and I propose to argue the case for change and offer some solutions.

A road map for this book

This book is structured along two axes. We start with a discussion of the foundation of private wealth management. We consider the wealth management process, investor psychology, tax efficiency, and the issue of multiple asset locations, and introduce a more sensible tax-efficient portfolio structure. Each of these first six chapters provides an opportunity to examine the building blocks needed to understand the balance of the book.

The 12 subsequent chapters follow the four steps of the wealth management process. We start with an investigation into topics related to understanding the opportunities and the issues, focusing on a brief history of capital markets, and the need for, and means of, developing rational investment expectations. We look into one of the wealth management problems most frequently experienced by entrepreneurs: what to do with highly concentrated and low-cost equity holdings. This is followed by a discussion of the different ways to be an 'active' manager. The next group of chapters deals with planning a wealth management strategy, considering the pitfalls of a traditional analysis and the value of integrated wealth planning. We also revisit the question of market timing, but this time in an after-tax context. The section on implementing the wealth management plan comprises four chapters, which delve into highly practical issues: tax-efficient portfolio management, tax-efficient security selection, the dangers of style diversification, and manager selection. Our final section is dedicated to supervising and monitoring the process, with a focus on performance measurement and performance assessment. We conclude with an essay describing the changes that must take place if a traditional portfolio manager is to morph into a successful private wealth manager. Illustrations distilled from my own and colleagues' experiences have been included throughout, shaded for ease of reference.

---

[1] See Arnott, Robert D., Andrew L. Berkin, and Jia Ye, 'How Well Have Taxable Investors been Served in the 1980s and 1990s?,' *The Journal of Portfolio Management*, Summer 2000, pp. 84–94.

[2] Swensen, David F., *Pioneering Portfolio Management – An Unconventional Approach to Institutional Investment*, New York: The Free Press, 2000.

[3] Shafir Eldar, Peter Diamond, and Amos Tversky, 'Money Illusion,' Chapter 19, pp. 335–55, of Daniel Kahneman and Amos Tversky, eds., *Choices, Values, and Frames*, Cambridge: Russell Sage Foundation, Cambridge University Press, 2000.

[4] See Rom, Brian M., 'The Psychology of Money: Its Impact on Individual Risk Tolerance and Portfolio Selection,' *The Journal of Wealth Management*, Fall 2000, pp. 15–19. This author mentions Kahneman, Daniel, and Amos Tversky, 'Advances in Prospect Theory: Cumulative Representation of Uncertainty,' *Journal of Risk and Uncertainty*, 1992, pp. 297–323.

[5] McCabe, Bernard J. 'Monte Carlo Analysis of the Impact of Portfolio Volatility on After-Tax Wealth.' *The Journal of Private Portfolio Management*, Winter 1998, pp. 22-23.

[6] McCabe, Bernard J. 'Analytic Approximation for the Probability that a Portfolio Survives Forever.' *The Journal of Private Portfolio Management*, Spring 1999, pp. 43-48.

[7] Meyers, Darryl L. 'Volatility and Mortality Risk Considerations in Estate Planning.' *The Journal of Wealth Management*, Winter 2000, pp. 52-58.

[8] Brunel, Jean L.P., 'The Upside-Down World of Tax-Aware Investing', *Trust and Estates*, February 1997, pp. 34–42.

Chapter 1

The wealth management process

Understanding the wealth management process may well be the most important element of a successful relationship between an individual investor and his or her professional advisor(s). Exhibit 1.1 illustrates the idea that the wealth management process is both multiphased and iterative. This has three important implications, which will underpin many of the themes developed in the rest of this book:

- one needs to take the time to go though the whole process, so that all appropriate targets and expectations are set;
- one needs to recognize that different problems beget different solutions and eschew 'cookie cutter' approaches; and
- one needs to recognize that technology is going to facilitate change and make it considerably easier to enhance the wealth management services currently provided to individuals, through mass customization.

Exhibit 1.1

The wealth management process

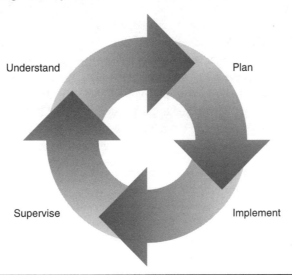

The process is iterative

The first and probably most important attribute of the wealth management process is that it is iterative. Understanding the iterative nature of the process is essential, because it clearly says that individual investors will 'travel on the road to optimality,' rather than reach it in one fell swoop. They will need to learn about the opportunities and about themselves. They will need to get used to and comfortable with markets and strategies, before being fully committed to them.

Pete sold his retail business to a large conglomerate. He was self-made, having started with little more than a great idea. He had spent all his working life developing his business and had never taken much time to think of or invest in the public capital markets. Initially, the contrast between the two of us with respect to the way in which we looked at 'volatility' was striking. Having been in a business that saw him 'lose' money 10 out of 12 months a year, Pete was comfortable with volatility. Yet, the volatility he knew was predictable and seasonal, as U.S. retailers know they make a disproportionately large share of their revenues in the last two months of the year. At that time, I had also spent a lifetime in a single business, which had made me comfortable with volatility. Yet the volatility I knew related to capital markets, as the business in which I had toiled was investment management.

Pete was comfortable with volatile monthly results, but not with volatile asset valuations. By contrast, being in a business where monthly revenues were highly predictable, I was uncomfortable with revenue volatility, but did not unduly mind seeing capital market levels fluctuate. Around the Pacific Basin, I had seen my share of bear markets followed by sharp recoveries.

Pete's initial portfolio was predominantly invested in fixed-income instruments, as he felt that he could not deal with any significant monthly fluctuations in market values. Similarly, he was not comfortable enough with complex investment processes to consider market-neutral or hedged strategies. As time passed, however, *the evolution in the structure of Pete's portfolio was very interesting and illustrated the iterative nature of the wealth management process*.

We had made it a point for him to own small commitments to a variety of volatile markets, so that he could gain experience with them. Seeing a few of them go down then up, and a few others go up then down, Pete learned two lessons. The first was that he could tolerate some volatility, provided he understood the underlying principles of the relevant markets and strategies. The second is that volatility is usually associated with higher returns. Over time, the portfolio shifted to riskier strategies and today only a minute portion of Pete's portfolio is invested in fixed income. In fact, today his fixed-income investments account for less than 10% of his financial assets and are in high-yield bonds.

Pete's story has at least two important implications. First, Pete took his time to travel the road to the optimal strategy for him and his family. Had we moved to that point too quickly, Pete would have likely been shocked by one or another sharp market gyration, and might have even been 'spooked' and given up a long-term asset allocation privileging returns over risk. Second, the need for iteration has to do with 'getting comfortable' with both the strategies eventually used in the portfolio and their ongoing behavior. This requires substantial personal education, a point to which we turn next.

The importance of investment education

Tom, an individual whose fortune had been made in real estate development, told me that he would react differently to a 20% decline in the value of a U.S. equity portfolio than to the same decline in the value of a portfolio invested in emerging market equities. He would not be happy, but could tolerate a 20% decline in U.S. equity prices, because he felt comfortable with the country's economy and its institutional framework. He would be very uncomfortable with a similar decline in emerging market equities, because he did not know the countries in which these companies operated and did not trust their regulatory frameworks to the same extent as he did the United States's. Tom needed to educate himself, just as Pete did. Over time, Tom learned about the nature of emerging economies and got used to the volatility of their markets before he could invest in them.

Client education

Similarly, Linda, who founded and headed her own advertising agency, needed time to learn about hedge funds and the strategies employed by their managers before she could accept the proposition that they offered significant diversification potential. To her, it initially sounded too good to be true that you could have good returns, low volatility and high diversification potential in the same strategy. She needed to understand how that might be.

Pete, Tom, and Linda all needed to understand emotionally, rather than just intellectually, the issues of concern to them. For Pete, the question related to the risk of short-term losses and the impact that would have on a fortune he had worked so hard to build. For Tom, it had to do with the need to understand the economic and institutional framework of the areas in which he invested. For Linda, it involved discovering the difference between manager and market risk. *The educational process needed to integrate both intellectual and emotional elements.*

Emotions

The four distinct phases in the wealth management process

There are four distinct stages in the wealth management process. Each stage requires a different focus. Understanding the nature of the process and appreciating the resources that need to be brought to bear at each stage are two of the keys to a successful execution.

Dave had been a successful entrepreneur and become liquid as a result of the sale of his business. Trained as an engineer, he had been involved in the design and manufacturing of a whole range of electronic products. He was an impulsive individual, and this almost caused his financial demise. Dave did not want to 'waste time' on the early steps of the process, or even on the idea that there should be a process. When confronted with my questions as to his goals and preferences, he wanted to move on and not be involved in all that 'subjective mumbo-jumbo.' He did not have the time to plan: 'I have a lot of cash in the bank and I need to get it invested.' He succumbed to the siren's song of a competitor who got him involved in a wide variety of individual investments and strategies, seemingly with little common thread. He bought into most of the then current 'fads.'

In his haste to invest his money, Dave had in fact missed a number of crucial steps, which soon came back to haunt him. A year and a half into the process, Dave began to worry that quite a number of his investments were not doing well, falling in value or substantially underperforming the rest of the market. He did not understand why and was getting concerned. He soon discovered that his portfolio made very little sense. There was little diversification, as he was simply making the same few bets in a variety of different ways.

Instructed by the experience, Dave then proceeded through the various steps in the right order. He understood that he needed a much deeper investment education. He further realized that his wife and four children also needed some education, as they would have to handle the wealth and its management should anything happen to him. When we turned to investment planning, he found out that he had significant philanthropic goals that he had not even considered. Even more importantly, he discovered that he needed to be concerned about estate planning issues, to ensure that his 'dynastic' objectives were met.

During the implementation part of the process, Dave took the time to evaluate strategies and managers, and found himself actually selecting approaches that, he said, he had rejected out of hand a year earlier because they were 'boring.' Finally, he appreciated and understood the need to create a solid governance structure to monitor and supervise the management of his wealth. Earlier in the process, he looked up his portfolio on the internet on an almost daily basis. Now, he receives monthly reports and, in fact, focuses sharply on the portfolio only during quarterly reviews, when managers visit and discuss their results.

You need to execute all phases of the process. They are all equally important. Deliberately sidestepping the first two phases because 'cash is burning a hole in the pocket' of the investor exposes him or her to serious consequences. In fact, these consequences can be doubly painful to the taxable investor: you not only have to accept unsatisfactory investment performance, but you may have to pay taxes for the privilege of setting the portfolio on a new, better footing. Similarly, careful implementation and monitoring are essential. Without them, investors are exposed to buying into fads, to selecting the wrong manager or to finding out about a problem after it has become both big and painful.

Finally, individuals will often naturally feel more attracted to certain phases of the process than to others. Depending on their 'money personality,' as Kathleen Gurney calls it,[1] they may well be more prepared and willing to deal with one phase, and less with another.

Bob was exceptionally comfortable during the first and second phases of the process. He literally enjoyed learning about himself and 'being educated' in investment management, a discipline he did not know. He took it beyond the theoretical, and developed a particularly well designed and complex plan. Bob's problem, though, was that, in his words, he was uncomfortable 'pulling the trigger.' Further, he has since shown little interest in the regular monitoring of the portfolio and the managers. Yet, since he understood that personal weakness, he decided to appoint an 'external chief investment officer' to do the monitoring for him.

By contrast, individuals such as Dave are typically not very interested in the early phases, which are insufficiently 'action-oriented,' but enjoy the implementation and monitoring, because they need to make decisions and enjoy making them. The external help they require is principally focused on education, planning and process issues.

The challenge therefore set before both investors and advisors is to recognize the nature of the wealth management process. Investors must have the patience to go through the process, even if certain steps do not naturally appeal to them. Advisors must first explain to their clients why the process is so important. They must then take the time to go through the process and 'walk the walk.' This may be difficult for those advisors who are subjected to the need to keep generating net revenues for their firm. Yet experience demonstrates over and over again that taking the time to build a relationship is usually a very cheap and highly rewarding investment.

Understanding opportunities and issues

Quite often, this first step is not carried out, but, consciously or subconsciously, is assumed away. Therein lie a number of failures, whether they involve relationship problems or major investment missteps. Why is this step not formally taken? Answers abound, and the fault does not always reside with the service provider, though it often does. The most frequent cause is the conflict in which many service providers find themselves. On the one hand, many do see themselves as trusted advisors and would naturally like to serve the needs of their client, the individual investor. Yet, they also often work in an organization that requires them to generate net new revenues. Thus, they tend to default into a sales, or 'product pushing' mode, which prevents them having the right kind of dialog with their clients. Another frequent cause for a lack of initial focus on developing a full understanding of opportunities and issues actually can be traced to the individual investor. Moved by a 'desire for action' or by a preference for having several distinct advisors (to avoid having to confide too much in any one of them, whom they naturally tend to distrust), individual investors at times jump to conclusions and operate in a 'product buying' mode. Then, they tend to ignore the opportunity to investigate their own values, needs and goals or to validate their perceptions as to actual capital market or structural opportunities. By 'structural,' I mean the vehicles through which assets can be held, owned or controlled.

'Investor, know thyself'

There are many dimensions to this need to understand opportunities and issues. In my view, at the top of the list is the requirement for every investor to know himself or herself. Particularly important is the need to appreciate the way in which they will react to adversity, defined here as a strategy producing unexpected and disappointing results. Ensuring that the investor will be able to define his or her 'comfort zone' is one of the most important elements of the planning process. There has been a suggestion that more than half of the investors in the Magellan Fund, probably one of the most successful mutual funds in the United States, have in fact lost money. If true, this cannot be because the fund did not perform well: it did very well by most standards. I suspect that this was because investors bought shares late in the cycle, after a period of particularly strong absolute fund performance, or sold them when the going got tough.

Understanding values, goals, and needs

Equally important, and still a 'soft' issue, is the question of value, needs and goals. You can break the whole decision process down into three simple questions (suggested to me by Larry Hause of the Minneapolis law firm Frederickson & Byron): Where am I? Where do I want to go? How do I get there? Many investors unwittingly hurt themselves by ignoring the need to take themselves through these questions. In fact, these questions are particularly relevant to investors dealing with family wealth. Multi-generation wealth management involves a lot more than simply generating the highest possible return.

Vince Rossi, a former U.S. Bank colleague, suggested a more personal question that may help put the concept in the proper perspective: would you rather have 16 husbands or wives, or 16 million dollars? I am told that most people respond that they do not have room or energy for 16 marital partners. What they are telling us then is that they have gotten to know how much is enough for them. The same occurs with respect to wealth. There is a point at which too much really can be too much. The effort or strain associated with getting certain results is not worth it. This can happen when getting that marginal extra million destroys family values or unity. Understanding these values, understanding that they may evolve from one generation to another, and understanding how these values determine and interact with the family's goals are all major parts of the wealth management process.

Getting to know needs is equally important, particularly when these needs are expressed in both objective and subjective form, or, worse yet, in strictly subjective terms. I was once having a conversation with a client on the advisability of short-term currency trading. I was suggesting that the kind of trading he was doing was unlikely to be successful, for a variety of solid investment reasons. He answered by telling me that short-term currency trading was his way of proving to himself that he was still capable of making decisions. This was an important need for an individual who had recently relinquished the chief executive position in a large company that still bore his name. The 'return' associated with his activity was not measured in the same dollars and cents as the balance of his portfolio. We will come back to this later, when we discuss the repositioning of the risk/return trade off, which we will replace with a 'comfort/reward' trade-off.

Developing rational investment expectations

Formulating rational investment expectations is another issue that investors and their advisors need to explore before setting out on an irreversible course. Behavioral finance, common sense, and experience all suggest how frequent it is for individuals not to have fully rational expectations. In fact, Meir Statman[2] suggests that individuals suffer from cognitive biases and advises them to use the 'scientific method' to evaluate options. Scientific method here means considering theory, proposing a hypothesis, and testing it with empirical evidence. Statman's insight is that empirical evidence and appropriate framing will help identify and compensate for these cognitive biases. Thus, though investors and their advisors do not need a whole treatise on capital market history, it is highly relevant to look into the past. Such an analysis is important therefore, not in the sense that it describes patterns or presents data that we do not know, but because it helps us identify the issues that should be raised when an individual or a family starts the·

wealth management process. Thus, they can begin to appreciate what it is reasonable for them to expect and what should make them worry. They can understand which asset classes or strategies make sense for them, and which are likely to make them uncomfortable, for some intermediate period of time or more permanently. Finally, they can learn how the constraints that they would like to impose will or will not significantly affect the returns that they can expect.

Planning a wealth management strategy

Investment management is not a tactical game. What are the chances of anyone hitting their target if they have not taken the time to identify and locate it? The messages of the late 1990s were that a great deal of money could and would be made through day trading, and that just having access to information or certain electronic tools would pave the way to great wealth. Both fictions disguised the simple fact that there is a lot more to wealth management than picking a few stocks or mutual funds. The cynic will observe that these tendencies to be just tactical are just an aspect of the typical bull market: they would point to the observation often made in Hong Kong that the top of the market is reached when *amahs* (domestic helpers) or cab drivers start buying stocks. The sharp equity price reversal experienced in the 1990s in Japan illustrates the impact of a good bear market on investor psychology. Housewives, traditionally among the leading private investors in Japan, would let their brokers collect their savings from their 'Ryo piggy banks.'[3] They would then invest them at will in the house mutual funds. Since the massive market reversal started in December 1989, Japanese individual investors, housewives and their husbands, have seemingly sworn off the equity market. One may wonder what it will take to bring them back.

The impact of taxes

One very powerful reason for being careful and developing a wealth management plan has to do with taxes. In contrast with the blessed environment in which a tax-exempt investor lives, the world of the taxable investor penalizes mistakes very heavily. This is one of the areas where the need to have a total portfolio focus comes alive.

Assume that you do *not* have to pay taxes and that you have adopted a strategy that experience subsequently demonstrates is not appropriate. For instance, you may have selected an active equity manager. Now, you realize you should have opted for a passive solution, as the active manager seemingly is not able to earn enough after-tax value added to justify his management fees. Assume further that equity prices have moved up in the interim, and that your portfolio, though not doing as well as expected, is still up from where it was when you selected the active manager. Changing from the active to a passive strategy simply requires you to liquidate your actively managed portfolio and reinvest the proceeds in a passive strategy. The only costs you will have incurred related to brokerage commissions and bid-ask spreads, which have come down substantially and are relatively quite low.

Now, let us revisit the transaction in the case of a *taxable* investor. He or she will not only have to pay the same comparatively low transaction costs, but will also have to incur capital gains taxes on the market appreciation of the portfolio that is liquidated.

Taxable investors can thus be hurt twice by a poor decision: they must live with disappointing performance *and* accept the tax costs associated with any subsequent change. We will have ample opportunities to come back to this point in later chapters.

Developing an investment policy

Though critical, developing a strategic wealth management plan is a complex exercise. The ultimate outcome of the planning process is an investment policy. Charles Ellis[4] frames the issue well:

> Clients of investment managers all too often delegate or more accurately abdicate … responsibilities which they should keep for themselves. Their undelegatable responsibilities are: setting explicit investment policies consistent with their objectives; defining long-range objectives appropriate to their particular fund; and managing their managers to ensure that their policies are being followed.

I view an investment policy, in practical terms, as a letter that a family or an investor writes to himself or herself. It should discuss values, goals and needs. It should cover philosophical preferences with respect to wealth management issues, together with important constraints. It should describe both strategic asset allocation and the general ranges within which portfolio rebalancing will be conducted. Finally, it should specify the governance structures to administer and control the process, and the way in which investment decisions will be made and implemented.

The importance of asset location

Recognizing that most individual investors have more than one pocket is another crucial piece of the private wealth management puzzle. I have come to refer to the problem as '*asset location*,' in part to recall its better-known alter ego, 'asset allocation.' At a minimum, private investors will often have a tax-deferred pocket, usually holding their retirement assets, and taxable personal savings. As the individual's wealth increases, so do both the justification for more comprehensive financial and estate plans, and the incentive to carry them out. Though multiple, these locations eventually fall in one of four main categories:

- taxable personal accounts;
- structures designed to shelter personal assets from the impact of current taxation;
- structures designed to facilitate intergenerational wealth transfers; and
- structures designed to carry out charitable endeavors.

Multiple asset locations increase the complexity of any solution we eventually select, as we will see in Chapter 5.

Integrated wealth planning

Integrated wealth planning brings together and integrates three different disciplines that interact when dealing with individual investors: estate, financial and investment planning. Estate planning has to do with the transfer of wealth across generations in the most tax-efficient fashion. Financial planning is concerned with meeting cash flow needs, now and in the future,

Investment planning deals with the selection of investment strategies. Integrated wealth planning has to do with selecting investment strategies that most appropriately take advantage of the opportunities afforded by each location and meet the cash flow, generational (or dynastic) and emotional needs of the investor.

Though often a complex exercise, this integration is an absolute must. I often ask a simple question: 'would you rather operate an abacus or a calculator?' An abacus is simple to make, but complex to learn to operate. Contrast that with the user-friendliness of a calculator, which it is much more difficult to design and manufacture. The message is easy to understand: complexity is only a problem if it makes it difficult to act. Engineering complexity for the sake of operating simplicity is not only *not* a problem, it may well be viewed as a virtue.

Portfolio optimization

The *optimization process* associated with wealth planning is one of the areas where the lessons of the institutional investment management industry must be learned and appropriately applied. Traditional pre-tax, single-location, single-period models demonstrate the value of a disciplined approach to addressing the risk-return trade-off. However, they fall short of the mark when it comes to individual wealth planning, for two main reasons.

First, they fail to recognize that the appropriate conceptual framework requires an after-tax, multi-location and multi-period framework. Moving an existing portfolio to a better mix and rebalancing the portfolio on some regular basis both involve substantial costs, principally, but not solely, associated with taxes. Portfolio rebalancing reflects the need to avoid, or at least manage, portfolio drift. Almost more importantly, it also reflects the fact that individuals expect the portfolio to accommodate certain cash flow needs, most of which require assets to be bought and sold, and thus capital gains to be realized and taxes on them paid. This brings the multi-period dimension into the picture.

Second, tax-oblivious institutional models typically do not provide for a sufficient focus on the consequences and management of decision risk, nor for the uncertainties associated with investor reaction to market gyrations or their cash flow needs.

There is also a need to *redefine the way an individual perceives or experiences the investment trade-off*. The real trade-off for an individual investor should most often be expressed, not in terms of risk and return, but in terms of comfort and reward. Thus, the optimization process should incorporate simulation features to allow the investor to see the full range of possible outcomes and evaluate his or her likely reactions to certain outcomes. In Australia, I selected a few notable historical time periods and simulated the performance of a possible portfolio mix during these periods. I then asked clients to try to 're-live' the past, in particular asking: 'can you imagine how you would have felt then if the following outcome happened?' This helped us determine the suitability of a strategy, as the historical context 'brought the alternative to life.' In short, it is another instance that illustrates the belief that investors need to understand issues both intellectually *and* emotionally.

Finally, the process must incorporate a *reality test*. It should also allow you to gauge whether the proposed asset mix will effectively interact with the underlying attributes of estate planning strategies, not only in the most likely case, but across a full range of potential market patterns. There would indeed be little point in a strategy that involves an investor paying important upfront costs, yet has a meaningful probability not to produce the expected result. For instance, it might be worth considering the issue of who bears the residual investment risk in a charitable endeavor. An overly aggressive strategy in a charitable pocket would not be a good idea, if the investor were not explicitly seeking to have the charity bear residual investment risks. By contrast, too conservative a strategy in a defective grantor trust would make little sense, as it might prevent any significant wealth being passed on to the beneficiaries of this very useful U.S. estate planning technique.

Implementing the wealth management plan

For many individuals, implementing the strategy is the real start of the action. It is true that it involves making decisions, but these decisions must be well informed and carefully made. Implementing the wealth management plan principally is concerned with manager selection and management, but it also involves several important other issues, such as market timing and tactical portfolio rebalancing, the use of derivative instruments and, most importantly for newly liquid investors: initial portfolio funding.

Differentiating individual strategies

Though the development of the wealth management plan has required us to focus on a number of potential strategies, it is the implementation of the plan that is critical. The plans that I have helped investors design usually draw a sharp distinction among individual strategies, particularly with respect to the extent to which a manager is expected to add value and what value that manager is expected to generate. An important item of caution, to which Chapter 9 is dedicated, concerns the often-used dichotomy between 'active' and 'passive' management. I feel that it obscures the nature of the true choice. A so-called 'passive' strategy may actually be viewed as 'passive with respect to security selection' and 'active relative to taxes.'[5] However, even within the traditional definition of active management, there are a number of nuances that many individuals do not take the time to consider during the planning phase. For instance, how do we approach the choice between two equity managers, one of whom might hold 50 large capitalization stocks in a portfolio designed to beat the S&P 500 Index, while the other wants to hold 150? Similarly, how do they deal with the choice between two fixed-income managers, one of whom makes significant duration bets, while the other focuses solely on credit or sector decisions? Being able to understand and appreciate these nuances, and to make decisions in a sensible fashion is the crux of the problem.

Other old habits worth discarding

At the top of the list, you find the tendency to divide portfolios into too many sub-portfolios. Many investors, probably in part instructed by an institutional experience, want to differentiate between and diversify across investment styles. In an equity context, they often extend that to the desire to differentiate between large and small capitalization stocks, if not taking that segmentation further, when they want to distinguish and select among large, small and mid-capitalization equities. Experience, however, consistently illustrates the futility of such an effort. The more narrowly you define your investment strategy, the more you are defaulting into the sequential portfolio optimization mode, which should be rejected. Indeed, you tend to increase the needs for portfolio rebalancing, with its attendant tax costs.

Assume that you want to break your equity portfolio between two competing styles: 'growth' and 'value.' Though a sensible idea in a tax-oblivious mode, it is not likely to work in practice for the investor who needs to worry about taxes. This is because many individual stocks will tend to migrate back and forth between these styles as their price and earning cycles interact. Thus, investors who create two sub-portfolios, one a 'growth portfolio' and the other a 'value portfolio,' will find themselves exposed to the impact of capital gain taxes as the underlying managers rebalance their sub-portfolios to reflect changes in the indexes describing their respective universes. A style-neutral or blended portfolio would not be exposed to these shifts, because individual stocks, though they migrate across style-defined universes, remain within the overall broad equity world. A similar case could be made with respect to a size-based segmentation.

Coming a close second on the list is the tendency to want to time markets or strategies. Clearly, it would be foolish to argue that it does not make sense to look into the relative attractiveness of individual strategies. A periodic look at overall portfolio balance can be rewarding, but a healthy dose of humility is required. Thinking of the whole portfolio indeed makes it necessary also to review the traditional portfolio management paradigm. Though many individual investors may not immediately recognize it, it is a fact that our industry has an incredibly high rate of 'error.' In fact, a quotation attributed to Sir John Templeton says it best: 'even the best portfolio manager is not right more than 65% of the time!' The corollary of this must be that the best portfolio manager is wrong at least one third of the time, and that most of us are wrong much more often than that. Would you take a cruise if the ship had a 35% chance of sinking? Enter taxes. Often, the taxable investor will pay taxes for the privilege of seeing a decision that they did not need to make go awry.

Finally, individuals might be well served rethinking the role of derivative instruments. Though there may be two decision axes (asset allocation and security selection), there is only one execution mechanism: buying and selling individual securities. Except when implemented through derivative instruments, an approach relying on substantial shifts across assets, strategies or managers is fraught with danger. The decision sequence we all follow explains why it is so. In a world of physical securities, the sequence comprises four steps: I have an investment idea; I execute the portfolio shift suggested by that idea (buying and selling individual securities); I pay the taxes associated with the sell side of that trade and – I pray, because I do not know whether the initial idea will work out or not. If it works out, everything is fine. If it does not, I will have paid capital gains taxes for the privilege of making a poor decision.

Contrast this with the sequence that we follow when we use derivative securities. The first two steps are the same, though the execution of the trade takes place through an 'opening derivative trade,' rather than through the purchase and sale of individual securities. Note

.

that this property of derivatives applies in all jurisdictions where taxes are only due when a trade is 'closed.' However, the latter two are inverted. Indeed, my third step is not to pay taxes – as taxes are due not on the opening leg of a trade, but, generally, on the outcome of the trade when it is 'closed' – but to watch as the investment consequences of that trade work out. Then, if it was a good idea, I will have to pay taxes, as I need to close the derivative trade and realize a capital gain. But if the idea was not a successful one, I will not only not have had to pay taxes, but may in fact be able to take a loss that can be used to shelter a gain elsewhere in the portfolio. The point, however, is that I have avoided paying taxes for the privilege of making a bad trade.

A further, second-order cost of periodic portfolio reallocations has convinced me to keep tactical portfolio moves not executed through derivative instruments to a minimum. Whenever I need to reduce portfolio exposure to a manager, I have to ask that manager to sell some of the assets entrusted to him or her, in order to generate the cash proceeds I need to raise the portfolio's exposure to another. These trades inject a degree of portfolio management inefficiency into the investment process of that manager, and force him or her to make a difficult and unnecessary choice: should I forgo tax efficiency and reduce each position proportionately? Or should I strive for tax efficiency and accept that I will be maintaining a less well balanced portfolio to ease the pain for my client?

Manager selection

Having selected the appropriate strategies, the next crucial step is to select the manager. Another healthy dose of humility is helpful, as manager selection is not really a science. It is another one of those areas where the interaction between investment and psychological issues is both richest and most important. Even in a world where there are no taxes, and only a few psychological likes and dislikes, manager selection is a particularly difficult exercise, because time series do not tell the whole story and because managers change. The classic danger to be avoided is to rely on the past to select managers. For instance, consider the behavior and composition of the quartiles of one of the leading manager surveys, compiled by the consulting firm Campbell and Cooke in Australia. In the mid-1980s, a manager in the top quartile in any given quarter had a better than 50/50 chance of finding himself below the median in the subsequent 12 months. Others have performed similar analyses,[6] which suggests that these surveys are best used in an intermediate to long-term time frame, principally to select managers out. Indeed, managers who do poorly in competitive terms seem more likely to stay at the bottom of the surveys than those who do very well. Those indeed rarely stay at the top for a large number of short-term periods. Statisticians would add that historical performance analysis is made particularly difficult because of 'survivorship bias.' Survivorship bias results from the fact that you can only look at the managers who survived the full period you are considering, as any manager who dropped out during the period will be ignored, though you might have selected him or her without the benefit of hindsight.

In the end, you need to look for at least three attributes (discussed in more depth in Chapter 17). First, for those strategies where tax efficiency is important, I am ruthless and insist on the process described by the manager being tax-efficient. I am particularly careful to avoid 'forensic tax efficiency' (a great phrase coined by Peter Torvik, a former colleague at U.S. Bank), which has to do with concluding that a process must have been tax-efficient if the observed tax efficiency is above average. How wrong this is. There are market circumstances that promote unintentional tax efficiency and can turn suddenly. For instance, a sustained period of relative success for a particular industry or theme in the equity world can promote low portfolio turnover. This will lead to apparent tax efficiency, together with the substantial accumulation of unrealized capital gains. Yet there will almost surely come a time when the manager feels that he or she needs to rebalance away from the hitherto successful industry or theme, triggering massive unrealized capital gains and causing distressfully poor tax efficiency.

Second, I also insist on a process that is well-defined and makes sense. Though marketing literature can cover a multitude of sins, a careful questioning of the portfolio manager will usually bring to life the difference between insights and biases. Insights are the raw materials that a portfolio manager transforms into superior performance. Biases can at times produce spurious performance, as a manager who dislikes a particular category of equities, for instance, will do well when that category is out of favor; or vice versa. The experience of non-U.S. equity managers from 1990 to 1995 is a good example. Any manager who was biased against Japan looked like a hero, as Japan was doing very poorly, but, early in the period at least, accounted for nearly two thirds of the index. Change the performance assessment period to the preceding five years, 1985 to 1990, and the bias against Japan was extremely painful. To eliminate or at least to manage potential bias, I always aim to evaluate performance over a full cycle.

Third, and finally, I look for portfolio managers who have lived through at least one and preferably two full cycles in their respective areas of specialty. The crucial insight here is this: you should not confuse a bull market with genius. Further, experiencing at least some adversity will promote the necessary humility and increase the likelihood that the manager will not alter his or her style to manage through a difficult market environment. Experience indeed consistently suggests that, except in the hedge fund world, style rotators seem to have the worst performance records.

Manager coordination

Manager selection in the world of taxable individual investors also presents a coordination problem that does not really exist in the world of tax-oblivious or tax-exempt investors. Individual investors need to temper the natural tendency to look for manager diversification and weigh it against the risk of different managers trading in the same securities. Two managers trading in the same security can create 'wash sales,' defined as instances where a trade in a security occurs within less than 30 days on either side of another trade that generated a capital loss. Wash sales can be insidious, as, except when you specifically focus on the issue, it can be years before you identify the problem, at which point you are faced with the need to reconstruct long and complex transaction histories.

Investors must also coordinate the activity of all managers, across multiple asset classes.

There may indeed be times where total portfolio tax efficiency may be gained by inviting a manager in a poorly performing asset to take losses, even if that manager is doing well relative to the relevant benchmark. These losses can then be used to rebalance a portfolio that has drifted too far from its strategic balance or to allow another manager to refresh the tax basis of a portfolio in risk of lock-up. Portfolio lock-up or freeze arises when unrealized capital gains are so large as to make any trade not reasonable. Asking a manager to take losses can be one of the most difficult decisions, as it can involve seemingly penalizing a manager doing well in relative terms to help another one who may be trailing the market. Yet, in total portfolio terms, the decision clearly makes sense.

This naturally leads us into the supervising and monitoring phase of the process, to which we turn next. Before we do so, however, allow me a final comment in support of the idea of keeping small manager stables and aiming to establish long-term relationships with these managers. The difficulty associated with certain implementation decisions has led me to conclude that the relationship that individuals build with their managers needs to be more subtle and more oriented to the long term than might be the case in the institutional world. A greater sense of partnership will make it easier to coordinate across managers and promote the right kind of total portfolio focus on the part of all managers, such as the suggestion that you might take some money away from me for some time, because that will help the whole portfolio. This altruistic attitude can only be expected from a manager who will be rewarded with more assets when that makes sense, and who will not be unduly penalized for some short-term performance problem.

Supervising and monitoring progress

The initial effort to outline value, goals, and needs, and to enhance individual understanding of opportunities and issues, goes a long way toward raising the probability that the wealth management process will be successful. However, there remains the need to monitor progress. In a world where returns are uncertain at best, a few of the assumptions originally incorporated in the modeling of the portfolio strategy are likely to appear far-fetched at one point in time or another.

Certain strategies will fall substantially short of the mark from time to time, and risk will also appear to have been greatly understated. Remember that, in a normal distribution, there is a 66% probability that actual outcomes will fall within a one standard deviation band around the mean expected return. That probability rises to 95% when the band is widened to two standard deviations and to 99% when the band extends to three standard deviations. Unfortunately, with the riskier end of the return spectrum, looking at the 99% confidence interval usually involves a range of possible returns so wide as to seem almost meaningless. Many investors tend to develop a 99% confidence in the return range consistent with the 66% interval, creating the wherewithal for substantial surprises, most of which are unpleasant.

Similarly, with the relatively high error rate that each manager must endure, there will be periods of time where one's expectations will not be met. A manager will have to go through a tough patch when his or her insights seem 'out of synch' with market realities.

A private client once asked me to advise him on whether to change the manager of his firm's pension fund. The manager had made a decision that was totally consistent with the style he had advertised, yet the results were proving to be quite poor. I advised the individual to stick with that manager until the cycle fully unfolded and then review the decision. He might decide to terminate that manager because he, the client, had been uncomfortable with the implications of the manager's style. But he should not penalize the manager for doing what he had said he would do and simply getting a big bet wrong. A solid monitoring process can therefore help control the 'decision risk' associated with manager performance difficulties.

The challenge faced by individual investors and their advisors takes on three main dimensions. The first has to do with the *design and delivery of a reasonable portfolio appraisal*. At issue here is the fact that reasonableness is very much in the eyes of the beholder. Earlier, we met Dave, who liked to see his portfolio virtually daily and who now looks at it quarterly. It goes without saying that the kind of information available on a daily basis will be very different from the data that can be presented quarterly. Designing the contents of the desired periodical reporting package is the first step to a successful wealth management process. The right package is the 'body language' of my management process (just as John T. Lane, a former colleague at J.P. Morgan, once told me that a compensation program is the 'body language' of the organization). The idea is that the contents of the report and its design must reinforce the decision process I have put in place. The report must ostensibly provide the information on which I will base the decisions I want to make, in the way I say I want to make them.

The second challenge faced by individual investors relates to *performance measurement and assessment*. I once suggested[7] that performance measurement is trivial in a pre-tax environment and that it becomes considerably trickier when taxes are taken into account. We can take this further to say that pre-tax performance assessment requires care in a pre-tax world and becomes even more difficult when dealing with taxable portfolios. In a pre-tax world, the determination of investment returns is simply formulaic. Yet a number of assumptions must be made before being able to compute a sensible after-tax return, in many jurisdictions. Do we want to think in pre-liquidation or post-liquidation terms? How do we deal with cash flows? Does it make sense to look at any individual portfolio pocket?

The question of performance assessment is even more perplexing. Assessing returns requires the computation of some benchmark, which becomes quite an involved endeavor, as one can argue that there is no obvious uniform benchmark for any portfolio. Indeed, after-tax returns are dependent upon both portfolio activity and market opportunities (just as is the case in a pre-tax environment), but the problem is compounded by the fact that they also depend upon the starting conditions. This is the security selection equivalent to the 'cost of getting there,' which we discussed earlier, when dealing with the strategic asset allocation problem. In fact, I once concluded, only partially mischievously, that there are twice as many benchmarks as there are portfolios. Each benchmark must reflect the specific circumstances of each portfolio, and there must be one pre- and one post-liquidation benchmark for each.

The third challenge relates to the need to *provide for governance* in circumstances where it is not always natural. I am speaking here of the need to create a process through which decisions will be made, and to stick to that process.

> Don and his wife, a couple of young entrepreneurs, whose fortune had become liquid through the sale of their single concentrated holding, intuitively sensed the need for a process. In fact, they told me that they were not fully comfortable with the way their wealth was managed, because they did not know for sure how all decisions were made. They insisted on the need to develop a clear decision structure to ensure that they knew who was responsible for what part of which decision.
>
> Jack's family, whose wealth was also based on the sale of their investment in the company in which Jack was a senior executive, had the same problem, except that it extended beyond the first generation. He wanted his two children involved in the management process and the need was therefore clear for a supervisory structure where parents and children had equal votes.

Though Don and Jack understood the need for family governance, most families are happy to operate under the watchful but kindly eye of the patriarch or matriarch. A lack of family governance often leads to significant challenges and at times open conflicts, which can persist beyond the financial matters that triggered them. Thus, being able to handle business dynamics in a family context is one of the most difficult problems faced by individual investors. Yet, when addressed successfully, it can provide by far the most satisfaction.

I serve on the board of a family office, which itself has an explicit and formalized structure for the relationship between members of the family. It has survived and even prospered through multiple generation changes over more than a century and kept more than 100 individuals united in the family. This achievement, which undoubtedly also reflects the unique family values that are taught to each generation, illustrate the importance of the appropriate structure. I cannot resist mentioning one of these wonderful values, which I find particularly inspiring: 'we are the stewards of the family's wealth, for the benefit of future generations.'

Summary and implications

The nature of the wealth management process and its distinct, yet iterative phases is one of the most visible illustrations of the need for a new wealth management paradigm.

First, you must take the time to *go through the whole process*. I was once admonished (by Pierre Daviron, who in the late 1970s was head of international investment research at J.P. Morgan): 'learn to waste time!' Take the time to think, even if it does not seem that anything concrete is being produced at that time. Many individual investors see the first two phases of the wealth management process as a waste of time. They might be tempted to avoid any effort to develop a better understanding of their own and their family's psychology. Yet I know I am not overstating the case when I state that many wealth management problems can be avoided with careful and thoughtful planning. Time 'wasted' on planning will pay huge dividends when the world takes an unexpected turn.

Second, *different problems will naturally require different solutions*. Recognizing that an individual investor's situation will require him or her to adopt an individual solution is a crucial step toward success. The need for an 'individual solution,' in this instance, conveys two different messages. On the one hand, it tells me that I may not be appropriately served by the solution adopted, with success, by my neighbor, friend or acquaintance. Thus, I need to be careful to take the right part of any advice and to make sure that I do not simply transpose the solution to my own circumstances. On the other hand, it tells me that the fact that I need to be concerned about taxes means that I should be careful when someone offers what looks like an institutional, cookie-cutter solution. I need to be prepared to go through the process of determining my own needs, the constraints that apply to me – and not necessarily to others – and to design and implement my own strategy. The professional advisor needs to appreciate that making the solution as individually tailored as possible is the key to a long and successful relationship.

Third, *technology is making the advisors' jobs easier.* Imagine a world where there is no internet and only limited computer power. Designing the wealth management plan would be very difficult, because we would not have the necessary optimization power, or, even more simply, a way to provide the education needed to develop rational expectations. Providing customized portfolio reports would be extremely difficult, not to say impossible in a profitable environment. Contrast that with where we are today. We can run the most complex optimization without the investor needing to 'lift and look under the hood.' The computer has made it simpler to address complex problems, and to provide simple and yet relevant trade-offs to facilitate individual decision-making. Highly sophisticated computer graphics and simulation capabilities allow us to provide relevant education on capital markets, and illustrate what a change in pattern might mean. Finally, the age of the internet has ushered in mass customization. Though it is still a rare commodity, I am convinced that we will soon be able to access our portfolios directly through the internet, customize the views to reflect exactly what we want to see, and be able to order those reports printed and sent to us.

---

[1] See Kathleen Gurney, *Your Money Personality*, New York: Doubleday, 1988.

[2] Meir Statman is the Glenn Klimek Professor of Finance at the Leavey School of Business, Santa Clara University. He made the comment referenced here at the 8th Annual Family Office Forum, hosted on June 25 and 26, 2001 by the Institute for Investment Research in Chicago, Illinois.

[3] See Alletzhauser, Al, *The House of Nomura*, London: Bloomsbury, 1990, pp. 144–45. This refers to the 'Million Ryo Savings Chest' campaign launched in 1953 by Tsunao Okumura, then President of Nomura.

[4] See Ellis, Charles, *Investment Policy: How to Win the Loser's Game*, second edition, Homewood, Illinois: Business One Irwin, 1993, p. 2.

[5] See Stein, David M., and Premkumar Narasimhan, 'Of Passive and Active Equity Portfolios in the Presence of Taxes,' *The Journal of Private Portfolio Management*, Fall 1999, pp. 55–63. David Stein is President of Parametric Portfolio Associates and Prem Narasimhan is one of his colleagues.

[6] See Christopherson, Jon A., and Andrew L. Turner, 'Volatility and Predictability of Manager Alpha,' *The Journal of Portfolio Management*, Fall 1991, pp. 5–12; Bogle, John C., 'Selecting Equity Mutual Funds,' *The Journal of Portfolio Management*, Winter 1992, pp. 94–100; Bailey, Jeffery V., 'Are Manager Universes Acceptable Performance Benchmarks?,' *The Journal of Portfolio Management*, Spring 1992, pp. 9–13; Goetzman, William N., and Roger G. Ibbotson, 'Do Winners Repeat?,' *The Journal of Portfolio Management*, Winter 1994, pp. 9–18; Bauman, W. Scott, and Robert E. Miller, 'Can Managed Portfolio Performance Be Predicted?,' *The Journal of Portfolio Management*, Summer 1994, pp. 31–40; and Beckers, Stan, 'Manager Skill and Investment Performance: How Strong is the Link?,' *The Journal of Portfolio Management*, Summer 1997, pp. 9–23.

[7] Brunel, Jean L.P., 'The Upside-Down World of Tax-Aware Investing', *Trust and Estates*, February 1997, pp. 34–42.

Chapter 2

Understanding investor psychology

In the Introduction, I emphasized the need to change the paradigm as we moved from investment to wealth management. On the surface, this may seem like a small change; splitting hairs or an exercise in semantics. Yet the fundamental differentiating features of the individual asset management process are, first, the impact of taxation, and, second, the interaction between investor psychology and the uncertainties associated with capital markets and individual cash flow needs. In this chapter, I will focus on investor psychology

Appreciating that we are dealing with individuals is not a new idea

Many portfolio managers or investment advisors have understood for a long time that managing individual assets requires a different approach.[1] However, until the early 1980s and the development of behavioral finance, that different approach did not really help individual investors.

> When I became the chief investment officer of J.P. Morgan's Global Private Bank, I kept hearing a phrase that puzzled me: 'it is his (or her) money.' The phrase typically came in response to a query as to why a portfolio manager was doing something that I found surprising, and that I was invariably told had been specifically requested by the investor. Intuitively, it appeared that something was amiss, as the phrase by itself made only limited sense. Granted, on the one hand, there was nothing obviously objectionable, for 'it' was indeed the individual's money. We had to make adjustments to the investment process to recognize the individual nature of the investor. On the other hand, it did not make sense that an individual should hire a professional investment manager and then proceed to tell that professional what trade should be carried out in the portfolio. As my father was a surgeon, an analogy came to mind: you do not go to see your physician and ask for an appendectomy, you tell him or her about a stomach ache and then wait for the diagnosis.

Dealing with individuals requires us to adopt different approaches, but this goes quite a bit beyond simply pandering to their 'worst' instincts. We need to take the time to understand what issues and problems they bring to the table. Our job is then to develop the best possible solutions to their problems. For instance, in 1998[2] I was trying to understand why individual investors would select an investment strategy that, to an investment purist, seemingly made no sense. The focus of that analysis was on absolute return strategies, executed through a combination of physical securities and options. Discussing decision and opportunity risks, I concluded:

investors with performance assessment horizons of up to five years ought to consider absolute return strategies seriously, in effect trading some reduction in decision and opportunity risks for lower long-term return expectations.

What I had discovered was simply that individuals do behave sensibly, even when they seem to break certain objective rules, if 'soft' issues are taken into account. *The challenge revolves around taking these soft issues into account and integrating them in a professional response to the investment problem at hand.*

A different decision framework

The first important step is to recognize that individuals follow a different decision framework. Monsieur De La Palice was a Maréchal de France (born in 1470, died in 1525) who is remembered not for his war prowess but for the naiveté of his poetry, which always seems to state the obvious. If asked to differentiate between an institutional and an individual investor, he would probably have stated that the principal difference is that the latter is an individual! From that obvious statement a kernel of insight emerges.

Institutional investors typically look at their investment problems in the context of an asset/liability decision.[3] Consider a defined benefit pension plan. The pension manager's job is to make sure that the employer's contribution can be minimized while preserving the integrity of the plan. That integrity is defined in terms of being able to meet the plan's required payments to retirees. You can use standard actuarial processes to estimate the flow of benefit payments to current and future retirees. The challenge is thus to manage the assets so that they match or exceed the present value of these future benefits. There may be the need, from time to time, to add to the plan through employer contributions, but the ideal circumstance is when no such contribution is needed. We saw in the previous chapter that a process framed in an asset/liability context imposes a discipline on the pension manager. There are a number of analytical tools available to him or her to describe the behavior of the liabilities. For instance, one can compute the interest sensitivity of these liabilities (their duration).[4] Another level of discipline comes from the need to report to a board, which will tend to focus on decision processes as well as performance.

A wealthy investor usually has no such constraint. At lower levels of wealth, one can argue that saving for children's college education or for retirement can create some form of intellectual discipline. At higher levels of wealth, these considerations no longer seem relevant, as they can be handled through 'petty cash.' Yet it is clear that, throughout the wealth spectrum, the investor is not emotionally detached from either the decisions or their outcome. Frustrated by the limitations ostensibly imposed by standard finance theory, researchers developed behavioral finance.

A historical perspective on behavioral finance

According to Brian Rom,[5] behavioral finance is not new: it grew out of the field of cognitive psychology having to do with the investment world in 1951. Behavioral finance differs from standard finance to the extent that it does not assume that people aim to maximize their utility.[6] In that context, maximizing one's utility should be understood to mean that people would be guided by the goal and act to 'get the biggest bang for whatever buck they have'. Scott Budge[7] makes the same general point:

> interest in the psychology of investments has begun to intensify, even though the associated issues are as old as time. At this point, the psychology of investments can be said to provide a rubric under which the apparently irrational behavior of both lay and professional investors can begin to be understood.

There are two sets of reasons why behavioral finance is attracting so much attention. The first relates to the fact that individual investors have surpassed institutional investors in terms of the assets they control, in part because of a shift from defined benefit to defined contribution pension plans and in part because of a substantial increase in private wealth.[8] The second has to do with the commoditization of investment products, which is in part a function of the increasing role of investment consultants, who have pushed managers to adopt well-specified styles. It also, in part, reflects the fact that investment management has become a big business, where large institutions must manage business risk and thus ensure that individual portfolio managers do not take excessive risks.

Behavioral finance proposes both explanations of apparently surprising individual behavior when dealing with financial decisions and a set of principles to help individual investors improve the quality of these decisions. Robert Olsen[9] had even higher expectations for behavioral finance: he felt that it might provide an explanation of 'excessive' stock-price volatility.

Principles of behavioral finance[10]

Howard Raiffa[11] introduced the idea that there are three approaches to the analysis of decisions. *Normative* analysis focuses on the ideal that actual decisions should strive to approximate. *Descriptive* analysis is concerned with the manner in which real people actually make decisions. *Prescriptive* analysis deals with practical advice and help that people may use to make rational decisions. Daniel Kahneman and Mark Riepe[12] define the role of financial advisors in that framework:

> Financial advising is a prescriptive activity whose main objective should be to guide investors to make decisions that best serve their interests. To advise investors effectively, advisors must be guided by an accurate picture of the cognitive and emotional weaknesses of investors [as they make investment decisions].

These weaknesses come in three main flavors and each can have a major impact on the success of wealth management plans. First, investors can make a faulty assessment of their own interests and true wishes. Second, they can ignore important relevant facts. Finally, there are limits to the ability of investors to accept advice and to live with the decisions they make.

According to Meir Statman,[13] individuals at times tend to be too intelligent for their own good. He cites an experiment to which both humans and rats are subjected. Each is asked to press one of two buttons, A or B. The 'right choice' will lead humans to get monetary reward, while rats will get food. Clearly, the success associated with each button is not known in advance. Looking at the results, he then tells us that A has a one in five chance of winning, while B offers a four in five chance of being successful. The decision pattern followed by human and rats is very interesting. Both species initially use a random approach to 'learn' the success ratio associated with each button. After a while, rats keep pressing B, though, one time out of five on average, they are not rewarded. Humans, by contrast, keep experimenting, though they end up averaging choosing B four out of five times. The point of the story is that intelligence involves searching for patterns, yet, at times, it can also lead us to jump to conclusions. As individuals, we suffer from *cognitive biases.*

Cognitive biases lead people to be deceived or misled by their minds because they do not frame decisions in the right manner.[14] Consider the classic visual illusion shown in Exhibit 2.1. Though I know that the two horizontal lines are equal in length, and though I can in fact convince myself of that fact by using a ruler, I still see the second line as longer than the first. I see it that way until it is appropriately framed in (1b). Behavioral finance helps investors and their advisors deal with the problem, teaching them about cognitive illusions and decision-making, and developing the skills to recognize situations in which a particular error is likely.

The mistakes of intuitive reasoning are not easily eliminated. Making a decision, whether in the investment world or in everyday circumstances, in effect involves selecting one choice among different options. Decision theorists argue that each choice – they call them 'gambles' – is characterized by the range of its possible outcomes and by the probability of these outcomes. The rational decision-maker looks at these probabilities, based on his or her beliefs, and selects the one that appears to be preferable.

Yet individuals are not always rational; they commit cognitive errors. Rational people, in Statman's words, do not 'confuse noise with information,' but individuals often do. They do so because errors creep into the process through two doors. First, there are errors of judgment, which many authors call 'biases.' Second, there can be errors of preferences.

Exhibit 2.1

The Muller-Lyer Illusion

Sources: Daniel Kahneman and Mark W. Riepe, 'Aspects of Investor Psychology,' *Journal of Portfolio Management,* Summer 1998, p. 53; Heidi L. Schneider and Alyssa A. Lappen, 'Behavioral Finance: Old Wine in a New Bottle,' *Journal of Wealth Management,* Fall 2000, p. 11.

Judgment biases

Many authors have looked into and discussed these biases.[15] Kahneman and Riepe propose four broad categories of judgment biases: overconfidence, optimism, hindsight and over-reaction to chance events.

Overconfidence

Being overconfident means that we do not assume the right probability of a certain outcome relative to another. Imagine the simple case of a decision with a binary outcome: you can earn or lose money. Overconfidence will lead you to overestimate the probability that you will earn money and underestimate the potentially negative consequences. To illustrate the extent to which one can be overconfident, Hersh Shefrin[16] uses a 'trivia test,' which first appeared in a book by Edward Russo and Paul Schoemaker.[17] The point of the test is to answer each of the 10 questions – found in Exhibit 2.2 below – but with a twist. You are not expected to provide the 'right answer.' Rather, you must provide the extremes of a range within which you are 90% confident the actual answer will fall. A rational individual would select a single point if he or she knew the answer; a narrow range if he or she had a fair idea of what the answer was; and a very wide range if he or she had no idea of what the answer might be.

The evidence from this test suggests that we are not rational. One would expect most people to miss just one out of the 10 questions, if they were really 90% confident in their answers. In fact, Shefrin reports that most miss four to seven and that barely 1% of people miss only one question. This means that the other 99% are *overconfident* and thus not rational.

Being overconfident means that you will be surprised more often than 'normal'. In reality, the important insight is that you often will receive a *negative surprise*. A negative surprise is defined as an unforeseen event that produces a negative outcome. It does not mean that the surprise will always be unpleasant in itself. For instance, a negative surprise could still be a sharp market rally when you were expecting a further fall. It is pleasant if you still held stocks, but it could be a negative surprise if your equity exposure was lower than it would normally be, since you could have earned a higher return. Shefrin illustrates this:

Exhibit 2.2

Trivia test*

1. How old was Martin Luther King when he died?
2. How long, in miles, is the Nile River?
3. How many countries were members of OPEC in 1989?
4. How many books are there in the Hebrew Bible?
5. What is the diameter, in miles, of the moon?
6. What is the weight, in pounds, of an empty Boeing 747?
7. In what year was Wolfgang Amadeus Mozart born?
8. How long, in days, is the gestation period of an Asian elephant?
9. What is the air distance, in miles, from London to Tokyo?
10. How deep, in feet, is the deepest known point in the ocean?

*see end of chapter for answers

---

people get surprised more often than expected. Sometimes the surprise is pleasant, as when a bull market continues when the consensus was for a reversal, and the investor has been long in equities. But, occasionally, the surprise is quite unpleasant, as happened in 1994 when the Federal Reserve Board raised interest rates six times.

Optimism

Optimism is, to a certain extent, a variant on the overconfidence theme. Many individuals hold optimistic beliefs and tend to exaggerate their talents. Consider the pretty common statistic advanced by many behavioral specialists to prove that point: over 80% of all drivers, when asked, rate themselves 'above average.' Kahneman and Riepe propose another, just as instructive, observation: 'most undergraduates ... believe that they are less likely than their roommates to develop cancer or to have a heart attack before the age of 50.'

There are two other aspects of optimism that can have a direct impact on the way in which individuals handle their wealth. First, they tend to underestimate the likelihood of bad outcomes over which they have no control. Second, optimists are also prone to an illusion of control. Note that both aspects relate to the idea of control. This is particularly important when dealing with individuals in general and recently liquid entrepreneurs in particular. Wealthy individuals are used to being in control and to having a high level of knowledge. The world of financial assets comes as a surprise to many of them, leading to a number of potentially challenging circumstances.

Individuals tend to underestimate the role of chance in human affairs and to misperceive games of chance as games of skill. However, the potentially explosive combination of optimism and overconfidence needs to be recognised. Applied to the world of investment decision making, *optimism combined with overconfidence will naturally lead individual investors to overestimate their knowledge and their ability to control events, and to underestimate risks.*

Optimism, overconfidence and 'momentum bias'

An interesting consequence of optimism and overconfidence is that they help explain the apparent built-in 'momentum bias' observed in individuals.[18] That momentum bias is visible in the fact that people tend to be optimists in bull markets and pessimists in bear markets.[19]

Two interesting statistics[20] illustrate the point. First, in March 2000, individuals expected U.S. equities to return 14.4% in the following 12 months.[21] In April 2001, individual expectations for equity returns over the next twelve months had fallen to 7.2%. The sharp equity price correction had led them to 'discern' a new pattern. Second, in the same surveys, it is worth comparing the expectations of these individual investors for the market and for their own portfolios. In March 2000, they expected their personal portfolios to return 15.3% versus 14.4% for the market. In April 2001, they still thought that they would do better than the market, with a 8.7% personal portfolio return versus 7.2% for the market.

These two sets of statistics show that individuals have higher expectations when the environment has just been more favorable and lower expectations after a difficult period. They also show the optimism and overconfidence we just discussed, in their feeling that they will do better than average. Behavioral scientists would view this momentum bias as affecting the way risks are perceived. In good times, the risk of a potential downturn is underestimated, while, in bad times, it is the risk of a market rise that is underestimated. In short, optimism can be viewed as an overestimation of the chances that your view (whether you predict a pleasant or unpleasant event) will come to pass. This naturally has the potential to lead to both over- and under-valuations, which, to simplify, we might call 'bubbles' and 'crashes.'[22]

Hindsight

People tend, after the fact, to exaggerate their prior beliefs that the event would take place. The important facet of hindsight in the context of the relationship between an investor and his or her advisor is that it can damage trust. Indeed, once something has happened, individuals can feel 'betrayed' because an expert did not predict what now appears so simple. As the event, by now, appears to them obvious, they wonder how their advisor can be capable if he or she did not anticipate it, with all the information and skills at their disposal. Further, a decision that you might have made in a very reasonable way and that appeared quite sensible at the time can now appear so 'dumb' as to put your capabilities in doubt.

Note that a pattern is beginning to emerge here. Just as overconfidence and optimism are related, so is hindsight, to both of them. Hindsight, or rather the feeling derived from hindsight, tends to promote overconfidence. It is also related to the final category, to which we will turn next, as hindsight can make you think that the world is a more predictable place than it is, or that events that are totally random can be viewed as predictable.

An important implication of the need to deal with hindsight is that advisors should be forthright with individual investors and help them understand that they, the advisors, have severe limitations. It is true that it is hard to complete a sale when focusing your prospective client on your limitations, but wealth management is one of the areas where there is no real alternative. Investment managers will get things wrong a fair percentage of the time and investors need to know it. *An honest effort to educate clients on the vagaries of capital markets and to help them develop the right kind of expectations can go a long way toward dealing with hindsight.*

Overreaction to chance events

Overreaction to chance events is the tendency to discern patterns where they do not really exist. Imagine that you are asked to pick six numbers out of 50, say in a lottery. How likely do you feel you would be to pick 1, 2, 3, 4, 5, and 6? Most people would argue that it would be much too unlikely for the six numbers to be in a sequence such as that, yet the probability that this combination will come out is exactly the same as for any other combination of six numbers.

Experts have been investigating this tendency to find order where only randomness exists. One of the seminal pieces of work discusses the 'hot hand' fallacy, initially documented in a study of basketball players.[23] Believers in the fallacy claim that a player who has scored a number of baskets from the free-throw line, for instance, is more likely to sink the next one than someone who has missed his or her last attempt. Yet probability theory convincingly shows that streaks can happen and appear unbreakable – until they are broken. For instance, assume that you have an 80% chance of something happening and that such outcome has come to pass 14 times in a row. The probability that you will have the same outcome a 15th time is still almost 4%, by no means a negligible reading.

Knowing that people potentially overreact to chance events is only one half of the insight. The other half involves being able to predict, or at least anticipate, how they will react. Experience seems to suggest that, in the world of investors, there are two responses. The 'momentum' players tend to feel that the hot hand is likely to continue, while the 'contrarian' players want to bet in the opposite direction. I had to struggle with this issue when studying probability theory and Pascal's Law, which discusses the fact that certain events are independent. Think of the classic question: is there any greater chance that a bus will come in the next instant when you have waited at a bus stop for a long time? The answer is 'no,' if you are thinking truly of the next instant, but it might be different if you mean in 'the next several instants,' as in 'the next few minutes.' *The important lesson is that investors and their advisors must learn to identify real patterns and differentiate them from randomness.* We will turn to that in the next chapter, as we look at the main facets of capital market history.

Errors of preference

Errors of preference have a different character, in that they occur because individuals do not necessarily make 'rational' choices. Blaise Pascal (born 1623, died 1662) provides us with a great introduction to this topic. Pascal was simultaneously a mathematician, a physicist, a philosopher, and a theologian. Having, with Pierre de Fermat, created a basis for the theory of probabilities, he used a probabilistic dialog in a book entitled *Les Pensées* (Thoughts)[24] to discuss the existence of God. (Pascal had experienced a night of religious ecstasy on November 23, 1654: he then decided to consecrate his life to faith and piety). More specifically, he offered the argument, often called 'Pascal's Wager,' that we have everything to gain and nothing to lose from believing in God. The relevance of this anecdote to the point at hand was not lost on Peter Bernstein:[25]

> The only way to choose between a bet that God exists and a bet that there is no God down that infinite distance of Pascal's coin-tossing game is to decide whether an outcome in which God exists is *preferable* [emphasis added] – more valuable in some sense – than an outcome in which he does not exist, even though the probability may be only 50–50.

This is where the notion of preferences comes into the decision process, as individuals will tend to view risk and reward as a totality. The consequences of being right or wrong are both evaluated, in relation to broader goals.

Behavioral scientists list a number of errors of preference, but three are most relevant to the issue of understanding the opportunities and issues associated with wealth management planning.

Value function

The first error of preference to be considered here has to do with the individual's value function. People react in different ways to the same outcome, processing it through their personal value prisms to decide whether they are satisfied or not.[26] It is therefore important to make these value functions explicit rather than keep them implicit and thus unspecified.

Consider an instance where investor and advisor embark on the wrong relationship because the advisor projects his or her preferences, or 'value function,' onto the investor. Imagine that the investor is worried about losing wealth. Will the advisor's greater comfort with risky assets or strategies lead the investor astray? The reverse is just as true. The investor may be willing to tolerate risk because he or she feels that there is so much money that day-to-day needs could still be met even if half of the money were lost. Could a risk-averse advisor, projecting his or her own fear of being without money, lead the investor toward too conservative an investment strategy?

This carries an important practical implication. When discussing the formulation of an investment policy, you should aim to make the investor's value function explicit. For instance, one might ask what it would take for that investor to feel 'un-wealthy' (a term coined by David L. Brigham, who was CEO of J.P. Morgan Investment Management, Inc. in the mid-1990s).

One of the most crucial aspects of individual behavior is directly related to the value function: *loss aversion*. Shlomo Bernartzi and Richard Thaler[27] have worked extensively on the topic, and three of their findings are particularly relevant. First, people tend to be risk-seeking in the face of loss – they are prepared to risk a larger loss to avoid the immediate pain of a small but certain loss.

Second, individuals tend to evidence risk avoidance when they have a gain, even when they could rationally expect to do better with the risky choice.

Finally, an investor who considers a longer horizon will be willing to take risks that an individual oriented to a shorter term will reject, even if the investors' underlying aversion to risk is the same – this is often labeled 'myopic loss aversion,' after the short-term focus of the investor.[28] Interestingly, myopic loss aversion is not the same for everyone, thus requiring careful questioning to ensure that you fully appreciate the appropriate level for each situation.

In short, fully understanding the individual value function and its evolution over time is one of the most important rules for a private wealth manager.

Shape and attractiveness of gambles

The second error of preference that we will examine here relates to the preferences that individuals have when considering decisions, or gambles. Individuals do not all value gambles in the same fashion, but they do seem to prefer situations combining a high probability of a moderate gain and a small probability of a very large gain. Lola Lopes[29] states it best: individuals like gambles that combine a high level of security with some upside potential, and these prospects are associated with much hope and little fear. This probably explains why individuals are naturally attracted to options, which provide for well-specified pay-off functions, with set downside risk (defined as the risk of being wrong) and unlimited upside potential (when we are right). In that, they differ from 'professional investors,' who might be tempted to look at the way in which the option is priced and to evaluate whether volatility is priced cheaply or expensively, or whether its time value is reasonable. Individuals like options because they offer a gamble to which they are naturally attracted.

Mental accounting

The third relevant error of preference relates to the fact that individuals tend to keep 'mental accounts' of their investments.[30] A very frequent error of preference occurs when individuals think of the purchase price for a particular investment as the reference point. Hersh Shefrin and Meir Statman[31] arguably predicted that such would be the case when they coined the term 'disposition effect' to describe 'the disposition to sell winners too early and to hold losers too long.' Shefrin argues that 'get-even-itis'[32] is a part of the disposition effect, to the extent that investors have a 'tendency to try to get even rather than realize a loss.' Further, individuals tend to keep several mental accounts, and can thus frame a decision in either a narrow or a broad frame. In a narrow frame, individuals look at each problem one at a time rather than in the context of the whole.

Living with the consequences of decisions

As we have seen, one of the weaknesses of individual investors is that they can have difficulties accepting advice and living with the consequences of their decisions. This underpins my belief that decision risk is one of the greatest risks faced by individuals. Mark Hulbert[33] offers a great illustration of the issue. He writes that the recommendation that 'investors should focus on equities, because they perform better than bonds over the long term,' may be the worst possible advice that can be given to an individual. He notes that 'you can get run over by a truck on a highway that averages only one truck a day – especially if you panic when it arrives.' *Hulbert's insight is that individuals must guard against the risk of shifting to a more conservative strategy at the point of maximum pain, or to a riskier strategy at the point of maximum greed. A corollary of this is that we must select a strategy that we can live with over a full cycle.*

Regret

Regret and risk both have to do with the feelings we have when things do not work out as expected. Yet regret is fundamentally different from risk. Statman suggests that risk is about the future, while regret is about the past. At the same time, understanding the full effect of decision risk requires appreciating the nature of regrets,[34] more specifically the distinction between regrets of omission and regrets of commission.

A regret of omission is felt by an investor who has elected not to make a particular change in his or her portfolio and now knows that, had he or she made that change, the value of the portfolio would be higher today than it actually is. The investor's regret is focused on a missed opportunity.

A regret of commission is felt by an investor who elected to make a particular change in his or her portfolio and now can see that the portfolio value would be higher had that decision not been made. The investor's regret is focused on a loss sustained.

Interestingly, there seems to be a relationship between the form of regrets people experience and their willingness to hold equities. In an unpublished survey, Kahneman and Thaler asked more than 100 wealthy investors to bring to mind the financial decisions they regretted the most, and to identify whether those decisions had been to do something or not to do something. As in other groups, most of these wealthy people reported that their worst regret was about some action that they had taken. The minority of individuals who reported regrets of omission tended to have another characteristic in common: they generally held unusually high proportions of their portfolios in stocks.

All this suggests that a simple, though rough, test would be for investors to ask themselves the following question: what do I tend to regret most, something I did or something I did not do? Those who regret some inaction on their part, would, in this interpretation, be more likely to remain comfortable owning stocks in bad times than those who regretted action they took.

Hersh Shefrin argues that regret is one of the important dimensions of the disposition effect: 'regret is an emotion which augments a loss.' He takes the issue one step further, suggesting that 'acknowledging an erroneous decision is similar to closing a mental account at a loss,' an action that naturally triggers pain. Further, though it may be natural for us to want to delay the realization of pain, if regret prevents us making good decisions, we face a self-control problem. A solution well worth considering, for investors and advisors alike, might be to use formal decision rules as a means of dealing with loss realization as a self-control problem.

Regret is a very important element of the psychology of an individual investor. It must be well understood because the form of regret felt by an individual can serve to predict his or her ability to deal with riskier investments. Regret can also be very effectively channeled, through appropriate education, to help individuals learn from their mistakes and thus 'travel on the road to optimality.'

Money personality

Kathleen Gurney's book *Your Money Personality*[35] offers an interesting illustration of the need for and power of behavioral finance. Observing that each individual has a 'money self,' alongside his or her physical, emotional and social selves, she argues that:

> most of us fail to realize the extent to which our money personality impacts our financial habits and affects the degree of satisfaction we get from what money we have. There is an inseparable link between our unconscious feelings about money and the way in which we earn it, spend it, save it, and invest it.

Gurney believes that knowing one's money personality is an important first step toward being able to deal with the aspects of our life that relate to money. I would extrapolate from this the conclusion that knowing our own or our clients' money personality is a critical step to successful wealth management planning.

Summary and implications for wealth planning

In this chapter, our main goal was to look into the mind of the individual investor in order to gain insights into how best to help him or her plan the management of their wealth. Behavioral finance is invaluable, as it allows us to develop a better understanding of the biases that investors may bring to the table, and of the reactions that should be expected. In particular, an important insight, as suggested by Brian Rom, is that 'individuals make *satisfactory* rather than *optimal* decisions.' This has three interesting implications, to which we turn now.

Better investment questionnaires

Understanding the behavior of individuals can help substantially improve the design of an effective risk-tolerance questionnaire that can be used to assist individuals in selecting appropriate investment portfolios. Note, however, that a well-designed risk-assessment instrument should have a number of 'adaptive' questions designed to measure and validate the consistency of responses. Adaptive questions are those that change according to the answer to the previous question. Without such questions, you may be left assuming, rather than being convinced, that you have really understood the values, needs, and goals of the investor. Brian Rom proposes five key admonitions to avoid common errors:

- don't assume that everyone has the same *downside reference point*;
- don't assume that individuals know what their risk preferences are;
- don't assume that risk preferences in other areas, such as skydiving or bungee jumping, are relevant to an individual's attitudes to investment risk;
- don't confuse long-term investment strategy with day-to-day cash flow issues; and
- don't make assumptions about the relationship between past behavior and risk tolerance.

Evolution of investment strategies

A better understanding of investor psychology should mitigate the surprise at seeing individuals varying their 'optimal' strategies over time, even when their financial circumstances do not change. Decision risk can indeed be managed down over time, if we accept that we are all the product of our own experiences. Why should we be surprised that an individual who has spent the bulk of their life so far building wealth through *operating business decisions* should not necessarily be familiar with the intricacies of the world of investment decisions? In particular, note that there is a significant difference between investment and operating businesses. Operating a business day-to-day is concerned with income statement issues. By contrast, day-to-day investment activities are concerned with balance sheet issues. This arises from the fact that the main determinant of short-term investment success lies in the observation of the impact of day-to-day price fluctuations on the value of a portfolio. Moving from an operating to an investment environment requires one to become comfortable with the randomness associated with many day-to-day price fluctuations.

Experience suggests that many investors gradually become comfortable with short-term portfolio volatility and consequently a greater degree of investment aggressiveness. The same observation applies to the ability and willingness of many investors to participate in strategies or markets that may initially befuddle them, if not frighten them outright.

Making sense of suboptimal strategies

Adam Smith in *The Wealth of Nations* suggested that the best collective outcome for the economy may be obtained by an 'invisible hand' guiding us individually. The principle is applicable to our industry. Though the invisible hand has favored strategies that may not be optimal from an investment standpoint, these can become much more reasonable when decision risk is thrown into the equation.

A good example would be dollar-cost averaging. Bernhard Scherer[36] eloquently demonstrates that investing gradually, rather than in one fell swoop, is not optimal. This is an assertion that numerous other authors have also made. Yet we all know that individual investors prefer to move gradually. The element that reconciles everyone is that, though more efficient, investing all new cash at once exposes the investor to the risk that he or she abandons the original strategic plan if the markets in which the portfolio is invested experience a sudden decline, even though that decline might be both predictable and well within the statistical tolerances that describe its long-term return and risk potential.

Thinking more deeply about the real needs of an investor, from both financial and psychological standpoints, has led me to reformulate the traditional proposition that the whole thing is really about managing a risk/return trade-off. I now prefer to think of that particular choice as a *comfort/reward* trade-off. Interestingly, this also offers the potential to think in terms of the fourth dimension of the individual investment universe. We have already discussed the three dimensions of risk, return, and tax efficiency. The last dimension is *comfort*. While this may appear unacceptably 'soft,' behavioral finance teaches us how important it is. Our role as advisors, or even as investors, is not necessarily to pick the solution that is 'best' in absolute terms, but rather to pick the solution that we and our clients can best live with. In an environment where the individual must still 'pull the trigger,' we cannot ignore the question of the confidence that he or she will need to have in each decision.

---

1 See Zeikel, Arthur, 'Memorandum to My Daughter,' *Financial Analysts Journal*, Vol. 51, No. 2, March/April 1995, pp. 7–8. For an early piece focusing on the issue of individual investor behavior, see Nagy, Robert A., and Robert W. Obenberger, 'Factors Influencing Individual Investor Behavior,' *Financial Analysts Journal*, Vol. 50, No. 4, July/August 1994, pp. 63–68.

[2] See Brunel, Jean L.P., 'A Second Look at Absolute Return Strategies,' *The Journal of Private Portfolio Management*, Spring 1998, pp. 67–78.

[3] For an early discussion of this topic, see Ezra, D. Don, 'Asset Allocation by Surplus Optimization,' *Financial Analysts Journal*, Vol. 47, No. 1, January/February 1991, pp. 51–57.

[4] This led to the idea of immunizing liabilities by creating a portfolio of assets designed to behave in exactly the same manner. Bond portfolio immunization is one such technique. See Granito, Michael R., *Bond Portfolio Immunization*, Lexington, MA: Lexington Books, and Toronto: D.C. Heath and Company, 1984.

[5] See Rom, Brian M., 'The Psychology of Money: Its Impact on Individual Risk Tolerance and Portfolio Selection,' *The Journal of Wealth Management*, Fall 2000, pp. 15–19.

[6] See Kahneman, Daniel, and Amos Tversky, 'Prospect Theory – An Analysis of Decision under Risk,' in Daniel Kahneman and Amos Tversky, eds., *Choices, Value, and Frames*, Cambridge: Russell Sage Foundation and Cambridge University Press, 2000, pp. 17–43; or, in the same book, Kahneman, Daniel, and Amos Tversky, 'Advances in Prospect Theory – Cumulative Representation of Uncertainty,' pp. 44–65.

[7] See Budge, G. Scott, 'The Psychology of Investments: An Overview of Emerging Insights,' *The Journal of Wealth Management*, Summer 2000, pp. 39–52.

[8] See Albrecht, Steven. 'Changes in the Private Wealth Marketplace,' *The Journal of Wealth Management*, Fall 2000, pp. 59–67.

[9] See Olsen, Robert A., 'Behavioral Finance and its Implications for Stock-Price Volatility,' *Financial Analysts Journal*, Vol. 54, No. 2, March/April 1998, pp. 10–19.

[10] Thaler, Richard H., and Werner F.M. De Bondt, eds., *Advances in Behavioral Finance*, Cambridge: Russell Sage Foundation and Cambridge University Press, 1994, contains a number of very pertinent articles on this topic.

[11] See Raiffa, Howard, *Decision Analysis*, Reading, MA: Addison-Wesley, 1968.

[12] See Kahneman, Daniel, and Mark W. Riepe, 'Aspects of Investor Psychology,' *The Journal of Portfolio Management*, Summer 1998, pp. 52–65.

[13] Meir Statman is the Glenn Klimek Professor of Finance at the Leavey School of Business, Santa Clara University. He made the comment referenced here at the 8th Annual Family Office Forum, hosted on June 25 and 26, 2001 by the Institute for Investment Research in Chicago, Illinois.

[14] See Johnson, Eric J., John Hershey, Jacqueline Meszaros, and Howard Kunreuther, 'Framing, Probability Distortions, and Insurance Decisions,' in Daniel Kahneman and Amos Tversky, eds., *Choices, Value, and Frames*, Cambridge: Russell Sage Foundation and Cambridge University Press, 2000, pp. 224–300.

[15] For instance, see Camerer, Colin F. 'Prospect Theory in the Wild – Evidence from the Field,' in Daniel Kahneman and Amos Tversky, eds., *Choices, Value, and Frames*, Cambridge: Russell Sage Foundation and Cambridge University Press, 2000, pp. 288–300; in the same book, Kahneman, Daniel, and Amos Tversky, 'Conflict Resolution – A Cognitive Perspective,' pp. 473–87; or Camerer, Colin F., and Dan Lovallo, 'Overconfidence and Excess Entry – An Experimental Approach,' pp. 414–23.

[16] The Mario L. Belotti Professor of Finance at Santa Clara University, Hersh Shefrin authored 'Recent Developments in Behavioral Finance,' *The Journal of Private Portfolio Management*, Summer 2000, pp. 25–37.

[17] Russo, Edward, and Paul Shoemaker, *Decision Traps*, New York: Simon & Shuster, 1989.

[18] See Daniel, Kent, and Sheridan Titman, 'Market Efficiency in an Irrational World,' *Financial Analysts Journal*, Vol. 55, No. 6, November/December 1999, pp. 28–40. Readers might also be interested in Schiereck, Dirk, Werner De Bondt, and Martin Weber, 'Contrarian and Momentum Strategies in Germany,' *Financial Analysts Journal*, Vol. 55, No. 6, November/December 1999, pp. 104–16.

[19] See Nesbitt, Stephen L. 'Buy High, Sell Low: Timing Errors in Mutual Fund Allocations,' *The Journal of Portfolio Management*, Fall 1995, pp. 57–61. For a discussion of the impact of investor overreaction on capital markets, see Bauman, Scott W., C. Mitchell Conove, and Robert E. Miller, 'Investor Overreaction in International Stock Markets,' *The Journal of Portfolio Management*, Summer 1999, pp. 102–11; also, Shefrin, Hersh, 'Irrational Exuberance and Option Smiles,' *Financial Analysts Journal*, Vol. 55, No. 6, November/December 1999, pp. 91–103.

[20] From the article cited above, note 9.

[21] Gallup survey quoted by Meir Statman in the article cited above, note 9.

[22] For a discussion of one of the most famous bubbles and its applicability to equity markets, see Hirschey, Mark. 'How Much is a Tulip Worth?', *Financial Analysts Journal*, Vol. 54, No. 4, July/August 1998, pp. 11–17. See also Treynor, Jack, 'Bulls, Bears, and Market Bubbles,' *Financial Analysts Journal*, Vol. 54, No. 2, March/April 1998, pp. 69–74. For a discussion of crashes, see Fergusson, Robert, 'On Crashes,' *Financial Analysts Journal*, Vol. 45, No. 2, March/April 1989, pp. 42–52.

[23] See Gilovich, Tom, Robert Vallone, and Amos Tversky, 'The Hot Hand in Basketball: On the Misperception of Random Sequences,' *Cognitive Psychology*, 1985, pp. 295–314.

[24] Published in 1670, and thus after Pascal's death, the book comprises the notes he had compiled for a work to be entitled Apologie de la Religion Chrætienne (Apologia for the Christian Religion), which he never finished.

[25] Bernstein, Peter L., *Against The Gods: The Remarkable Story of Risk*, New York and London: John Wiley & Sons, 1996, pp. 69–70.

[26] For a discussion of one such value function, called the 'money illusion,' see Shafir, Eldar, Peter Diamond, and Amos Tversky, 'Money Illusion,' in Daniel Kahneman and Amos Tversky, eds., *Choices, Value, and Frames*, Cambridge: Russell Sage Foundation and Cambridge University Press, 2000, pp. 335–55; or Miller, Ross, and Evan Schulman, 'Money Illusion Revisited,' *The Journal of Portfolio Management*, Spring 1999, pp. 45–54.

[27] See Bernartzi, Shlomo, and Richard H. Thaler, 'Myopic Loss Aversion and the Equity Premium Puzzle,' *Quarterly Journal of Economics*, February 1995, pp. 73–92.

[28] For an early discussion of this insight, see Riley, William B., and K. Victor Chow, 'Asset Allocation and Individual

Risk Aversion,' *Financial Analysts Journal*, Vol. 48, No. 6, November/December 1992, pp. 32–37.

[29] See Lopes, Lola, 'Between Hope and Fear: The Psychology of Risk,' *Advances in Experimental Social Psychology*, 1985, pp. 255–95.

[30] See Thaler, Richard H., 'Mental Accounting Matters,' in Daniel Kahneman and Amos Tversky, eds., *Choices, Value, and Frames*, Cambridge: Russell Sage Foundation and Cambridge University Press, 2000, pp. 241–68.

[31] See Shefrin, Hersh, and Meir Statman, 'The Disposition to Sell Winners Too Early and Ride Losers Too Long: Theory and Evidence,' *Journal of Finance*, 40 (1985), pp. 770–790; also, Barber, Brad M., and Terrance Odean, 'The Courage of Misguided Convictions,' *Financial Analysts Journal*, Vol. 55, No. 6, November/December 1999, pp. 41–55.

[32] Leroy Gross coined the term in *The Art of Selling Intangibles: How to Make Your Million ($) by Investing Other People's Money*, New York: New York Institute of Finance, 1982.

[33] Hulbert, Mark, 'Money and Investments: Which Eggs, Which Baskets?,' *Forbes*, October 23, 1995, p. 334.

[34] See Clarke, Roger G., Scott Krase, and Meir Statman, 'Tracking Errors, Regret, and Tactical Asset Allocation,' *The Journal of Portfolio Management*, Spring 1994, pp. 16–24.

[35] New York: Doubleday, 1988.

[36] See Scherer, Bernhard, 'Cost Averaging – Fact or Myth?,' *The Journal of Private Portfolio Management*, Winter 1998, pp. 18–21; also, Statman, Meir, 'A Behavioral Framework for Dollar-Cost Averaging,' *The Journal of Portfolio Management*, Fall 1995, pp. 70–79; Rozeff, Michael S., 'Lump-Sum Investing versus Dollar-Averaging,' *The Journal of Portfolio Management*, Winter 1994, pp. 45–50.

* The answers to Exhibit 2.2 are: (1) 39 years; (2) 4,187 miles; (3) 13 countries; (4) 39 books; (5) 2,160 miles; (6) 390,000 pounds; (7) 1756; (8) 645 days; (9) 5,959 miles; (10) 36,198 feet.

Chapter 3

Understanding tax efficiency

Tax efficiency was a novel concept as recently as the early 1990s.[1] Since then, however, it has permanently entered the vocabulary, though it still means different things to different people.

Defining our terms

I define tax efficiency as the art of avoiding unnecessary taxes and deferring unavoidable taxes. There are, therefore, two components to tax efficiency.

The first is to avoid paying taxes, which can be done either through the use of better or more appropriate holding structures, or by using an investment process focused on avoiding the wrong decisions.

The second is probably even more important, as it contains the seed of one of the main insights: deferring taxes[2] is equivalent to having the opportunity to earn a return on monies that would otherwise be paid to the tax authorities. In the words of Robert Arnott,[3] tax deferral strategies can be viewed as 'interest-free loans from the government.' The power of compound interest takes off from there.

Though tax efficiency is a compelling concept, it is important to understand both its strengths and its limitations. The main limitation relates to the time horizon of the investor. This reflects the fact that a large part of the benefits associated with tax efficiency relates to the 'interest free loan' implicitly received from the government when tax liabilities are deferred. It should not be surprising that it takes time for the compounding effect of earning returns on assets that would otherwise be paid out to become significant in relation to total wealth. An important implication of the need to be able to think long term is that investors with relatively short time horizons are unlikely to derive significant net benefits from adopting a tax-efficient approach to investing.

The different forms of taxation

You will also have noted that the definition discusses 'taxes,' in an unspecified manner, for tax efficiency applies to both the two main forms of taxation.

First, taxes on incomes and capital gains can also be called taxes on investment returns. Indeed, though tax regimes vary from country to country, there is often some form of tax on investment returns. Certain countries do not differentiate between what U.S. investors know as 'income' and 'capital' items. That does not mean that capital gains are necessarily tax-free in such countries: it may simply be that capital items are treated as a part of income. Recall

ASSET LOCATION

47

the example of the Chiang family of Singapore (see Introduction), who wanted to be treated as investors rather than traders because in Singapore in the early 1980s capital gains were taxable or nontaxable depending upon whether the taxpayer was an investor or a trader.

Second, estate and gift taxes, which we might call ownership transfer taxes, are also critically important. They relate to the potential loss of assets as they are transferred between generations or across different ownership vehicles within the same overall family wealth management structure. Ignoring that aspect of tax efficiency, or applying an extreme focus on 'investment return taxes,' will both expose the investor to the risk of winning a battle but losing the war.

One should avoid an excessive focus on one or other form of taxation, and rather focus on all forms of tax drag.

This definition of tax efficiency is also instructive in a different sense: *tax efficiency is not about making investment decisions strictly driven by tax considerations.* In the end, this would be about as foolish as the idea of managing your money until it is all gone, or generating tax losses to offset gains at the expense of investment performance.

Tax efficiency is about managing a three-dimensional trade-off that incorporates return and risk – or, if you prefer, comfort and reward – together with tax efficiency. Tax efficiency is about combining investment and tax considerations, because making investment decisions in a tax vacuum is probably about as uninspired as making strictly tax-driven investment decisions. A simple example illustrates this.

Assuming that risk is unchanged and that you are an investor who must consider taxes, which of the following two return combinations would you prefer:

- a 10% pre-tax return, with 90% tax efficiency, or
- a 12% pre-tax return, with 70% tax efficiency?

'Tax efficiency,' in this context, refers to what is left of pre-tax returns once taxes have been paid. In this sense, 90% tax efficiency means that the effective tax rate is 10%, while 70% tax efficiency means that it is 30%. A typical individual would certainly not hesitate long once he or she has realized that the first alternative produces a 9% after-tax return and the second only 8.4%.

Therefore, the only relevant performance measure for a taxable investor should be the after-tax return earned in any period, or, better yet, the compound after-tax return earned over some meaningful period of time. Those who believe that taxes do not matter that much, or that the smart investor should first aim to outperform the reference index and then worry about tax efficiency, are simply missing the point.

The trade-off is indeed fully three-dimensional, because each of the three dimensions – pre-tax returns, risk, and tax efficiency – affect the other two. Consider the following three situations.

First, you might be able to increase the expected return on your portfolio by selling a few of your investments. Yet doing this would require you to realize hitherto unrealized capital gains, and thus pay capital gains taxes. To what extent is the increase in expected return enough to offset that initial tax drag?

Second, you might be able to reduce the expected risk of your portfolio by selling some of the appreciation recorded by a couple of positions that have become very large in relation to the rest of the portfolio. Yet, again, doing this would require you to realize hitherto unrealized capital gains, and thus to pay capital gains taxes. To what extent is the reduction in risk enough to offset that tax drag?

Finally, you might design a better portfolio management process that focuses on generating after- rather than pre-tax returns. Yet applying this process will require the manager to forgo certain investment opportunities, involving either risk reduction or return enhancement. To what extent is the increased tax efficiency of the process enough to offset its cost in terms of pre-tax returns and risk levels?

Expanding the issue to incorporate estate and gift taxes makes the problem only more complex, as it forces the investor to think in terms of multiple periods rather than single periods. The three-dimensional trade-off remains the same, but it needs to be applied across time.

From a practical standpoint, tax efficiency is thus about the need to understand the implications of our investment activity, in a perspective that states that we are in the business of earning after-tax returns. When managing portfolios, we must consider what we get to keep, not what we get. That activity incorporates the management of investment returns and gift or transfer taxes.

Taxes matter

It is often tempting to think of taxes as a necessary evil. Many traditional investors have fallen into the trap of believing that they will not let the tax tail wag the investment dog. Other investors have tended to refrain from making any investment decision, for fear of its tax implications. They have thus adopted a 'buy and hold' approach.[4]

Quantifying the impact of taxes is a first step in the right direction.[5] It shows that the problem is serious, but it also provides some guideline as to how serious it is and thus creates the parameters needed to manage the three-dimensional trade-off effectively.

The impact of taxes on after-tax wealth

Exhibit 3.1 shows the results of a simple experiment. Imagine that you invest US$1.00 today and achieve a 12% annual compound pre-tax return on that investment. Now imagine that your goal is to maximize the terminal after-tax value of that 'wealth' in 100 years, which you can take as a rough proxy for three generations. Finally, assume that there will be two generational transfers over that period, taking place respectively after 33 and 67 years. Two important dimensions must enter into your thinking:

- what have you done about estate planning? and
- what are you doing about investment management?

The horizontal axis of the graph in Exhibit 3.1 addresses estate-planning issues. We considered three rates of estate taxation, using, as an illustration, the rates currently in effect in the United States. The two extreme rates, 0% and 55%, reflect the instances where the investor has an exceptionally effective estate plan, or where there is no plan at all. The middle rate, 28%,

Exhibit 3.1

The impact of taxes on long-term wealth (logarithmic scale)

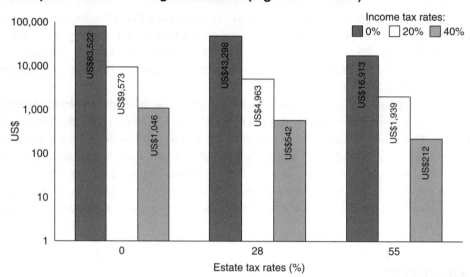

implicitly assumes that the investor has been able to shelter some, but not all, of his or her estate from taxes. Arguably, we could also vary assumptions across the two transfers, assuming that the investor was able to shelter all the first-generation transfer, but none of the second. (Though this would certainly change the ultimate outcome, the point of this illustration is to be simple enough that we can get a good sense of the dynamics of the problem. Making it unduly complex, though possibly more realistic, might well prevent the point from coming out as clearly.)

The vertical axis on the graph relates to income and capital gain taxes, and there are three possible levels here as well. The first, provided more for reference than as a realistic alternative, assumes that the investor has been able to defer taxes for the full 100-year period. In that case, all income and capital gains would be tax-free, and his or her after-tax return would equal his or her pre-tax return. At the other end of the spectrum, the worst-case scenario is that the investor not only did not focus on tax implications, but also selected investment strategies that rely solely on income and short-term capital gain realization for their investment returns. In other words, the pre-tax return is taxed in full, and the effective tax rate (again as focused on a U.S.-resident investor, excluding state and local taxes and using the highest current federal tax rate) is 40%. Finally, a third alternative contemplates circumstances where the investor has been able to achieve some degree of tax efficiency, effectively incurring an average 20% tax rate each year.

Exhibit 3.1 clearly illustrates that ignoring taxes can only be done at one's peril. The difference between the totally tax-oblivious approach (40% taxes every year and no estate planning) and the maximally tax-aware process (total tax deferral) is dramatic. A perfect tax-deferral approach would transform the initial US$1.00 into US$83,522 over the next 100 years, while a totally tax-oblivious process would yield only US$212 over the same period.

The impact of taxes on compound average annual returns

What does this difference in terminal wealth 100 years from now mean in terms of annual returns? Exhibit 3.2 helps address this question, showing virtually the same experiment, and using three different annual return assumptions, 11%, 12% and 13%. The only difference between this and the previous experiment is that we have removed the intermediate estate tax rate, for the sake of presentational simplicity. Clearly, the interaction between the various forms of taxation and the timing of the taxable event produces a range of outcomes, with some subtle variations. An exact cost that would apply to all circumstances is difficult to generate, but Exhibit 3.2 suggests that tax-oblivion might cost between 2% and 3% each year.

Remember that we only seek to *avoid unnecessary and defer unavoidable taxes*. We therefore intentionally do not consider the absolute extremes, involving the transformation of an investor's situation from fully taxable to effectively tax-exempt. Thus, starting with income tax-efficiency, in the context of a 100-year time horizon, a more realistic application of that definition is to assume that one has been able to convert all taxable income from a 40% to a 20% tax liability. With respect to estate tax efficiency, the same rationale leads us to a definition that settles somewhere between no taxes for either generational transfer to half the maximum tax rate for each transfer.

Exhibit 3.2

Value of US$1.00 in 100 years under various return and tax assumptions

	Income tax rates (%)	Expected compound return (US$)		
		11%	12%	13%
No estate tax	0	34,064	83,522	203,163
	20	4,601	9,573	19,811
	40	597	1,046	1,828
55% estate tax	0	6,898	16,913	41,140
	20	932	1,939	4,012
	40	121	212	370

Exhibit 3.2 can thus be transformed to show compounded average annual rates of return, to allow a better understanding of the dynamics of the analysis. Exhibit 3.3, below, shows the effective after tax rate of return in six different tax circumstances (three income tax rates and two estate tax situations). It suggests the following three broad conclusions:

1. The difference between paying full or no estate taxes for both generational transfers amounts 1.7% to 1.8% compound over time. We can see that by looking at the difference between pairs of returns in the first three and last three lines of the table, respectively (for instance 11%-9.2% = 1.8%).
2. Total investment tax inefficiency from the point of view of income and capital gains taxes (defined as going from 0% to 40% income tax rates) creates a cost ranging from 4.3% to 5.2%, compound over time. We can see that by looking at the difference in each column between the 0% and the 40% lines (for instance 11%-6.6% = 4.4%).

Exhibit 3.3

Effective after tax rates of return in selected circumstances

Estate tax (%)	Income tax (%)	Assumed (%)	Pretax (%)	Return (%)
		11	12	13
0	0	11	12	13
0	20	8.8	9.6	10.4
0	40	6.6	7.2	7.8
55	0	9.2	10.2	11.2
55	20	7.1	7.9	8.7
55	40	4.9	5.5	6.1

3. Looking at the difference between the two pairs of 20% and 40% lines, we can see that moving from total tax-inefficiency to tax-efficiency as defined above saves 2.2% to 2.6% (for instance 11%-8.8% = 2.2%). If we use a similar definition for estate tax efficiency (i.e. settling somewhere between no tax for either generational transfer to half the maximum tax rate for each transfer), we would arrive at the general conclusion that estate tax efficiency could save between 0.8% and 0.9% over time (basically dividing the range shown under point 1 above by 2).

Bringing the two together would suggest that this form of tax-efficiency across both dimensions would save somewhere between 3.0% and 3.5%. Clearly, There can be greater savings if one can manage to bring either tax lower still, and the computations repeated here involve substantial simplifications, if only in terms of the timing of the payment of any tax (compounded over time equally rather than at some precise point in time, which would bring in the time value of money). There could equally be lesser savings if one has not been able to reach the implicit 20% income tax and 27.5% estate tax rate averages.

Using the Morningstar mutual fund Principia Pro universe to put this cost in perspective, we investigated how many mutual funds appeared to be able to earn 2% to 3% more than their relevant benchmark index. The idea behind this simple experiment was as follows: we would conclude that 2% or 3% was not a difficult hurdle if a large number of funds managed to beat the index by that margin. Conversely, the data would tell us that it is a tall hurdle if funds found it hard to generate that level of value added, net of fees.

Using the 'Large Blend' grouping of U.S. large capitalization equity funds, the most recent data points to a sobering conclusion: 2% to 3% proved to be a very difficult margin of outperformance for that sample of managers. Specifically, for the trailing five years, 98 out of 421 funds beat the index, but only 32 out of the same 421 beat the index by 200 basis points or more (on the basis of annualized compound returns). The trailing three-year data are no more comforting. Out of 725 funds, 230 beat the index and 127 beat the index by 200 basis points or more. *Ignoring taxes requires the investor to generate that performance regularly, over a three-generation time frame, just to stay even with a simple indexing strategy.*

The U.S. tax framework

All tax codes are quite complex, and can vary across states, provinces or regions, and certainly across international borders. What follows is no more than a simple summary of the framework in the world's leading economy, which helps put abstract principles into proper perspective. It should not be relied upon by anyone as tax advice.

In a recent presentation, Darryl Meyers[6] provided an excellent framework to conceptualize income tax regimes. He outlined three income tax theories:

- *accretion-based* – income is the money value of the net accretion to economic power between two points in time;
- *expenditure-based* – income is defined as the change in value of the net accretion to economic power between two points in time, minus the amounts reinvested in productive activity;
- *schedular tax* – income is determined by sources, i.e., 'the gain derived from capital, from labor, or from both combined.'[7]

Meyers suggests that 'accretion tax' is the U.S. baseline and that 'basis' is the key to its maintenance, with two important exceptions. The first is known as the 'realization requirement,' which leads to the definition of income as 'an undeniable accession to wealth, clearly realized, and over which the taxpayers have full dominion.'[8] The second important exception relates to qualified plans, such as retirement plans, where income is not taxable until some future date.

Further, the schedular feature of the U.S. tax system requires taxpayers to distinguish between passive and active activities, and between different forms of income character: capital versus ordinary income, and long-term versus short-term realization intervals. Broadening the horizon, it is fair to say that there are three important elements to taxation: the basis on which we pay taxes, the rate at which taxes are computed, and the timing of our obligation.

Income and capital gains

The U.S. tax code differentiates between three broad components of return, each taxed at a different rate. Income, which is typically composed of interest and dividends, is currently taxed at a maximum federal tax rate of 39.6%. Realized short-term capital gains (gains on securities held for less than 12 months) are taxed at the same rate as income. Realized long-term capital gains are taxed at a maximum of 20%. Capital gains are taxed only when realized, and unrealized capital gains are therefore usually not taxed, except in certain circumstances. For instance, selected derivative contracts must be marked to market annually for tax purposes.

Short-term and long-term capital gains can be generally offset by short-term and long-term capital losses. However, capital losses cannot be used to offset more than a very small portion of income (currently limited to US$3,000). Certain interest income is tax-free and certain investors are subject to other than the regular income tax regime. The U.S. Congress has

53

enacted an 'alternative minimum tax' (AMT) regime to ensure that everyone pays a minimum amount of tax. The computation of the AMT involves different steps than the process used in the regular income tax regime, principally with respect to the way in which certain deductions are allowed or disallowed. The AMT rate is currently 28%.

Dealing with unrealized gains

Jim Poterba[9] takes this one step further. He suggests that one should not ignore unrealized capital gains in the measurement of current after-tax returns. Indeed, though the tax rate on unrealized capital gains *appears* to be zero, he argues that in fact: 'capital gains that are not realized in one period are carried forward to future periods, creating "contingent future tax liabilities" for the investor.' He proposes a conceptual framework that could be used to describe the expected present value of the taxes that an investor may pay in the future on a gain that accrues today.

[handwritten: Part of investor liabilities on Balance sheet]

Wash sales

An important aspect of the U.S. tax code relates to the process through which capital losses are realized. The code prohibits 'wash sales,' which are defined as circumstances when a loss is taken in a security in which the investor is trading within a 61-day period centered around the date at which the loss was realized (i.e. 30 days before and after that date).

This is an important difference between the regime found in the United States and the regimes prevailing in several other countries. In France, for instance, the tax authorities do not worry about wash sales and allow the investor to perform 'round trips' within one day.

Wash sales present an important constraint in at least two areas. First, a loss realized as a result of a wash sale is disallowed. Second, though the loss cannot be considered realized and thus used to offset a realized gain, the investor is allowed to build that loss into the tax basis of the security bought as a result of taking that loss.

Defining a sale – the concept of 'constructive sale'

Another important consideration relates to the definition of a sale. Mark Anson[10] helps frame the concept of 'constructive sales.' He states:

> Section 1259(c) [defines] a taxpayer as having made a constructive sale of an appreciated financial position … if the taxpayer:
>
> - enters into a short sale of the same or substantially identical property;
> - enters into an offsetting notional principal contract with respect to the same or substantially identical property; or
> - enters into a futures or forward contract to deliver the same or substantially identical property.

Thus, for a transaction to cause an investor to have to realize a capital gain, there does not need to be a formal sale of the appreciated asset. Any transaction that, in effect, substantially eliminates the risk associated with holding a security may result in the unrealized capital gain associated with that position having to be realized. Anson seems to believe that the U.S. Treasury would likely apply the same criteria to define 'substantially identical' as those used in Section 1091 of the Internal Revenue Code. There, securities are considered 'substantially identical' if, in Anson's words, 'they are not substantially different in any material feature or in several material features considered together.' He adds that: 'a constructive sale may also occur if the taxpayer enters into one or more transactions that have "substantially the same effect" as the three transactions described above.'

Practical experience suggests that a simple rule of thumb, which should be checked with tax advisors, may simply be that a constructive sale occurs when substantially all the risks associated with holding that appreciated security have been eliminated. The converse would be that a constructive sale might not be deemed to have occurred if some of those risks, defined here as sensitivity to upside and/or downside, are retained. It is important to note that Anson argues that the Act does not discuss constructive sales when dealing with depreciated security positions.

Estates and gifts

Though the whole issue of whether 'death taxes' will remain in place is at the top of the U.S. political agenda as this is being written, it is worth noting, in the words of Jim Poterba,[11] that: 'the estate tax is the most concentrated tax in the United States tax system, with marginal rates among the highest anywhere in the tax code.'

The same is not necessarily true outside the United States. Japan has for many years had the most onerous estate tax system in the developed world, although with a number of loopholes to bring the effective rate down, while European countries often find themselves imposing somewhat lower tax rates than the United States, but make those rates apply considerably sooner as well.

Jim Poterba offers an interesting insight into the scope of the estate tax system in the United States:[12]

> the estates of just 231 decedents accounted for more than one-sixth of federal estate and gift tax revenues. More than half of federal estate and gift tax collections were accounted for by the 2,000 estate tax returns filled on behalf of the wealthiest decedents. To place these statistics in context, roughly 1.4% of deaths in the United States currently result in taxable estate tax filings.

The U.S. estate tax system is based on two principles. First, there is a high exemption to ensure that only the largest estates are taxed. The Unified Tax Credit is set at US$675,000 for 2001, and is scheduled to rise gradually and to reach US$3,500,000 in 2009, falling back to US$1,000,000 in 2011 (estate taxes having been repealed in respect of 2010, they are to be reinstated in 2011). Exhibit 3.4 provides the details of the current schedule.

Second, the code sets relatively high rates for amounts that exceed the threshold. In the paper referenced above, and thus using 1999 tax rates, Poterba observed that:

> the marginal estate tax rate on the 650,001st dollar of taxable estate is 37%, while the highest statutory marginal estate tax rate is 55%. Yet, as a result of an estate tax surcharge that phases out the progressive estate tax structure, the highest effective marginal estate tax rate is 60% and applies on estates valued at between $10 and $17 million.

Exhibit 3.4

U.S. estate and gift tax schedules, 2001 to 2011 and beyond

	Estate tax exemption amount (US$)	GST tax exemption amount (US$)	Gift tax exemption amount (US$)	Maximum estate and gift tax rates (%)
2001	675,000	1,060,000	675,000	55 (5% surtax)
2002	1,000,000	1,060,000*	1,000,000	50
2003	1,000,000	1,060,000*	1,000,000	49
2004	1,500,000	1,500,000	1,000,000	48
2005	1,500,000	1,500,000	1,000,000	47
2006	2,000,000	2,000,000	1,000,000	46
2007	2,000,000	2,000,000	1,000,000	45
2008	2,000,000	2,000,000	1,000,000	45
2009	3,500,000	3,500,000	1,000,000	45
2010	Estate tax repealed	GST tax repealed	1,000,000	35 (gift tax only)
2011 and beyond	1,000,000	1,060,000*	1,000,000	55 (5% surtax)

* as adjusted annually for inflation.

Source: Cummings and Lockwood – Letter to Clients and Friends, June 30, 2001.

Gifts *inter vivos*

In the United States, though *inter vivos* giving attracts the same tax rates, and benefits from the same broad exemptions, as transfers upon death, gift tax laws further allow individuals to make certain gifts without incurring gift tax liability. Currently, an individual may give US$10,000 each year to each recipient without incurring a liability. Further programs allow an individual to make selected other tax-free gifts, for instance a US$50,000 gift to an education account. Contrast this with provisions found in France, for instance, where tax-free gifts are considerably more difficult to execute, being limited to FF300,000 every 10 years between parents and children.

Individuals in the United States also have a choice of using their unified tax credit. In particular, individuals can use some or all of their credit to make tax-free gifts during their lifetime. When they do so, the exemption applied to their estate will be equal to the residual of the unified tax credit, calculated by subtracting *inter vivos* gifts (other than those falling in one of the tax-free categories) from the unified tax credit.

Generation-skipping gifts

The U.S. tax code also provides for at least another important exemption, which allows individuals to make generation-skipping gifts. These gifts can be made, for instance, by grandparents to their grandchildren, skipping the parents' generation and thus avoiding the tax that might have become due upon the death of the parents. The code is designed so as to prevent wealth transfers skipping one or more generation, with one exception. Typically, the relevant gift tax is applied to gifts that skip generations, as many times as appropriate, given the number of generations that are skipped. However, it is currently provided that up to US$2.1 million can be transferred across generations with the payment of only one gift tax. Note that a couple that elects to transfer US$2 million to their grandchildren, for instance, can first use their unified tax credit (US$1.35 million in 2001) for a truly tax-free gift and then pay the applicable gift tax on the balance.

The costs of being tax-efficient

What are the costs associated with tax efficiency? Answering the question requires taking a few steps back. It may be tempting to think in terms of a paradigm according to which different investments will be differently attractive to taxable and tax-exempt investors. I feel that you should avoid this temptation. As we shall see in Chapter 15, it is possible to argue that you may amend the equity investment research process to account for the fact that a taxable investor should consider discounting dividends at a different rate than capital gains. However, I prefer the idea that tax efficiency takes a two-dimensional problem into a three-dimensional space, as a better logical construct to tackle the issue.

This leads to two important observations. First, it is not unreasonable to think in terms of absolute, risk-adjusted investment attractiveness. Were taxes not to be a part of the problem, you could identify investments that would naturally move the portfolio further in the desirable northwesterly direction in the efficient-frontier plane. Thus, it would make sense to identify trades, and, by implication, portfolios that could be considered 'ideal,' given a particular investor's risk/return trade-off point.

Second, tax-efficient portfolio management involves solving the problem created by the fact that moving to a position dictated by pure investment considerations will usually involve a tax cost.[13] In short, the optimal portfolio will reflect the interaction between a desired portfolio target and the portfolio's current position, with its own built-in set of tax bases. This is what I have dubbed the cost of getting there (discussed more fully in the context of strategic asset allocation issues). Note, however, that this cost is an integral part of every facet of the investment process, whether strategic or tactical. The cost of getting there is equal to the tax incurred on any capital gain that must be realized in order to move from a current position to another, deemed more desirable from the standpoint of a pure risk/return trade-off.

The critical issue therefore faced by a tax-efficient portfolio manager is to determine whether the 'cost of getting there' overwhelms the expected increment in value added or not. If the after-tax expected value added is negative, then the transaction must not be executed. On the other hand, it can be implemented if there is still positive after-tax value added. In this context, after-tax value added must be understood to mean 'risk-adjusted excess return.' Indeed, a transaction that does not produce significant incremental return but substantially reduces expected portfolio risk must be viewed as generating positive value added. A corollary must be that *there will be transactions that might generate significant expected pre-tax value added but will not 'make the cut' on an after-tax basis.*

Further, it should generally be true that adding a tax dimension to the problem will at best leave expected pre-tax value added unchanged and more likely be at least in part 'pre-tax alpha invasive.' That is, tax efficiency should be expected to prevent a portfolio manager realizing the full extent of his or her pre-tax value added potential, as certain transactions will need to be forgone in order to keep focusing on risk-adjusted after-tax returns. At a recent conference, David Stein presented very illustrative data,[14] which is reproduced in Exhibit 3.5. It shows the excess return required of any trade in order for it to make sense over a stated time horizon, given varying assumptions as to the difference between tax basis and current market value, measured in terms of 'market to book ratio.' For instance, you would need to think that the stock you are buying will outperform the stock you are selling by 11.4%, if the stock you are selling had a book value equal to half of its market value and if you wanted the trade to break even in a year.

Exhibit 3.5

Excess return on a buy required to justify a capital gain on the sale, per year for holding time

	0	*0.1*	*0.2*	*0.3*	*0.4*	*0.5*	*0.6*	*0.7*	*0.8*	*0.9*	*1.0*
One year	25.7	22.6	19.6	16.7	14.0	11.4	8.9	6.6	4.3	2.1	0.0
Two years	12.2	10.8	9.4	8.1	6.8	5.6	4.4	3.2	2.1	1.0	0.0
Three years	8.0	7.1	6.2	5.3	4.5	3.7	2.9	2.1	1.4	0.7	0.0
Four years	5.9	5.2	4.6	4.0	3.4	2.8	2.2	1.6	1.1	0.5	0.0
Five Years	4.7	4.2	3.7	3.2	2.7	2.2	1.7	1.3	0.8	0.4	0.0

Source: See endnote 14.

The mechanics of tax efficiency and time horizon considerations

Understanding the mechanics of tax efficiency helps frame the issue and explain the intuitive importance of time horizons. Since tax efficiency is principally an activity concerning tax deferral, the time horizon is a critical variable. The original question can be reformulated as follows: to what extent does the expected compound return earned on deferred taxes exceed the expected excess return on the transaction which would give rise to that tax payment? It should logically follow that, unless alpha invasion, or the loss of investment value added, is minimal, there must be some minimal period during which return on those monies is allowed to compound before it makes sense to accept forgoing that excess risk-adjusted return.

An analogy might help make this clearer. Consider the last time you refinanced your borrowings on your primary residence to take advantage of lower prevailing rates of interest. You probably went through a computation to ensure that the closing costs associated with the transaction did not wipe out the interest rate differential. Bankers generally tell their clients that they have a good deal when it takes three years or less to recover these closing costs.

Measuring the impact of time on a pre-liquidation basis

Typically, the tendency is to compare the terminal value of two hypothetical portfolios, one managed in a tax-efficient manner and the other in a tax-oblivious fashion. To the extent that alpha invasion is rarely equal to the expected effective tax rate, the outcome of the comparison is effectively pre-ordained: it always makes sense to be tax-aware. However, these portfolios are only assessed on a pre-liquidation basis.

An illustration shows the importance of the issue. Consider the following two possible circumstances: you may receive a gift of US$10,000 in cash, or you may receive it in appreciated securities, the price of which is substantially higher than their tax basis (or cost). Are you really indifferent as to which form you receive the gift in? In the first instance, you receive a cash gift and will be free to use the full amount to do what you please, whether investing or consuming it. In the second instance, you are receiving a gift of appreciated securities. If you like the portfolio that you have received and want to invest the gift, you can keep it as is, and the US$10,000 will be compounding in full at whatever rate of return you earn. On the other hand, if you do not like the portfolio, or wish to consume the gift, you will need to sell the appreciated securities and pay some capital gains tax. In the end, the gift will not be US$10,000, but a smaller amount. (We will come back to this very point in Chapter 18, when we look into after-tax performance measurement and assessment.)

It follows that a pre-liquidation analysis is probably faulty. However, let us look at the results of the analysis, which we will then compare to a post-liquidation scenario. Exhibit 3.6 illustrates several sets of such possible comparisons.

The table suggests two broad observations. First, note that, *on a pre-liquidation basis*, time horizon does not matter. This is logical, since the tax-efficient strategy advantage is simply measured by comparing after-tax returns, which are a function of the 'alpha advantage' of the tax-oblivious strategy and of the 'tax efficiency advantage' of the tax-efficient strategy.

Second, note that, among the combinations selected, there is no combination of 'alpha

Exhibit 3.6

Tax efficiency and time horizon: pre-liquidation analysis (%)

	Pre-liquidation tax-efficient strategy advantage					
Difference between	*Three-year*			*20-year*		
tax-efficient and	*Tax efficiency of tax-oblivious strategy*					
tax-oblivious alpha	*80*	*70*	*60*	*80*	*70*	*60*
0.50	1.25	2.40	3.55	1.25	2.40	3.55
1.00	0.85	2.05	3.25	0.85	2.05	3.25
1.50	0.45	1.70	2.95	0.45	1.70	2.95
2.00	0.05	1.35	2.65	0.05	1.35	2.65

advantage' and 'tax efficiency advantage' that produces an advantage to being tax-oblivious. Though one could have imagined a broader array of manager value added or of tax efficiency ratios, the sample is still broad enough to illustrate the point.

As expected, the pre-liquidation analysis produces intuitively unsatisfying results. In reality, it fails the test, as it does not consider the important question of what happens at the end of the time horizon. Before going on to a post-liquidation analysis, it is worth revisiting the question of the difference between investment and performance horizons.

Investment and performance horizons

We have already touched on the issue of the difference between investment and performance horizons, particularly when dealing with investor psychology (in Chapter 2). The investment horizon of an individual should be defined as the period of time within which his or her investment objectives are expected not to change dramatically. Though objectives may not change, investment strategy might. Strategy is driven by comfort with the interaction between perceived opportunities, the willingness of the investor to assume the attendant risks, and the goals set by the investors. By contrast, performance horizon can be defined as the period of time over which the investor is likely to evaluate returns and risk, and during which strategic changes are unlikely. There could still be manager or tactical asset allocation changes during that period, reflecting the investor's satisfaction, or lack thereof, with the performance of the individual manager, and the relative opportunities that the investor perceives among the major asset classes or strategies.

That distinction between investment horizon and performance horizon is important, as it incorporates the implicit assumption that assets should remain invested throughout the investment horizon. By contrast, a change of strategy at the end of the investment horizon could require some or all of the assets to be liquidated. Therein lies the critical issue that leads a pre-liquidation analysis of the impact of time horizon on tax efficiency to suggest an intuitively wrong answer.

Post-liquidation analysis of the interaction between time horizon and tax efficiency

An investor with a shorter-term investment horizon will implicitly make the assumption that the assets will be liquidated, wholly or in part, at the end of that horizon. One can imagine the circumstances of an investor saving to buy a house, to pay for children's education, or to retire. At the end of the horizon, the financial assets set aside to meet that goal must be liquidated to pay for (say) the house in full or make a down payment.

It therefore seems that the appropriate evaluation of the interaction between tax efficiency and time horizon must consider the question on a post-liquidation basis. This, as shown in Exhibit 3.7, makes the playing field somewhat more level. It shows that there must be some time commitment before tax efficiency starts being worth the effort. Specifically, note that there are selected combinations of 'alpha advantage' for the tax-oblivious strategy and 'tax efficiency advantage' where, over the short term, being tax-efficient is actually not a sensible strategy.

Exhibit 3.7

Tax efficiency and time horizon: post-liquidation analysis (%)

	Post-liquidation tax-efficient strategy advantage					
Difference between	Three-year			20-year		
tax-efficient and	Tax efficiency of tax-oblivious strategy					
tax-oblivious alpha	80	70	60	80	70	60
0.50	0.43	1.05	1.66	0.80	1.67	2.51
1.00	0.07	0.72	1.36	0.42	1.33	2.21
1.50	**-0.28**	0.39	1.06	0.03	0.98	1.91
2.00	**-0.64**	0.07	0.76	**-0.36**	0.64	1.61

Tax efficiency and the difference between the portfolio's market value and tax cost

An important dynamic is at work here. A tax-oblivious investment process does cost the investor more ongoing taxes, as a larger share of the annual return on the portfolio is made up by income and realized capital gains. However, note that, as gains are realized and the proceeds are reinvested, the tax basis of the portfolio is continuously 'refreshed.' Therefore, the ratio of the portfolio's market to book value remains relatively low. By contrast, consider a tax-efficient process. On the one hand, it does allow the investor to defer taxes, as a substantial share of the return is earned in the form of unrealized capital gains. Thus, ongoing after-tax returns are higher, because the tax drag is lower. However, as these unrealized gains accumulate, the ratio of the portfolio's market to book value rises over time. This means that the tax impact of liquidating a tax-efficient portfolio will typically be higher than would be the case with a tax-oblivious portfolio.

Summary

Exhibit 3.8 presents a graphical comparison of tax-efficient and tax-oblivious returns over different time periods in pre-liquidation and post-liquidation contexts. It suggests that tax efficiency is most suited to investors with a horizon exceeding 10 years. Admittedly, however, the difference between tax efficiency and tax obliviousness arguably becomes significant after five years, if our alpha invasion assumption for the tax-efficient process and our tax efficiency assumption for a tax-oblivious process are both reasonable. In this specific instance, we are assuming a tax-oblivious alpha advantage of 100 basis points (i.e. 12% pre-tax return for the tax-oblivious strategy and 11% pre-tax return for the tax-efficient process), and a tax-oblivious tax efficiency of 75%, versus 95% tax efficiency for the tax-efficient process.

Exhibit 3.8

Tax efficiency and time horizon: comparing pre-liquidation and post-liquidation analyses

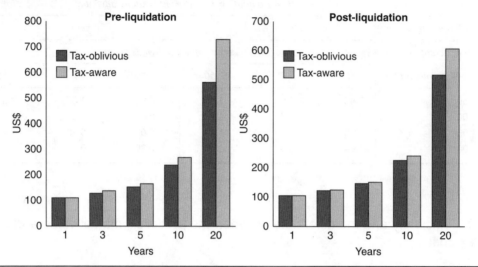

Static versus dynamic tax efficiency

Our discussion of time horizons brings up another important issue of tax efficiency: the difference between 'static' and 'dynamic' tax efficiency. We have just looked into the main insight: a tax-efficient investment process naturally leads to accumulation of unrealized capital gains. David Stein and his colleague Premkumar Narasimhan[15] frame the issue, and the resulting 'portfolio lockup,' particularly well:

> as time passes, the investor may be faced with a problem of portfolio lockup, when the cost basis of each lot is substantially below its market value and to sell any security requires a large tax cost.

Stein and Narasimhan point to the fact that lockup is more likely in a concentrated portfolio than when it is well diversified, but, if the time period is sufficiently long, lockup is almost inevitable. Roberto Apelfeld and his two co-authors[16] echo this observation. Discussing their tax-aware equity management process, they observed that:

> toward the end of the simulation period, turnover drops to between 10% to 30% as the portfolio began to run out of losses that could be taken to offset gains. Eventually, losses would have been completely depleted.

This risk arises because each transaction in considered in the light of *static* tax efficiency. The objective of the process is indeed to maximize the expected value of the portfolio's after-tax return appropriately corrected for its tracking error.

Dynamic tax efficiency

Managing that risk requires thinking in terms of *dynamic* tax efficiency. Dynamic tax efficiency adds an important dimension to the static process. It requires the investor to think of the future consequences of any current action. For instance, as a dynamically tax-efficient investor, you might question whether avoiding *any* net current capital gain realization is appropriate, given the risk it creates that you will have to accept greater tracking error or need to take potentially greater capital gains at some future point. Roberto Apelfeld, Michael Granito, and Akis Psarris[17] address the issue from a highly quantitative standpoint. They confirm that it might make sense, in the appropriate circumstances, to forgo some short-term tax efficiency to reduce the risk of portfolio freeze at some future point. In fact, they show that a model can be used to analyze that trade-off. In its most complex incarnation, the model is a fully dynamic program.

Simpler alternatives are conceivable, though admittedly probably less intellectually robust or satisfying. You might consider accepting some standard rate of acceptable capital gain realization. David Stein, for instance, reports that, in the early years of a portfolio initially funded with cash, normal market volatility might allow a manager to realize some net capital losses, thus improving the tax efficiency of the broader portfolio. These net capital losses might amount to as much as 2% to 4% over the first few years. Using some of these net losses to raise the tax basis of the portfolio could substantially postpone the inevitable lockup.

Similarly, one could imagine constraining the market-to-book ratio of the portfolio, forcing greater net capital gain realization in instances where substantial market appreciation has led to an unhealthy accumulation of unrealized capital gains. That constraint could be either client-driven or influenced by the likelihood that the client might benefit from future basis step-up. This is another concept that applies to U.S. residents: the tax basis of a portfolio is marked up to market without the need to pay capital gains taxes as assets pass into an individual's estate upon that individual's death. More work is needed on this front to quantify the trade-off and provide more specific guidelines to investors and their advisers alike. (An interesting dimension of the problem is that it is conceptually similar to the quandary faced by an investor with substantially concentrated low-basis holdings, a topic investigated in more detail in Chapter 10.)

Summary and implications

Tax efficiency is a very important dimension of the individual wealth management process. Individuals broadly pay taxes, while most institutional investors do not. Understanding the impact and the role of taxes requires appreciating how much of a drag taxes can impose on long-term portfolio returns. These taxes comprise not only those associated with the return on the portfolio assets, but also those that arise when a transfer of ownership occurs, still within the investors' 'broad family.' That broad family is defined here to include related or unrelated entities that the investor wishes to see derive some benefit from the assets, be it in the form of income from the assets or in the form of outright ownership of these assets. Thus, incorporating taxes into the process is equivalent to introducing a third dimension to the traditional two-dimensional space defined by return and risk.

However, one of the most important considerations should be for the investor to question his or her real time horizon, as experience shows that there is a clear trade-off between the pure investment cost of being tax-efficient and the long-term wealth implications of being tax-oblivious.

[1] Even the original work by Bob Arnott and Robert Jeffrey was not published until 1993. See Arnott, Robert D., and Robert H. Jeffrey, 'Is Your Alpha Big Enough to Cover its Taxes?,' *The Journal of Portfolio Management*, Spring 1993, pp. 15–25.

[2] For an early discussion of the effect of deferral on returns, see Holton, Glyn A. 'Transient Effects in Taxable Equity Investment,' *Financial Analysts Journal*, Vol. 49, No. 3, May/June 1994, pp. 70–75.

[3] See Arnott, Robert D., Andrew L. Berkin, and Jia Ye, 'Loss Harvesting: What's It Worth To The Taxable Investor?,' *The Journal of Wealth Management*, Spring 2001, pp. 10–18.

[4] For a discussion of the impact of capital gains taxes on portfolio management, see Appelbach, Richard O., Jr., 'The Capital Gains Tax Penalty?,' *The Journal of Portfolio Management*, Summer 1995, pp. 80–88.

[5] For an early discussion of the topic, applied to the institutional assets held by nuclear decommissioning trusts, see Meehan, James P., Daihyun Yoo, and H. Gifford Fong, 'Asset Allocation in a Taxable Environment: The Case of Nuclear Decommissioning Trusts,' *Financial Analysts Journal*, Vol. 49, No. 6, November/December 1993, pp. 67–73.

[6] Darryl Meyers, a Vice President at Wells Fargo Private Client Services, offered the insights quoted here at the AIMR Conference: *Investment Counseling for Private Clients III: Integrated Wealth Management, Taxes, Estate Planning, and Wealth Transfer*, in Atlanta, GA, March 27–28 2001. Session II: Integrated Wealth Management.

[7] *Eisner v. Macomber*, 252 U.S. 189 (1920).

[8] *Commissioner v. Glenshaw Glass*, 348 U.S. 426 (1955).

[9] See Poterba, James M., 'Unrealized Capital Gains and the Measurement of After-Tax Portfolio Performance,' *The Journal of Private Portfolio Management*, Spring 1999, pp. 23–34. Dr. Poterba is a professor at the Massachusetts Institute of Technology.

[10] See Anson, Mark J.P., 'The Impact of the Taxpayer Relief Act of 1997 on Derivatives Transactions,' *Journal of Derivatives*, Summer 1998, pp. 62–72.

[11] See Poterba, James M., 'Estate Tax Avoidance by High Net Worth Households: Why Are There so Few Tax-Free Gifts?,' *The Journal of Private Portfolio Management*, Summer 1998, pp. 1–10.

[12] See also Eller, M.B., 'Federal Taxation of Wealth Transfers, 1992–1995,' *Statistics of Income Bulletin*, Winter 1996–97, pp. 8–63.

[13] This is the insight discussed at length by two of the seminal writers on the topic, Robert D. Arnott and Robert H. Jeffrey, in the article cited in note 1 above. See also the article by Richard O. Appelbach cited in note 4.

[14] David Stein, chief investment officer of Parametric Portfolio Associates, presented the data at the AIMR Conference already cited in note 6 above – Session IV: The Trade-Offs between Tax Efficiency and Tracking Error.

[15] See Stein, David M., and Premkumar Narasimhan, 'Of Passive and Active Equity Portfolios in the Presence of Taxes,' *The Journal of Private Portfolio Management*, Fall 1999, pp. 55–63.

[16] See Apelfeld, Roberto, Gordon Fowler, Jr., and James Gordon, Jr., 'Tax-Aware Equity Investing,' *The Journal of Portfolio Management*, Winter 1996, pp. 18–28.

[17] See Apelfeld, Roberto, Michael Granito, and Akis Psarris. 'Active Management of Taxable Assets: A Dynamic Analysis of Manager Alpha,' *Journal of Financial Engineering*, Vol. 5, No. 2, 1997, pp. 117–46.

Chapter 4

Five principles of tax efficiency

Having defined tax efficiency and reviewed the three most important environmental variables relating to tax efficiency – taxation principles, time horizon, and objective (static versus dynamic) – let us now look into the five major principles that underpin tax-efficient portfolio management. The list of these principles could be expanded, and probably will be, as new thoughts emerge as to critical variables. The five principles to which we turn now are those that appear, at least currently, to merit the greatest attention:

- challenge conventional wisdom;
- volatility may be valuable;
- two types of transactions;
- focus on the whole portfolio; and
- portfolio drift is not trivial.

These principles are broad philosophical guideposts that can be used in day-to-day circumstances to answer the question I keep asking myself: am I as tax-efficient as I can be? This is a question that should be asked by individual investors, by their advisors, and by tax-aware portfolio managers.

Challenge conventional wisdom

Arguably, this is the most basic principle. In practice, it substantially underpins the others. We have seen that taxes introduce a new dimension to the classic two-dimensional investment management problem. It is intuitively logical that a new dimension would have the potential to change both the nature of the problem and the framework within which it is evaluated. The question then is: how much of a change is required? We shall find that the change is both dramatic and substantial.

The asset management industry has spent a number of years developing sophisticated approaches to the problems of institutional, usually tax-exempt investors.[1] These approaches did upset the apple cart in some ways, introducing a number of innovative solutions to institutional asset management. These included, for example, a greater focus on risk; systematic approaches to asset allocation; multimanager constructs, as specialist management mandates were recommended by emerging and then flourishing investment consultants; and a sharp focus on the active/passive management debate. The advent of actively traded derivative markets also contributed to further innovation, such as tactical asset allocation, currency management overlay programs, portfolio protection (known until the debacle of October 1987 as 'portfolio insurance'), and sophisticated multisecurity strategies, often found in hedge funds.

This litany of innovation is mentioned to illustrate the point that the asset management industry has been neither overly tradition-bound nor averse to change. In fact, it has been willing and able to develop new solutions to old problems. However, innovations have typically followed a process of marginal improvement applied to the most important segment of the industry's business: institutional clients. Under that process, a current solution is modified at the margin as new opportunities arise. As these modifications compound one another, the end result may be quite different from the original approach. Yet the process has been incremental rather than revolutionary.

Unfortunately, dealing with taxable individuals makes such an incremental process at best ill suited and, arguably, unable to produce the desired outcomes. While certain of the solutions developed for tax-exempt institutional investors will likely remain relevant, and potentially profitable, to taxable individual investors, we must caution ourselves that many of them may not.

Considering the composition of investment return

Certain strategies may not be relevant, in large measure because they rest on assumptions that are not valid in the individual investor world, or because they do not take other important issues into consideration. An example illustrates the point.

An important development observed in the institutional world over the past 30 years or so is a shift in investor focus away from accounting definitions of income and toward the concept of total return. This shift makes sense, for a tax-exempt investor should be indifferent to how return is generated, whether via income, realized capital gains or unrealized capital gains. Unless one assumes highly significant transaction costs, any disbursement required to satisfy a negative cash flow need can be satisfied through a sale of principal assets. In this context, trading costs are defined as commissions, bid-ask spreads or substantial market impact.

Clearly, such an assumption is invalid in the world of taxable investors; and this for two reasons. First, return components are subject to at least three different taxation regimes – in the United States and, with variations, elsewhere too – depending upon whether they are classified as income, realized capital gains or unrealized capital gains. Second, should income, in an accounting sense, not be sufficient to meet disbursements, assets must be sold, with the potential to attract capital gains taxes.

Thus, taxable investors and their advisors must focus on the nature of return components, while a tax-exempt portfolio manager does not have to. Any strategy or investment approach that implicitly or explicitly ignores the way in which return is broken down into its individual components is likely to provide taxable investors with inaccurate, if not outright misleading, insights.

We can think of several other instances where conventional wisdom is misguided when it comes to managing individual investor assets. In general, it is reasonably simple to detect such errors, as they seem almost always to proceed from the faulty assumption that we are still dealing in a two-dimensional world, defined by return and risk. The moment we begin to think of the third dimension – tax efficiency – things take on a totally different character.

Note in passing that there is also a fourth dimension that can interact with tax efficiency. We considered it earlier, in the broader wealth management context: investor comfort with the strategy that he or she has chosen. However, comfort extends beyond staying the course and coping with decision risk. Different individuals have different levels of comfort, or discomfort, with taxes. Certain individuals display a strong allergy to any tax payment, to the point that they may elect to forgo certain returns to avoid paying anything to the government. Others accept that paying taxes is 'fair' and simply aim to keep that payment within their definition of fairness.

Performance assessment issues

Conventional wisdom has it that performance measurement is trivial and that performance assessment is complex, but mathematically simple. Yet, if we insert tax efficiency into the problem, performance measurement becomes complex and performance assessment becomes extremely difficult. We will consider this issue in more detail at the end of this book, but the main point is that after-tax performance is 'path-dependent.' Path-dependence means that the return that you earn on a portfolio is, in an after-tax space, dependent upon where you started and how you got there.

The *starting point* matters because the extent to which the initial portfolio substantially differed from where you would like it to be, and had significant unrealized capital gains, will determine how close to your desired target portfolio you can get and how much of an initial return penalty you will accept.

The *path you take to get there* also matters, because the nature of the transactions occurring from time to time, for instance cash flows into or out of the portfolio, will exacerbate or mitigate the challenges posed by the initial state of the portfolio.

Practice management issues

Challenging conventional wisdom is just as important when thinking of investment processes as when focusing on practice management (in the case of investment advisors) or advisor qualifications (if dealing with affluent investors). With a few notable exceptions, the investment management industry has not demonstrated a lot of forward thinking in the way it has dealt with individual investors. Though this might have been understandable early on, when individuals did not control a significant fraction of the assets entrusted to the industry, it is more difficult to understand now that they have overtaken institutions in terms of total financial assets. The temptation has seemingly been too great for many to try to fit a square peg in a round hole, in a bid to continue to capture the growth in individually owned assets without having to change business model or product array.

In European countries with strong traditions of private banking, the trend has been to serve the private investor through a mix of individually designed processes and a joint decision-making approach. This solution at times has seemed to blur the distinction between delegated and self-directed asset management activities.

In countries with strong institutional traditions, particularly in the United States, the trend has been to envision the business model in an almost bimodal fashion. A part of the industry replicated the European model, mixing portfolio manager and broker roles, with potentially dramatic legal consequences as and when markets behaved in unexpected ways. (Then, individual investors queried the appropriateness of decisions made in their name, without specific mandate to do so, and brokers often found themselves having to compensate clients. The reciprocal of that observation has been found in successful litigation, where a named fiduciary, with a discretionary mandate, listened 'too much' to his or her client, and agreed to decisions that eventually proved fateful). The remainder of the industry delivered institutional, tax-oblivious solutions to unsuspecting individuals, who were convinced that they were buying the most sophisticated possible product. Though many proved highly satisfied, a rising number of individuals has been found complaining of the adverse tax consequences of tax-oblivious trading, which did not seem problematic when markets were rising, but all of a sudden are quite costly when they fall.

Challenging conventional wisdom in this context involves being quite clear in your own mind as to three questions:

- What does it means to manage money on behalf of an individual who has to pay taxes?
- Am I prepared to design a different business model and thus to differ from the bulk of my competition?
- Can I articulate a philosophy centered on the individual and his or her needs, irrespective of the fact that it may require the investment advisor to develop purpose-designed services?

For example, creating a family of tax-sensitive mutual funds or similar commingled investment structures should be viewed as a necessity and not as a marketing gimmick. The family should be a complete one, and not simply group funds that could not be sold otherwise or simply happened to demonstrate ex-post tax efficiency. Peter Torvik of U.S. Bank (mentioned in Chapter 1) rightly referred to that kind of activity as 'forensic tax efficiency.' Forensic tax-efficiency is both insidious and misleading. First, it is insidious as many funds started at the point of maximum (coincidental) tax-efficiency often see their tax-efficiency fade over time. Second, these funds are marketed to both taxable and tax-exempt investors, while the latter do not need to bear the costs associated with tax-efficiency.

Being prepared to challenge conventional wisdom is the cornerstone of the tax-efficient management edifice. Over time, it would be reasonable to predict that the asset management industry will evolve into two well-differentiated segments, one focused on tax-oblivious portfolio management and the other on tax-efficient wealth management. Though the wealth management segment has, paradoxically, a longer history, it may have lost a few steps in terms of the sophistication of the solutions that it offers to individual investors. Yet there is no reason to think that, with individuals now controlling more assets than their institutional counterparts, the industry will not develop a set of highly sophisticated and customized approaches. To do that effectively, however, it needs to be prepared to cut the umbilical cord that still ties it to institutional asset management, and, in the process, to create a new conventional wisdom for its own specific circumstances.

Volatility may be valuable

Appreciating the potential value of volatility is in itself a striking example of the need to challenge conventional wisdom. In the pre-tax world, volatility is usually viewed as the investor's enemy. After all, are we not describing the conventional pre-tax investment problem as a trade-off between our friend return and our enemy risk, or volatility, the cost we must pay to get return? Yet it can be argued that volatility can be the investor's friend in an after-tax context – albeit with a couple of important caveats.

A loss can be valuable

The main reason why volatility can be the investor's friend is that a loss can be valuable. Before going any further, it is worth restating the obvious: no one should invest money with the explicit goal of losing it. However, once a loss exists, and losses will tend to be routinely created by random market volatility, the contrast between taxable and tax-exempt investors could not be more striking.

The tax-exempt investor cannot see the loss as anything other than a nuisance. It would require a very high level of enlightenment to view it as tuition in the art of investing. By contrast, the taxable investor can see the loss as an opportunity to shelter a gain, today or in the future, to rebalance the portfolio's asset allocation or to raise the tax basis of the portfolio, with the goal of reducing future tax liabilities.

An unrealized capital loss can indeed be viewed as a free option. Roberto Apelfeld, Michael Granito, and Akis Psarris[2] offer a methodology to value that option.

Diversifiable volatility is an asset

The potential value of a loss makes diversifiable volatility a potential asset. In 1997, we reported on a simple experiment to investigate and evaluate the point.[3]

Let me start with an example. Considering two different investment opportunities, a rise in the price of one accompanied by a fall in the price of the other, creates the opportunity to realize 'tax-free' capital gains in the investment whose price is rising. This occurs because you are able to realize the loss by selling the security whose price is falling and to use that loss to offset the gain, which you would also realize by selling the security whose price is rising.

A combination of extreme factor exposures and volatility in individual asset classes or securities can give rise to more opportunities to create free options for sheltering gains. A 'factor,' in this context, is defined as a common trait that explains some of the riskiness of an investment.

The industry in which a company operates can be such a factor: all the companies in that industry will tend to suffer or prosper along with the industry as a whole. Recall the 'bank effect' in the first quarter of 1985 in Japan, or the health care effect in the United States when Hillary Clinton was leading a task force aimed at changing the structure of the industry. In both instances, most, if not all, of the stocks in those industries behaved in very comparable ways, with Japanese bank stock prices rising sharply and U.S. health care stock prices falling just as substantially.

Other factors can be more complex and relate to common risk considerations, such as whether earnings growth is steady or cyclical, whether the company relies on foreign sales, whether its balance sheet is leveraged, whether it is labor intensive, and so on. 'Investment styles' can be viewed as an ultimate form of factor, since among the most important determinants of whether a stock falls in the 'growth' or the 'value' camp are its long-term earnings growth for the former and the ratio of its price to book value for the latter.

Valuing that asset

The experiment we conducted was based on four portfolios, each comprising just two securities or asset classes. These securities came in four flavors. They all had the same expected returns, but two had a low volatility (13% standard deviation), while the other two had a high volatility (23%). Further, two of the securities were negatively correlated (-0.6), while the other two were positively correlated to the same extent (0.6). The four portfolios each comprised a pair of securities and were rebalanced to a 50/50 mix at the end of each year. We then looked at all four portfolios at the end of 10 years and compared their respective tax efficiency, and did that on both pre-liquidation and post-liquidation bases.

Exhibit 4.1 shows the results of the experiment. On a *pre-liquidation* basis, the portfolio combinations with the higher volatility have greater tax efficiency than those with lower volatility. The higher tax efficiency of the portfolio where the assets are positively correlated seems counterintuitive: why would highly correlated assets produce a more efficient outcome? The outcome is explained by the fact that low correlation requires more frequent rebalancing, which leads to higher net capital gains realization and thus lower pre-liquidation tax efficiency.

Exhibit 4.1

The impact of volatility on tax efficiency

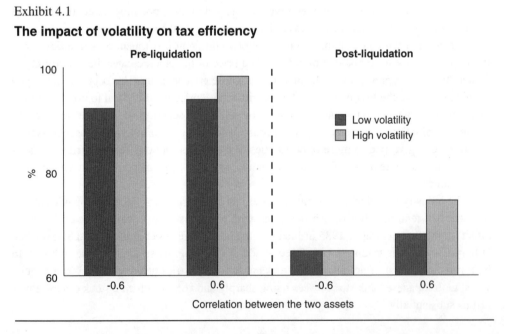

On a *post-liquidation* basis, volatility seems to be a positive attribute, as the portfolios comprising higher-volatility assets have a higher tax efficiency. The surprising correlation impact observed in the pre-liquidation picture reverts to a more intuitively logical outcome, as the more frequent portfolio rebalancing associated with the lower correlation produces a continuing upward adjustment in the tax basis of the assets held. Thus, when they are eventually liquidated, the terminal capital gain payment is smaller. This is another illustration of the difference between static and dynamic tax efficiency (discussed in Chapter 3).

The psychological dimension

Though volatility may be the investor's friend and realizing a hitherto unrealized capital loss may make a great deal of sense, advisors and investors need to understand that they are likely to be caught in a psychological bind. This arises from the notion of mental accounting and the disposition effect (both of which we encountered in Chapter 2). Hersh Shefrin[4] proposes an excellent example of 'get-even-itis' that captures part of the disposition effect:

> Scott Szach is the former CFO of Griffen Trading Company, a commodities-trading firm. Outside of his formal duties, and without authority, Szach began to trade using the firm's money. Initially he traded small amounts. During August 1997, his first month of trading, he lost $10,656. And so 'get-even-itis' set in. Szach's losses mounted over the course of the next year. The *Wall Street Journal* reports that '[i]n the last three months of the year, his trading became furious, with commissions alone running, respectively, $97,543, $84,401, and $65,321, and his combined losses finally reaching $2 million.' Griffen Trading was a small operation. Szach's losses broke Griffen Trading's back.[5]

The point of the example, again in Shefrin's words, is that:

> People generally sell their winners too early and hold their losers too long. Realizing a loss is painful, despite the possibility of a tax advantage. An investor who recognizes the tax benefit, but finds the psychological cost too painful, experiences a self-control problem. Some investors find ways to realize tax losses eventually, notably by using December as a deadline.

Thus, investors and portfolio managers need to learn to control their natural behavior, and realize the value of hitherto unrealized losses in their portfolios. Further, as aptly proposed by Robert Arnott and his co-authors,[6] loss harvesting should be a year-round activity:

> The *so-called* tax-sensitive investment manager, who engages in loss harvesting only once at the end of the fiscal year, has probably seen numerous loss-harvesting opportunities appear and disappear in the course of the year.

Two types of transactions

A direct consequence of the potential to use 'loss harvesting' as a factor to raise portfolio tax efficiency is that you need to look at individual transactions in a different way. This is yet another illustration of the need to challenge conventional wisdom. In a tax-exempt or tax-oblivious environment, the only sensible rationale for executing a transaction must be that the transaction will improve the portfolio, by raising the expected return, lowering the expected risk or some of both. You can call such a transaction an 'alpha generating' transaction. In this context, alpha is the term of art to describe investment value added.

However, the tax-efficient investor, advisor or portfolio manager may need to consider another transaction, which could be called 'alpha enabling.' An alpha-enabling transaction would be one that does not in and of itself produce any incremental alpha, but makes it possible for another transaction to create after-tax alpha, usually by sheltering an unrealized gain on the sell side of the transaction.

One of the problems associated with tax efficiency is that there may be instances where a transaction, though it might make sense on a pre-tax basis, does not make sense when it is considered in terms of its contribution to after-tax returns. An example illustrates this.

Imagine two investors or portfolio managers, both of whom are convinced that the stock of Ford will outperform the stock of General Motors over some specified investment horizon. Now, imagine that one of them holds General Motors at a tax cost relatively close to the current market price, while the other has held the stock for a long period of time and has a significant unrealized capital gain. Will it make sense for both investors, or portfolio managers, to shift from General Motors to Ford? Or should one hold on to his or her General Motors stock, while the other does the trade?

In the previous chapter, we looked at a table, drawn from a presentation given by David Stein,[7] which showed the implied value added that you must expect from a trade for it to make sense on an after-tax basis. The table clearly demonstrated the intuition that the larger the unrealized capital gain, the larger the implicit alpha must be. Thus, though the 'buy Ford, sell General Motors' transaction might make sense for one investor, it might not for the other. The transaction might not make sense if the excess return expected from Ford relative to General Motors over the investment horizon is insufficient to cover for the fact that the 'appreciated General Motors holder' has to pay capital gains taxes on the position and thus reinvest a smaller dollar amount in Ford.

Imagine that the investor who holds the substantially appreciated position in General Motors also happens to hold Pfizer at some loss. Also imagine that the investor is indifferent as to the prospects of Pfizer relative to Merck. An alpha-enabling transaction would be to sell Pfizer and buy Merck. Though that transaction would not add to nor detract from the portfolio's expected return or volatility, it would generate a capital loss. That loss could then be used to offset some or all of the unrealized gain in General Motors, thus allowing the investor to sell General Motors and buy Ford, in a profitable after-tax fashion.

The example could equally have included an international dimension. Rather than holding Pfizer at a loss, the investor may have held Nippon Steel at a loss, either because the stock fell in the Japanese market, or because of the weakness of the yen relative to the U.S. dollar. The investor might sell Nippon Steel and buy into another integrated steel-maker in Japan, such as Sumitomo Steel, and achieve the same results.

We can take this further. The pairs of transactions would still make sense if the investor expected Merck to underperform Pfizer, for as long as the underperformance of Merck was not expected to be substantial enough to offset the outperformance expected from Ford over General Motors, and for as long as there was no other pharmaceutical stock, which was expected to perform similarly to Pfizer.

Alpha-enabling transactions arise more frequently than one might think. We will reconsider this when dealing with tax-efficient security selection, but consider the broad market circumstances. A careful analysis of the performance of capital markets over time shows that there are times when a whole industry, or even a whole market, goes down for a variety of reasons, none of which point to a serious risk of the ultimate demise of the industry or the market. Let us simply call this an over-reaction to a recent over-reaction in the opposite direction. In these circumstances, which we might label 'wholesale market moves,' there are plenty of opportunities to use 'noxious random volatility' to our advantage. Even if it means foregoing a holding in a stock which we really like for the long term, the opportunity can be very tempting to use those random price moves to execute a transaction that previously appeared impractical, or simply to raise the tax basis of the portfolio, moved by a concern for dynamic tax efficiency.

Alpha-enabling transactions should also not be limited to the world of individual equities, or even individual securities. They can very profitably be considered across asset classes, as the example of Nippon Steel and Sumitomo Steel suggests. This naturally leads us to the next of our five major principles.

Focus on the whole portfolio

A tax-efficient investor cannot afford to allow his or her focus to be diverted from the whole portfolio to individual portfolio pockets. It is a truism that one pays taxes on the whole of one's wealth, and not on individual pockets. Thus, sequential optimization, which is the rule in the world of the tax-exempt investor, must give way to a simultaneous optimization in the taxable world.

Sequential optimization versus simultaneous optimization

In a tax-exempt environment, it is not unusual to think in terms of decision-making sequences. The idea is that, if one can optimally combine individually optimal sub-portfolios, the resulting overall portfolio will likely be optimal. This will generally be the case unless the extreme parceling of the portfolio among multiple strategies and managers creates costly administrative burdens, or dilutes the investor's bargaining power to the point that the management fees rise dramatically. Combined with the observation that specialization may produce higher manager skill, practicing sequential optimization has led to the current environment, where many institutional portfolios differentiate between a wide diversity of individual pockets.

It is not unusual, for instance, for an institutional equity portfolio to be broken down into four or six individual mandates, one each of large, mid- and small capitalization ranges, each broken down into growth and value style biases. Add to this the tendency to have more than one manager for each mandate, and the problem associated with overseeing a multimanager stable becomes quite complex.

This sequence immediately appears faulty in the case of a taxable investor. Even if each of the submanagers were to be individually tax-efficient, how would we know that the tax-sheltering activity performed within each subportfolio has not 'wasted' unrealized losses that would be more valuable elsewhere in the portfolio?

Imagine the case of an investor having U.S. equity and Japanese equity mandates within his or her portfolio. Over the last 10 years, the overall value of the U.S. equity market has more than doubled, while the Japanese equity market has lost more than half of its value. Thus, a U.S. equity portfolio manager might have found it at times difficult to execute certain trades because of having to deal with unrealized capital gains. Conversely, the Japanese equity manager was probably not fretting over his or her unrealized losses. Yet these losses might have been very helpful to the U.S. equity manager.

How do you know that you have taken maximum advantage of the potential afforded by multiple portfolio pockets, each with its own tax status and overall circumstances? Here, the issue relates to the way in which individual investment strategies are held. We will spend a whole chapter later on asset location, but suffice it to say that it might make more sense to hold tax-efficient strategies in taxable pockets and tax-inefficient strategies in pockets that either are tax-free or benefit from the potential to defer taxes. Examples of the latter might be a life insurance contract in France or a retirement plan in the United States.

How do we know that the interactions that naturally take place between security selection and asset allocation decisions are optimal? As we will discuss in a later chapter, asset allocation decisions are often implemented through the purchase and sale of individual securities. Thus, we need to ensure that activity related to asset allocation, for example, has been conducted in a way that has not counteracted efforts made on the security selection front.

In short, sequential optimization must give way to simultaneous optimization, with two important consequences. First, individual mandates are created only if there is a clear and measurable benefit to specialization, once the total portfolio picture has first been taken into consideration. Second, a proactive global coordination effort is designed to ensure that activity across the different mandates is harmonized and made to work for the benefit of the overall portfolio.

Implementation considerations

This challenge to conventional wisdom may be among the most difficult to manage, because it strikes at the core of the habits that have developed among institutional investment managers. The industry is indeed incredibly set in its ways on this front and the issues are hard to explain using the inspired soundbites that now seem to rule the day. The challenge indeed requires each investor or advisor to debunk three important myths, in whose stock there have been very substantial investments.

1. The style diversification myth

Style diversification does not always make sense (we will return to the issue in more depth in Chapter 16). Here, it is worth mentioning David Stein's work again. He argues that a U.S. equity portfolio managed into four building blocks (large-capitalization value and growth, and small-capitalization value and growth) will require some annual turnover, simply to rebalance the portfolio to the desired neutral balance. The observation is based on the fact that individual companies migrate from certain parts of the universe to others.

For instance, Exhibit 4.2 suggests that 6% of the universe migrates from 'large value' to 'large growth,' as value stocks become more expensive because their prices have risen. Similarly, some large stocks become small, while selected small stocks become large, as they outperform or underperform their respective peer groups. Yet, from the point of view of the whole universe, there is no migration, as each of the four components is kept in balance, with the large-cap and small-cap sectors being defined as the top 80% and bottom 20% of the universe, respectively, and growth and value both being allocated half of the universe as well. Stein computed that the average annual turnover required to maintain that neutral balance across the four sectors is around 22%.

In an environment where we expect equity prices to rise over time, the cost of such a turnover cannot be underestimated. A simple computation suggests that a 22% average turnover, in a market returning an average of 10% (made up solely of capital gains), would create a tax drag in the range of 44 to 88 basis points, depending upon whether the capital gains thus realized attract a 20% tax rate or a 40% tax rate. Clearly, the problem is more complex in real life, but this average still offers a reasonably good order of magnitude, which ought to bring one to think again before automatically opting for a simple four-way split of an equity portfolio.

2. The multiple manager myth

It may not always be good to try to diversify manager risk by having multiple managers (we will come back to this point in more depth when looking at manager selection issues). When we looked at selected taxation principles, we discussed the concept of 'wash sales,' which is so important in the United States. In a single manager context, this is something that can be effectively monitored, as systems can be put in place to ensure that the portfolio manager does not sell at a loss something that he or she has bought within the last 30 days. They also need to ensure that the portfolio manager does not repurchase something that was sold at a loss within the last 30 days.

In a multiple manager environment, the situation becomes considerably more complex and difficult to handle. Trades by both managers will be consolidated from the point of view

Exhibit 4.2

Typical annual turnover

From *To*	*Large* *Growth*	*Large* *Value*	*Small* *Growth*	*Small* *Value*
Large growth	32	6	1	1
Large value	6	32	1	1
Small growth	1	1	7	1
Small value	1	1	1	7

Source: David Stein[8]

of their individual investor client, if they both manage assets that are held in pockets with the same taxpayer identity. Thus, there is the potential for wash sales to be triggered across managers. The administrative complexity associated with pre-approval of all trades, to ensure that no such sales can occur, is both time-consuming and cumbersome, and may prevent either or both managers from giving their client the best performance they can generate.

3. The commingled structures myth

Mutual funds or similar commingled structures may not always be better than individual accounts. The problem is particularly acute in the United States or in countries where some of the return on the mutual fund is taxable to the investor, even if he or she has not sold out or reduced his or her position in the fund. In the United States, for instance, the rules associated with the Investment Company Act of 1940 require that 90% of the income (interest, dividends, and realized capital gains) be passed on to mutual fund shareholders each year, so that the fund can retain its own tax-exempt status. Note that they cannot upstream losses. In countries where similar rules apply, just as in the United States, mutual funds are rarely tax-efficient.

By contrast, in many countries, particularly on the European continent, transactions within a mutual fund are not taxable to the mutual fund holder, except when he or she sells the share in the mutual fund at a profit. There may be exceptions for certain money market funds, in certain circumstances. In France, for instance, an exception applies when money market fund units are sold in excess of a certain amount. Individuals have taken advantage of a loophole that allowed them to transform taxable income into capital gains by diverting deposits to money market mutual funds, and then selling some of their mutual fund holdings to replace the interest income generated by deposits. However, these exceptions do not change the general point we are making.

A mutual fund can be viewed through two lenses, similar in essence to the idea of inside and outside tax basis in partnership accounting. You can think of two types of transactions: those that take place within the mutual fund and those involving the purchase or sale of units in a mutual fund. Most jurisdictions look at the second type of transaction as giving rise to some taxable income. Many do not concern themselves with transactions within the activity that is taking place within the fund, though the United States certainly does want to tax those as well, at the investor's level.

This actually creates interesting investment opportunities, on which Roberto Apelfeld and I have reported.[9] In particular, we focused on the fall in the price of the mutual fund when it distributes dividends or, more importantly, net realized capital gains. We concluded that there was the potential to use these accounting losses to the benefit of the overall portfolio. In particular, we found that:

> at least for the period tested, a global balanced mutual fund portfolio could benefit from incorporating an evaluation of the tax liability associated with capital gain and income distribution in the investment process. Proactively dealing with taxes and incorporating them into an integrated investment process seems to have played an important role in enhancing the performance of portfolios of mutual funds.

However, while there may be some such silver lining, the general rule still is that a mutual fund, at least for countries with a system such as that in the United States, is generally not a tax-efficient vehicle. Which investor has never been hurt by the fact that a mutual fund he or she owned distributed realized capital gains on which taxes would be due in a year when the market subsequently went down? This seems to many investors to be adding insult to injury. Further, this can become quite painful, should, for instance, a mutual fund experience significant net redemptions. Indeed, the shares sold to meet redemptions may well involve significant unrealized gains, which are then realized, so that the shareholders who remain in the fund have to pay the taxes associated with the activity of shareholders who have left the fund.

Mutual fund sponsors are fond of downplaying the issue, claiming that individual investors may well benefit, on balance, from the fact that funds 'normally' experience positive cash flows, thus providing the investor who cannot add to his or her holdings the average cost benefits that accrue from dollar cost averaging. This is true. Yet it could be argued that what may be true at the level of an individual fund could well not be true for the industry as a whole.

In fact, the weakness of mutual funds or similar commingled structures is compounded when an investor starts thinking of changing managers. Indeed, most mutual funds will not allow investors to purchase shares by tendering securities, nor will they allow investors to redeem their shares in kind. Selected mutual funds do offer the ability to redeem holdings in kind, to mitigate the disadvantages discussed here, and, in fact, they can use these provisions to enhance the tax efficiency of their portfolios beyond the individual transaction.

Imagine now that you have a portfolio of individual securities whose current prices, on average, are somewhat higher than their tax bases. Also imagine that you are unhappy with the manager currently in charge of the portfolio. Buying a mutual fund will require you to sell your portfolio, realize capital gains, and reinvest the proceeds, minus the appropriate tax provision, in the mutual fund. Similarly, selling a mutual fund to move to a different manager will require the realization of any unrealized capital gain in your position. Using portfolios of individual securities can make either change less traumatic, as you may require that the new manager receive the securities in kind and adapt their management strategy to the fact that certain securities involve too large an unrealized capital gain for them to be sold.

In summary, it is not hard to become convinced that portfolios of individual securities might be preferable, except in circumstances where the costs inherent in an individual portfolio – diversification, custody, transaction, and the like – are so prohibitively expensive as to require the lesser of two evils, the use of a mutual fund. Clearly, the industry today does not really like this idea, as it is considerably more comfortable and efficient for a manager to handle a commingled structure than a multiplicity of individual accounts. Yet technology will most likely eventually force the asset management industry to follow other industries and move toward mass customization.

Portfolio drift is not trivial

The last of our five main principles concerns investors or portfolio managers who, seeking to minimize taxes, let the portfolio drift. (We will return to the issue when discussing strategic asset allocation and the efficient frontier framework.) Portfolio drift affects all aspects of portfolio management. It has an obvious impact on strategic asset allocation, and it has an equally important impact on the day-to-day portfolio management activity of an investor who only holds a number of individual stocks.

Illustrating portfolio drift

Exhibit 4.3 illustrates portfolio drift in a somewhat dramatic fashion – yet, while it may seem unrealistic for someone to remain absolutely passive for 50 years, the example does make the important point that the consequences of inaction are serious. The exhibit depicts the respective weights at the end of various time horizons of two hypothetical assets, assuming that one returns a compound 12% while the other returns only 8%. Though drift is not overly meaningful for the first few years, note that passively holding these assets without

Exhibit 4.3

Illustrating portfolio drift

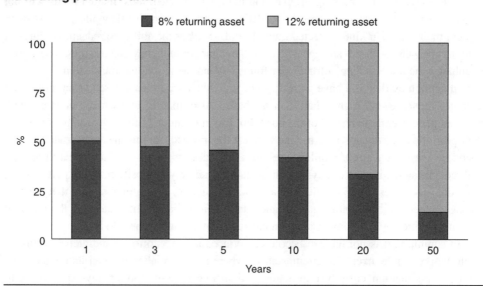

rebalancing would lead the 50/50 initial mix to move to 55/45 by the end of the fifth year, to 59/41 by the end of the 10th year, to 67/33 by the end of the 20th year, and to 86/14 by the end of the 50th year.

With the higher-returning and therefore presumably riskier asset rising in weight throughout the period, the portfolio's risk profile rises over time. Does the investor's risk profile rise as well? This change in risk

Exhibit 4.4

Expected portfolio risk at different period ends (%)

First year	11.6
Third year	11.8
Fifth year	12.1
10th year	12.6
20th year	13.6
50th year	16.1

is definitely not trivial. Assuming that the 8% returning asset has a standard deviation of returns of 8% and that the 12% returning asset has a standard deviation of returns of 18%, we can compute the implicit expected risk of each portfolio. Exhibit 4.4 displays these, assuming that the correlation between the two assets is set at 0.5.

Dealing with portfolio drift

Though a tax-exempt investor does not need to be concerned with the issue, as periodic portfolio rebalancing can be assumed to be a cost-free exercise, the same cannot be said for a taxable investor. Portfolio rebalancing will be costly, particularly if one assumes that capital markets produce positive returns over time. Indeed, the portfolio imbalance results from the fact that one asset outperforms another. Portfolio rebalancing would require the investor to realize hitherto unrealized gains and pay the associated capital gains taxes. This takes us back to the issue of static versus dynamic tax efficiency. A tax-sensitive investor focusing on dynamic tax efficiency will probably be more willing to accept the costs associated with some continuous portfolio rebalancing, as he or she will likely believe that these costs will reduce the need for a more difficult choice later on: whether to accept significant portfolio drift or incur material realized capital gain taxes.

Summary and implications

It is important to understand fully the rules under which we must operate, the issues that they create, and the principles that must guide us. There are two principal implications to adopting a tax-efficient approach to managing one's wealth: think differently and keep focusing on the broadest possible picture.

Be prepared to think differently

This simply echoes the first principle: challenge the conventional wisdom. Thus, individual investors and their advisors need to be prepared to be different, because the circumstances of the investor are different. I would suggest that there are two dimensions to this idea of being prepared to think differently.

The first involves controlling the natural reaction of applying 'tried and tested' principles, even though they were tried and tested in a totally different environment. Three simple examples illustrate the point. Individual investors or their advisors must ask themselves whether multimanager diversification really makes sense. They must ask themselves whether they really need to consider style diversification, that is, having both a growth and a value mandate, rather than one single blended portfolio. Finally, they must ask themselves whether the traditional aversion toward volatility is really applicable to their individual circumstances.

The second involves being prepared to design totally different solutions if they make sense. Three more examples will make the point. Individual investors and their advisors need to be concerned with the multigenerational nature of the investment problem and ensure that they have designed an integrated wealth plan, bringing together financial, estate and investment planning issues. They need to reconsider the traditional segmentation between active and passive management processes, and see that one can be active with respect to security selection, just as one can be active relative to tax management (see Chapter 9). Finally, they need to reconsider a natural aversion toward volatility or derivative securities. Both may well have a role in improving overall portfolio after-tax returns.

Being prepared to think differently means two things. First, one must pause to ask a simple question: am I doing this because that is the way it has been done in the past? Avoiding the trap of following the well-trodden path out of habit, rather than by choice, is made easier when one states assumptions formally. This typically prevents one going too far down a blind alley. Indeed, with clearly stated assumptions, one can usually quickly see whether they are or are not relevant to the circumstances of the individual investor. Second, and more generally, more resources need to be dedicated to conducting research into wealth management and many of its arcane corners. We are starting to see some interest on the part of academia in the issues surrounding the circumstances of individual investors, but a lot more is needed. Further, there is a need to integrate these findings, as they are still quite specialty-specific, with researchers focused on taxation issues and behavioral finance issues, to name only two. The real solution requires the whole picture to come into focus.

Keep focusing on the broadest possible picture

This also echoes one of the five principles, the need for a total portfolio focus. Yet it actually goes further. Wealth management ideally should be viewed in a multigenerational, dynastic context. At times, clients or investors themselves will not be willing or able to think in such broad terms. Yet the challenge remains to keep the broadest possible perspective, as local optimization can be the enemy of total optimization.

Earlier, we noted that tax efficiency is concerned with both income and capital gains taxes, on the one hand, and estate and gift taxes on the other. Focusing narrowly on the situation of one individual, while ignoring estate or gift tax considerations, can turn an otherwise good solution into a serious problem.

Imagine an entrepreneur who does not consider the structure through which he or she owns a private company until after the company has become listed on a stock exchange. Think of how much easier it would have been to pass some of that ownership down to other generations, with the appropriate discount, at a time when the actual value of the gift was hard to determine and the gift was wholly illiquid.

Again, in the world of less wealthy investors, consider individuals adopting distinct and independent strategies for their taxable and tax-deferred pockets. Not viewing one's individual retirement account, for instance, as a component of a total picture is likely to lead the investor to a suboptimal solution. Admittedly, selected plans have challenging constraints, but would it not be easier to mitigate these constraints in the broader context of the whole portfolio?

Finally, consider the investor who falls into the trap of not considering all their investment strategies as a whole. How about the individual who asks for and executes the most tax-efficient strategies possible in the part of his or her assets entrusted to someone else to manage (either directly or through a mutual fund vehicle), and then totally eschews tax efficiency in a personal trading activity?

In summary, an important step to tax-efficient wealth management across generations is to keep in mind the fact that tax efficiency requires a shift from a two-dimensional conceptual framework to a three-dimensional one. Viewing that third dimension as a full equal to the other two is the essence of the challenge and the seed of the solution.

---

[1] As aptly chronicled by Peter Bernstein in his book *Capital Ideas*, New York: Free Press, 1992.

[2] See Apelfeld, Roberto, Michael Granito, and Akis Psarris, 'Active Management of Taxable Assets: A Dynamic Analysis of Manager Alpha,' *Journal of Financial Engineering*, Vol. 5, No. 2, 1997, pp. 117–46.

[3] See Brunel, Jean L.P., 'The Upside-Down World of Tax-Aware Investing,' *Trusts and Estates*, February 1997, pp. 34–42.

[4] See Shefrin, Hersh, 'Recent Developments in Behavioral Finance,' *The Journal of Private Portfolio Management*, Summer 2000, pp. 25–37. Hersh Shefrin is the Mario L. Belotti Professor of Finance at Santa Clara University.

[5] See Ewing, Terzah, and Jeff Bailey, 'Dashed Futures: How a Trading Firm's Founders Were Blindsided by Bombshell,' *The Wall Street Journal*, February 18, 1999.

[6] See Arnott, Robert D., Andrew L. Berkin, and Jia Ye, 'Loss Harvesting: What's It Worth To The Taxable Investor?,' *The Journal of Wealth Management*, Spring 2001, pp. 10–18.

[7] At the AIMR Conference: *Investment Counseling for Private Clients III: Integrated Wealth Management*, Taxes, Estate Planning and Wealth Transfer, Atlanta, GA, March 27–28 2001, Session IV: The Trade-Offs between Tax Efficiency and Tracking Error.

[8] Stein, David M. 'Equity Portfolio Tracking Risk in the Presence of Taxes,' AIMR Conference Proceedings: *Investment Counseling for Private Clients III*, March 27-28, 2001, pp. 45-53.

[9] See Apelfeld, Roberto, and Jean L.P. Brunel, CFA. 'Asset Allocation for Private Investors,' *The Journal of Private Portfolio Management*, Spring 1998, pp. 37–54.

Chapter 5

Multiple asset locations

One of the most important differentiating features of individual investors must be the fact that they typically hold their assets in multiple pockets. The simple case will often involve an individual having both some form of retirement account and some personal savings vehicle, but the number of pockets can expand substantially. This creates both a number of exciting opportunities and a great deal of complexity in their investment circumstances.

Generically, there are three principal reasons why individuals will typically have more than one investment pocket. The first relates to the wish on the part of most individuals to transfer some of their wealth to their heirs. The second reflects the structure of the typical tax code. The third derives from the philanthropic spirit, which drives many to want to share some of their good fortune with others.

This chapter will be particularly focused on the United States, but will still be highly relevant for investment professionals residing overseas. It should provide them with important insights that should help them compete more effectively for the business of U.S. prospects. Also, it will make it easier for them to deal with circumstances where the spouse or a child of a non-U.S. tax-resident happens to be subject to the U.S. tax regime. I should add that, in those few instances when I have had the opportunity to deal with non-U.S. residents, I have found that similar principles do apply to those that we will be discussing here. For instance, I had the opportunity to assist a French resident deal with wealth management issues in a structure that included both a personal account and a life insurance contract. The same location issues that we discuss below apply to him, though the specific tax provisions and solutions are naturally somewhat different.

Tax codes and multiple accounts

There are two essential reasons for having multiple account structures, and they arise from the fact that there are two principal forms of taxation: the taxation of income and investment returns, and the taxation of generational wealth transfers through *inter vivos* gifts or estates. In several countries, and certainly in the United States, having these two different regimes offers substantial opportunity for 'arbitraging' the different provisions incorporated into each.

Structurally, income tax codes incorporate a number of legislative initiatives designed to create incentives for taxpayers to behave in the ways legislators wish them to. For instance, legislators in many countries have long wanted to find ways to encourage citizens to save money for various purposes. They have often created special tax treatments for retirement accounts. More recently, other savings incentives have been created. In the United States, for instance, special treatment is offered for education savings accounts (529(a) accounts, which allow an individual to place up to US$50,000 in a savings account where return can accumulate in a tax-deferred manner). In France, laws provide incentives for diverting some savings toward investments in the French equity market, directly or through tax-protected special accounts. Similarly, several annuity or life insurance contracts are provided with a tax-deferred status.

The second significant source of multiple investment pockets comes from the estate and gift sections of the tax code, which allow individuals to set up a variety of fiduciary structures. These are designed to help them transfer wealth from one person to another. Also, several structures are available to allow investors to donate some of their wealth to charity in a variety of ways, which can include gifting a stream of income, or an asset, to the income for which they may, or may not, retain title.

These structures create both opportunities and significant complexities. The different tax status of each structure and the ability, at times, to transact among them in a tax-protected manner open up a number of wealth planning avenues. These avenues make it possible to raise the overall tax efficiency of the total portfolio while achieving a variety of distinct goals. At the same time, the need to deal with a significant number of individual holding pockets, a few of which may have their own quirks, creates both conceptual and administrative complexities. Conceptually, a multilocation-holding structure requires the investor to be able to plan not only across both asset classes and strategies, but also across individual locations.[1]

A feasible set of wealth structures

Darryl Meyers and I once crafted the diagram presented in Exhibit 5.1 (Darryl Myers was formerly one of my colleagues at U.S. Bank and is now a vice president at Wells Fargo, Private Client Services). Our original purpose was to trace the flows associated with the assets held by an individual in the U.S. tax system, in order to try and find simple common principles and solutions. The extreme complexity of the diagram demonstrates that the issue is not a simple one. It therefore needs to be addressed with great care.

Our diagram identifies four distinct states or phases to the ownership, control and tax-responsibility flows.

The first state relates to the origin of the wealth that the investor enjoys today. We decided that there are only two realistic alternatives. Either the money belonged to the investor, or he or she was a beneficiary of some fiduciary structure created by an earlier generation, or by some other benefactor. In either case, the individual had the discretionary power to use the income generated by these assets, though he or she may or may not have had control over the underlying assets. The individual would not have control over the underlying assets if they were held in trust and he or she was solely an income beneficiary.

The second state of the family wealth disposition diagram relates to the generic ways in which one can invest or dispose of wealth. The investor may elect to keep the assets in his or her name, and invest them through taxable, tax-exempt or tax-deferred accounts; or he or she may transfer that wealth, through charitable or noncharitable giving – there are several options in either instance.

Exhibit 5.1

Family wealth disposition diagram

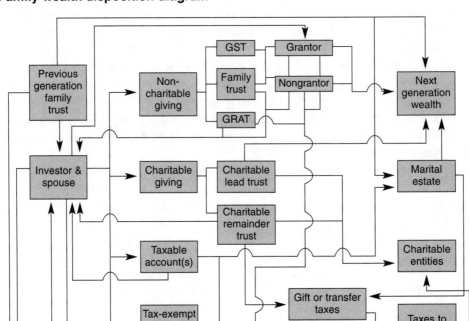

The third state deals with the tax implications of any of the transactions. In selected instances, the transactions involve no taxes and the return earned on the assets involves no income or capital gain tax liability to the investor either. The latter may occur because the structures provide some taxation shelter, of a permanent or deferred nature, or because the ownership of the assets has passed to someone else, who is now responsible for all taxes associated with investment returns. In other instances, the transfers will require the original owner of the wealth to pay gift taxes, but these transfers will, again, be permanent enough to relieve the grantor of any liability for taxes on investment returns. This offers an opportunity to highlight an important difference among various tax codes. While certain regimes, as is the case in the United States, require the person making the gift to pay taxes, others place the tax obligation onto the recipient of the gift. This requires the advisor to differentiate between net and gross gifts. In yet other instances, the grantor may or may not incur gift or transfer taxes, but can retain the liability for taxes on investment returns. In the United States, this happens in the case of trusts generally classified under the 'defective trust' heading. They are defective because certain provisions make them effective from an estate tax standpoint, but defective from the standpoint of the income tax code.

The final state of the wealth disposition diagram relates to the ownership of the investor's or the family's wealth at some future point in time. There are potentially four parties with a claim on some of these assets:

- the government, as taxes, whether associated with a transfer or caused by ongoing investment returns, naturally accrue to the taxing authority;
- relevant charities and individual beneficiaries, as provided in the instruments creating gift structures;
- members of the individual's family, upon maturation of the vehicle through which the assets are held; and
- the original investor's estate.

Wealth planning alternatives

Though the number of alternatives is limited only by the creativity of the investor and his or her advisors, there are seven structures that seem to be most often used, at least in the U.S. context.[2] These are:

- personal accounts;
- grantor trusts;
- generation skipping trusts;
- charitable trusts (generally, in the United States, charitable remainder trusts or charitable lead trusts);
- variable life insurance policies;
- tax-deferred pension vehicles; and
- foundations (public or private).

Beyond these specific structures, there are several strategies that can and should be used to maximize cross-generational after-tax returns. It is worth exploring them first before turning to a brief description of the seven possible holding structures.

Three intergenerational transfer strategies

Intergenerational loans

Jay Hughes[3] introduced the notion of 'family allocation' in a wonderful book dedicated to family wealth planning. He described the family wealth planning effort as a process designed to 'minimize the size of the chair reserved for the Internal Revenue Service at the family's table.' He observed that families often find themselves in a quandary and suggested that intergenerational loans may be a solution. Managing money across multiple generations would be most successful if the assets with the highest expected returns were owned by those members of the family with the longest life expectancies. However, usual family circumstances provide for the older members of the family to have the easiest access to excess cash and thus the greatest opportunity to invest in higher-returning investments.

Intergenerational loans arise when a member of an older generation lends money – on 'arm's length' terms, to avoid adverse tax circumstances – to one or several members of another generation. They may allow younger members to own the higher returning assets or the best current investment opportunities, despite the fact that they would usually not have excess liquid assets. At a minimum, this allows the investment return in excess of the cost of servicing the debt to accrue in the name of a member of a younger generation, free of estate or gift taxes.

Intergenerational loans could be viewed as the older generation's fixed-income exposure, though this may impose liquidity constraints on the assets held by the younger generation and work against the tax efficiency of these investments. Another variant on this approach relates to intergenerational loan guarantees. Loan guarantees issued by a member of the senior generation may allow younger family members to have access to capital on terms more attractive then normal commercial rates. While there is uncertainty on how tax authorities would treat guarantees from a gift tax perspective, guarantees may prove an attractive strategy in providing younger generations with access to capital.[4]

Transactions with defective trusts

Defective trusts are trusts whose terms do not satisfy all provisions of both income and estate tax codes. For instance, a gift might qualify as a gift for estate tax purposes, but not for income tax purposes. These trusts provide for substantial opportunities to raise the net after-tax returns within the trusts, by allowing the grantor to pay the taxes on income and net capital gains generated within the trust. Further, they provide an opportunity to have the trust buy assets (packaged in a partnership, for instance) rather than have the assets gifted to the trust.

These transactions can allow the family to benefit from valuation discounts, which can further raise the effective returns earned by the trust. Imagine a situation where a wealthy individual wants to donate US$3 million to her children's trust. She really has two options available to her. The first would involve writing a check to the order of the trust, which would in turn invest these assets, hypothetically in a fund of hedge funds. The other alternative involves the creation of a partnership, which she initially owns, and which is funded with cash. That partnership in turns invests these US$3 million in a fund of hedge funds. Interest in the partnership can then be gifted to the trust. Because there are certain liquidity limitations in the underlying investments, the wealthy individual may be able to argue successfully that the US$3 million she has given is really only 'worth' only US$2 million.

Thus, any gift tax that would typically be due on the gift would be reduced to the extent of the gift tax rate multiplied by the discount on the valuation of the partnership. At the same time, the actual amount of the gift accruing to the trust is exactly the same.

Purchases by or on behalf of defective trusts can be funded either by outright cash gifts (within the constraints of the unified tax credit[5]) or, in some instances, through loans or loan guarantees.

Family partnerships

Family partnerships can be set up to share family assets among several members. Such a structure can help meet at least two important wealth and family planning objectives[6]. First, as we just saw, placing assets into a partnership and gifting shares of the partnership, either on a gradual basis (to take advantage of the annual gift exclusion of US$10,000 per person available to U.S. taxpayers), or in one move into defective trusts, can help a family reduce its likely estate tax liability. As important is the second possible objective served by a partnership: to provide administrative simplicity, cost reduction or simply access to strategies for each of the individual family members. The concept is applicable across a wide range of country-specific situations.

Imagine a family that comprises five individual members, each of whom has wealth of US$25 million. The family has been advised that it needs to own a minimum of two funds of nondirectional hedge funds to achieve satisfactory diversification. Yet each of these funds has a minimum account size of US$5 million. Each member would need to invest US$10 million, of 40% of his or her wealth, in hedge funds to obtain that diversification. The family agrees with the advice that this would be too large a commitment to this single strategy. Should it abandon the opportunity to invest in hedge funds, or accept a lower diversification? There is a solution that allows the family to achieve all of its objectives. Creating a family partnership allows the family's minimum hedge fund exposure to fall to 8%, as the partnership must only hold US$10 million, which is a much smaller share of the family's collective wealth of US$125 million. The partnership has provided the family with *feasible access* to the desired strategy.

Imagine now a different family, with three generations and financial assets of US$90 million. Imagine further that each generation owns an even one third of the total assets and that they have significantly different investment objectives. For the sake of simplicity, let us assume that there are only two possible asset classes, bonds and equities. Let us also assume that the older generation needs a 75/25 mix of bonds and equities, the middle generation a 50/50 mix, and the younger generation a 25/75 mix. Creating two family partnerships, one dedicated to bond investments and the other to equity assets, will allow the family to benefit from the economies of scale associated with two accounts of US$45 million each. By varying the percentage ownership of each generation in either of the asset class partnership, the family will also be able to offer tailored strategies. Thus, the partnership approach provides them with *cost, customization, and administrative benefits*.

Five criteria to evaluate wealth planning solutions

There are five main criteria that best describe the attributes of individual wealth planning alternatives. I am sure that an estate lawyer would deem these descriptions too general. Nevertheless, the fundamental role of a wealth planner is not simply to design these structures, but rather to *understand how they interact with the other dimensions of the process:* investment and financial planning. The former concerns the development of the appropriate investment strategy, defined in terms of its expected return, expected risk, tax efficiency, and comfort from the point of view of the decision-maker. The latter is principally concerned with the development of an appropriate liquidity strategy, defined in terms of providing the family with appropriate access to the wealth, as and when income is needed or additional savings need to be invested. These five criteria are:

- term – is the holding vehicle designed to last in perpetuity, for life or for some specific period?
- access – how much access does the investor have to the underlying assets (liquidity)?
- control – who controls the investment management options?
- valuation – are there particular opportunities for valuation discounts?
- tax efficiency – does the structure help enhance a strategy's tax efficiency?

Seven wealth planning and management alternatives

Personal accounts

Clearly the simplest holding structure, a personal account, as its title implies, is an account established in the name of the owner of the wealth.

In the context of this analysis, we define the *term* of a personal account as the life of the owner, or the longest among the lives of multiple owners when the account is set up as a joint account with a right of survivorship. By definition, the owner has both total *access* to, and *control* over, the assets, but he or she has no opportunities to benefit from any *valuation discount*, as ownership of the assets is not transferred. Typically, a personal account would be viewed as *tax-inefficient*, to the extent that returns earned within a personal account are taxed at the individual's marginal tax rates.

Grantor-retained annuity trusts

In a grantor-retained annuity trust (or GRAT),[7] the owner of the assets places them in a trust for the benefit of specified individuals. The owner remains entitled to an annuity flow from the trust, which can be defined either as a fixed annual payment or as a payment determined at the beginning of each period by applying a set percentage rate to the value of the assets held in the trust at that time (the GRAT would be referred to as a 'unitrust' in these circumstances).[8] The document governing a GRAT may provide for the grantor – the original owner of the assets – to be able to substitute principal, meaning that he or she can replace a certain holding in the trust with another, of like value at the time of the transfer. When the trust matures, the beneficiaries receive, free of estate and gift taxes, an amount equal to the difference between the actual value of the assets in the trust at the time and the value the original assets would have at maturity, had the assets earned the 'applicable federal rate' (or AFR). Section 7520 of the U.S. Internal Revenue Code prescribes the interest rate to be used in valuing annuities, term interests, and remainder interests. The 7520 rate is equal to 120% of the federal mid-term rate in effect (under Section 1274 of the Code) on the date of the gift.

If the trust is funded as a gift to the beneficiaries, the grantor will pay a gift tax on the 'gift value' implicit in the transfer. This value is equal to the difference between the terminal value of the trust, assuming that it earns the AFR each year, and the present value of the annuity accruing to the grantor. During the life of the trust, the income accruing in the trust is taxable to the grantor, though he or she may elect to be reimbursed for that expense by the trust.

Note that therein lies an important benefit of the structure. To the extent that the grantor elects not to be reimbursed by the trust for taxes paid by the grantor on the income of the trust, the grantor is effectively 'gifting' to the trust an amount equal to that tax, tax-free. Note also that, at maturity, the assets in a GRAT accrue to the beneficiary at their tax basis within the trust.

The *term* of a GRAT usually varies between two and 10 years. Very long-term GRAT terms are rare, as the estate planning benefits of a GRAT are negated if the grantor dies before the GRAT matures. *Access* to the assets in a GRAT is somewhat limited, once the GRAT's terms have been set, but the grantor has *control* over these terms.

Indeed, control of the strategies used within a GRAT is relatively high, though the grantor must take into consideration the competing interests of the beneficiaries in setting investment policy and tactics. The grantor may, for instance, elect to retain a greater part of the assets in his or her estate, for instance by selecting a high annuity payment. However, usually, one would only do that to minimize gift tax payments, as the very reason to create such a vehicle is to pass wealth on to named beneficiaries in a tax-efficient manner.

Depending on one's point of view, a GRAT may or may not be viewed as *tax-efficient*, although we prefer the perspective that views it as a tax-efficient vehicle. Tax efficiency has two dimensions here. First, a GRAT is a tax-efficient wealth transfer vehicle, both because of the provision that can allow the grantor to pay income taxes on the GRAT's behalf, and because it can be funded in a way that allows *valuation discounts* to be applied to the assets held in the GRAT (when these assets are held through a corporate – such as Limited Liability Companies (LLC) – or partnership structures given to the GRAT). Second, a GRAT is not necessarily a tax-efficient vehicle from the GRAT's own standpoint. Indeed, there is no provision allowing the GRAT to shelter investment return or defer the taxes associated with investment results, other than by having the grantor pay for them. Note, however, that transactions between the grantor and the GRAT are not taxable from an income and capital gains standpoint, which opens opportunity for dynamic asset allocation.

Generation-skipping trusts

A generation-skipping trust (or GST) is set up for the benefit of future generations, in a way that avoids at least one level of estate tax payment. In the absence of a GST, assets flowing from the first to the third generation of a family would typically attract estate taxes twice: once when they pass from the first to the second generation and a second time when they pass from the second to the third generation.

Generation-skipping trusts may be established as grantor ('defective') trusts. This can be achieved by incorporating one of several provisions that have the effect of allowing the grantor to continue to have enough control over the beneficial disposition of the assets to have those assets viewed as being a part of the grantor's assets from an income tax standpoint. That status typically disappears upon the death of the grantor. When GSTs are defective from an income tax standpoint, the grantor can effectively enhance the net value of his or her gift to future generations by paying the taxes on the trust's investment activities (capital gains and ordinary income). When a GST is created, the grantor may be liable to a single gift tax for those assets whose value exceeds the uniform tax credit but does not exceed the GST exemption, which in the United States is currently set at US$1 million per person, or US$2 million per couple. At maturity, the assets in a GST would generally pass to the beneficiary at their tax basis within the trust.

The *term* of a GST is usually longer than one generation. Though many states in the United States still have statutory limits on the terms of trusts, (which are set at 21 years after the death of the last 'life in being' at the time of the establishment of the trust) certain states now allow dynasty trusts lasting in virtual perpetuity. *Access* to the assets in a GST is totally forfeited from the point of view of the grantor. Usually, a GST is set up in such a manner that the gift is completed from the point of view of estate taxes, though it may be completed or not from the point of view of income taxes. The characterization of a GST on our other evaluation criteria is broadly similar to that other grantor trusts, such as GRATs.

Charitable trusts
Charitable trusts are set up so that an individual may direct some of his or her assets for the benefit of charitable causes. They generally come in two flavors, which can be viewed as direct alternatives if the grantor's goal is to share the assets 50/50 with a charity.

In a *charitable remainder trust* (or CRT), the grantor retains a beneficial interest in the assets, in the form of some annuity paid to the grantor, whether fixed or governed by a unitrust structure. At the CRT's maturity, the assets in the trust are turned over to the charity named in the document, whether that charity is related to the grantor or not. It could be the grantor's private foundation in certain circumstances, for instance. The value of the gift made in a CRT is calculated by subtracting the ratio of the present value of the income stream from the expected terminal value of the trust (using the IRS 7520 rate mentioned above). For the trust to qualify as a CRT, the value of the gift passing to charity must equal at least 10% of the fair market value of the assets contributed to the trust at the time of the creation of the trust.

A *charitable lead trust* (CLT) is a trust that pays an annuity to one or more charitable organizations for a term of years. At the end of the term, the remaining trust property is distributed to the grantor's descendants. Upon creation of the CLT, the grantor makes a gift to the charity of the present value of the charity's right to receive the annuity payments, discounted by the AFR. Simultaneously, the grantor makes a gift to the grantor's descendants of the remainder interest in the CLT. The value of the gift is equal to the value of the property transferred to the CLT, minus the value of the annuity payments the charity will receive during the trust term.

One 'psychological' benefit of CLTs is that they can be viewed as allowing each generation an opportunity to reformulate their charitable or philanthropic philosophies. Indeed, once a CRT has terminated, the assets formerly owned by the family have passed on to a charity, which may continue to involve future generations in gifting strategies. Yet the amount of money given to charity remains as set by the original benefactor and it can be argued that future generations simply implement an ancestor's philanthropic strategy. In a CLT, the assets originally placed in the trust revert to the family. This exposes future generations to the need to decide whether, and how much of, their wealth should be dedicated to the charity. The amount might be smaller or greater than what an ancestor might have selected. Thus, each generation has the opportunity to have an impact on the formulation of the family's values.

Let us now consider how charitable trusts stand up to our five criteria. The *term* of both CRTs and CLTs can vary, though they usually do not exceed 20 years, except in the case of a CRT, the term of which can be set to equal the lifetime of the beneficiaries. *Access* to the assets in a charitable trust is severely restricted. In the case of a CRT, access to the assets is governed by the term of the annuity payment, which provides some access during the life of the trust. In the case of a CLT, access is limited, except at maturity, at which point the assets accrue to the named beneficiary. Note that, at maturity, the assets in a CLT accrue to the beneficiary at their tax basis within the trust.

In both forms of charitable trust, the original owner of the wealth retains a significant amount of *control* over the management of the assets in the trust, subject to certain rules, which, for instance, tend to prohibit strategies generating unrelated business income, such as hedge funds.

Valuation discounts are generally available, but would only be used when the principal purpose of setting the trust did not involve seeking to receive an income tax deduction for the value of the gift to charity.

Charitable trusts are relatively *tax-efficient*, to the extent that they provide useful vehicles for deferring or eliminating the taxes associated with the sale of a low-basis security occurring within the trust.

In a CRT, account is taken of the character of the income generated within the trust, and the distributions made to trust beneficiaries are taxed according to very specific ordering rules (under U.S. Internal Revenue Code Section 664). These rules can create surprising results. For example, distributions can be taxed to trust beneficiaries as capital gains, even if the income is generated within the trust through a tax-exempt investment, if that income is less than the required trust payout.

CLTs are governed by tax rules that are very different from those for CRTs, and the interplay between these rules and the asset management strategy will determine whether or not the trust is conducive to a tax-efficient outcome. Most typically, a CLT is taxed as a separate entity, or trust, for income tax purposes. Under this regime, the asset being contributed to the trust carries with it the original income tax basis, so sale of the asset would then produce a capital gain at the trust level. Offsetting the gain, however, is the so-called IRC Section 642 (c) deduction, which is an offset (or deduction) against trust income for the payments made each year to qualified charitable organizations. Thus, if the asset in question is low-basis stock that will be sold, the initial sale within the CLT will generate a capital gain at the trust level that will normally be much larger than any offsetting deduction for a required annual payout. After the year of sale, then, whether the trust is tax-efficient will depend upon whether the portfolio gains and income within the trust exceed the required 642 (c) deduction.

Variable life insurance policies

A variable life insurance policy is a whole life insurance contract that allows its policy-owner to select the investments underpinning the policy, in exchange for taking the investment risk. Sandra Manzke[9] distinguishes between modified endowment contracts and nonmodified endowment contracts. She argues that the main determinant of this distinction is the relationship between the amount of premium paid and the death benefit provided under the policy. The policy will be considered a modified endowment contract if the accumulated premiums paid at any time during the first seven years after the policy is established exceed the sum of the net level premiums that would have been paid on or before such time if the future benefits provided in respect of the policy were deemed to be paid up after the payment of seven annual premiums.

The most significant taxation difference between the two types of policies relates to the treatment of loans taken by the policy-owner against the policy. In a modified endowment contract, loans are treated as withdrawals from the policies and are subject to tax on a 'last in, first out' basis. If received before the age of 59, the distribution would also be subject to a 10% tax penalty, such as the one imposed on such distributions from annuities or individual retirement accounts. Both types of policy impose certain broad investment diversification restrictions.

The *term* of a variable life policy is the life that it is deemed to cover. *Access* to the underlying assets is dependent upon the status of the policy: nonmodified endowment policies allow policy-owners to take loans against the policy, effectively enjoying the benefits of some liquidity despite the inherently illiquid nature of the contract.

There are two limitations to the *control* that the policy-owner has over the underlying investment strategies. First, there are certain statutory diversification requirements. Second, the portfolio can only invest in strategies and vehicles approved by the insurance carrier.

These contracts offer little scope for benefiting from *valuation discounts*, as they are typically funded with cash, either in one payment or with several annual payments, the latter designed to earn the nonmodified endowment contract designation.

Variable life insurance contracts are highly *tax-efficient*, to the extent that, subject to the diversification rules imposed by law, investment returns within the policy compound on a tax-deferred basis.

Tax-deferred pension vehicles

Ignoring the cash value of a defined benefit pension program as an investment vehicle in this analysis, there are still many tax-deferred pension vehicles.[10] For the purpose of this analysis, we will consider a generic U.S. resident individual retirement account (or IRA) and assume that there are no annual cash flows into or out of the IRA for the foreseeable future. Typically, assets held in an IRA come from one of two sources. They may have first accumulated in a company sponsored defined contribution plan (such as a 401(a), 401(k), 403(b), 457, IRA, or Keogh), which was subsequently rolled over into an IRA when the individual ceased being employed by the plan's sponsor. Second, they can be funded by individual contributions, currently limited by U.S. law to US$2,000 per year.

Generally, the *term* of an IRA is the life of the individual who owns it: upon the individual's death, the assets accrue to his or her estate. New approaches are, however, just appearing, under the terms of which an individual may nominate a child as a trustee of an IRA and thus extend its life beyond his or her own.

Access to the assets held within an IRA is strictly limited, being generally prohibited before the beneficiary reaches the age of 59 and a half. Before that age, withdrawals attract an additional 10% tax, except in certain emergency circumstances. After that age, the tax status of the assets withdrawn depends upon the type of account. Generally, if the assets contributed to the IRA are in the form of pre-tax dollars (a standard IRA), the assets taken out of the IRA will attract income tax at the individual's marginal rate. By contrast, if the assets contributed to the IRA are in the form of after-tax dollars (a Roth IRA), the assets taken out of the IRA will not attract income taxes.

The owner of an IRA has wide discretionary *control* over the investment strategies that can be employed, provided they are acceptable to the institution responsible for their custody and administration.

With cash the typical source of funding of an IRA, there is virtually no significant opportunity to benefit from a *valuation discount*.

While an IRA is in place, it is generally quite *tax-efficient*, to the extent that investment income accumulates within the portfolio in a tax-deferred manner. At the same time, IRAs can be particularly tax-inefficient if they still contain significant assets at an individual's death, as these assets would attract two levels of taxation: income and estate taxes.

Foundations

A foundation is an entity created to allow funds to accumulate and be distributed over time to further a particular purpose. The principal difference between a *private foundation* and a *public foundation* is that a private foundation is not allowed to seek contributions from the public. Private foundations can help an individual or a family achieve a number of apparently contradictory goals: to create worthwhile philanthropy, to perpetuate family values, to benefit from income tax deductions and asset protection, to maintain family control over the assets, to increase cash flow to the family, and to provide a training process for heirs.[11] Our principal focus will be on private charitable foundations whose goals are to allow a family to institutionalize a process through which funds are distributed to worthy causes, while the assets contributed to the foundation can escape both estate and income taxes. An important attribute of a private foundation is that it can help a family congregate around certain central charitable values, so that one generation can teach its descendants how to deal with and share wealth.

The *term* of a foundation is typically indefinite, in that it exists until wound up. Once the assets have been gifted to the foundation, the only *access* that the benefactors can have to them is in the form of payments of management fees or reimbursement of certain expenses, particularly in the case of 'operating foundations'.

Assuming that the benefactor wishes to retain management *control* over the foundation, in terms of both disbursements and the deployment of the assets, it can be argued that control over the assets remains high. However, the benefactor should manage the assets of the foundation with the interests of the foundation in mind, and not in a way that reflects his or her own interests.

Valuation discounts are typically not applicable in the case of a foundation, as the value of the assets transferred can be deducted, within the limits of the relevant laws and regulations, from the benefactor's income. Given this situation, why would anyone want to deflate the value of a deduction against income?

Management of the endowment of a foundation is highly *tax-efficient*, as investment income is virtually tax-exempt for as long as the foundation distributes a set minimum amount of monies to eligible recipients. In the United States, for example, current rules stipulate that a foundation should make charitable contributions equal to at least 5% of the market value of its corpus each year. These contributions incorporate a number of specified

93

expenses incurred in the process of carrying out the mission of the foundation, such as officer and director compensation or due diligence and related expenses.

An illustrative case study

The most effective way to understand such a potentially complex topic probably is to see the various concepts at work in a case study.[12]

> The Burgers are a hypothetical family, bringing together a number of common factors often found in wealthy investors. Bill and Linda Burger estimate their financial net worth at approximately US$100 million. Of that total, approximately US$50 million is made up of a virtually zero basis holding in ABC Conglomerate, which, three years ago, purchased the company, Burger Industries, that they had co-founded 20 years before and taken public five years before. The bulk of the balance, about US$40 million, is still in cash, resulting from the after-tax profits they made on the exercise of their last nonqualified stock options, which was required when the Burgers left the management ranks of their company according to the terms of the agreement governing the sale of Burger Industries to ABC Conglomerate. The balance of their financial wealth is split evenly between their IRAs, which are both invested in U.S. large-capitalization equity portfolios worth, together, about US$5 million; and a $5 million 'rainy day' municipal bond portfolio.
>
> The Burgers are in their mid-50s, and have three children aged 25, 21, and 17. They are sorry to admit that they were so focused on growing their business that they ignored all but the simplest estate planning issues, and that the children do not yet own any substantial financial assets. The Burgers own three homes, worth around US$10 million in total, and indicate that they do not wish to invest in 'financial real estate,' feeling that they have a sufficient exposure to that market through their homes. We will not be incorporating these real estate assets in the Burgers' financial profile. Experience has taught us to distinguish between 'financial assets' and 'other assets,' which we have at times called 'toys' with selected clients. The definition of a 'financial asset' in this context is something that people are prepared to sell at a price: owner-occupied real estate seems not to fit under that heading. (At the same time, of course, the Burgers' comment that they do not want to own 'financial real estate' because of the fact that they own three homes does make the decision to classify these homes as other assets less clear-cut.)
>
> The Burgers summarize their financial objectives in five simple propositions:
>
> First, our goal is to maximize the value of our assets over multiple generations.
>
> Second, we do not want our children to be spoiled by our wealth and in fact would like them to have the opportunity to experience the exhilaration of creating their own wealth. Thus, we would like the children to have access to some of our wealth, but prefer for them to view themselves as the stewards of that wealth for the next generations, rather than as users of it.
>
> Third, we believe that God has been very kind to us and that we should have significant philan-

thropic activities for the balance of our lives. We intend to fund a private foundation with $10 million of our appreciated stock and would like to find ways to add to those charitable assets.

Fourth, we need about $1 million after tax [per year] to maintain our current standards of living and would like the children to have access to $100,000 per year each. We do not believe we will need to invade our principal over the foreseeable future, but would still like to have access to at least $9.5 million in the event the entrepreneurial bug bites us again and we want to buy or start another business.

Finally, we define risk as the probability of negative returns over any rolling three-year period and we do not want to see that probability rise above 10%.

Discussing specific investment strategies, the Burgers indicate that they are comfortable with private equity investments, despite their relative illiquidity, and with hedge funds, provided two conditions are met. They do not wish more than 35% of their assets to be invested in these two strategies and they want their hedge funds[13] to be truly 'nondirectional' (where the manager hedges the market risk fully and thus generates 'market neutral' returns). They do not disbelieve that active managers can add value and are thus not fixated on indexed security selection strategies, but they do measure returns on an after-fee, after-tax basis.

Formulating a solution

We know that the Burgers are starting with two structures, their personal account and their respective IRAs, which, for the purpose of this analysis, we will consider as one. We also know that they want to create a foundation, funding it with US$10 million worth of their low-basis stock. However, to meet their goals the Burgers will need to create four additional structures: a generation-skipping trust (GST); a defective grantor trust (DGT); a charitable lead trust (CLT); and a variable life insurance policy.

A generation-skipping trust

The first order of priority is for the Burgers to start planning for some transfer of their wealth to their children and eventual grandchildren. Arguably, they could use their uniform tax credit to pass wealth on to their children, but this would not be the most efficient use of that credit. Indeed, it makes more sense to use the credit in the vehicle that has the longest term, thus allowing the greatest possible compounding of the return on the assets until they reach the ultimate beneficiary. It is thus sensible to use that credit to fund a GST, though they may elect to provide their children access to some income from the trust. They should use the full amount of their allowable generation-skipping exemption. They would likely magnify the impact of that exemption by gifting cash to the GST and having the GST buy into a partnership holding the required investments, to allow the GST to benefit from purchasing the interest in the partnership at some discount to net asset value.

We will assume that they have been able to purchase US$3 million worth of assets in the

GST (assuming, in turn, that the Burgers are able to negotiate a 33% discount when purchasing the interest in the partnership). Note that owning interest in a partnership will require the GST to own the same asset mix as the other owners of that partnership. In order to retain future management flexibility and to maximize the tax efficiency of their overall investment strategy, the Burgers would likely elect to make the GST defective for income tax purposes.

A defective grantor trust

Next, though the Burgers have exhausted their ability to make gifts to their children in a tax-free manner, they can still work to transfer some additional part of their wealth to them using low-to-no transfer tax strategies. One such strategy is to sell assets to a defective grantor trust (DGT).

The Burgers might fund this DGT with a gift of US$1 million, on which gift tax will have to be paid. We are assuming that they will eventually want the DGT to have US$10 million in cash to buy interests in the family partnership at a discounted price. A typical safe-harbor recommendation is that the trust be initially funded with 10% of the amount of the planned installment note. Here, we will assume that the total funding is US$10 million, comprising a US$1 million cash gift and a US$9 million installment note. The Burgers might then sell assets to the trust, receiving back a US$9 million installment note, which they can use, together with the initial US$1 million cash gift, to purchase US$15 million worth of assets held within a family investment partnership or limited liability company. As the DGT will buy into the same partnerships as the GST, the asset allocation of DGT and GST will be the same. Since the Burgers must pay the tax on income generated by the trust, the trust can build pre-tax income to service and/or pay off the note. If the assets compound at an annual rate greater than the AFR, then the excess is a free gift.

Note that an alternative design would have the Burgers make the gift and create the structure for their grandchildren. The gift tax on the initial US$1 million would be more onerous, but the eventual excess return relative to the AFR would accrue to the grandchildren

A charitable lead trust

As we have seen, the Burgers have also indicated that they want to dedicate more of their resources to charity. They choose a CLT rather than a CRT, as they prefer to provide funds to these charities now, rather than at some future point in time. They elect for that CLT to have a 15-year life, and for the value of the gift to be 40% of the US$10 million that they commit to that structure.

The Burgers' attraction to a CLT is twofold. First, they do not need the additional income that a CRT might have produced. Second, they want their children to participate in a family review of its charitable policy upon the maturity of the CLT.

A variable life insurance policy

The Burgers decide that a variable life insurance policy would be a good vehicle to shelter some of their nondirectional assets from current income and capital gains taxes. They elect to fund several policies, covering the lives of both parents and children. They want to maximize access to these funds by working through nonmodified endowment contracts, funding these insurance policies with only US$5 million. This would also provide them with sufficient flexibility in the choices of investment managers and strategies.

A private exchange fund

The final wealth-planning step taken by the Burgers is to create a private exchange fund for the share of their low-basis holdings that they cannot diversify through gifts to charitable vehicles.

The final structure

Exhibit 5.2 presents an illustration of the structure of the Burger family's wealth once this planning has been completed. Note that the Burgers elected to create a second family partnership – not shown in the diagram (to avoid clutter) and yet important – to hold a portion of the family's exposure to international assets. Indeed, the individual pockets that might need to participate in that strategy does not hold sufficient assets to allow them a customized individual portfolio. Combining their needs into one pool provides them the critical mass needed to get a cost-effective individual portfolio. Note that the diagram also shows a possible allocation to specific broad asset classes and strategies. (We will come back to this topic, and to the Burgers in Chapter 12.)

Exhibit 5.2

Proposed asset disposition for the Burgers

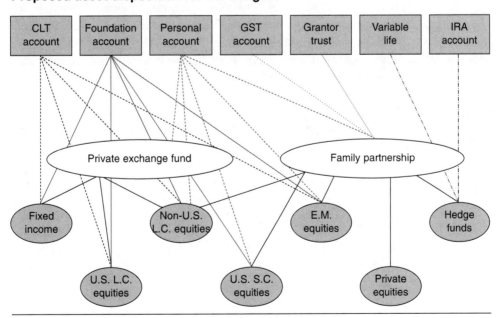

Note: the lines distinguish between the various ownership flows originating with each individual structure.

97

The creation of this complex structure allows the Burgers to achieve three important goals. First, it raises the expected after-tax return on their wealth and thus the expected after-tax value of their wealth in the future. Second, it reduces the risk inherent in the management of that wealth, measured here in terms of achieving a lower probability of negative rolling 36 month returns. Finally, it reduces the initial portfolio reorganization cost, principally reflecting here the cost associated with diversifying their low-basis stock holding.

Dynamic asset location

Dynamic asset allocation can be considered in two different contexts. The first relates to the multi-period nature of the strategic wealth planning process (discussed in Chapter 12). The second involves using the potential for principal exchanges between a grantor and his or her grantor trust.

Grantor trusts can indeed be drafted to give the senior generation grantor a power to reacquire and substitute trust assets. The relevant rules, in the United States, are in Section 675 (c)(4) of the Internal Revenue Code. A grantor's power to substitute or reacquire trust assets is presumed to be held 'in a fiduciary capacity,' where, as an example, the grantor serves as trustee or co-trustee of the trust. If the grantor exercises a power and also serves as trustee, the power would likely be held in a 'fiduciary capacity,' and the power, alone, would not cause the trust to be treated as a grantor trust. If, on the other hand, a person who is not trustee holds the power, such power would be held in a 'nonfiduciary' capacity, with the result that the trust would be treated as a grantor trust. Since the Internal Revenue Service will not rule on whether a power is held in a nonfiduciary capacity, advisors will generally use additional powers to create grantor trust status, not depending solely upon Section 675 to obtain favorable grantor trust status. Thus, if this power is held in a nonfiduciary capacity, the power will cause the grantor and the trust to be treated as one and the same for income tax purposes. These exchanges provide the investor with a great opportunity to enhance the portfolio's overall tax efficiency, on both the return and the transfer tax fronts.

Let us focus on this second dimension. There are three possible strategies involving such principal exchanges:

- reducing the forward-looking volatility of a successful GRAT;
- capturing the appreciation potential of a depressed, attractive security; and
- reducing potential capital gains for GRAT remaindermen.

Each of these strategies effectively requires the grantor of the defective trust to be able to exchange principal with the trust without incurring tax consequences. These transfers are feasible if allowed under the document governing the trust. Indeed, a defective trust usually views the assets in the trust as still being a part of the grantor's assets from an income tax viewpoint, though not for estate tax purposes. Thus, asset transfers taking place during the lifetime of the grantor do not give rise to tax consequences, as the income tax regime does not view these assets as having been transferred in the first place. The essence of these asset transfer strategies is to determine whether the performance of certain assets within these trusts can be utilized for the greater good of the family.

Reducing the forward-looking volatility of a successful GRAT involves a circumstance where a security held within a trust has appreciated either beyond its potential or at least sufficiently to satisfy the grantor's original gifting intent. Then, the grantor may be able to exchange that security for another with equal fair market value at the time of the exchange but with a more predictable forward-looking investment potential. In its ultimate incarnation, the strategy has the grantor exchange the appreciated security for cash. In this case, the grantor effectively 'freezes' the value of the gift made in the trust.

In an opposite set of circumstances, it is possible to address the problem caused by a depreciated GRAT asset. Imagine that a security placed in a GRAT or another form of defective trust has so depreciated that the likelihood is next to nil that the trust will be able to earn the minimum return required for there to be a gift upon its maturity. In such cases, and assuming that the grantor still sees strong potential in the security, it might make sense again to exchange that security for a like value low-risk investment and to create a new trust, using the security now seemingly even more attractive. The goal is to capture the appreciation potential of a depressed but still attractive security.

Finally, it is important to remember that the assets in a defective trust will usually pass to the final beneficiaries with a tax basis equal to the tax basis these assets have in the trust, increased by any gift taxes paid on the transfer. Thus, the trust will often hold appreciated assets that will be subject to capital gains tax if (when) the trustee wishes to rebalance the portfolio. Here, two tax benefits may accrue from the grantor (or other nonadverse party) exercising this power. First, the low basis portfolio can be pulled back into the grantor's estate, with the benefit of eliminating the built-in gain, by passing the securities through an estate, or two, or deferring the gain by contributing these securities to a charitable lead trust. Second, the income tax basis of the assets within the grantor trust can be 'brought to market,' effectively shifting the income tax liability back to the grantor for elimination or deferral. If the trust was a dynasty trust, one could envision the grantor exercising the power on more than one occasion, refreshing the income tax basis when optimal, while enjoying the benefit of having realized losses flow through to the grantor to offset capital gains.

Summary and implications

Though individual investors have to consider and pay taxes on their investments, the legal framework in most countries provides them with a number of opportunities to work around and benefit from the complexity that tax laws create. Asset location issues represent the first level of interaction between investment and estate planning issues, but they go beyond that. Indeed, they offer an opportunity to look to inefficiencies between the various parts of the overall tax code and to behaviors that legislators want to encourage, in both cases finding ways to enhance the tax efficiency of the overall wealth management process and thus meet the ultimate goal of most individuals: keeping more of what they get.

It has long been accepted that strategic wealth planning involves the need to consider a number of issues that would traditionally fall into the 'financial planning' category. This is the reason why many planners will ask investors to discuss their liquidity needs, among other similar topics. Yet the realization is only starting to dawn that asset location issues must also be incorporated into that same overall planning exercise.

Asset location issues arise from three different angles. The first relates to the fact that most wealthy families are thinking in dynastic terms. Whether illustrated by the current debate in the United States on the appropriateness of 'death taxes' or reflected in the commercial that invites the viewer to remember 'who you work for' – implying that you really work for your family and not for an employer – most of us still feel that one of our goals is to transfer some wealth to our descendants. The moment we start to think beyond our own selves, the issue of the efficiency of that transfer to future generations comes to the fore. The power of compound interest tells us that the earlier we use the tools provided for us by legislators, the greater will be our reward. However, these transfers will force us to start dealing with different ownership structures.

Darryl Meyers[14] proposes breaking these down into two important sets of questions. The first has to do with access to the property: who can benefit from the property, who can make the investment decisions, and what investment decisions may they make. The second focuses on taxation and relates to who pays what tax and when.

Another element of the relevancy of asset location relates to the opportunities provided by the tax code to enhance total portfolio tax efficiency. As a first step, it is worth remembering that the principles underpinning the tax code vary between the sections dealing with income and capital gains, which I call 'investment return focused,' and the sections dealing with gift and transfer taxes. Thus, it is possible for certain transactions to be appropriate from the point of view of one section and not from another, giving rise to interesting opportunities to arbitrage among the relevant provisions. The best illustration of this is the role that defective trusts can play in wealth transfers. The second step has to do with the use of structures put in place to encourage some activity which the legislature felt was desirable. By providing tax-exempt or tax-deferred status to selected structures, legislators are allowing individuals to partition their wealth more effectively and thus to benefit from favored tax provisions.

Finally, asset location issues arise as a result of the fact that most individuals feel the need to have some form of philanthropic activity. Being an activity that the U.S. Congress, like many other legislatures, has always wanted to encourage, charitable giving receives favorable tax treatment. However, the most important issue that an individual needs to address relates to whether it is appropriate to view assets reserved for philanthropy as a part of his or her total wealth, or not. Gregory Friedman[15] has a wonderful way of looking at this issue: he suggests that you should ask who is taking the residual investment risk. Certain gifting strategies indeed concentrate the residual investment risk on the charity, while others place the risk on the benefactor or his or her estate. Understanding who takes that risk can help you decide whether it is appropriate to incorporate the charitable asset pool in the overall plan or not.

---

[1] One of the first papers on the topic was Shoven, John B., 'The Location and Allocation of Assets in Pension and Conventional Savings Accounts,' Working Paper 493, Center for Economic Policy Research, Stanford University, March 1998. It was followed by Shoven, John B., and Clemens Sialm, 'Long Run Asset Allocation for Retirement Savings,' *The Journal of Private Portfolio Management*, Summer 1998, pp. 13–26, and by a large body of work

by William Reichenstein, a professor at Baylor University – see note 9 below.

[2] For a broad perspective on the topic, see Manning, Jerome A., *Estate Planning – How to Preserve Your Estate for Your Loved Ones*, New York: Practicing Law Institute, 1992.

[3] Hughes, James E., Jr., *Family Wealth: Keeping It in the Family*, Princeton Junction, NJ: NetWrx, 1997, pp. 61–66. See also Hughes, James E., Jr., 'Modern Portfolio Theory, Estate Taxes, and Investor Allocation,' *The Journal of Private Portfolio Management*, Spring 1998, pp.8–12.

[4] See *Bradford v. Commissioner*, 34 T.C. 1059 (1960). Rev. Ruling 84–25, 1984 – C.B. 191. Letter Ruling 9113009.

[5] Under the U.S. tax code, for gifts made in 2001 the applicable exclusion amount is equal to US$675,000 per individual.

[6] For a discussion of the pros and cons of family partnerships, see Thompson, Patricia M. 'Family Limited Partnerships: Pros and Cons.' *AIMR Conference Proceedings: Investment Counseling for Private Clients III*, pp. 84–93.

[7] See Macklin, Lawrence J., 'Wealth Management Through Dynasty Trusts,' *The Journal of Wealth Management*, Spring 2001, pp. 43–48.

[8] See Bruce L. Paulson and Gregory Owens, 'The Economics of Charitable Remainder Trusts and Related Asset Management Issues,' *The Journal of Wealth Management*, Winter 2000, pp. 33–38, for an illustration of unitrust principles.

[9] Sandra L. Manzke, 'Private Placement Life Insurance,' *The Journal of Private Portfolio Management*, Summer 1999, pp. 45–48. Sandra L.Manzke is the Chairman and Chief Executive Officer of Tremont Advisors. See also Cohen, James R., Jeffrey S. Bortnick, and Nancy L. Jacob, 'Tax-Efficient Investing Using Private Placement Variable Life Insurance and Annuities,' *The Journal of Private Portfolio Management*, Winter 1999, pp. 27–36; and Blazzard, Norse, and Robert Stone, 'Offshore Variable Insurance Products,' *The Journal of Private Portfolio Management*, Winter 1999, pp. 37–40.

[10] See the following four articles by Reichenstein, William: 'Savings Vehicles and the Taxation of Individual Investors,' *The Journal of Private Portfolio Management*, Winter 1999, pp. 15–26; 'Frequently Asked Questions Related to Savings Vehicles,' *The Journal of Private Portfolio Management*, Summer 2000, pp. 66–82; 'After-Tax Wealth and Returns Across Savings Vehicles,' *The Journal of Private Portfolio Management*, Spring 2000, pp. 9–19; and 'Calculating the Asset Allocation,' *The Journal of Wealth Management*, Fall 2000, pp. 20–25. See also Spitzer, John J., and Sandeep Singh, 'Optimizing Retirement Savings,' *The Journal of Wealth Management*, Winter 2000, pp. 30–44; and Caliendo, Frank, W. Cris Lewis, and Tyler J. Bowles, 'New Findings on Strategic IRA Investing,' *The Journal of Wealth Management*, Spring 2001, pp. 49–53.

[11] See presentation by Thomas Quinlin, 'Private Foundations: an Old Tool for the New Millennium,' *The 8th Annual Family Office Forum*, organized by the Institute for International Research, June 25–26, 2001, Chicago.

[12] See Brunel, Jean L.P., 'Asset Location – The Critical Variable: A Case Study,' *The Journal of Wealth Management*, Summer 2001, pp. 27–43.

[13] For more information on the topic, see Brunel, Jean L.P., 'The Role of Alternative Assets in Tax-Efficient Portfolio Construction,' *The Journal of Private Portfolio Management*, Summer 1999, pp. 9–26; or Anson, Mark, 'Selecting a Hedge Fund Manager,' *The Journal of Private Portfolio Management*, Winter 2000, pp. 45–52; or Lamm, R. McFall, Jr., and Tanya E. Ghaleb-Harter, 'Do Hedge Funds Belong in Taxable Portfolios?,' *The Journal of Wealth Management*, Summer 2001, pp. 58–73.

[14] Meyers, Darryl L., 'Tax Minimization Strategies for the Taxable Investor,' presentation to *The Investment Counseling for Private Clients III Conference*, organized by the Association for Investment Management and Research, March 27 – 28, 2001, in Atlanta, GA.

[15] See Friedman, Gregory R., 'The Role of Philanthropy in Estate Planning,' presentation to *The Investment Counseling for Private Clients III Conference*, organized by the Association for Investment Management and Research, March 27–28, 2001 in Atlanta, GA. Also, Friedman, Gregory R. 'Philanthropy in Estate Planning'. AIMR Conference Proceedings: *Continuing Education. Investment Counseling for Private Clients III,* March 27-28, 2001, pp. 65-72. Gregory Friedman is a principal of Greycourt & Co.

Chapter 6

A tax-efficient portfolio construction model

As we have seen in previous chapters, dealing with taxable individual investors forces us to rethink many of the principles and approaches that have been viewed as gospel truths. Rethinking is also needed in the construction of diversified portfolios.

Value added and portfolio activity

The first piece of the puzzle concerns the relationship between portfolio activity and expected value added.[1] In this context, we will define value added as the return earned over and above the relevant market benchmark, as a result of decisions that move the portfolio away from that index.

Consider the case of several portfolio managers. To keep things simple, assume that the expected value added associated with any investment decision is proportional to the size of the decision. Thus, if a manager makes a trade that results in changing 1% of the portfolio, we will assume that he or she expects that a value added of 0.05% has been generated. If

Exhibit 6.1

Portfolio activity and expected value added

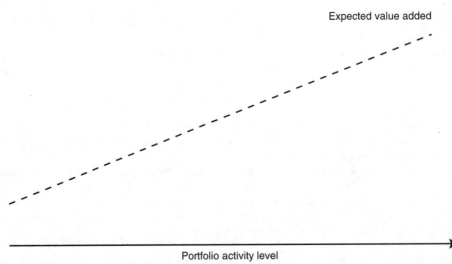

Expected value added

Portfolio activity level

Source: Brunel, Jean L.P. 'A Tax-Efficient Portfolio Construction Model,'
The *Journal of Wealth Management*, Fall 2001, pp.43-50

another manager makes a trade that results in changing 5% of the portfolio, we will assume that he or she expects to earn a value added of 0.25%. Now, if this framework appropriately describes the reality of the investment process a simple conclusion should follow: *there should be a linear relationship between the manager's activity level and the portfolio's expected value added*. This framework is actually not unreasonable, given the observed tendency of portfolio managers to scale their bets in ways that reflects their convictions.

Exhibit 6.1 allows us to visualize the relationship, which, predictably, looks like a straight line. Note that we are not talking of the observed value added, which depends upon the manager's success; we are depicting only the value added that the manager *expects* to generate. Note also that we do not need to limit ourselves to a return-based definition of value added. We could risk-adjust it, assuming that the manager also has a tracking error expectation associated with the value added.

A tax-oblivious business implication

In a tax-oblivious environment, it would naturally follow that portfolio managers would design strategies with activity levels that maximized their business-risk-adjusted return. They would then be as active as they could afford to be, given two considerations.

The first of these considerations is the extent to which making fewer and larger decisions absorbs too much of the managers' trading capabilities to grow their business to the level they want to grow it, given the fees that their clients agree to pay. This consideration would lead them to address the typical number of positions that they should have in each portfolio, on average. Indeed, given a set 'investment capacity,' measured in terms of ability to protect the expected value added, a manager will need to resolve a trade-off between a smaller number of concentrated portfolios or a larger number of more diversified portfolios. This trade-off reflects the extent to which the insight that the manager develops can be absorbed in trading costs. For instance, assuming that the manager expects to make 10% on a particular trade, but 'spends' 1% of that in commissions and 8% on market impact (as he or she first buys and then sells the given security), the residual value added, as perceived by the client would be only 1%. Assume that the client pays a 1% management fee and the result of the mandate is an index performance, presumably with more volatility than the index. In any case, another factor compounding the complexity of the decision will be the fact that the fees earned by the manager will vary depending upon the expected value added associated with the strategy, and thus be higher for a concentrated portfolio.

The second consideration is the extent to which the probability of success for any given decision exposes managers to the risk of having to report dramatically poor investment performance. Indeed, the more concentrated the portfolio and, thus, the larger the relative size of each decision, the greater the risk that a manager could experience a run of 'bad luck.' This 'bad luck' could expose the manager to substantial business risk.

The 'business arbitrage' that tax-oblivious managers must address therefore involves setting the appropriate level of portfolio activity given their capacity to generate value added and their appetite for business risk.

However, a tax-aware investment manager cannot look at the trade-off in such terms, because of the relationship between tax efficiency and portfolio activity. Indeed, the way in which the manager will need to assess business success must be based upon after-tax investment returns.

Tax efficiency and portfolio activity

Robert Arnott and Robert Jeffrey[2] have eloquently demonstrated that tax efficiency does not relate in a linear fashion to portfolio turnover. I prefer a slight variation on the theme, because I do not like to think of portfolio turnover as a decision variable. Thus, rather than focusing on portfolio turnover, portfolio managers should focus on the decisions they must make and the transactions they must execute to maximize the relevant value added accruing to their clients. Portfolio turnover should be seen as the residual of sensible portfolio activity.

We have established that there are both alpha-generating and alpha-enabling transactions (see Chapter 4). Though an alpha-enabling transaction might raise portfolio turnover, it would tend to improve tax efficiency. Consequently, it is best to think in terms of portfolio activity defined as the net capital gain realization rate. This tells us that the observed tax efficiency of a portfolio is therefore a function of two distinct factors:

- the degree to which a manager's portfolio activity generates gross capital gains; and
- the degree to which a manager's tax sensitivity will allow some of these gains to be sheltered by realized capital losses.

Tax efficiency and net capital gain realization

If portfolio activity and tax efficiency are indeed related, how does the relationship work? Exhibit 6.2 illustrates the truism that tax efficiency falls rapidly as portfolio activity rises. A highly passive investment process is relatively tax-efficient for as long as it is applied to an investment strategy where the bulk of the return is earned in the form of capital gains. Then, as activity picks up, one of two things can happen.

First, if the investment process is tax-oblivious the rate of net capital gain realization rises as well. This reflects both the need for portfolios to pay taxes on realized gains and the 'cost of compounding.' The cost of compounding is due to the fact that the portfolio no longer has the opportunity to earn a return on the assets that have been paid out.

Second, if the investment process is tax-sensitive the manager will strive to offset realized gains with random losses or to wait until the holding period allows the gains to attract the lower long-term capital gains tax rate. The direct tax drag will be reduced and there will be an opportunity to earn a compound return on the monies that have been retained in the portfolio.

However, as the level of portfolio activity increases significantly, it may simply become impossible for the manager to be able both to earn investment alpha and to pay attention to taxes. Thus, toward the right-hand side of the graph in Exhibit 6.2 the tax efficiency ratios of both tax-oblivious and tax-sensitive strategies have converged.

Consider an interest rate arbitrage between a government bond and a corporate bond. Assume that you expect the difference in the yields between a government bond and a cor-

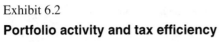

Exhibit 6.2

Portfolio activity and tax efficiency

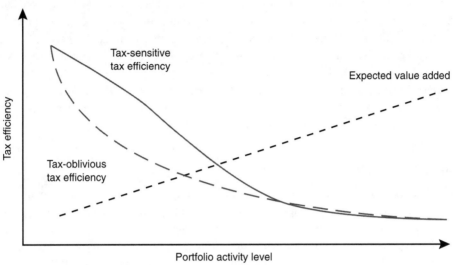

Source: Brunel, Jean L.P. 'A Tax-Efficient Portfolio Construction Model,'
The *Journal of Wealth Management*, Fall 2001, pp.43-50

porate bond to decrease. You will typically buy a corporate bond, or a portfolio of such bonds (to diversify away the bond-specific risk if the move you are trying to capture is generic to the corporate bond market rather than to an individual bond), and sell short an equivalent notional amount of government bonds with the same maturity. Though you may have some time frame in mind when the transaction is initiated, you will surely close the trade when you feel that the gap, or spread, between the two yields is back to normal, or even expensive. You may thus find yourself having to realize a short-term gain, but that would be preferable to waiting and not booking any gain, or worse, booking a loss.

However, the level of activity likely to trigger severe tax inefficiency will vary from strategy to strategy. In the preceding example, we saw that one form of arbitrage, in this case fixed-income arbitrage, must usually be seen as somewhat tax-inefficient. On the other hand, risk, or merger arbitrage can be somewhat tax-efficient when mergers are done on a stock-for-stock basis. Indeed, in the typical merger arbitrage trade, the manager will take a long position in the target company and short an equivalent number of shares (post-merger) in the purchasing company. Upon completion of the merger, the manager will be short and long an equal number of shares in the same stock, as the shares of the target company have, by then, been converted into shares of the surviving entity. Rather than closing out the transaction on that day, which would normally be less than one year away from the date the trade was put on, a tax-sensitive manager may hold on to both sides of the trade, in effect staying with a synthetically created 'short against the box' position, until the character of the capital gains changes from short term to long term. By doing so, the manager, if transacting on behalf of a U.S. taxpayer, has effectively enhanced the tax efficiency of the trade.

'Short against the box' is a strategy used by an investor who holds a position in a company, and would like to eliminate the risk associated with that stock, but for some reason, usually to do with capital gains, does not want to decide to sell the stock that he or she owns. He or she borrows an equivalent amount of stock from a broker and sells the borrowed stock. Thus, the net position of the investor is to be short and long the exact same number of shares in the same company. He or she has achieved the risk management goal. Recent changes in U.S. tax law, however, mean that such a transaction is now classified as a 'constructive sale,' which makes it no longer feasible if the goal is to avoid paying capital gains taxes. However, the reclassification has not led to synthetic 'short against the box' positions being treated in the same manner, because an investor who establishes such a position through a risk arbitrage takes on the risk that the merger is called off.

The problem with the 'murky middle'

The typical portfolio manager occupies what can be called the 'murky middle,' maintaining portfolio activity that sits somewhere between replicating the index and becoming a very active trader. This should be no surprise. The average investor likes to strike a balance between no activity and a lot of activity, and manager activity in many ways equates with manager risk. The higher the level of manager activity, the higher the risk that the manager's bets will not work out and, therefore, the higher the risk that the performance of the portfolio will be unsatisfactory. Diversifying manager risk thus equates with seeking a portfolio activity level sitting somewhere else than at an extreme position on the spectrum, with the average investor ending up on some mid-point between these extremes.

Further, from the point of view of the manager, being in the middle of the pack, targeting value added and tracking error, can be a smart business risk management strategy. The further the manager deviates from the average, the greater the risk that his or her performance will deviate from that of their peers and thus potentially disrupt client relationships.

Though the positioning of the average manager does not create a problem and in fact makes a great deal of sense in a pre-tax, or tax-oblivious, business model, it is potentially quite damaging for someone who needs to worry about taxes. Exhibit 6.2 tells us that, by the time the investment process has the level of activity associated with the 'murky middle,' it will more likely than not have reached almost minimal tax efficiency, particularly if the manager is not tax-sensitive. Note, however, that while tax efficiency has just about disappeared, the level of potential investment value added is still substantially short of the maximum.

Note also that we pay taxes on total return and not solely on value added. Therefore, assuming normal, average market returns, it would not be unusual for a 'murky middle' manager to produce positive pre-tax value added and negative after-tax value added at the same time.

Assume that the equity market has returned 10% and that our 'murky middle' manager has produced a pre-tax value added of 2%. Further assume that the portfolio's tax efficiency is around 70%. The after-tax return on that portfolio is 8.4%, as we will have paid 30% of 12% in taxes, or 3.6%. Assuming that the index has a tax efficiency of around 98% (which is probably more unkind than kind to the index), the after-tax return on the index would be 9.8%. The manager has done a great pre-tax job and cost the investor 1.4% relative to the

106

index, plus the difference in management fees between the manager in the 'murky middle' and the manager of an index fund.

Even if the investor needs a level of portfolio activity equivalent to what would normally be delivered by a 'murky middle' manager, in order to control the overall level of manager risk in the portfolio as a whole, there must be a better solution.

An alternative design: core and satellite

An alternative is offered by the opportunity to think in terms of 'barbelling' the portfolio. Instead of placing all our eggs in the basket located in the middle of the portfolio activity spectrum, we can actually divide the portfolio into two strategic baskets, which do not need to have the same size (as we shall see later). The first of our two baskets, or subportfolios, aims to produce the highest possible tax efficiency, and is therefore designed with the possibility in mind that no value added will be generated at all. The second subportfolio aims to produce the highest reasonable value added, and is therefore designed with the possibility in mind that it will be very tax-inefficient. Exhibit 6.3 illustrates the alternative design.

The balance between the two baskets should be designed to reflect the kind of manager risk with which the investor is comfortable. That comfort can be based on philosophical beliefs, for instance on whether the investor believes that active management, at least as traditionally defined, can add value in a cost-efficient manner. Investor comfort can also be based on a more specific risk management process.

A numerical example will help illustrate the difference that such a design can make. Going back to the earlier example, assume that an index fund generates 9.8% after-tax

Exhibit 6.3

Moving away from the murky middle : a core and satellite approach

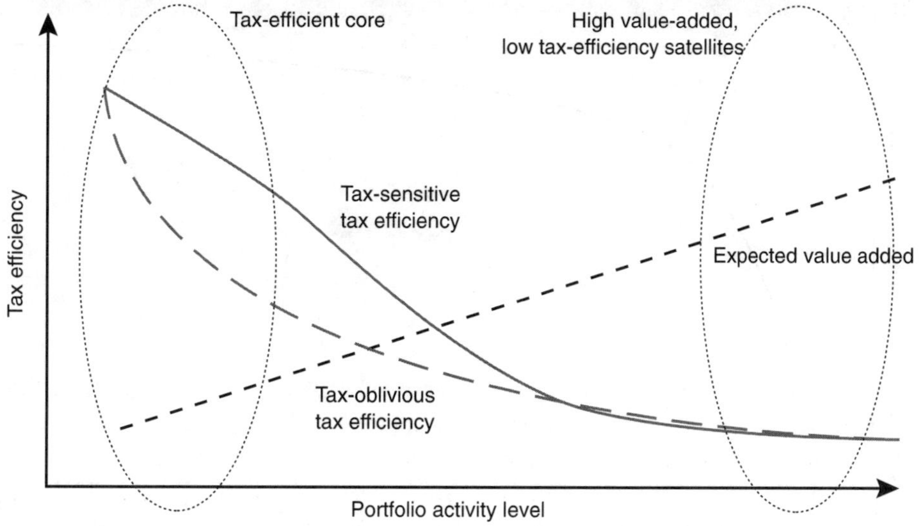

Source: Brunel, Jean L.P. 'A Tax-Efficient Portfolio Construction Model,'
The *Journal of Wealth Management*, Fall 2001, pp.43-50

returns, and that a satellite strategy will have a 60% tax efficiency. Note that, in this context, we are looking at a simplified version of U.S. circumstances. Indeed 60% is the minimum tax efficiency possible if we consider only federal taxes. The maximum marginal tax rate was 39.6% as of the middle of 2001 (when this chapter was written). The worst possible investment outcome, from a tax standpoint, is for the return to comprise only dividends and realized short-term capital gains, which, in the United States, both are taxed at the taxpayer's marginal tax rate. It follows that any satellite able to generate 16.3% pre-tax returns, or a 6.3% value added, will match the after-tax performance of the index.

This example underlines two important points. First, one needs a lot of pre-tax value added to beat an index after-tax. Second, combining a tax-efficient core and a tax-inefficient satellite might produce a higher risk-adjusted after-tax return than a 'murky middle' alternative. Note further that, though this satellite would have a higher risk than the index, it would offer potential tax efficiency benefits over time, as that volatility would produce opportunities to use realized capital losses to offset some of the gains.

'Hyper-tax-efficient' strategies

The core and satellite design further illustrates the importance of thinking in total portfolio terms. Imagine that, instead of using a standard passive index fund, we decide to invest in an active tax-managed strategy. Such a strategy potentially has a tax efficiency in excess of 100%, as it generates net realized capital losses while matching the performance of the index. Even after accounting for dividend income, it is not unreasonable to aim for a 101% tax effi-

Exhibit 6.4

Required satellite pre-tax alpha at various portfolio exposure levels (%)

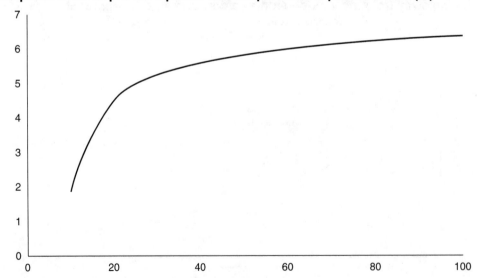

Source: Brunel, Jean L.P. 'A Tax-Efficient Portfolio Construction Model,'
The *Journal of Wealth Management*, Fall 2001, pp.43-50

ciency, meaning that the strategy would actually produce tax-exempt returns, plus some tax credit that may be used to shelter tax-inefficient returns elsewhere in the portfolio. The 101% tax efficiency target is reasonable, given the approximate 2–3% net realized capital losses that David Stein, Robert Arnott, and their respective colleagues obtained in their experiments,[3] at least in the earlier years, on average. Now, if we just aim to beat the 9.8% after-tax return of the index, we can afford to combine a 'hyper-tax-efficient' passive structured strategy with some less efficient subportfolio, with a high expected value added.

Exhibit 6.4 illustrates the different combinations of expected satellite value added and satellite portfolio exposure needed to match the after-tax performance of the index. Note that the hyper-tax-efficiency of the passive structured approach allows the satellite strategy to offer minimal alpha at very low levels of portfolio exposure to that strategy. Yet at higher levels of satellite portfolio exposure, the required alpha quickly becomes very imposing.

Arguably, this design is even more compelling when considered in the context of a multi-asset class or strategy portfolio. Examples of strategies that one might find in the core portion of such a portfolio would include passive portfolios, actively tax-managed portfolios, municipal bonds, and private equity funds. By contrast, the tax-inefficient satellite portion of the portfolio might comprise taxable bonds, concentrated portfolios or hedge funds, directional or nondirectional.

Making the 'core and satellite' decision

At least two factors might help an investor decide on the relative sizes of the two subportfolios. The first is of a philosophical nature, while the second relates to whether he or she prefers static or dynamic tax efficiency.

An individual who does not believe that managers can add value through active portfolio management will likely tend to privilege tax efficiency at the expense of active strategies. For instance, such an individual may decide that the only management activity reasonably likely to produce significant, risk-adjusted value added lies in the hedge fund world. At the same time, he or she might also believe that the nonmarket risks associated with hedge funds, as well as their possible lack of liquidity, militates in favor of capping his or her total portfolio exposure to that sector at, say, 20%. In this example, the investor would end up with a portfolio 80% allocated to the tax-efficient core.

The question of static versus dynamic tax efficiency is somewhat subtler. We looked into an important aspect of this debate in Chapter 3. Our focus here is on the relationship between the investor's preference for static or dynamic tax efficiency and the balance that he or she might strike between core tax-efficient strategies and satellite tax-inefficient strategies.

Static tax efficiency is focused on minimizing tax drag over the immediate term, accepting the potentially adverse consequences associated with the risk of 'portfolio freezing,' as discussed by Roberto Apelfeld, Gordon Fowler, and Jim Gordon in an article on tax-aware equity management (to which we will return in Chapter 15).[4] Again, this risk involves either forfeiting the potential to keep earning after-tax value added – as the level of unrealized gain in each position makes it increasingly hard to justify any sale – or accepting higher portfolio tracking error. This arises because the portfolio, by definition different from the index, will keep drifting away from the index as its individual holdings generate different returns than those of the index. When the portfolio freezes, it becomes impossible to rebalance it closer to the index, and the risk inherent in that drift becomes increasingly significant over time. Though Robert Jeffrey[5] argues that this is not an important issue, it must still be factored in, as it is a risk for which one is not compensated and that can be quite material, particularly when considered in a multi-generational context. (The ultimate incarnation of the problem is known as low-basis portfolio concentration, discussed in Chapter 10.)

By contrast, a dynamically tax-efficient process would look to maintaining a balance between tax efficiency, risk management, and the potential to earn value added over the long term. A dynamically tax-efficient investor would be concerned with the risk of too wide a gap developing between the portfolio's market value and its tax basis. He or she may thus be potentially more willing to incur some short-term tax drag, provided he or she expects to earn a fair after-tax and risk-adjusted compensation over the long term. *Such an investor might be therefore more inclined to have a greater proportion of the portfolio in tax-inefficient satellite strategies.* These tax-inefficient strategies might, over time, provide him or her with greater flexibility to adjust the portfolio's balance.

Asset location considerations

These portfolio construction considerations must finally be looked at in the context of the structure through which the wealth is held. An important concern here is to refrain, when attempting to create a delicate equilibrium, from creating complexity for the sake of it, or from designing a strategy that can eventually come back to haunt the investor.

An example will make the point. I recently had to deal with a situation where an investor did not feel comfortable opting either for a full passive structured approach or for a fully active strategy. The logical way out of the dilemma seemed to be to have some of both. Unfortunately, that solution exposed the individual to significant 'wash sale' risks, as the chances were high that, at some point, a net loss realization sale in one subportfolio would be offset by a value purchase in the other, creating tax accounting nightmares, particularly if not caught early on. This was particularly relevant as the investor had a philosophical bias in favor of 'value investing.' In this case, you would naturally expect 'value investing' to work at cross purposes with the passive structured strategy. Indeed, the passive structured manager would tend to sell any stock that recently experienced a price decline, to capture the tax loss. At the same time, the value manager would likely be tempted to purchase that stock, thus invalidating the tax benefit associated with the trade made by the passive structured manager and creating substantial accounting difficulties for the investor caught in the middle. (This is not so important a problem outside the United States, particularly for investors in a number of European countries, where the concept of wash sales does not exist.)

The solution involved observing that there were at least two distinct ownership pockets within the family's wealth. It was therefore possible to locate one strategy in one pocket and the other strategy in the other pocket. Had the family not been able to benefit from the multi-location opportunity combining the two strategies, this could have led to later unpleasantness.

Portfolio optimization issues

Issues related to asset location, as well as investor preferences for static or dynamic tax efficiency, should all be made a part of the quantitative portfolio optimization process. Indeed, a well-designed optimization tool should provide for individual preferences in terms of tax sensitivity, which can help address static versus dynamic tax efficiency issues. The investor's return and risk expectations for each asset class or strategy will inevitably reflect his or her philosophical beliefs in terms of the ability of active managers to create value added.

Thus, it is not unreasonable to expect that a well designed strategic portfolio optimizer should produce recommended portfolios that have a barbell structure. One could, therefore, argue that focusing on a barbell structure does not require conscious effort on the part of the investor: the model would take care of it. I disagree with this contention. As David Swensen has observed:[6]

'Unconstrained mean-variance runs usually provide solutions unrecognizable as reasonable portfolios.' Richard Michaud,[7] in his critique of mean-variance optimization, writes, 'The unintuitive character of many "optimized" portfolios can be traced to the fact that mean-variance optimizers are, in a fundamental sense, "estimation-error maximizers" … Mean-variance optimization significantly overweights (underweights) those securities that have large (small) estimated returns, negative (positive) correlations, and small (large) variances. These securities are, of course, the ones most likely to have large estimation errors.'

Thus, realistic models will need to be appropriately constrained[8] (as we shall see in Chapters 11 and 12), and these constraints must reflect the professional insights as to what is reasonable and what is not. I was driven to formulating the core and satellite architecture by a question I kept asking myself: why is the unconstrained optimizer producing such a quirky portfolio structure?

It is therefore important to segregate these issues in a conceptual sense, to help understand why an optimizer provides solutions that may otherwise appear strange. Having a solid understanding of why such a structure makes sense can also help an individual investor or professional advisor make simple decisions when they do not feel the need to use a complex quantitative tool.

Summary and implications

The core and satellite strategy illustrates one of the most significant differences between tax-oblivious and tax-sensitive portfolio management. The need to keep a total portfolio focus forces investor and manager alike to reconsider long-practiced approaches.

Interestingly, the core and satellite design echoes practices I encountered years ago among European and Asian investors: having a high proportion of a portfolio in virtually risk-free assets and a small part exposed to the risk of total loss. Examples include cases of individuals invested in money market instruments and in a handful of stocks. Another illustration is an individual invested in low-coupon long-term government bonds – for instance, British War Loans, selling at 15 cents on the dollar and paying a 3% coupon – with a minor exposure to warrants on a small number of Hong Kong stocks. These barbell practices were designed to help the investor manage risk, which was then ostensibly defined in terms of absolute downside risk. The conceptually similar core and satellite approach is, however, designed to enhance total portfolio tax efficiency.

---

[1] For a tax-oblivious early discussion of the topic, see Grinold, Richard C., and Mark Stuckelman, 'The Value Added/Turnover Frontier,' *The Journal of Portfolio Management*, Summer 1993, pp. 8–17.

[2] Robert D. Arnott and Robert H. Jeffrey, 'Is Your Alpha Big Enough to Cover its Taxes?,' *The Journal of Portfolio Management*, Spring 1993, pp. 15–26.

[3] See Stein, David M., and Premkumar Narasimhan, 'Of Passive and Active Equity Portfolios in the Presence of Taxes,' *The Journal of Private Portfolio Management*, Fall 1999, pp. 55–63; and Arnott, Robert D., Andrew L. Berkin, and Jia Ye, 'Loss Harvesting: What's It Worth To The Taxable Investor?,' *The Journal of Wealth Management*, Spring 2001, pp. 10–18.

[4] See Apelfeld, Roberto, Gordon Fowler, Jr., and James Gordon, Jr., 'Tax-Aware Equity Investing,' *The Journal of Portfolio Management*, Winter 1996, pp. 18–28.

[5] See Robert Jeffrey, 'Tax-Efficient Portfolio Management: Easier Said than Done,' *The Journal of Wealth Management*, Summer 2001, pp. 9–15.

[6] Swensen, David F., *Pioneering Portfolio Management – An Unconventional Approach to Institutional Investment*, New York: The Free Press, 2000. A similar caveat was expressed in a broader piece dedicated to the mechanics of portfolio optimization: Kritzman, Mark, 'What Practitioners Need to Know ... About Optimization?' *Financial Analysts Journal*, Vol. 48, No. 5, September/October 1992, pp. 10–13.

[7] Michaud, Richard, 'The Markowitz Optimization Enigma: Is "Optimized" Optimal?,' *Financial Analyst Journal* Vol. 45, No. 1, January/February 1989, pp. 31–42.

[8] For a discussion of certain constraints and their impact, see Fisher, Kenneth L., and Meir Statman, 'The Mean-Variance Optimization Puzzle: Security Portfolios and Food Portfolios,' *Financial Analysts Journal*, Vol. 53, No. 4, July/August 1997, pp. 41–50.

Understanding the opportunities and the issues

Chapter 7

Defining the capital market opportunities

In this chapter, we focus on three main topics: the value of looking at past data; defining asset classes and strategies; and the broad lessons that we have learned from the past.

As we look at any past data, we must develop an understanding of how the past speaks to us, making sure we identify the right messages. An important first step is to agree definitions for the major asset classes and strategies. This has two dimensions. First, the concept of asset class has substantially evolved over the past several decades. It is therefore useful to appreciate the issues and limitations associated with any of the main definitions that can be used. The main insight is that the set of asset classes or strategies used must be sufficiently complete to provide a full picture, while the various definitions must be sufficiently distinct to ensure as little overlap among the various possibilities as possible. Second, the interaction between asset class or strategy and investor psychology tends to make certain strategies more or less suitable to various individual investors.

Two broad topics are subsumed into this discussion. First, it is worth revisiting the issue of risk, in particular the debate on time diversification: does risk decline or rise with time? We will see that disagreements on the answer to the question arise from different definitions of risk. Second, a study of the past is, by necessity, conducted on indexes. It stands to reason that one never really looks at history in a perfect sense. The analogy of a photograph might help illustrate this point better. Imagine that you are looking at a picture of a room in someone's house. If the picture was taken with a wide-angle lens, the image will seem to have a great deal of breadth and the room typically will look larger. That same room photographed with a telephoto lens will appear much smaller. Yet the room, itself, will not have changed.

The same is true of capital market history. The lens that we are using is often the index that depicts market movements. Thus, indexes with different construction and composition may provide dramatically different pictures, and lead the observer to dramatically different conclusions.

We then turn to a few useful truisms gleaned from an investigation of the historical returns and risks associated with a number of commonly accepted asset categories or strategies. The point is not to replicate the work so ably done by many observers, but rather to illustrate a few of the most important relationships that will eventually be used to support any framework developed to create rational forward-looking expectations.

How the past speaks to us

Though the past is rarely the most reliable guide to evaluating future opportunities, it is a good point to start. Starting with the past allows us to build in our mind a set of guideposts that describe what has been possible and why. As David Swensen has observed:[1]

> While past patterns provide important inputs for assumptions about the future, historical data must be modified to produce a set of numbers consistent with expected market realities. Thoughtful investors strike a balance between respect for history and concern for analytical consistency.

The philosopher George Santayana once wrote: 'Those who cannot remember the past are condemned to repeat it.' Therein lies the need to understand the past. The past can indeed teach us about the relationship between individual asset classes or between broad economic circumstances and capital market behavior. We can also learn about the relationship between certain individual biases and the most suitable strategies that individuals might consider. In fact, the data suggest that, despite all the changes, there are many relationships that have been amazingly stable, when appropriately understood, modified or calibrated.

On the other hand, there are many good reasons why one should not excessively rely on the past to consider the future. Consider two of the most frequent mistakes investors make. The first is to extend the recent past into the indeterminate future. The second involves glossing over structural change, which might make some past pattern, at best, unlikely to be repeated in the future, if not simply irrelevant.

The financial scene in Australia since 1980 provides a useful illustration of two important points. First, major change can occur, but, second, such changes are usually few and far between.

In 1982, the Australian Treasurer (finance minister) changed the government bond issuance program from a 'tap' to a 'tender' system. In a tap system, the Treasurer sets out the level of interest rate at which the government is willing to issue bonds at each maturity and accepts requests for purchases by intermediaries willing to buy at these prices. In a tender system, the Treasurer sets out the quantity of bonds that the government wants to issue, sets out a tender date, and asks for bids comprising both a yield and a quantity. After the bids have been ranked from the highest to the lowest interest rate, the Treasurer starts accepting bids from the lowest yield (and therefore the lowest cost to the state) onwards until the government has met its financing needs. Moving to a tender system changed the way interest rates were determined and made them, *ceteris paribus*, more volatile. An analysis of the past must recognize structural change and account for it when using the past to gauge the future.

In 1988, the Treasurer changed the tax status of pension funds, making equity holdings relatively more attractive than bonds because of the franking credit, which is meant to prevent double taxation. Any analysis of the past that did not recognize the rise in the marginal propensity to hold equities on the part of Australian pension funds would be bound to provide misleading conclusions.

Defining asset classes and strategies

Though the asset allocation process has become second nature and almost automatic for most investors, it has substantially evolved over the past quarter century. As we moved from the simplest definition in place a few decades ago to the more complex and differentiated approaches of today, we may have sidestepped a number of important questions.

An analogy helps focus the mind. Consider the story of the frog and the pan full of water. Throw the frog in a pan full of hot water and it will jump out and survive. Throw it in a pan full of cold water, place that pan on the stove and gradually heat it up and the frog will die: the temperature changes will be too gradual and it will allow itself to be cooked rather than be shocked into escaping.

Similar circumstances apply to the world of asset allocation and, in particular, to the definition of asset classes. The change we have experienced may have been so gradual that we failed to appreciate how definitions changed. It is thus important to take a step back and make sure that we understand what we mean by 'asset class.' At the outset, arriving at a reasonable definition of what an asset class is, or should be, is very important, to ensure that investors are able to view a complete picture. At the same time, the individual pieces that are combined to create the picture must be defined in appropriate terms relative to each other.

From individual securities to asset classes

Historically, the process through which asset classes were effectively 'created' reflects the increase in the sophistication of the asset management industry, in part in response to developments in modern portfolio theory. Jeffrey Horvitz[2] suggests that

> asset allocation is a consultant's concept that is now several decades old. It was a major advance, not as theory, but as a paradigm for investing. It is a paradigm, in that it creates a framework for conceptualizing normative investment behavior and in this respect shifted, in material ways, the investment focus from the security level to the portfolio level. This change in paradigms was not in a vacuum. Modern portfolio theory (MPT) is closely related to asset allocation and predated it.

Modern portfolio theory transformed a problem often viewed through its single return dimension to a two-dimensional space, defined in both return and risk terms. The first step in that transformation process was to group securities within 'asset classes'. Originally, the three basic asset classes – cash, bonds, and equities – were broadly defined and assumed to comprise publicly quoted securities.[3] The thought process through which asset classes were 'created' directly followed the tenets of modern portfolio theory. Everything starts with the idea that risk is broken down into two components: market risk and nonmarket risk. The point of portfolio optimization is to diversify a portfolio sufficiently – but not too much – so that one maximizes the opportunity to earn attractive returns without taking any risks for which one cannot rationally expect to be compensated. Individuals seem to have no problem understanding the concept of avoiding risks for which they cannot expect to be compensated. This is in effect similar to the teaching of modern portfolio theory that the portfolios on the efficient frontier are such that one cannot expect a higher return on any one of them without incurring a higher level of risk.

Theory holds that nonmarket risk can be diversified away by holding a well diversified portfolio of the securities comprising that market, with that portfolio being left with market

117

risk, also called systematic risk. The process goes on to assume that a well diversified portfolio, comprising exposure to different market risks, will also have a lower risk than any one of its components taken individually. Asset classes thus became simply the construct allowing one to view these larger building blocks.

David Swensen takes an interestingly different tack on defining asset classes: 'Careful investors define asset classes in terms of function, relating security characteristics to the role expected from a particular group of investments.' Yet he would probably agree that, over time, the increasing push to identify manager strategies in greater detail has produced a proliferation of labels, many of which have in turn been used to define 'new' asset classes. Horvitz puts it best: 'what was intuitively obvious in the three-class system is now lost: homogeneity within classes and heterogeneity across classes.'

A three-attribute framework for defining asset classes

To avoid the trap identified by Horvitz, we need a sharp definition of what constitutes an asset class. Looking at the three original constituents of the three-class system, we can see that there are important fundamental differences among them. These differences can be analyzed in terms of three major variables.

The relative importance of income in total return

Both cash and bonds should be expected to provide the bulk of their total return through income. In fact, by definition, cash only provides income, whether that comes from interest payments, as would be the case for a bank deposit, or through the amortization of a discount on the initial purchase price, as typically happens with a Treasury bill. Bonds provide both income and capital gain (or loss) potential, as their prices fluctuate in response to changes in the shape or level of the yield curve. Equities principally provide potential capital gains.

The relative predictability of income

If credit risks assumed away for a moment, both cash and bonds can be said to offer relative certainty as to expected income payments. Equities can offer significant income potential, but they do not provide the same certainty, as dividends can be cut or raised at will by management.

The term of the instrument

While cash and bonds offer fixed terms, equities are effectively perpetual. The holder of a cash deposit or a bond knows that he or she will eventually be repaid in full – again, credit considerations aside – at the maturity of the deposit or of the bond. The only way an equity holder can think of getting his or her money back is to assume that the equity will find a buyer at some point in the future.

From asset classes to groups of strategies

Though agreeing with Horvitz's comments with respect to asset classes, we need to develop a more powerful model to be able to analyze and thus understand the variety of strategies available to individual investors. We can approach the issue from a different angle, drawing a distinction between asset classes and groups of strategies. Using the foregoing three attributes to 'define' the base asset classes, we can expand the framework to include at least two additional dimensions.

Liquidity

Though liquidity is not readily modeled into the customary way of evaluating expected risk and returns for asset classes, it must be taken into account. Thus, it is reasonable to look at illiquid strategies as one broad additional category. Illiquid strategies have two important features that make them particularly relevant to many individual investors. First, their lack of liquidity means that the investor must constrain the total allowable portfolio exposure to ensure that his or her liquidity needs are met. Second, they are not necessarily priced as frequently as other assets. This can have significant impact on the comfort that an investor will have with the investment.

The source price fluctuation risk

Though it is tempting to focus solely on the notion that the common feature of all strategies within an asset class should be that they are exposed to the same 'broad market risk,' this is too restrictive an approach. Price fluctuation risk can indeed arise from both market and manager risk.

Thus, I view hedge funds[4] as a separate group of strategies. Though they tend to be exposed to substantially lower 'market risk' in the traditional sense, they are principally exposed to 'manager risk.' Admittedly, each of the main hedge fund strategies is substantially different from the others. The group therefore may seem somewhat heterogeneous, failing one of our earlier tests. However, I believe that Horvitz's definition may be too narrow: '[The] most homogenous features [of hedge funds are] the legal ownership structure and the profit sharing arrangement [and] have nothing to do with the underlying investment activities.' In an asset allocation context, being principally exposed to manager risk is their most significant common feature, and they are homogeneous with respect to it. Further, because they are substantially different from the traditional classes, as they have a different source of price risk, they will tend to be less correlated to other asset classes or groups of strategies. Thus, they should provide more portfolio diversification. As David Swensen explains:

> Nontraditional asset classes provide powerful tools for investors attempting to reduce risk by constructing well-diversified portfolios and augment returns by pursuing active management opportunities. Absolute return strategies and real estate holdings add diversifying power, while private equity investments improve portfolio return prospects.

Summary

The five criteria set out above can serve as the primary determinants of major strategic groupings and allow us to take the analysis further, as we define any number of asset strategies within these asset groupings. This framework will allow us to differentiate among strategies that investors would view as different, such as domestic equities versus foreign equities, large-capitalization equities versus small-capitalization equities, government bonds versus high-yield bonds, directional hedge funds versus nondirectional hedge funds,[5] and public equities versus private equities.[6] A framework comprising five basic groups will provide us with individually different sets of strategies from which to choose *and* will be broad enough to cover most of the choices that we will need to make.

Using this framework for portfolio optimization, we will be able to set asset class or strategy group exposure constraints. This will make it possible for us to ensure that we fully understand the features of the resulting portfolio in terms of the five criteria.

Summary and implications: lessons on risk

There are two important dimensions of risk that should be of particular concern to individual investors. The first relates to the notion of time diversification, which has to do with the following question: does risk increase or decrease over time? The second takes the issue further, and explores the question of the definition of risk.

Time diversification

As we begin to look at the past to gain an understanding of the future, the notion of the behavior of risk over time is never far away from the surface.[7] Indeed, individual investors are frequently subjected to a barrage of information on the need to think long term. The rationale often emphasizes the idea that thinking long term will allow investors to avoid short-term market disappointments. Implicit in that statement is that risk decreases over time. Let us investigate this latter point.

Exhibit 7.1 sets the stage for the debate on the interaction between time and risk. It shows the volatility of returns over various time frames for the three main traditional asset classes. It illustrates the basic tenet of time diversification: the longer the holding period, the less volatile the compound return. Dennis Hammond[8] phrases best one side of the debate:

> over long periods the issue [of negative performance] disappears altogether. For example, when the time horizon is lengthened from a single annual period to rolling three-year periods over the past fifty years the incidence of negative periods is eliminated.

Charles Jones and Jack Wilson[9] disagree:

> the issue of time diversification is concerned with whether the risk of holding a portfolio of stocks increases or decreases over time. This controversy continues today, with numerous observers often declaring that risk decreases over time, while some academics, such as [Paul] Samuelson,[10] argue that this is simply untrue. Samuelson states that the risk involved is the amount of terminal wealth an investor may acquire increases over time.

In fact, both sides are right, once we have taken the time to appreciate the fact that they have a different definition of risk. Jones and Wilson have put it best:

The key to understanding the time diversification controversy is to separate annual average total returns from cumulative wealth. Then, the following statement can be made: Risk, as measured by the probability distribution of returns around a per-annum average total return over multiple time periods, decreases over time. Risk, as measured by the probability distribution of returns around the cumulative mean of total returns over multiple time periods, increases.

Exhibit 7.1

Volatility of rolling returns for the traditional three main asset classes, 1925 to 2001 (%)

	Short-term Treasury bills	*Long-term Treasury bonds*	*Large-capitalization equities*
One year	3.21	9.06	22.07
Five years	3.07	4.72	8.58
10 years	3.01	3.94	5.52
20 years	2.74	2.91	3.44

Source: Author, data from Ibbotson Database and others.

Implications for individual investors: defining risk

This is an important consideration, as it places the onus on the investor and his or her advisor to define risk in appropriate terms. Behavioral finance tells us of the Pavlovian behavior of many individual investors, who recoil at the thought of volatility of return being a good descriptor of risk. They prefer to think of risk in the more traditional sense of 'losing money,' rather than in terms of return volatility, or even in terms of volatility of terminal wealth. Yet the notion of losing money itself is rather vague.[11]

Indeed, when you begin to think in terms of 'losses,' you will inevitably have to ask yourself: what do I mean by loss? Do you think in nominal terms? Do you think in real, or inflation-adjusted terms? Jones and Wilson[12] have analyzed the probabilities associated with losses and shown that:

> the probability of earning 0% or less inflation-adjusted return, on a compound annual basis, decreases fairly rapidly over time. But, nevertheless, the risk of loss in this sense is significant, particularly for short periods of time. For example, for a five-year horizon, the probability of a 0% or less compound annual inflation-adjusted rate of return [from equities] is 20%, while with bonds the same probability is 27%. For a ten-year horizon, the respective probabilities are 12% and 19%. Even with a fifteen-year horizon, the probability is approximately 14% of experiencing an inflation-adjusted annual compound rate of return of 0%, or less, from corporate bonds, and about 7% from common stocks.

Thus, bonds can actually be viewed as riskier investments than stocks, when risk is defined as experiencing inflation-adjusted losses. Though this observation should not cause surprise when one recalls the experience of savers during times of hyperinflation, it is still important

121

to keep it in mind. It tells us of the need to be specific in setting out the dimensions of our individual problem, to make sure that we focus on those items that are important to the investor with whom we are working at the time.

In *The Art of War*, Sun Tzu[13] reminds us that a critical element of any successful campaign is to know who the enemy is:

> If you know the enemy and know yourself, you need not fear the results of a hundred battles. If you know yourself, but not the enemy, for every victory gained you will also suffer a defeat.

We cannot effectively address our own risk/return preferences if we do not know what we call 'risk.' Is it the fluctuation in the value of our wealth at some future point in time? Is it the fluctuation in the return earned on our portfolio? Is it the probability of our being able to meet certain financial requirements at some future point or over some period of time? To each definition, there corresponds one 'lens' through which we can look at the past and identify how that past may be relevant to our future.[14]

Index biases

Indexes are tools that allow us to comprehend a market or a part of a market. These tools are designed to depict the behavior of a large number of individual securities over multiple periods of time, in a single number or set of numbers. The problem, by definition, is that these tools are designed to answer very specific questions, because they are governed by the laws of statistics.

Consider the following example to appreciate the need to understand the question to which you may seek an answer. Imagine that you are looking for a school for your child and are interested in the average class size. There are at least two different valid answers to the question. One could approach the school's principal and ask two questions: how many students do you have? and how many classes are there in the school? The average class size would be found by dividing the number of students by the number of classes. Alternatively, one could approach each student and ask one question: how many students are there in your class? The average class size would be found by averaging the answers provided by all students. Intuitively, one would imagine that the second approach would provide you with a larger average class size than asking the principal. Indeed, there are more students in larger classes. Yet the principal's answer would certainly also be correct.

The lesson from this example is that you need to make sure that you understand the question you are asking and that it is indeed the question to which you need an answer. If we are trying to find out about the stock market's performance yesterday, we must make sure that we know what data are relevant, and how the lens through which we look at the issue may produce a distorted picture. Are we interested in the average stock, the average large-capitalization stock, or the average small-capitalization stock? Are we interested in a broadly diversified portfolio of stocks, a concentrated portfolio, or even a portfolio principally invested in a small number of economic sectors? The conclusion is that indexes will naturally comprise biases, reflecting the way in which they were constructed and the questions to which they were meant to provide answers.

A discussion of index biases must be broken down into two components. First, we must look at the way in which the index is constructed. Second, we must check whether the index's construction or composition tends to create biases, which we must then take into account.

Three index construction methods

There are three main approaches to index construction, as discussed by John Shoven and Clemens Sialm,[15] and each has its own set of attributes: price weighting, weighting by market capitalization, and equal weighting.

The actual value of a *price-weighted index* can be determined using the following formula, which takes the Dow Jones Industrial Averages Index (DJIA) as an example (the Japanese Nikkei 225 index is another broadly used example):

$$DJIA_t = \frac{1}{d_t} \sum_i P_{i,t}$$

The price of the stock of company i at time t is denoted by $P_{i,t}$ and the divisor is given by d_t. The divisor is needed to allow the index to maintain a continuous history in circumstances where its composition may change. The divisor of the DJIA originally equaled the number of companies in the average. Since 1928, however, the divisor has changed each time a member stock split or paid a large stock dividend, or each time the composition of the index changed.

Though easy to compute and arguably potentially better targeted at the stocks that an individual might hold, a price-weighted index suffers from a very important drawback: the price level of each index component drives its weight. To some extent, this may be acceptable in 'normal circumstances,' as changes in the price of individual stocks will indeed create comparable changes in the value of the portfolio and in the relative weight of a stock in a portfolio. However, consider what happens if the change in the price of a stock does not reflect a decrease in the value of the company. For instance, the weight of a company in the index drops whenever its stock splits. Thus, assuming that an investor constructed a portfolio to replicate or approximate the performance of that index, he or she would need to sell that stock which has just split, to reflect the fact that it now has a smaller weight in the index.

A *market capitalization-weighted index* can be computed as follows:

$$VWI_t = VWI_{t-1} \sum_i w_{i,t} \frac{P_{i,t}}{P_{i,t-1}}$$

where

$$w_{i,t} = \frac{P_{i,t-1} N_{i,t-1}}{\sum_i P_{i,t-1} N_{i,t-1}}$$

Here, *VWI* denotes a value-weighted index and the formula simply says that the value of the index at point in time t is equal to the value of the same index at period t-1, modified by the changes in the prices of each of the component stocks, each weighted by its own market capitalization. Thus, the relative market capitalization of company i in the previous period is denoted with $w_{i,t-1}$. $N_{i,t-1}$ is the number of shares outstanding in the previous period. A stock split does not affect the value of a value-weighted index unless it affects the holding period returns of the stock. The changes to a value-weighted index correspond to the changes of the total market value of all the companies included in the index. Investors trying to match the index only need to adjust their portfolio when a constituent company issues new stock or repurchases shares.

The main criticism of such an index is that the size of a company is not necessarily the best criterion for determining its weight.[16] This is particularly true in instances where certain stocks are particularly illiquid, often, for instance, because of ownership circumstances. The circumstances of many Asian markets come to mind, though similar points could be made with respect to several of the large continental European markets. Substantial crossholdings, such as those in Japan or Germany, mean that the floating shares available for investor purchases are considerably less than the total market capitalization of these companies. Yet the weight of the company in the index often reflects both floating and nonfloating shares.

Finally, an equal-weighted index gives each of the n companies in the index the same weight:

$$EWI_t = EWI_{t-1} \frac{1}{n} \sum_i \frac{P_{i,t}}{P_{i,t-1}}$$

The number of shares in each company that an investor would need to hold in order to replicate an equally-weighted index would be proportional to $1/P_{i,t}$. Investors would hold more shares in the low-priced stocks such that the dollar-amount invested in each stock is identical. Investors desiring to hold an equal-weighted index continuously would need to readjust their portfolios in each period, by selling shares in companies that had outperformed the index in the previous period and by buying shares in the companies that had underperformed the index. Such a strategy that would generate considerable tax liabilities for investments in taxable portfolios.[17]

While having the substantial advantage of creating the greatest possible simplicity, an equal-weighted index does not necessarily offer a true picture of the set of investment opportunities available to the broad investment community. Indeed, it is not realistically replicable for substantial investors, for instance large institutions, which would need to buy overly large dollar exposures to small companies.

How are dividends accounted for?

Beyond the way in which the index is constructed, the way dividends are accounted for can have a very significant impact on the returns you look at over time. Certain indexes assume that dividends are reinvested, while others do not. Ignoring dividends can have a very significant impact. John Shoven and Clemens Sialm explain it best:

> a value-weighted index of the Dow components, including dividend payments, would have closed at 293,001 at the end of December 1999, had it started off in October 1928 at 239.43. The actual DJIA closed at 11,497. Adding dividends increases the value of the index after 70 years by a factor of more than 25. Including dividends mitigates the effects of the Great Depression. A new all-time high is reached in January 1945 instead of November 1954 if dividends are included.

Applying this to the circumstances of individual investors involves an additional question. Individuals can rarely keep the whole of the dividend payments they receive. Typically, they will need to pay taxes, and will therefore only reinvest after-tax dividends.

Within a given country, individuals will tend to see their portfolios underperform an index with gross dividends reinvested. Indeed, the long-term compounding effect inherent in that computation will fail to recognize that only a fraction of the dividends has been reinvested.

For investors investing outside their home countries, the problem is compounded by the fact that certain countries impose withholding taxes. Interestingly, the Morgan Stanley Capital International indexes provide computations with 'net dividends reinvested,' which I find of greater value than any of the purely domestic indexes available to investors.

Skewness

Among the several biases that can creep into the analysis of the unsuspecting investor, the most important one relates to 'skewness.' Skewness deals with the extent to which the distribution of returns, in any given period, is symmetric or asymmetric. Discussing the impact of skewness on the evaluation of a manager's performance relative to an index, David Ikenberry, Richard Schockley, and Kent Womak[18] noted that, in most years, 'skewness tends to be positive (right-tailed) and harms the relative performance of managers, however, its impact varies from year to year.' The rationale for this observation is that, as skewness increases, a random portfolio will occasionally draw stocks with extremely high returns relative to the median or 'typical' portfolio, which is largely unaffected by skewness.

Five broad historical observations

Capital market history is both rich in potential insights and full of pitfalls as to the nature of the opportunities available to individual investors. There are five observations that have proven broadly true and are likely to retain a great deal of validity.

First, *there is a reasonably clear trade-off between return and risk*. History can seem at times to cloud the theoretical definition of the capital market line, which has the return and risk (defined as the volatility of that return) of all asset classes neatly aligned in an upward sloping manner. There have been instances where the relative proportionality of risk and return has appeared to go awry. Yet history has so far not been able to disprove the general truism according to which exceptional returns come together with exceptional risks, and *vice versa*.

This is a particularly important issue for individual investors, for at least two reasons. One is that investing in public financial markets has rarely been the most successful way to build a personal fortune; it is often best viewed as a reasonable way to protect wealth and grow purchasing power modestly: 'Investors get rich by being concentrated … but they stay rich by being diversified.'[19] The other is the oft quoted phrase illustrated in the investment world daily, 'if it looks too good to be true, it probably is.' (We will come back to this in Chapter 17, when we consider manager selection.)

Second, *there is a diverging relationship between risk measured as the risk of short-term capital loss and risk defined as the loss of long-term purchasing power.* In terms of short-term volatility, short-term fixed income, such as cash or money market instruments, provide the highest level of likely capital protection, credit considerations aside. Over the long term, equities, which typically are more volatile over the short term, tend to provide the lowest probability of negative inflation-adjusted returns. The position of medium- to long-term fixed-income securities is not clear-cut, as there must be careful attention paid to the duration of the period defined as 'long-term' and the time to maturity of the bonds.

Third, *risk, as measured in terms of volatility of compound average annual returns, decreases as the time horizon lengthens*. Though the range of possible terminal wealth outcomes broadens as the time horizon lengthens, the risk many investors seem to consider the most important – losing money – will tend to decrease over time, if the point of reference is static. By contrast, it will not decline if investors keep moving the base point, effectively defining a loss as having less money today than yesterday. This underpins the general belief that investors with real long-term horizons should focus principally on riskier assets, a belief that remains true only in circumstances where behavioral finance considerations do not lead the investor to unwind the strategy at the worst possible time.

Fourth, *defining asset classes and strategies is paramount to identifying opportunities and formulating an overall wealth management strategy*. Identifying opportunities arguably requires a preciseness in the analysis that must be at least partially unwound when it comes to formulating an overall wealth management strategy. It is important to dig sufficiently deep into the details to ensure that one has gained all the insights necessary to form a solid opinion of the opportunities. Particularly when dealing with taxable funds, experience suggests that it may be more opportune to focus on more broadly defined asset classes or strategies.

Finally, *asset classes and strategies can be analyzed into three basic groups*. Over both short and long time horizons, three basic asset classes dominate the landscape: cash (or money market), bonds, and equities. Most other traditionally accepted sub-asset classes can in fact be defined in relation to the three base asset classes. This indicates that they share the principal risk and return characteristics of the three main assets, while offering the potential for higher return, usually at the expense of higher risk. Taxable individual investors need to go beyond passive indexes and focus on actively managed strategies, whether traditional or nontraditional ('alternative'[20]), and whether the manager's activity is dedicated to security selection or to tax management.

[1] See Swensen, David F., *Pioneering Portfolio Management – An Unconventional Approach to Institutional Investment*, New York: The Free Press, 2000. See also Gray, William S., 'Historical Returns, Inflation and Future Return Expectations,' *Financial Analysts Journal*, Vol. 49, No. 4, July/August 1993, pp. 35–45.

[2] See Horvitz, Jeffrey, 'Asset Classes and Asset Allocation: Problems of Classification,' *The Journal of Private Portfolio Management*, Spring 2000, pp. 27–32.

[3] For a discussion of 'asset class-ness', see Greer, Robert J., 'What is an Asset Class Anyway?,' *The Journal of Portfolio Management*, Winter 1997, pp. 86–91. See also the book by David Swensen cited in note 1 above.

[4] Three books are well worth reading to get a better appreciation of hedge funds, their nature, their potential and their role. Grerend, William J., *Fundamentals of Hedge Fund Investing – A Professional Investor's Guide*, McGraw-Hill, 1998; Lederman, Jess, and Robert A. Klein, eds., *Hedge Funds – Investment and Portfolio Strategies for the Institutional Investor*, Irwin, 1995; and Lederman, Jess, and Robert A. Klein, eds., *Market Neutral – State-of-the-Art Strategies for Every Market Environment*, Irwin, 1996. For a discussion of the historical performance of hedge funds, see Liang, Brian, 'Hedge Fund Performance, 1990–1999,' *Financial Analysts Journal*, Vol. 57, No. 1, January/February 2001, pp. 11–19.

[5] For a discussion of long/short strategies, see Jacobs, Bruce I., and Kenneth N. Levy, 'Twenty Myths About Long-Short,' *Financial Analysts Journal*, Vol. 52, No. 5, September/October 1996, pp. 81–85; also, Michaud, Richard O., 'Are Long-Short Equity Strategies Superior?,' *Financial Analysts Journal*, Vol. 49, No. 6, November/December 1993, pp. 44–49.

[6] For a discussion of the growth in alternative investments in general and international private equities in particular, see Healey, Thomas J., and Donald J. Hardy, *Financial Analysts Journal*, Vol. 53, No. 4, July/August 1997, pp. 58–65.

[7] See Levy, Haim, and Yishay Spector, 'Cross-Asset versus Time Diversification,' *The Journal of Portfolio Management*, Spring 1996, pp. 24–35; Thorley, Steven R., 'The Time-Diversification Controversy,' *Financial Analysts Journal*, Vol. 51, No. 3, May/June 1995, pp. 67–75; Hansson, Björn, and Mattias Persson, 'Time Diversification and Estimation Risk,' *Financial Analysts Journal*, Vol. 56, No. 5, September/October 2000, pp. 55–62; Merrill, Craig, and Steven Thorley, 'Time Diversification: Perspectives from Option Pricing Theory,' *Financial Analysts Journal*, Vol. 52, No. 3, May/June 1996, pp. 13–19.

[8] See Hammond, Dennis R., 'Cloudy Days and Sunny Days,' *Journal of Investing*, Spring 1995, pp. 82–83. See also Levy, Haim, and Deborah Gunthorpe, 'Optimal Investment Proportions in Senior Securities and Equities Under Alternative Holding Periods,' *The Journal of Portfolio Management*, Summer 1993, pp. 30–36; Gunthorpe, Deborah, and Haim Levy, 'Portfolio Composition and the Investment Horizon,' *Financial Analysts Journal*, January-February 1994, pp. 51–56; Fergusson, Robert, and Yusif Simaan, 'Portfolio Composition and the Investment Horizon Revisited,' *The Journal of Portfolio Management*, Summer 1996, pp. 62–67.

[9] See Jones, C.P., and J.W. Wilson, 'The Incidence and Impact of Losses from Stocks and Bonds,' *The Journal of Private Portfolio Management*, Summer 1998, pp. 31–40. See also Butler, Kirt C., and Dale L. Domian, 'Risk, Diversification, and the Investment Horizon,' *The Journal of Portfolio Management*, Spring 1991, pp. 41–48; Siegel, Laurence B., and David Montgomery, 'Stocks, Bonds, and Bills after Taxes and Inflation,' *The Journal of Portfolio Management*, Winter 1995, pp. 17–25; Wilson, Jack W., and Charles P. Jones, 'Long-Term Returns and Risk for Bonds,' *The Journal of Portfolio Management*, Spring 1997, pp. 15–28.

[10] See Samuelson, Paul A. 'The Judgment of Economic Science on Rational Portfolio Management: Indexing, Timing and Long-Horizon Effects.' *The Journal of Portfolio Management*, Fall 1989, pp. 4–12. 'Asset Allocation Can Be Dangerous to Your Health.' *The Journal of Portfolio Management*, Spring 1990, pp. 5–8. 'The Long Term Case for Equities.' *The Journal of Portfolio Management*, Fall 1994, pp. 15–26. Also: Levy Haim, and P.A. Samuelson. 'The Capital Asset Pricing Model with Diverse Holding Periods.' *Management Science*, 38 (1992) pp. 1529–1542. Levy, H. 'The CAPM and the Investment Horizon.' *The Journal of Portfolio Management*, Vol. 7, 2 (1980), pp. 32–40. Levy H. 'The CAPM and the Investment Horizon: Reply.' *The Journal of Portfolio Management*, Vol. 9, 1 (1982), pp. 66–68. Levy, H. 'Measuring Risk and Performance over Alternative Investment Horizons.' *Financial Analysts Journal*, Vol. 40, 2, (1984), pp. 61–68. Kritzman, Mark. 'What Practitioners Need to Know … About Time Diversification?' *Financial Analyst Journal*, Vol. 50, No. 1, January-February 1994, pp. 14–19. Gunthorpe, D. and Haim Levy. 'Portfolio Composition and The Investment Horizon.' *Financial Analyst Journal*, Vol. 50, No. 1, January–February 1994, pp. 51–56. Ferguson, Robert, and Yusif Simaan. 'Portfolio Composition and The Investment Horizon Revisited.' *The Journal of Portfolio Management*, Summer 1996, pp. 62–68. Levy, Haim, and Allon Cohen. 'On the Risk of Stocks in the Long Run: Revisited.' *The Journal of Portfolio Management*, Spring 1998, pp. 60–69. Bierman, Jr., Harold. 'A Utility Approach to the Portfolio Allocation Decision and the Investment Horizon.' *The Journal of Portfolio Management*, Fall 1998, pp. 81–87.

[11] For a discussion of 'experts' definitions' of risk, see Olsen, Robert A., 'Investment Risk: The Experts' Perspectives,' *Financial Analysts Journal*, Vol. 53, No. 2, March/April 1997, pp. 62–66.

[12] See Jones, C.P. and J.W. Wilson, 'Probabilities Associated with Common Stock Returns,' *The Journal of Portfolio Management*, Fall 1995, pp. 21–32. See also Siegel, Laurence B., and David Montgomery, 'Stocks, Bonds, and Bills after Taxes and Inflation,' *The Journal of Portfolio Management*, Winter 1995, pp. 17–25.

[13] See Sun Tzu, *The Art of War*. Edited and with a Foreword by James Clavel. Delacorte Press, Bantam Doubleday Dell, NY, 1983, pp. 18.

[14] For a discussion of the statistical dimension of the issue, see Shula, Ravi, and Charles Trzcinka, 'Research on Risk and Return: Can Measures of Risk Explain Anything?,' *The Journal of Portfolio Management*, Spring 1991, pp. 15–21. See also Sharpe, William F., 'The Sharpe Ratio,' *The Journal of Portfolio Management*, Fall 1994, pp.

49–59. On a less serious note, one might also read Musumeci, Jim, 'Comment: Statistics Never Lie,' *The Journal of Portfolio Management*, Winter 1994, pp. 81–83.

[15] See Shoven, John B., and Clemens Sialm, 'The Dow Jones Industrial Average: The Impact of Fixing Its Flaws,' *The Journal of Wealth Management*, Winter 2000, pp. 9–18. See also Clarke, Roger G., and Meir Statman, 'The DJIA Crossed 652,230,' *The Journal of Portfolio Management*, Winter 2000, pp. 89–94; and Larsen, Glen A., Jr., and Bruce G. Resnick, 'Empirical Insights on Indexing,' *The Journal of Portfolio Management*, Fall 1998, pp. 51–60.

[16] See Haugen, Robert A., and Nardin L. Baker, 'The Efficient Market Inefficiency of Capitalization Weighted Stock Portfolios,' *The Journal of Portfolio Management*, Spring 1991, pp. 35–40; and Strongin, Steven, Melanie Petsch, and Greg Sharenow, 'Beating Benchmarks,' *The Journal of Portfolio Management*, Summer 2000, pp. 11–28.

[17] See Dickson, J.M., J.B. Shoven, and C. Sialm, 'Tax Externalities of Equity Mutual Funds,' *National Tax Journal*, 53, 3.2, 2000, pp. 607–28.

[18] See Ikenberry, David, Richard Schockley, and Kent Womak, 'Why Active Fund Managers Often Underperform the S&P 500: The Impact of Size and Skewness,' *The Journal of Private Portfolio Management*, Spring 1998, pp. 13–26.

[19] I am indebted to Scott Welsh, Director of Equity Risk Management at CMS Financial Services, for this quotation, from an anonymous source, cited at the 8th Annual Family Office Forum organized by the Institute for Investment Research, June 25–26, 2001, in Chicago.

[20] For a discussion of one of the aspects of the inclusion of alternative assets in a traditional portfolio, see Brush, John S., 'Comparisons and Combinations of Long and Long/Short Strategies,' *Financial Analysts Journal*, Vol. 53, No. 3, May/June 1997, pp. 81–89.

Chapter 8

The need for capital market forecasting

In the previous chapter we discussed the need to *understand* the nature of the opportunities offered by capital markets. We now turn to the *evaluation* of these opportunities. Our fundamental goal is to be able to develop rational investment expectations. Without rational expectations, we cannot go through the objective part of the integrated wealth planning process.

This process requires us to address strategic asset *allocation* and *location* issues. Strategic asset allocation provides the answer to the following question, asked from the point of view of the individual investor: which assets or strategies should I own in order to achieve my goals? Strategic asset location answers a different, equally important question, which we discussed in Chapter 5: how should individual assets or strategies be located in the various structures through which an individual's or family's wealth is owned, to maximize the efficiency of the effort?

A cynic might ask why he or she needs to go through a complex process to develop these expectations. He or she might even point to evidence on how hard it is to do. Behavioral finance teaches us that we frame our gambles in a variety of ways and make our decisions based on preferences or biases. The real answer to the original question is simply that if you do not take the time to make your expectations explicit you will work from implicit expectations instead. Given what we know about the human tendency to be influenced by the very recent past, and given that we also know that the recent past is rarely a good predictor of the future, there is a great deal of safety in taking the time to make expectations explicit.[1]

There is another aspect to the need to go through such a complex process. Given the relatively poor record of forecasters, would it not be just as good to make relatively broad guesses and live with the lack of precision associated with them? One of the points that I will articulate in this chapter is the need to be able to react to surprises or disappointments. Having a clear forecasting framework, even though it may be indeed more complex than its outcome is accurate, provides a way to go back up the decision tree when a surprise occurs. This maximizes the chances that we will not compound a possibly erroneous decision at some point in time by bailing out at the worst possible moment, a tendency that gives rise to 'decision risk.'

Understanding the real set of opportunities likely available in the future and formulating rational forward-looking expectations require both a review of the past, and an analysis of the changes that could make the future different from the past. At one level, it could be argued that an intuitive or subjective forecast of the main variables – return and risk – may well be as good, or as faulty, as more systematic, model-based approaches. Yet nonsystematic forecasts seem insufficient, unless they are used in an equally intuitive and qualitative manner. For instance, they might be used to gauge the relative attractiveness of some asset class over another. However, whenever they are to be used in a quantitative form, the integrity of the forecast, in its totality, is primordial, following the principle 'garbage in, garbage out' (GIGO). A structurally sound approach does not guarantee a better forecast, but it does provide for more consistency in that forecast. This covers both the need for all the individual numbers to be internally consistent and for there to be a means to change them in a systematic fashion, should a change in assumption be necessary at some future point.

Defining an achievable goal

Many of the arguments against forecasting markets are indeed right. Those who feel that there is value in predicting the likely level or volatility of the return on a particular asset class for the next 12 months may be sadly mistaken. It is true that markets never seem to perform in the way they are expected to perform, and when a forecaster seems to be doing well he or she may be only weeks or months away from failure and dismissal. Individuals such as Joe Granville, Elaine Gazzarelli, or, more recently, Abby Cohen or Herbert Kerschner have at least two things in common. First, they were at one point or other exceptionally successful in predicting certain market developments. Second, they also missed important turns. The surprise should be, not about the fact that they missed some forecast, but about the fact that they proved to be prescient at some point and for a reasonable period of time.

What, then, can be considered a reasonable goal? It may be hard to develop absolute return insights, which I define here as forecasting long-term to medium-term market returns at any particular point. It may actually be easier to create the right 'predicted hierarchy of returns' among individual asset classes or strategies. Specifically, I may not be able to tell whether equities will generate 5% or 15% returns in the next several years, but I may well be able to tell that equities will generate 2% to 3% more than bonds. At a more detailed level, it is possible, using the same logic, to identify the relative expected returns of large-capitalization equities in the Eurozone and of high-yield U.S. dollar bonds, for instance. Finally, the same general principle applies to a discussion of risk.

The goal of the forecasting process is not to arrive at solid 'point forecasts,' but rather to establish appropriate hierarchies of return and risk forecasts, *based on a common set of assumptions*.

Note that generating the right hierarchy is just as effective in terms of strategic investment planning as having the ability to forecast with a great deal of precision and sharpness. Indeed, the goal of the strategic process is to construct a long-term mix of assets, strategies, and locations that satisfies the investor's return expectations and, at least equally importantly, his or her risk tolerance. Assume, for example, that we have the right hierarchy, but we are off by 2% in terms of actual levels. We may be modestly surprised or disappointed by the actual return outcome, but we will still have held the right mix of assets and strategies if they performed reasonably in line with expectations *relative to one another*. By contrast, trying to be very precise and getting certain forecasts right, but others substantially wrong, could wreak havoc on the strategic asset allocation and location analysis that they drove.

Redefining one's goal away from an unachievable fantasy, and toward a more modest and more realistic target, is a very important element of the process. Further, because that goal is realistic, that in itself is a very strong reason to design and follow a systematic forecasting framework.

Reacting to surprises or disappointments

The appropriate hierarchy among assets and strategies is one that is based on a common set of assumptions, allowing us to 'climb back up the decision tree' when we are surprised by actual developments. Let me take a simple example to illustrate the point.

> A number of years ago, I was a security analyst and covered Philippine oil stocks, among others. These stocks were seemingly selling at very compelling valuations, involving low price-earnings ratios and, more importantly in that industry, very cheap reserves of oil in the ground. Initially, these stocks did very well, reflecting the fact that the country desperately needed cheap oil, given its large external deficits. One day, however, the stocks started going down and then they languished for quite some time. The catalyst had been an operational mistake, driven by political dictates, which had led to overpumping and losing some of the value of the reserves. The poor performance of the stocks was a clear disappointment, but having a clear set of assumptions behind our analysis made it possible to look ahead. We could see, first, that they were not going to go into bankruptcy and, second, that they represented value, based on a clear valuation model. Holding on to the stocks was made considerably easier and, eventually, they rewarded our patience. Without a well-defined model allowing one to keep confidence in companies in the face of adversity, it would probably not have been possible to hold the stocks and eventually profit.

When an outcome is significantly different from the original expectations, knowing specifically what assumptions have been made allows one to identify whether the surprise is due to a faulty assumption or to genuinely surprising market behavior. Understanding the difference between the two is absolutely critical, as a faulty assumption needs to be addressed, while you may simply need to wait out surprising market behavior. Recall the psychological tendency to be overconfident and optimistic, to overreact to chance events, and to have a selective memory when analyzing the past, and you will clearly appreciate the importance of having a well-defined forecasting framework with explicit assumptions.

Forecasters also need, from time to time, to react to anticipated changes.

> More than 20 years ago, I was one of four analysts at J.P. Morgan in Tokyo. Patrick Flavin, the head of the office, had assigned specific parts of the Japanese economy to each of us to monitor. One day, he was asked by the London-based director of international research to look into the consequences for Japan of a possibly substantial hike in oil prices. As analysts, we retreated to our own corners and first worked independently on our individually assigned parts of the economy. We then regrouped at the end of the week to discuss our findings. Three of us came up with projections that showed substantial changes in forecasts for the rate of inflation, the external accounts, corporate profitability, and consumer spending. One of us was an older Japanese gentleman, who was in charge of the forecast for capital spending. When his turn came to discuss the impact of

much higher oil prices, he surprised everyone else in the room by announcing that it would cause no change. We could not understand his conclusion. His eventual explanation serves, for me at least, as a strong argument for having structure in forecasts: 'my friend at the Economic Planning Agency says that it will not happen.' He could not evaluate the impact of a change of assumption because his forecast was totally intuitive. He did not have an architecture that would allow him to proceed from assumptions, through basic relationships, to related outcomes.

Now, let us fast-forward to the relatively recent past. Take yourself back to 1999, when many claimed that equity prices were going to keep on climbing forever because of a structural change to a 'new economy.'[2] Assume that you believed that the economy had changed for the better and that such a change should promote higher prospective equity returns. How much higher? Quite a few investors thought that returns twice as high as the historical norm was the right answer. Others went even further. Meanwhile, the careful analyst who built a forecast for equity prices based on a formal link to corporate profitability, through economic growth, sales growth, and profit margins, would have been heeding Alan Greenspan's comment on 'irrational exuberance.' A similar analysis, conducted in 2001, after a substantial bloodshed in technology stocks, would allow the rational investor to retain some confidence in a strategic allocation, or change it, by now reducing their strategic equity exposure.

Having confidence in a current forecast is one of the most critical elements of the strategic asset allocation process. Individuals need to be able to rely on some basic architecture to reduce the temptation to depend upon subjective perceptions. Having that framework will likely reduce the decision risk. It would be an overstatement to argue that having a solid framework will totally eliminate decision risk, as such processes do not remove our psychological shortcomings. However, they do offer considerable help, particularly to the investment advisor or to the leader of a family. We cannot expect to do away with biases, but we can take people through some logic and help them realize that they may have a bias. An even less ambitious goal would still be highly commendable: shaking the certainty associated with a perception that has no basis in fact, and raising confidence in an alternative forecast that reflects well thought-out assumptions and basic relationships.

Education

An interesting by-product of such a process is its educational value. Though education is an absolutely essential part of the wealth management process, it must be approached in the right spirit. As the father of four wonderful children, I can attest, based on an admittedly limited sample, to the fact that children, adolescents, and even young adults learn best when they *want* to learn. This requires two important ingredients: first, they need to be aware that there are things that they do not know, but should know; and, second, they need to see a purpose to the effort of learning.

Experience suggests that it is considerably easier for most individuals to learn about capital markets, investment strategies or even broad portfolio construction issues when they are most relevant. They tend to be most relevant when we start discussing the need for rational expectations, and when the investor can see why he or she needs to develop these expectations and looks for some historical or structural ground for going through the process. Addressing investment education at other times, almost as a separate topic, often strikes them as irrelevant or too theoretical, particularly when these individuals are not naturally attracted to the first two phases of the wealth management process, understanding and planning, and would rather move immediately to implementation.

We have a great opportunity to educate when investors are keen to understand why certain forecasts are made and why they may be different from their intuitive expectations. We can begin to discuss the key relationships between a few basic macroeconomic variables and the investment returns that investors see plastered across the newspaper every day. We can begin to discuss the notion of risk, and the relationship between risk and time horizon; the differences between an asset class and a variety of subsets of these main classes; the difference between an asset class and a strategy; and even the role of the investment manager, and the limits to what a manager can do when markets do or do not cooperate. I have found this to be an invaluable opportunity with the families with whom I work and, in fact, the leader of one such family requires me to send directly to him the full set of assumptions whenever they change. He wants to be sure he is fully in the loop. Note that he is under no false impression that the forecast is likely to come to pass: he fully understands that we are not to rely unduly on any specific numbers. Yet he has totally bought into the concept that the overall set of assumptions has strong internal consistency and is designed for any 'what if' analysis he might want us to do.

Thinking back to the Singapore family office mentioned in the Introduction, I catch myself wishing that I had had such a framework then, and wondering whether I could have used it to help educate the principal on capital market realities and thus helped him formulate rational expectations. In fact, I worked with another very substantial Singaporean investor a few years ago and saw then that he also found it difficult to understand the difference between marketing hype and reality. Knowing the impact that the 1998 crisis had on his wealth (still considerable, but somewhat less than a few years earlier), I wonder whether a more systematic approach would have made it easier for me to convey the critical message. I could thus have redirected his strategy toward more realistic and less risky approaches.

The value added to a systematic process

The final reason for having a framework has to do with the idea that any systematic process is better than none. Let me illustrate this idea.

The scene takes place in early 1987 in Melbourne, Australia. My colleagues and I had realized that our tactical asset allocation skills were at best somewhat limited, and yet we were intuitively aware of two facts. First, there had to be a way to make modest adjustments in diversified portfolios, in response to market developments, in order to earn additional value added for our clients. Second, our clients expected us to be able to both make these adjustments and to discuss them, as the industry, at that time, had not yet bought into the now widely accepted idea that security selection dominates relative manager performance.

We created a tactical model that functioned as a derivative overlay on top of asset class-specific subportfolios, where we only varied the dollar commitments to keep the portfolio balance around the neutral position. I was told a year ago by one of my former colleagues that the overlay portfolio, which could go from being 50% short one of the two assets (domestic equities and domestic bonds) to 150% long either of them, had a 10-year record that made it the best in its class and the best within the J.P. Morgan stable of tactical asset allocation tools.

The interesting facet, given our broader focus on the value of a systematic process, is that the initial incarnation of the model involved no formal insightful predicting effort. It used a risk premium approach to allocate between bonds and equities, but the fact is that the dividend discount rate used to compute that risk premium was based on a very simple rule, using a straight-line estimate of earnings growth over the ensuing two years and then a scaled convergence to some long-term value. The market earnings estimates for the current year were only adjusted when the year-to-date data made it clear that we would over- or undershoot our long-term trend. Though we eventually refined our analysis substantially, the performance of the model in the early days was still quite good.

How could we create value added, given the fact that we did not claim to have any insight? I believe that the answer is twofold. First, the fact that the model was systematic provided a discipline to our decisions and thus made us less likely to react like lemmings on the edge of a cliff. Second, the short-term discipline allowed us to capture some of the random volatility that markets customarily exhibit.

We can conclude that, while simply having a discipline will not necessarily provide us with a tremendously insightful strategy, it will help us avoid mistakes. A large part of our work, when dealing with private wealth management, has to do with avoiding mistakes. The power of compound interest is such that it takes a lot to offset a mistake. We have already seen that it takes a 25% return to get back to square one after we have lost 20% of our money. Being systematic, and thus avoiding the risk of being swayed by randomness or intuitively attractive but structurally faulty arguments, is a large part of the essence of success.

I cannot help but think back to 1999, when the hype about the internet led many investors astray. I remember many a conversation during which we discussed the idea that the internet was revolutionary, but disagreed over who would benefit: the companies that seemed obvious winners then, or some other group of companies, much like those that benefited from the invention of electricity or the railroad.

More broadly, when I look back at those instances when I was able to convince investors not to make excessive investments in companies whose business models were either nonexistent or substantially flawed, I can detect a common thread. *The argument carried weight only when I was allowed to go into the specifics of developing individual earnings forecasts.* It never worked when we just focused on trying to ascertain long-term growth rates in a subjective manner.

Forecasting: purpose and inputs

We have already established that structured forecasts are arguably most useful in the context of strategic wealth planning exercises. In that endeavor, the focus is on developing both:

- a *strategic asset allocation* that maximizes the chances of meeting our long-term investment goals, expressed in both return expectations and tolerance for risk; and
- a *strategic asset location* matrix that creates the opportunity to maximize after-tax wealth across generations.

The asset location effort capitalizes on the different tax status and ownership structures of the various holding pockets that an individual investor or family can create and manage. The ultimate purpose of a capital market forecasting effort is to *plan*.

There are three principal inputs that are needed to build individual forecasts, and a fourth that might help with certain families. The first is a set of long-term, 'equilibrium' pre-tax and after-tax returns for each of the major asset classes and strategies that, we believe, are relevant and suitable in the particular case of each individual investor. Equilibrium is defined here in relation to 'normal' economic and market conditions. Specifically, this applies to periods when the overall economic environment is perceived to be neither at the peak nor at the trough of a cycle. Also, capital markets should be assumed to be valued 'normally' – neither at a peak nor at a trough of investor emotions. Such a set of assumptions is necessary to correct for predictable temporary imbalances and to permit us to believe that the returns we forecast are sustainable over the long term.

The second principal input is a set of long-term 'equilibrium' pre-tax and after-tax return volatilities for the same set of asset classes and strategies. We will see later the incremental complexity associated with the need to think in both pre-tax and after-tax terms.

The third principal input is a matrix showing the correlations among the returns of all the asset classes and strategies. The concept of correlation is the critical component of the notion of portfolio diversification. Greg Friedman (a former partner of mine and now a partner at Greycourt & Co., an investment consultant to ultra-affluent families in the United States) once came up with a wonderful analogy that illustrates this concept. Imagine a world with three companies, each making, respectively, umbrellas, raincoats, and sunglasses. Would it not be logical to think that the makers of raincoats and sunglasses would experience completely opposite business fortunes? When the sun was out, sales of sunglasses would boom, but sales of raincoats would slump; and vice versa. The maker of umbrellas would fall somewhere in between, as umbrellas can be use to protect oneself from both rain and excessive sunshine. Statisticians would say that the correlation between the fortunes of the markets for raincoats and sunglasses is high and negative, while the correlation between the fortunes of either of them and those of umbrella manufacturers is modest and positive.

A fourth set of variables, a small number of medium-term 'modifiers' principally relating to key economic or market variables, may allow you to modify the long-term forecasts for particular structural imbalances perceived to apply at the point when the analysis is made. This helps when dealing with individual clients, as it promotes the image that the model is neither static nor detached from real life.

All this should ensure that the bulk of the precious conversation time available with an investor is spent on matters other than arguing capital market assumptions in absolute terms. Very valuable time may, however, be spent discussing the impact on long-term return and risk expectations of both structural changes and the current environment. However, one should be mindful that short-term to medium-term modifiers can introduce errors if they are not calibrated with a significant amount of humility.

Forecasting: three major principles

Forecasting capital markets is certainly not a science, although one should probably add that it is also not strictly an art form. It is important to understand the three major areas on which we need to focus: fundamental quantitative requirements, a hierarchy of influence, and the need for consistency and predictability.

Fundamental quantitative requirements

From a quantitative standpoint, our model will need to provide us with the first three sources of data just discussed: estimates of return and of the expected volatility of that return, as well as a correlation matrix covering the relationships between all pairs of assets and strategies. This latter requirement reflects the fact that *the volatility of the return on a portfolio comprising exposures to assets A and B is not equal to the weighted average of the two assets' individual volatility*. Rather, it reflects the extent to which the prices of the assets move together or not, and, for the quantitatively curious, is given by the formula:

$$\sigma^2_{A+B} = (W_A * \sigma_A)^2 + (W_B * \sigma_B)^2 + 2 * \rho_{AB} * [(W_A * \sigma_A) * (W_B * \sigma_B)],$$
where
σ_A and σ_B are the standard deviations of the respective average returns on assets A and B;
ρ_{AB} is the correlation coefficient describing the extent to which the returns on each of the two assets tend or do not tend to move together; and
W_A and W_B are the weights of assets A and B in the portfolio. The term $\rho_{AB} * (\sigma_A * \sigma_B)$ is called the covariance between the two assets.

One needs specific covariance forecasts to be able to calculate expected portfolio risk. The problem becomes even more challenging if the capital market forecasts are to be used in the context of portfolio optimization, when the correlation matrix needs to meet certain conditions. Mathematicians tell us that the matrix needs to be 'square' and 'nonsingular.' In practice, this should be translated as follows. First, a correlation matrix computed on the basis of historical data will always satisfy the required conditions. Second, it is unlikely, though not impossible, for a matrix whose cells are filled in subjectively to meet the required conditions, because we need each pair of data points to have relationships consistent with those implicit in the relationships of all other pairs. A specific additional procedure is typically needed to make the matrix conform to the required conditions, and that procedure may result in substantial changes needed in selected cells.

Computing the expected return of a portfolio of assets or strategies will be considerably easier than evaluating its risk, as the return of a combination of assets or strategies is equal to the weighted average return of its components.

Note that dealing with individual investors forces us to think differently and diverge from the well trodden paths of institutional asset managers. In the institutional asset world, going beyond the pure asset or sub-asset class is not absolutely necessary, because the strategic asset allocation process is applied in a pre-tax context. One can make the simplifying assumption that management fees and manager value added will be incorporated in one single net step, at the end of the process. Taxable individual investors do not have that luxury. They must worry about after-tax return and risk expectations.

Bill Reichenstein aptly notes in a recent article[3] that the introduction of taxes lead investors to share both risk and return with the tax authorities in the jurisdiction in which they reside. He observes that the individual's share of return and risk depends upon his or her approach to investing. More specifically, you need to focus on the interaction between manager activity and asset class characteristics. Thus, for instance, you would need to identify at least two distinct investment strategies for large-capitalization equities, depending upon whether the manager follows a tax-sensitive investment process or a tax-oblivious one.

In summary, then, when dealing with strategic asset allocation issues, individual investors need to evaluate the actual investments among which they will need to choose, rather than a theoretical set of market opportunities.

A hierarchy of influence

Given the fact that certain inputs seem easier to obtain than others, it is worth noting that inputs are not created equal. Indeed, as Vijay Chopra and William Ziemba[4] have argued, certain input errors are more important than others. Recognizing that forecasting errors are unfortunately a part of the landscape, Chopra and Ziemba asked themselves which of the three generic forecasts they needed to make would have the greatest impact on the results potentially derived from these faulty forecasts. These three variables were return, risk, and correlation, studied here through their covariances. Their work suggests that the most important statistic for a forecaster to get right is the mean return.

Jarl Kallberg and William Ziemba[5] suggest that errors in means are about 10 times as important as errors in variances (the variance of a statistical series is the square of the standard deviation of the series) and covariances. More to the point, they conclude that:

> the primary emphasis should be on obtaining superior estimates of means, followed by good estimates of variances. Estimates of covariances are the least important in terms of their influence on the optimal portfolio.

The need for consistency and predictability

We have established that the main reasons for having such a framework are the development of a reasonable hierarchy of expectations, the need to be able to react to surprises or change, the need to be able to educate investors, and, simply, the benefit associated with a formal framework when others may simply be guessing. This requires our framework to provide us with understandable results and to maintain total internal consistency across the various forecasts. A robust forecasting framework should therefore have at least three critical attributes: clarity of architecture, clarity of assumptions and clarity of perspective.

Clarity of architecture

Our first challenge is to firm up in our mind the various relationships in which we believe, philosophically. Going through that process will force you also to have gone through an analysis of history and a review of the structural changes that might take place, making history no longer the best guide.

The late John Weed (my first direct boss at J.P. Morgan and subsequently a good friend) taught me that the forecast itself is less important than the process. His point was simple, relating to individual company analysis, but yet fully applicable to our topic. You can debate a few basis points *ad nauseam*, but in the end you will have learned nothing. Debate the behavior of the components and you will understand your company well, and will be able to react as and when events surprise you.

The model that I have developed for my own use defines a clear hierarchy of forecasts, postulating that the universe of investable strategies can be broken down into three simple groups.

The first of these groups comprises the three base asset classes on which the whole model

Exhibit 8.1

Four critical building blocks

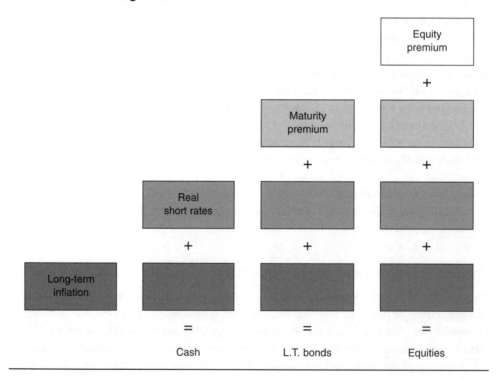

Exhibit 8.2

Two paths to an investment strategy

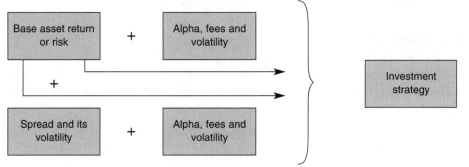

rests: cash, bonds, and equities. These are themselves defined based on four simple econometric building blocks, as illustrated in Exhibit 8.1.

The second group comprises a number of sub-asset classes, which, going back to Jeffrey Horvitz's point (mentioned in Chapter 7), are not sufficiently different from one another to be considered fully-fledged asset classes and yet deserve to be analyzed individually. These sub-asset classes are defined relative to the base asset classes through return and volatility spreads.

The third group comprises individual investment strategies, which are the actual portfolio building blocks. They are defined relative to the relevant asset or sub-asset classes, by adding manager value added and tracking error to the base returns and risk, as illustrated in Exhibit 8.2. Note that we also take fees and tax efficiency into account, and that this universe encompasses both traditional and nontraditional strategies.[6]

Clarity of architecture is particularly important when dealing with individual investors, as it usually is the starting point of any education process. Being able to discuss historical as well as prospective relationships, both between individual asset classes and strategies, and between them and the underlying economy, is a crucial ingredient. Consider the situation of the entrepreneur who has recently become liquid. He or she will need to be able to relate these new insights to the world that he or she knew previously. The connection between individual forecasts and the broad economy, the ability to discuss the difference between a security and a piece of a real business, and the relationship between history and the future are three major ingredients of our educational effort. Understanding the relationship between the economy and capital markets is made particularly difficult by the fact that we need to explain the difference between a security and the underlying business.

Very often, but particularly in the case of investors holding concentrated positions, I have found it crucial for the investor to appreciate that owning a stock, for instance, is totally different from owning a piece of a business. The critical insight is that there are two drivers to the value of a security: its intrinsic value and, more importantly, the price that someone is willing to offer to buy it from you. That price should reflect the company's underlying value, but it will not always do so, because of the distortions associated with the discounting of future prospects. Being able to appreciate that I have no real control over the fortunes of the underlying company and that I cannot sell it for more than someone else is willing to pay is one of the most important lessons. That lesson is much easier to understand when you have taken the time to identify the two drivers of value, and thus to show the nature and limitations of the connection between capital markets and the underlying economy.

Clarity of assumptions

Having a well-specified and logical architecture naturally leads to the need to understand each assumption fully, and to have evaluated it on its merits. There is always the temptation to tailor the assumption to the ultimate forecast you wish to see, but that should be resisted at all costs.

In Hong Kong in late 1981 the property market appeared overheated, but people were predicting major structural changes that would lead to an ever growing demand for quality office space: more trade with China and a great increase in the number of branches of foreign banks in Hong Kong. Focusing on the main drivers of the supply and demand for property, including the structural changes that were indeed taking place, suggested that a substantial oversupply was looming. Getting to that point required a few heroic assumptions, which were critical to being able to convince portfolio managers of the risk, despite an almost universal disagreement with that view on the part of the investment community. In the end, though we were early forecasting a bear market in the spring of 1982, the major decline in the fall of that year validated the forecast.

This example shows that the ultimate investment conclusion will have to rely on assumptions, a few of which may require fairly sizeable leaps of faith. Yet having these assumptions in black and white makes it possible for two processes to take place. The first might be called 'submission to Cartesian doubt,' while the second has to do with the ability to review and change assumptions over time, as circumstances or insights evolve. Seeing all the critical assumptions in black and white is an important element of the reality test, during which you will exercise intellectual honesty and ask how these estimates look, both individually and collectively. It will also allow you to have a rich and meaningful discussion with the investor or the family, and focus the discussion on items that usually do not inflame passions.

The set of assumptions therefore must be complete and internally consistent, as individual investors will often want to consider a broad investment universe comprising both traditional and nontraditional assets or strategies.[7] In the case of the model I have developed, my set incorporates both the drivers of the four basic building blocks and the various spreads, tracking error, manager value added, and risk, which allow me to proceed to the ultimate set of investment strategies to be considered by my investor client.

As an illustration, it might be worth looking at the way in which the four components of the base asset class return forecasts are defined.

First, *equilibrium inflation* is the long-term inflation level or target suitable for the relevant country. In a global capital market forecasting framework, we must start from some view of global equilibrium inflation and ensure that the main regional blocs that one defines have internally consistent, block-specific inflation assumptions. Beside a careful study of historical trends, there are several variables that one may consider when developing an equilibrium inflation forecast. The following three seem most helpful: flexibility of labor markets, freedom from government regulation, and the extent to which a country espouses a free trade philosophy. The first two go hand in hand and will tend to exert downward pressure on prices, particularly in a free trade environment.

Second, *real short-term interest rates* (short-term interest rates less inflation) are calculated to be consistent with noninflationary growth at that country's or bloc's potential GDP rate. Again, in the case of a global model, it is necessary to consider global equilibrium conditions. Though there are many variables that you might consider, you might select the following four, which seem the most relevant. The first two to be mentioned are labor force growth (population growth and participation rate) and evolution in the labor/capital ratio, which both have a direct impact on the extent to which the country can grow its production. The more excess capacity a country has now, or is likely to have in the future, the lower the inflationary pressures and thus the more flexibility afforded to its central bank to follow an accommodating monetary policy. The third is the global competitiveness of the country, which can generate insights as to the likely trade flows influencing the policy adopted by the central bank. Finally, the independence of the central bank and its determination to keep inflation under control play an important role.

Third, *maturity premium* is the spread between short- and long-term government bonds. When building a global model, it is useful to define long-term bonds as having a 10-year maturity, as that is the most common government bond benchmark around the world. The recent changes in outstanding U.S. Treasury bond balances make the choice even more logical. The maturity premium can be viewed as the excess return that an investor requires to take the price risk associated with the longer maturity. The two major risks that a longer-term bond investor is taking relate to inflation expectations, and to likely changes in the supply and demand for bonds. One might consider the indebtedness of the government, the general direction of fiscal policy, and factors that might trigger a change in inflation expectations. At the margin, an investor might also need to be concerned with the liquidity of the bond market. A liquid market allows the investor to sell the position if he or she perceives changes in fundamentals, something that an illiquid market does not allow. It makes sense to build an 'illiquidity premium' into the maturity premium.

Fourth, the *equity premium* is defined as the excess return required by an investor to accept the twin incremental risks associated with equity, relative to a long-term strategy of only investing in bonds: the volatility of the dividend and the lack of a fixed terminal value. This is probably one of the most difficult assumptions to finalize, as there has been considerable debate on the appropriate level for the equity premium.[8] History does not really help much.

Without these clear assumptions, the debate usually turns to a discussion of individual numbers, most of which cannot be seriously evaluated. At best, their reasonableness can be gauged relative to the past, recent or not, and you are exposed to the risk of extrapolation, or of failing to account for an important structural change.

Clarity of perspective
The final element of the equation is to be clear about what you are trying to accomplish with the forecasting framework. Explicitly, this also involves a clear understanding of what you

Exhibit 8.3

Examples of return and risk forecasts for 42 strategies (%)

	Pre-tax return	*Pre-tax risk*	*After-tax return*	*After-tax risk*	*Tax efficiency*
Cash and equivalents					
Taxable U.S. dollar cash	5.20	2.63	3.12	1.58	60.0
Tax-exempt U.S. dollar cash	3.90	2.63	3.90	2.63	100.0
Fixed-income instruments					
Tax-exempt U.S. bonds – active	5.06	8.65	4.91	8.39	97.0
Tax-exempt U.S. bonds – passive	4.69	8.51	4.69	8.51	100.0
Taxable U.S. government and corporate bonds – passive	6.53	7.82	4.08	4.89	62.5
Taxable U.S. government and corporate bonds – active	7.59	8.24	4.74	5.15	62.5
Taxable multistrategy bonds – active	7.95	9.32	4.97	5.83	62.5
Non-U.S. government bonds – passive, hedged	6.76	8.51	4.23	5.32	62.5
Non-U.S. government bonds – active, hedged	7.26	8.65	4.54	5.41	62.5
Emerging market debt – active	17.00	12.32	10.63	7.70	62.5
High-yield debt – active	9.25	7.81	5.78	4.88	62.5
Equities					
U.S. large-capitalization – active	11.40	16.24	7.98	11.37	70.0
U.S. large-capitalization – active core	10.25	14.82	8.20	11.86	80.0
U.S. large-capitalization – index plus	9.75	14.48	9.26	13.75	95.0
U.S. large-capitalization – passive	9.00	14.41	9.00	14.41	100.0
U.S. small-capitalization – active	14.40	24.12	10.08	16.89	70.0
U.S. small-capitalization – passive	12.00	22.93	12.00	22.93	100.0
Diversified non-U.S. – active	11.79	17.80	8.26	12.46	70.0
Diversified non-U.S. – active core	10.64	16.52	8.51	13.22	80.0
Diversified non-U.S. – index plus	10.14	16.21	9.64	15.40	95.0
Diversified non-U.S. – passive	9.39	16.15	9.39	16.15	100.0
European – active	13.03	17.80	9.12	12.46	70.0
Japanese – active	13.65	17.80	13.65	17.80	100.0
International small-capitalization – active	14.25	24.12	9.97	16.89	70.0
International small-capitalization – passive	13.10	22.93	13.10	22.93	100.0
Emerging market – passive	13.75	21.92	9.63	15.34	70.0
Emerging market – active	16.15	23.16	16.15	23.16	100.0
Alternative investments					
Private equity and venture capital	17.25	23.77	13.80	19.01	80.0
Nondirectional multistrategy	14.50	4.10	9.06	2.56	62.5
Directional multistrategy	17.25	13.25	11.21	8.61	65.0
Arbitrage	11.00	4.77	6.88	2.98	62.5

Exhibit 8.3 *continued*

Examples of return and risk forecasts for 42 strategies (%)

	Pre-tax return	*Pre-tax risk*	*After-tax return*	*After-tax risk*	*Tax efficiency*
Alternative investments *continued*					
Security nondirectional	13.00	5.64	8.13	3.52	62.5
Fixed-income directional	10.25	10.57	6.41	6.61	62.5
Equity directional	13.25	17.53	8.61	11.40	65.0
Short-sellers	9.75	20.08	6.34	13.05	65.0
Emerging markets	22.00	23.33	14.30	15.16	65.0
Sector-directional	13.25	17.53	8.61	11.40	65.0
Macrodirectional	15.31	19.21	9.19	11.53	60.0
Managed futures	12.50	10.33	8.25	6.82	66.0
Precious metals	4.50	9.00	4.50	9.00	100.0
Commodities	7.50	7.14	5.40	5.14	72.0
U.S. real estate – passive	11.50	7.04	10.93	6.69	95.0

are *not* trying to do. At issue here is the simple truth that no one has a solid, consistent predictive capability. Andrew Cormie (then a portfolio manager specialized in Australian equities in J.P. Morgan's Melbourne office) used to say that if you are going to forecast, forecast long-term or forecast often. His insight is that a healthy dose of humility is required for a forecaster to survive. However, as noted earlier, knowing that one is not always going to be right is no excuse for not trying. There is value in just applying a discipline where others may just be guessing. Making sure that you keep the debate focused on the hierarchy of returns, the relationship between return and risks, and the nature of the relationship between the expected returns of distinct asset classes and strategies ensures that the forecasts eventually derived through your model will be useful.

Exhibit 8.3 presents the set of forecasts that this model currently generates. The point of the table is clearly not to suggest that any of these individual forecasts offer any particular insight into the future of capital markets, now or at some future point. Rather, it is meant to illustrate the ability that such a model provides to create a set of internally consistent and rational capital market expectations, given a certain set of assumptions. Personally, I have found them invaluable, principally in helping individual investors get a solid handle on what to expect and what not to expect, and thus to move away from simple extrapolation from the recent past.

Summary and implications

Experience suggests that capital market developments are, at best, partially random, except in the very long term, and that the reliability of return and risk expectations formulated for short terms and medium terms is therefore always somewhat doubtful. Also, we saw earlier that the error rate in the investment management industry is substantial, which suggests that some humility is appropriate: your expectations will probably prove at least somewhat erroneous, if not completely off the mark. Yet this should not discourage you from trying. Indeed, the important aspect of the forecast is not that each individual element of the forecast be right, but that some hierarchy among the various elements be valid, even if actual numbers turn out to be wrong. When that hierarchy is preserved, optimization results based on these forecasts will likely hold, though overall expected risk and return statistics forecast for the portfolio as a whole may prove optimistic or pessimistic.

Further, it is equally important to appreciate that change will remain the only constant. As more information becomes available, and as errors are recognized, it is critical that the model or framework used to forecast capital market circumstances allows for consistent reflection of these required changes across all the individual forecasts. You can think of this in terms of a 'decision tree.' At some point, it will become obvious that the outcome that you expect to see at the end of a given branch of the tree will not happen. You will then want to be able to go back along the path you followed and make the changes that are needed. The ability to point to consistency and predictability is essential to any effort to develop rational capital market expectations.

---

[1] For a discussion of market bubbles, as one way in which recent trends can be extrapolated into excessive price movements, see Bierman, Harold, Jr., 'Bubbles, Theory, and Market Timing,' *The Journal of Portfolio Management*, Fall 1995, pp. 54–56. Another example is provided in Nesbitt, Stephen L., 'Buy High, Sell Low: Timing Errors in Mutual Fund Allocations,' *The Journal of Portfolio Management*, Fall 1995, pp. 57–61.

[2] At this point, it might be worth revisiting an article referenced in Chapter 2: Hirschey, Mark, 'How Much is a Tulip Worth?,' *Financial Analysts Journal*, Vol. 54, No. 4, July/August 1998, pp. 11–17.

[3] See Reichenstein, William, 'Asset Allocation and Asset Location Decisions Revisited,' *The Journal of Wealth Management*, Summer 2001, pp. 16–26.

[4] See Chopra, Vijay K., and William T. Ziemba, 'The Effect of Errors in Means, Variances, and Covariances on Optimal Portfolio Choice,' *The Journal of Portfolio Management*, Winter 1993, pp. 6–11.

[5] Kallberg, Jarl G., and William T. Ziemba, 'Mis-Specification in Portfolio Selection Problems,' in G. Bamberg and K. Spremann eds., *Risk and Capital: Lecture Notes in Economics and Mathematical Systems*. New York: Springer-Verlag, 1984.

[6] For discussions of certain of these strategies, see Jacobs, Bruce I., and Kenneth N. Levy, 'Long/Short Equity Investing,' *The Journal of Portfolio Management*, Fall 1993, pp. 52–63; Sharpe, Marc J., 'Constructing the Optimal Hedge Fund of Funds,' *The Journal of Private Portfolio Management*, Summer 1999, pp. 35–44; and Cattanach, Katherine A., Mary Frances Kelley, and Gail Marmorstein Sweeney, 'Hidden Treasure: A Look Into Private Equity's History, Future, and Lure,' *The Journal of Private Portfolio Management*, Summer 1999, pp. 27–34.

[7] For discussions of the relationship between real and financial assets, and the role of real assets in portfolio diversification, see Froot, Kenneth A., 'Hedging Portfolios with Real Assets,' *The Journal of Portfolio Management*, Summer 1995, pp. 60–77; Anson, Mark J.P., 'Maximizing Utility with Commodity Futures Diversification,' *The Journal of Portfolio Management*, Summer 1999, pp. 86–94; Edwards, Franklin R., and Mustafa Onur Caglayan, 'Hedge Fund and Commodity Fund Investments in Bull and Bear Markets,' *The Journal of Portfolio Management*, Summer 2001, pp. 97–108.

[8] See Finnerty, John D., and Dean Lestikow, 'The Behavior of Equity and Debt Risk Premiums,' *The Journal of Portfolio Management,* Summer 1993, pp. 73–82, together with comment and reply in the Summer 1994 issue. See also Reichenstein, William, and Steven P. Rich, 'The Market Risk Premium and Long-Term Stock Returns,' *The Journal of Portfolio Management*, Summer 1993, pp. 63–72; Yamaguchi, Katsumari, 'Estimating the Equity Risk Premium from Downside Probability,' *The Journal of Portfolio Management*, Summer 1994, pp. 17–27; Siegel, Jeremy J., 'The Shrinking Equity Premium,' *The Journal of Portfolio Management*, Fall 1999, pp. 10–17.

Chapter 9

Redefining active management

The background: the active/passive debate

The world of tax-efficient investing forces us to reconsider one of our most cherished distinctions: defining active investment strategies by contrasting them with passive approaches. On the one hand, passive approaches are defined as strategies designed to mimic some index, with no expected value added relative to that index. Even in the tax-oblivious investment world, passive strategies should be expected to underperform the index they aim to replicate, as the index bears no management cost while passive mandates attract some fees. On the other hand, an active strategy is simply defined as one that is not passive. The portfolio manager aims to produce some value added relative to a reference benchmark, be that an index or a combination of indexes. That value added may be set in absolute terms or in risk-adjusted terms.

The debate in the institutional world

The debate about active or passive management[1] found its genesis in the institutional investment management industry. A greater focus on the tenets of modern portfolio theory, and the burden imposed on the management of pension funds in the United States by the Employee Retirement and Income Safety Act, raised the reasonable question as to whether investors were being fairly compensated for the fees they were paying and the incremental risk they were taking by hiring active managers. Studies suggested that outperforming a market on a risk-adjusted basis and cost-efficiently was anything but easy to achieve. Other surveys proved that the average manager does not outperform the index. In itself, this is not a remarkable conclusion, given the fact that money managers account for the bulk of the market. They should be expected to have a hard time outperforming themselves, which would be the case if the average manager outperformed the market made up of the average of all managers.

The debate led to two main developments. First, it encouraged a strong belief that active management does not work, in the sense that it does not produce value added commensurate with the risk it involves or with the management fees associated with the mandate. Second, the debate has resulted in a proliferation of specialized strategies. Each such strategy was aimed at a narrow slice of the market, where the potential to generate value added seemed more believable. The process keeps iterating itself into infinity, as each step leads to the suggestion that managers are unable, or find it extremely hard, to add value. That suggestion, even at a narrower level, triggers a further inward iteration into the next level of specialization.

Extending the debate into the world of private wealth management

Following a trend that has been repeated over and over, the debate, over time, has shifted to the individual wealth management scene, using paradigms firmly established within the institutional management world. The question of 'bang for the buck' arose in the world of the individual investor as well. Yet it did not necessarily involve thinking about the circumstances that can make life different within the private wealth management sphere. A bull market dominated by a few large-capitalization stocks predictably made the task of the advocates of passive management easier, as it made active investment managers look particularly weak against indexes weighted by market capitalization. Similarly, the typical greed pointing to the much greater cheapness of index management drew support for index funds.

The move toward passive management in the private wealth management world has been accompanied by the same debate that took place in the institutional world. Yet this debate has not clarified the real issues. In fact, it has obscured them, and may have led many investors astray.

The actual performance of active managers

An analysis of historical data makes it very hard to support the conclusion that active managers as a group, or even a meaningful subset of the group, can generate significant value added. (We will come back to this point in Chapter 17, when we delve into the question of manager selection.)

William Fender and Brian Cunningham[2] provide useful statistics on the record of active managers. In particular, they quote a study by John Bogle,[3] the founder of the Vanguard fund group, which suggests that the average mutual fund manager underperformed the S&P Index by 2.4% for the period 1981–96. In his study, Bogle also found that the after-tax underperformance of active managers was even more dramatic, rising to 3.3%. He suggests that the index outpaced 84% of all mutual funds on a pre-tax basis, while 92% of the mutual funds

Exhibit 9.1

Relative pre-tax performances of active equity managers for periods ending December 31, 1998 (%)

	Three years	Five years	Seven years	10 years	15 years	20 years
S&P 500	28.2	24.1	19.5	19.2	17.9	17.8
Median Manager	24.0	19.8	16.6	17.1	15.7	16.5
Underperformance	*4.2*	*4.3*	*2.9*	*2.1*	*2.2*	*1.3*
20th percentile manager	27.1	22.3	18.2	18.9	17.0	18.0
Relative performance	*(1.1)*	*(0.8)*	*(1.3)*	*(0.3)*	*(0.9)*	*0.2*
10th percentile manager	30.0	24.1	18.8	20.6	17.5	19.7
Relative performance	*1.8*	*0.0*	*(0.7)*	*1.4*	*(0.4)*	*1.9*
First percentile manager	42.2	29.6	22.6	26.0	19.8	21.2
Relative performance	*14.0*	*5.5*	*3.1*	*6.8*	*1.9*	*3.4*

Sources: William E. Fender and Brian P. Cunningham; author.

fell behind the index on an after-tax basis. Exhibit 9.1, which uses data compiled by Callan Associates, Inc. representing a relevant sampling of large-capitalization mutual funds, confirms these findings, suggesting that underperformance of equity managers has been rampant both over the past 20 years and during rolling sub-periods. The typical 20th percentile manager – that is, one who did better than 80% of the peer group – still typically underperformed the index, though by a margin that roughly approximated the typical mutual fund fee.

Similar analyses can be carried out across other asset classes. Exhibit 9.2, for instance, depicts the results of an analysis carried out from the Morningstar universe, using the Morningstar Principia database. It shows the number of mutual funds outperforming the relevant index in each of three different additional asset classes: U.S. small-capitalization stocks, taxable (government and corporate) bonds, and municipal bonds, the latter analyzed on a national basis.

These results suggest two broad conclusions, neither of which contradicts the evidence presented so far against active managers:[4]

- small-capitalization stock managers seem to have a better relative performance record than their competitors who focus on large-capitalization stocks; and
- fixed-income portfolio managers fare considerably less well, but this may be in part due to the fact that the lower scope for value added in the investment grade world still has to absorb mutual fund management fees.

More generally, the data seems to support the notion that, on a pre-tax basis at least, the claim that active managers can broadly add value is somewhat hard to prove. This in turn suggests that believing in active management is more akin to an act of faith.[5]

Exhibit 9.2

Relative performances of selected managers in U.S. mutual funds for periods ending November 20, 2000

	One year	Three years	Five years	10 years	15 years
Small-capitalization equities					
Number of outperforming managers	650	427	228	51	30
Total number of managers	1078	822	474	148	77
Outperformance percentile	*60*	*51*	*48*	*34*	*38*
Government/corporate bonds					
Number of outperforming managers	114	75	62	25	8
Total number of managers	936	789	583	160	64
Outperformance percentile	*12*	*9*	*10*	*15*	*12*
Municipal bonds					
Number of outperforming managers	45	9	8	12	9
Total number of managers	545	491	416	158	84
Outperformance percentile	*8*	*1*	*1*	*7*	*10*

Source: Author's compilation, data from Morningstar Principia Pro Database.

Exhibit 9.3

Relative after-tax performance of active equity managers for periods ending December 31, 1998

	Three years	Five years	Seven years	10 years	15 years	20 years
S&P 500	28.2	24.1	19.5	19.2	17.9	17.8
Pre-tax requirement	32.2	27.4	22.2	21.8	20.2	20.1
Outperforming percentile	*5*	*3*	*2*	*4*	*1*	*7*

Source: Fender and Cunningham.

Fender and Cunningham extended their analysis to after-tax results. By doing so, they came up with evidence that seemed to be more damning for active managers, and that generally fit with the data shown by Bogle. They define the concept of 'pre-tax requirement' as the pre-tax return that would be required for a mutual fund to produce an after-tax return that equaled the S&P 500 index returns. Exhibit 9.3 demonstrates that the bar is indeed even higher when it comes to after-tax returns.

Refining the analysis: comparing the index and index funds

Though the evidence that outperforming an index is a rare achievement certainly seems compelling, it is worth noting that the dice are more than partially loaded. Conclusions should be taken with at least one caveat: the results of the industry incorporate fees, while the unmanaged index does not. Thus, a better basis for analysis would be a comparison between managed portfolios and index funds. Exhibit 9.4 shows the result of such an analysis, using mutual funds because the data on them is relatively accessible.

In this experiment, we ranked all large-capitalization U.S. equity mutual funds, and then displayed the rank of both the unmanaged index and of a composite average index fund. Our results suggest that the case for active management is still not strong, but that the relative advantage of indexing is less compelling. In fact, the cost of indexing is more readily apparent.

The table supports two interesting conclusions. First, active managers still do not do well relative to an unmanaged index. Over one-year and three-year periods, the market index is in the 43rd and 38th percentiles, respectively: it therefore beats 57% and 62% of all managers, respectively. Second, over the same periods the average index fund is in the 49% and 48% percentiles, respectively. This means that *the average index fund therefore only beats 51% and 52% of all managers*.

The statistic is close enough to 50% to offer a much more nuanced view of the relative strength of indexing relative to active management. This shows that management fees constitute an important difference between an unmanaged index and any managed strategy. This may well be another illustration of Adam Smith's 'invisible hand,' applied to the development and success of exchange-traded funds, which offer much the same features as index mutual funds at a lower cost.

Exhibit 9.4 shows that it can be misleading for anyone to compare a manager, whose per-

Exhibit 9.4

Comparing performances of an index and index funds – pre-tax*

| | | *Actual ranking* | | *Percentile ranking* | |
| | | *Large-capitalization* | | *Large capitalization* | |
	Total number of funds	*U.S. equity index funds*	*S&P 500 Index*	*U.S. equity index funds (%)*	*S&P 500 Index (%)*
One year	353	172	151	49	43
Three years	353	171	134	48	38
Five years	236	74	54	31	23
10 years	110	33	24	30	22
15 years	72	21	11	29	15

* We selected the Morningstar Large Blend domestic equity universe and created a composite of all funds with a R-Squared to the S&P 500 Index of 1.00 to represent index funds. We then eliminated all these 'index funds' from the universe, replacing them with their average. We attempted to eliminate all double counting by keeping only one class of shares per fund, the one that produces the best return to the investor (the one with the lowest expense ratio).

Source: data from Morningstar Principia Pro Database, February 28, 2001.

formance is measured after fees, to an index, which bears no fee, and assume that one could have earned that index performance. The relevant benchmark should not be the performance of an index, to which investors do not have risk-free access.

It could be argued that index performance might be earned through the use of index futures contracts. Though the performance of the contract will, over time, mirror that of the index, the investor is taking a basis risk. (Here, the word 'basis' is meant to reflect the difference in the performance of a derivative contract relative to its underlying physical security base.) However, though index futures contracts do track the performance of the underlying index, there can be significant divergences over short periods of time, reflecting two factors: the respective supply and demand conditions in the physical and derivative markets; and the cost of arbitraging the two. Arbitraging the two can be done (and is in fact done in a hedge fund strategy called statistical – or index – arbitrage) by exchanging futures contracts for baskets of securities exactly mirroring the composition of the index. In a perfect market, the difference between owning the basket and an index futures contract should reflect the cost of money, net of dividends paid by the stocks in the basket. A futures contract does not involve a significant outlay of cash and the owner of the contract thus earns the return on the futures contract plus the interest available on the cash value of the contract. Yet index arbitrage does involve some transaction cost, and the parity between the derivative and physical markets is not perfect. Sources of basis risk therefore involve both the day-to-day fluctuation in the premium/discount of the futures contract relative to fair value and the level of that discount or premium when the investor purchases the contract and sells it. A rational investor would want to be paid for that risk, and would not consider such a strategy a risk-free way of 'owning' an index.

Exhibit 9.5

Comparing performances of an index and index funds – after tax

		Actual ranking		*Percentile ranking*	
		Large-		*Large*	
		capitalization		*capitalization*	
	Total number	*U.S. equity*	*S&P 500*	*U.S. equity*	*S&P 500*
	of funds	*index funds*	*Index*	*index funds (%)*	*Index (%)*
One year	353	155	126	44	36
Three years	353	134	94	38	27
Five years	236	50	25	21	11
10 years	110	20	10	18	9
15 years	72	13	7	18	10

Source: data from Morningstar Principia Pro Database, February 28, 2001.

Instead, the benchmark should be the performance of index mutual funds. Predictably, all of them underperform the market index, and do so by an amount that approximates their expense ratios. Note, however, that, as the time horizon lengthens, the ability of managers to add value over time is still not proven. Exhibit 9.5 shows the same analysis on an after-tax basis, and the inherently greater tax efficiency of an index fund stands out, when compared to an actively managed fund with a tax-oblivious investment process.

The problem of index biases

Before moving on, it is also worth remembering that (as noted in Chapter 7) many indexes may be 'quirky.' Selected built-in biases can make it particularly difficult for a manager to outperform an index, especially when certain market conditions prevail.

Two simple hypotheses illustrate the point. First, the data presented above would not necessarily be as bad for active managers were it not for the cyclical favor found by the stocks with the largest market capitalizations in the last few years of the 1990s. The average mutual fund has tended to own companies with average market capitalization at most equal to that of the index. Thus, any outperformance by the largest companies will predictably have a larger proportional impact on the index than on a portfolio that not own them in the same proportion as their weights in the index.

Correspondingly, it is also conceivable that the data would not be so kind to small-capitalization equity managers had small-capitalization stocks not experienced such a dreadful time over the same period (with the exception of technology and related investments). Managers, many of whom tended to follow the Nasdaq index, which affords greater weight to the technology sector, might look particularly good when comparing themselves to the Russell 2000 index, which is less heavily weighted in technology.

It follows that it is important for investors to dig somewhat more deeply into the specifics of both the relevant index and the portfolio they are analyzing, to ensure that their conclusions do not fall victim to unintended statistical biases. Gerald Buetow and Hal Ratner discuss this issue in detail,[6] and, despite their caveats with respect to style-based analysis, it does make sense to use every tool available to ensure that the performance of an active manager is appropriately and fairly analyzed. In particular, though managers should not be given credit for value added that reflects their styles or biases rather than their skills, they should not be penalized for having stayed true to their style, even if it was out of favor. The reader is encouraged to review the data in more detail, to ensure that he or she is able to discern the real picture and thus distinguish the perennial from the time- or style-dependent.

Enhanced indexing

To fight the indexing trend, the institutional investment management industry has developed 'enhanced index' portfolios.[7] Enhanced indexing, whether executed synthetically or through tilts, has attracted considerable attention, as many managers have been able to point to solid relative performance records, even when adjusted for the fact that their management fees are often double to quadruple those charged by index managers.

The objective of these strategies is to control the risk of the portfolio relative to the index (in investment jargon, to control the 'tracking error' or the 'residual risk'), while still providing some small measure of value added. This allowed the active manager to argue that the investor is not locked into the classic loser's game, since, with an index fund, you are effectively assured of earning returns that are lower than those of the index (as illustrated in Exhibits 9.4 and 9.5). An enhanced index, aiming to generate some value added relative to the index, will therefore perform better than the index fund if the expected value added is greater than the difference in the management fees of pure index versus enhanced index funds.

Several types of enhanced index funds have surfaced over the past 10 to 20 years, but they generally fall into two generic categories: synthetic index funds and tilted portfolios.

Synthetic index funds

Synthetic index funds combine index futures with individual securities, usually selected from lower-risk asset classes. In this design, a portfolio of money market securities, for instance, is actively managed with a view toward generating some value added over the three-month Treasury bill rate typically incorporated into the pricing of a three-month index future contract. Managers offering such a strategy will typically argue that a modest 25–50 basis points of value added over the Treasury bill rate is achievable because of the 'natural' spread between government securities and high-quality corporate securities. The money market portfolio is then transformed into a synthetic equity portfolio through the purchase of equity index futures, such that the face value of these future contracts is equal to the market value of the underlying money market portfolio.

Though the resulting portfolio will necessarily have some tracking error relative to the pure equity index, the expectation is that such relative volatility will be close to that typically incurred in the management of the index portfolio. This volatility arises from either the volatility of the value added earned in the physical portfolio or fluctuations in the relative valuation of the future contract relative to the index, often called 'basis risk.' Clearly, such a

151

portfolio also involves some credit risk, as investments in high-quality corporate securities are, theoretically at least, not as safe as investments in Treasury bills. However, diversification and a focus on the highest credit quality can mitigate this risk. As we are talking of the volatility of a synthetic index fund relative to the underlying index, it is worth noting that index portfolios can experience some relative volatility too.

There are two generic approaches to the construction of an index portfolio. The first, which I call *replication*, involves constructing a portfolio owning all the shares in the index, in the exact same proportion to the weight of that security in the index. This approach, though generating the lowest relative volatility, can prove complex, as it requires a proportional reinvestment of each individual cash flow, be it external (such as investor decisions to buy or sell units in the portfolio) or internal (such as income events). The second, which I call *sampling*, involves the creation of a portfolio comprising many, but not all, of the securities in the index. Statistical algorithms are used to combine these securities, such that the expected risk of the portfolio approximates the risk of the index. Though considerably cheaper to manage, such a portfolio will typically experience relative volatility, as market dynamics tend to force the portfolio constantly away from the index. This occurs as stocks included in the sample outperform or underperform the index, while stocks in the index, but not in the portfolio, outperform or underperform as well.

Though a synthetic index fund will likely experience volatility relative to the underlying index, it is not alone in this predicament. An indexed mutual fund may well also experience some volatility, though, admittedly, probably less.

Tilted individual security portfolios
Managers typically tilt the portfolio toward securities that they believe are likely to outperform the equity index. The construction of a tilted portfolio is practically similar to the sampling approach to an index portfolio.

The first objective is to approximate the risk of the index. This can be done on a total portfolio statistical basis or with selected constraints. These constraints could limit the exposure to certain risk factors (for instance, industrial sector) or the possible deviation between the weight of any security in the portfolio and its weight in the index.

The second goal is to identify factors that might lead the sample to outperform the index. You can think of tilts toward or away from dividends, growth, value, financial leverage, the use of labor, the exposure to foreign markets or other similar broad 'macro variables.'

Note that tilting the portfolio toward likely outperforming securities can be done through a tilt excluding the bottom x% of the securities that make up the index, ranked in terms of relative attractiveness, whether that ranking is derived through quantitative or qualitative means. An example illustrates this. J.P. Morgan Investment Management developed an approach where they ranked all the stocks in the large-capitalization universe in terms of dividend discount rates. These dividend discount rates reflected the opinions of their research analysts as to the respective long-term prospects for their companies and thus created a means of ranking the stocks in terms of relative attractiveness. The manager of the 'Research Enhanced Index' strategy would then select out the bottom 20% of all securities in each industry and construct a portfolio approximating the characteristics of the index using the stocks in the top 80% in each industry.

Clearly, intentionally tilted portfolios must be viewed as 'riskier' than index funds, if the definition of risk is volatility relative to the index. The risk comes from the fact that their composition involves an intentional mismatch, which could just as easily backfire as be successful.

Tax efficiency issues

Interestingly, while pure index funds are usually perceived as tax-efficient (in large measure because of a low turnover, which minimizes the rate of net capital gain realization), the tax efficiency of enhanced index funds can vary substantially.

Synthetic funds – those that include money market investments and equity index futures – *are typically broadly tax-inefficient*. The bulk of the return is earned in the form of income and short-term capital gains. The income principally arises from the money market instruments, while capital gains are created by the maturation of futures contracts, whose term rarely exceeds 90 days.

Note, however, that, in the United States, gains on futures contracts are assumed for tax purposes to be split 60/40 between long-term and short-term time horizons, and thus typically attract a 28% tax rate. Short-term capital gains on physical security transactions are usually taxed at the highest federal marginal rate.

Tilted funds can be both tax-efficient and tax-inefficient. Thus, predictably, the critical determinant of the tax efficiency of a tilted fund is the extent to which the portfolio rebalancing process, which drives the rate of capital gain realization, is designed with tax efficiency in mind or not.

Clearly, an important point to remember is that enhanced index funds are not necessarily tax-efficient and can at times be exceptionally tax-inefficient. They may outperform index funds on an after-fee, pre-tax basis, but may not when taxes are taken into consideration.

Active tax management

A different definition of active management can help move the debate forward. The basic goal of an active manager is to beat the market. On a pre-tax basis, the only way to beat the index is for the manager, consciously or not, to make bets away from the index, choosing to hold a greater exposure to certain stocks or any exposure to nonindex stocks, and, conversely, eschewing selected index stocks in whole or in part. With this approach, an active manager constructs portfolios intentionally different from an underlying index, in order to earn returns in excess of those of the index.

This definition is helpful as it focuses on the principal difference between active and passive managers. The active manager accepts the possibility of incurring tracking error, in the expectation that such tracking error will provide excess returns. The passive manager simply strives to minimize tracking error. A manager who intentionally deviates from the index is said to be active, irrespective of whether the deviation is meant to generate excess returns from sensible stock picks, or from any other decision. A passive manager seeks to minimize deviations from the index.

This dichotomy is too simplistic in the world of after-tax wealth management. To understand the point, we need to contrast the way a manager aims to beat an index on a pre-tax basis with the options available to a manager who must beat the index on an after-tax basis.

We have just seen that the only way to beat an index on a pre-tax basis is to have a higher return than the index. The manager has only one investment option: to pick securities that will do better than the index he or she seeks to beat. In the case of an equity index, the manager must select stocks that, on average will outperform the index. He or she can do this by avoiding 'index catastrophes' or selecting 'unusual winners,' or as a result of conscious industry or theme bets or some combination of these alternatives. In a fixed-income environment, the situation is analogous, except for the fact that the relative homogeneity of the pool of available securities and the considerable role of interest rate variations allows the manager a simpler choice, between individual security-driven decisions or more macro-bets (such as duration, or sensitivity to changes in the level of interest rates), which may be implemented through interest rate futures.

By contrast, outperforming an index on an after-tax basis is no longer a one-dimensional endeavour, but can come from either or both of two different efforts. The manager *may attempt to beat the market on a pre-tax basis*. The after-tax challenge therefore faced by such traditionally 'active' managers is that they must protect their pre-tax value added by not being too tax-inefficient, in order to be able to offer attractive after-tax value added. Alternatively, the manager *may seek to be more tax-efficient than the index*. The challenge faced by these managers is to avoid incurring too large a pre-tax performance drag relative to the index, such that the higher tax efficiency relative to the index would not suffice to produce some after-tax value added.

Active tax management defined

The term 'active tax management' was coined by David Stein and Premkumar Narasimhan[8] to describe this latter alternative, which, in their words, 'seeks to maximize after-tax returns through the management of taxes rather than security selection.' They contrast this approach to the traditional active manager, who can be said to be 'passive with respect to taxes.'

Note that, in both instances – active security selection or active tax management – some tracking error is allowed relative to a reference index. Yet the point of taking that tracking error is radically different. An active security selector chooses to deviate from an index in a bid to produce better returns than the index, these excess returns usually being measured on a pre-tax basis. An active tax manager deviates from an index in a bid to be more tax-efficient than the index, by harvesting the random capital losses typically produced by a broadly diversified portfolio.

The benefits of loss harvesting

Active and systematic 'loss harvesting' is an important element of active tax management. Robert Arnott, Andrew Berkin, and Jia Ye[9] conclude that:

> loss harvesting adds a great deal of value, far more than most active strategies can hope to achieve, net of trading costs and capital gains taxes. We find that loss harvesting is remarkably robust, adding substantial value over time, whether markets are volatile or quiet, strong or soft.

Investigating active tax management in more depth has to start with a question that may well be seen as iconoclastic in many quarters – and is not an easy question to ask for someone who has spent more than 25 years in the world of active investment management: what would happen if we assumed that portfolio managers do not necessarily have the ability to generate value added from security selection? This forces us to ask two further questions:

- what is the value of an unrealized capital loss?
- what is the value of active tax management?

Let us investigate these in turn, using work published by two groups of leaders in this field.

According to Arnott, Berkin, and Jia
The value of a loss is the first building block in the analysis. In fact, Robert Arnott and his colleagues divide the question into two sub-questions:

- what is the value of loss harvesting?
- how do the results depend on the characteristics of market returns?

They describe a comprehensive experiment where they kept track of individual tax lots and harvested losses monthly, clearing tax obligations in the portfolio on a quarterly basis, using a 35% blended tax rate assumption. Their experiment involved 'approximately 10 billion simulated returns on individual tax lot holdings for each simulation run' – a massive undertaking. Their results are fascinating and can be summarized in four simple points.

First, the typical value added in the first year of a loss-harvesting program can be as large as 7%, for a portfolio that is funded initially with cash. However, it quickly declines, falling below 2% per annum before three years are finished, and below 1% per annum before five years are over. Yet, despite the gradual reduction in its scope, the loss-harvesting value added provides significant long-term accumulation: after 25 years, the cumulative gain from loss harvesting is roughly 27%.

Second, although there is a small liquidation tax drag, the benefit associated with earning a return on monies that would otherwise be paid out to the government adds over 50 basis points per annum, even after 25 years. Indeed, though harvesting losses does produce a welcome tax saving, it tends to lead to an accumulation of unrealized gains, which will eventually make the portfolio harder to manage and more expensive to liquidate. Robert Arnott and his colleagues estimate that there will 'actually be a slight negative liquidation value alpha in just over 25% of the portfolio in any given month.'

Third, and predictably, the turnover associated with a loss-harvesting strategy starts high and declines over time. In fact, turnover in the first year averages 50%, since almost half the stocks in the starting portfolio fall. As those assets fall and the loss is harvested, the proceeds are reinvested in new assets, almost half of which fall, and so forth.

There are two important implications to this pattern. One is that harvesting losses is an activity to be done every day and not, as has traditionally been the case, concentrated around tax payment time (mid-April in the United States) and the closing of the tax year (December in the United States). Robert Arnott observes that:

the *so-called* tax-sensitive investment manager, who only engages in loss harvesting once a year at the end of a fiscal year, has probably seen numerous loss-harvesting opportunities appear and disappear during the course of a year.

The other implication is that there exists a 'virtuous cycle' in any sort of assiduous effort to harvest losses, whenever they occur and whenever the tax alpha is large enough to justify the round-trip trading costs for the investor. In Arnott's words:

The more careful we are about pouncing on any meaningful loss-harvesting opportunity, the longer the loss-harvesting opportunities linger into the future, due to the new loss-harvesting opportunities created from the reinvestment of loss-harvesting proceeds.

Finally, the study confirms intuition and demonstrates that:

the tax advantages associated with loss harvesting are roughly linearly related to tax rates. The 25-year benefit of simple loss harvesting yields 14% more wealth for an investor in a 35% tax bracket than simple passive investing, an impressive gain. For the investor in a 50% marginal tax bracket, this marginal improvement in wealth leaps to 20% in 25 years.

According to Stein and Narasimhan

Stein and Narasimhan[10] produce results that are generally similar to those of Arnott and his colleagues, but their experiment deserves special mention as it tackles several additional important questions. Their experiment is based on 'the management of an indexed S&P 500 portfolio over a 10-year period.' The analysis is based on 'a careful stock-by-stock simulation of the constituents of the S&P 500.' They assume a 20% capital gains tax rate.

A computer simulation creates a portfolio that perfectly tracks the S&P 500 Index each month. Stein and Narasimhan use detailed security-level information on dividends, price return, and index constituent weights for each period. Their accounting tracks the average cost basis of each security. Portfolio evaluation and index rebalancing is performed each month. They assume no trading costs and hold fractional shares.

At the beginning, the portfolio is purchased from cash to match the index precisely. Each month-end, they evaluate the portfolio. Dividends received during the month are paid into the portfolio as cash, after paying taxes, and are reinvested to reduce tracking error. Certain securities enter or leave the index due to index reconstruction or corporate actions. Securities that leave the index are cashed out, incurring a tax consequence. For simplicity and to avoid loss carry-forwards, they assume the investor has other capital gains that can offset any loss incurred. They credit the portfolio with the value of the tax savings in the case of capital losses. They use any available cash to approach the index, and then determine whether additional transactions are still needed to obtain perfect tracking.

Introducing the concept of active tax management, Stein and Narasimhan offer three sets of data to illustrate the power, and the consequences, of a systematic loss-harvesting process. These are summarized in the following three exhibits.

Exhibit 9.6 presents the performance of a perfectly indexed portfolio replicating the S&P

500 for the ten years from 1987 to 1996, assuming an initial investment of US$1 million. The tax efficiency of a pure index during that period worked out to only 90%. One can assume that this may reflect the unusually high levels of mergers and acquisitions, and of index reconstruction, during the period.

Exhibit 9.7 presents the same statistics when a first level of active tax management is introduced. Here, the sole management activity is to attempt to offset unavoidable capital gains arising, for instance, because of corporate actions or index changes. The focus of that activity is still constrained to maintain tight tracking to the index. Note that, with loss matching, annual turnover increases substantially, but tracking remains very tight.

With loss matching, the tax efficiency rises relative to pure index replication: it goes from 90% to 91.3%. Note also that the process effectively defers capital gains into the 'liquidation horizon.' In the pure indexing approach, the ratio between the market value and final cost basis was 2.26, but it rises to 2.41 in the case of loss matching.

Finally, Exhibit 9.8 presents the same portfolio statistics, using an investment

Exhibit 9.6

A perfectly indexed S&P 500 portfolio, 1987–96

	Final value (US$)	Return per year (%)
Pre-tax	4,061,000	15
After-tax		
Market value	3,551,000	13.5
Final cost basis	1,573,000	
Liquidation value	3,148,000	

Source: David Stein and Premkumar Narasimhan.

Exhibit 9.7

A loss-matching portfolio, 1987–96

	Final value (US$)	Return per year (%)
Pre-tax	4,061,000	15
After-tax		
Market value	3,598,000	13.7
Final cost basis	1,495,000	
Liquidation value	3,177,000	

Source: David Stein and Premkumar Narasimhan.

process that is more aggressive with respect to active tax management. The focus now shifts to systematic loss harvesting. The study allows the portfolio to deviate from perfect tracking. When a security leaves the index, it may be held in the portfolio, which delays its taxation. On the other hand, Stein and Narasimhan reinvest dividends in order to track the index more closely over time. Interestingly, while turnover increases beyond 4% per year, it is below that of loss matching. Further, confirming the results of the other study, Stein and Narasimhan report that:

> turnover is particularly heavy in the first year, but drops below index turnover in later years. The tracking error grows from zero to 1.5% per year, averaging 0.75% over the period.

When a portfolio no longer tracks perfectly, its performance may differ from index performance because of random price fluctuations. The simulation results that Stein and Narasimhan present have been adjusted for any such performance difference. Note that the tax efficiency of the approach over the period rises further, to 94.7%. At the same time, the ratio between the market value and final cost basis rises to 3.24.

Active tax management and underlying market movements

The results just presented are, however, dependent upon both the design of the specific experiment and the actual market conditions that prevailed during the period analyzed. We discussed earlier the idea that an unrealized loss has many of the attributes of an option, and that value is in part driven by the volatility of underlying price movements. Thus, *the actual price pattern not only of the market as a whole, but also of each individual stock, should be expected to have an impact on overall results*. David Stein and Prem Narasimhan state the idea in greater detail:

> the investor has an option to pay a capital gain tax either at the present time or in the future. This option has a value that is higher when the underlying security has a higher volatility.[11] A portfolio manager who acts as 'Maxwell's demon,' realizing losses when they occur and letting gains ride, can obtain an after-tax advantage.

It is thus important to look into the relationship between the value added provided by an active tax management process on the one hand and the actual performance of the stock market during the period over which the relationship is evaluated. Let me use the experiment carried out by Stein and Narasimhan to discuss the point.

The experiment uses a Monte Carlo simulation of stock price movements based on historical data from the U.S. stock market. The results presented in Exhibit 9.9 below estimate the value of active tax management for market scenarios that are less generous than those experienced in the experiment whose results are reported in Exhibit 9.8.

The data provide insights as to the impact of market volatility on these results. They

Exhibit 9.8

A loss-harvesting portfolio, 1987–96

	Final value (US$)	Return per year (%)
Pre-tax	4,061,000	15.0
After-tax		
Market value	3,756,000	14.2
Final cost basis	1,158,000	
Liquidation value	3,236,000	

Source: David Stein and Premkumar Narasimhan.

Exhibit 9.9

Monte Carlo estimates of the value of tax management as a function of market return and stock volatility (%)

Market return	Large-capitalization U.S. stocks, with standard deviation 25% per year	Small-capitalization and international stocks, with standard deviation 32% per year
15	0.7	1.0
8	1.2	1.5
4	1.5	1.8

Source: David Stein and Premkumar Narasimhan.

clearly illustrate the point that the value of active tax management conforms to intuitive principles, suggesting two simple observations.

First, *the value of active tax management rises as compound market returns fall*. This should not be a surprise, as lower returns will both reduce the tax drag associated with capital gain realization and slow the inexorable rise in the ratio of the portfolio's market value to its cost basis.

Second, *the value of active tax management rises as return volatility increases*. This, again, should be no surprise, as the more volatile the price of a stock or of all stocks, the more likely random price movements will cause one stock to experience an unrealized loss, which can be realized to offset some gain in another stock. This can be viewed as a validation of our earlier contention that volatility has value for a taxable investor, when used in the appropriate manner.

An important element of the problem must be incorporated into the analysis: the time dependency of the value added by active tax management. We have seen that a principle of dynamic tax efficiency is that the opportunity for harvesting tax losses decreases over time, as the ratio between the portfolio's market value and its tax basis increases. Stein and Narasimhan report that in the simulation for the years 1987–96 'the size of the loss realized (as a fraction of the market value of the portfolio) decreases from about 7% in the first year to about 0.1% in the 10th year.' Assuming lower compound returns, such as the 8% scenario described in Exhibit 9.9, they show that 'the loss realized decreases from 7% in the first year to about 1% in the 10th. In this case, there are valuable harvesting opportunities even after 10 years.'

Summary and implications

Managing assets on behalf of taxable investors again forces a reconsideration of a debate that may have been couched in overly simplistic terms. If it is true that active management relates to a process under which a manager intentionally deviates from an index in the search for superior investment returns, then there are two forms of active asset management in the taxable world.

The traditional process, oriented to security selection, remains a practical solution for taxable investors, particularly when implemented in a tax-efficient manner. At the same time, fairness requires one to note how challenging it has proven to be to make the argument that managers are able consistently to produce after-tax value added. An alternative approach can also be considered, where the focus of the portfolio management process is firmly placed on minimizing taxes. In particular, there is a higher probability of generating after-tax value added relative to an index through a smart reduction of tax drag than through the heroic pursuit of the elusive security selection alpha.

There are two types of investors for whom it might make sense to consider an active tax management strategy, devoid of any effort to select stocks expected to perform better than the market averages: investors who do not believe that 'traditional' active management can add value; and investors involved in a portfolio transition.

For investors who do not believe in 'traditional' active management

A number of investors, together with numerous investment consultants, believe that it is not reasonable for anyone to expect to be able to find a manager capable of outperforming the market consistently. They believe that active security selection is not worth the price. The evidence presented earlier at the very least demonstrates that the challenge involved in selecting such a manager is daunting. Active tax management offers a useful alternative, because of four important attributes.

First, active tax management is *usually considerably cheaper*. Whether implemented by managers whose primary business is to offer active tax management (which we will call here 'passive structured management,' to avoid the potential confusion with the traditionally defined active management), or by others whose business is founded upon superior administrative capabilities (master custodians or master trustees, for instance), passive structured management usually costs a fraction of active management. It is not unusual for passive structured fees to be substantially less than half those charged by active managers.

The only exception to this general rule might be in the case of smaller portfolios. Indeed, once the portfolio becomes small, the economics of the process shift and require the investor philosophically determined against active management to invest through a commingled vehicle, such as a mutual fund, where many of the built-in advantages of the process fade somewhat.

Second, active tax management *offers considerable administrative ease*. Though often comprising a larger number of securities than a typical portfolio managed through active stock selection, passive structured strategies relieve the investor from the chores associated with frequent detailed portfolio monitoring. Careful attention placed at regular intervals on the tracking of the portfolio relative to the underlying index will normally suffice. Specifically, the need for a detailed review of all underlying individual securities is removed, as individual stocks are viewed as a set of investment characteristics rather than as representatives of underlying businesses.

Third, active tax management *has a high probability of outperformance*, particularly early on. The data presented by both sets of authors cited above strongly suggest that a passive structured portfolio can outperform an index in a meaningful manner, provided the starting portfolio is not too overly concentrated or already suffering from substantial appreciation relative to its cost basis. In fact, even after accounting for a typical management fee, the potential for some outperformance remains in the early years, which compares favorably to the experience of an index fund, which would likely underperform, probably to the extent of its management fee.

Finally, active tax management *maintains the potential for strategic theme investing*. Though investors may not believe in managers' (or their own) ability to pick superior stocks, they may believe in the potential for selected strategic themes to generate superior long-term returns. These themes may relate to industries, size or market capitalization, regional focus or any other broad macroeconomic factor. The algorithm used by most successful passive structured managers allows them to reflect these themes through the selection of the appropriate index and factor tilts.

For investors involved in a portfolio transition

Another aspect of the usefulness of active tax management is that the investor may be involved in a transition. Investors will, from time to time, want to change the manager responsible for handling their portfolios. Executing that change involves a cost, which, though not always made explicit, is nonetheless significant, all the more so when there are substantial unrealized capital gains. Indeed, whether the new account must be funded with cash or can take place through the transfer of securities, the change of portfolio manager will likely involve the realization of capital gains. This reflects the fact that individual portfolio managers have their own views as to the relative attractiveness of individual stocks, and it would be a minor miracle if both managers wanted to hold exactly the same securities in the same proportions.

Assuming that markets generally move up, the portfolio that is transferred will have many appreciated holdings, which the new manager may want to sell. Though a tax-aware manager will evaluate the advisability of these transactions carefully, one has to assume that some cost will be incurred, if only to allow the investor to benefit from the strategic change in management.

Separately managed portfolios using an active tax management process can greatly facilitate such manager changes, principally when the decision is driven by dissatisfaction with the current manager. It is indeed possible to transfer assets in kind, and to construct a portfolio around these securities, assuming that the investor also provides some cash inflow. Such a portfolio is at times called a 'completion portfolio,' or a 'completeness portfolio.' Exhibit 9.10, sourced from the work by Stein and Narasimhan, presents an illustration of the tax cost of a transition to an actively tax managed portfolio.

Moving from the initial portfolio to Portfolio 1 allows the investor to reduce the portfolio's tracking error to the broad Russell 3000 Index from 6.4% to 2%, with a minimal tax cost

Exhibit 9.10

Tax-sensitive transition analysis (US$ million except as shown)

	Benchmark Russell 3000	Initial portfolio	Portfolio 1	Portfolio 2
Securities (number)	2740	60	272	375
Beta (as calculated)	1.03	1.10	1.00	1.03
Yield (annualized; %)	1.24	1.00	1.26	1.26
Weighted average capitalization (US$ billion)	93	80	85	90
Market value	–	19.33	19.33	19.33
Cost basis	–	7.61	7.94	10.80
Short-term gains	–	0.81	0.67	0.41
Long-term gains	–	11.15	10.73	8.13
Short-term losses	–	0.12	0.01	0.01
Long-term losses	–	0.12	0.00	0.00
Liquidation cost	–	2.48	–	–
Transition cost	–	–	0.07	0.69

Source: David Stein and Premkumar Narasimhan.

161

of US$70,000. This is substantially less than the US$2.5 million that the investor would have incurred in moving from the initial portfolio directly to an index fund replicating the Russell 3000 index. Portfolio 2 takes this even further, aiming to reduce the tracking error to 1%. It requires the investor to bear a tax cost of US$700,000.

The value of an active tax management strategy at the time of a portfolio transition is thus significant. Let me use a specific example to illustrate it further, although the actual situation is more complex than the simple shifting of assets from one manager to another.

A wealthy family wanted to fund a passive structured strategy meant to improve the expected after-tax returns of the whole portfolio. They followed a three-step process. First, they decided how much of the total portfolio should be allocated to the passive structured strategy. The family had recently received a significant sum in cash, and its assets were then almost evenly divided between money market instruments and several individually managed portfolios comprising individual securities. In particular, they had significant pockets of appreciated equity securities, at least two of which were managed by institutions the family wished to retain. The decision was to have about two thirds of the equity assets managed through a passive structured approach and the balance managed through active security selection. The family held the assets through a series of appropriately structured vehicles so that there was no significant risk that transactions in one pocket could expose transactions in other pockets to wash sales.

Second, the family decided to fund the passive structured mandate with both cash and the appreciated equity securities. Though this initially made the passive structured portfolio have a greater tracking error than ideally possible, it allowed the family to defer the realization of the capital gains, at that point unrealized, within the managed portfolios.

Finally, the family replaced the physical securities taken away from the equity managers it wish to retain with an equivalent amount of cash. This allowed the family to enjoy the full benefit of the security selection value added that it believed the individual managers could provide, as it allowed those managers not to have to worry about realizing capital gains.

In this instance, the family was able to realize a tax saving equal to approximately 2% of their net worth, with no significant risk, just by implementing a carefully choreographed strategy.

The main message

In conclusion, the main message is twofold. First, the indiscriminate use of the words 'active' or 'passive,' as understood in the tax-exempt investment community, probably obscures rather than clarifies the debate in the taxable world. The world of private wealth management requires investors to redefine the words 'active' and 'passive,' and to use more refined definitions of individual investment strategies.

Second, active tax management, even when considered in the case of a manager having no ability to select superior securities, is a strategy that is well worth considering and seems superior to a simple pre-tax indexing approach. However, individual investors and their advisors should understand that passive structured strategies have limitations, particularly for smaller investment portfolios.

162

[1] For a discussion on the active/passive debate in the institutional field, see Sorensen, Eric H., Keith L. Miller, and Vele Samak, 'Allocating Between Active and Passive Management,' *Financial Analysts Journal*, Vol. 54, No. 5, September/October 1998, pp. 18–31. See also Ambachtsheer, Keith P., 'Active Management That Adds Value: Reality or Illusion?,' *The Journal of Portfolio Management*, Fall 1994, pp. 89–93. For a different perspective on the debate, suggesting that, appropriately defined, it is feasible for active managers to outperform indexing, see Etzioni, Ethan S., 'Indexing Can Be Beat,' *The Journal of Portfolio Management*, Fall 1992, pp. 24–26.

[2] See Fender, William E., and Brian P. Cunningham, 'What's the Chance of That Happening?,' *The Journal of Private Portfolio Management*, Winter 1999, pp. 51–56.

[3] See Bogle, John C., 'Mutual Funds: Parallaxes and Taxes,' speech to the Association for Investment Management and Research, November 12, 1997.

[4] For a discussion of a similar finding, see Gupta, Francis, Robertus Prajogi, and Eric Stubbs, 'The Information Ratio and Performance,' *The Journal of Portfolio Management*, Fall 1999, pp. 33–39. See also Goodwin, Thomas H., 'The Information Ratio,' *Financial Analysts Journal*, Vol. 54, No. 4, July/August 1998, pp. 34–43.

[5] For a somewhat different opinion, see Minor, Dylan B., 'Beware of Index Fund Fundamentalists,' *The Journal of Portfolio Management*, Summer 2001, pp. 45–50.

[6] See Buetow, Gerald W., and Hal Ratner, 'The Dangers in Using Return Based Style Analysis in Asset Allocation,' *The Journal of Wealth Management*, Fall 2000, pp. 26–38. See also Buetow, Gerald W., Jr., Robert R. Johnson, and David E. Runkle, 'The Inconsistency of Return-Based Style Analysis,' *The Journal of Portfolio Management*, Spring 2000, pp. 61–77.

[7] See Hill, Joanne M., and Humza Naviwala, 'Synthetic and Enhanced Index Strategies Using Futures on U.S. Indexes,' *The Journal of Portfolio Management*, 25th anniversary issue, May 1999, pp. 61–74; and Miller, Todd, and Timothy S. Meckel, 'Beating Index Funds with Derivatives,' same issue, pp. 75–87.

[8] See Stein, David M., and Premkumar Narasimhan, 'Of Passive and Active Equity Portfolios in the Presence of Taxes,' *The Journal of Private Portfolio Management*, Fall 1999, pp. 55–63.

[9] See Arnott, Robert D., Andrew L. Berkin, and Jia Ye, 'Loss Harvesting: What's It Worth to the Taxable Investor?,' *The Journal of Wealth Management*, Spring 2001, pp. 10–18.

[10] In the paper cited in note 8 above.

[11] See Constantinides, G.M., 'Optimal Stock Trading with Personal Taxes,' *Journal of Financial Economics*, 13, 1984, pp. 65–89.

Chapter 10

Low-basis stock

For many individual investors, the question of what to do about low-basis holdings is very significant. In this context, 'low-basis' simply means that the stock or stocks that they hold now have a much higher market value than their tax cost.

Defining the problem

What 'basis' means

Basis is a term, used principally for tax purposes, referring to the price that serves as the basis for the computation of capital gains. Though, under U.S. tax rules, the basis of an investment is not always the price at which it was purchased, net of any applicable commission or related transaction cost, it is often the case that tax cost is very often close to an accounting book value concept.

However, depending upon the actual means through which the investment was acquired, the basis might be different from its initial cost. The simplest illustration would be the case of a transmission through an estate, in which case the basis is 'stepped up' to the value of the investment at the time the estate matured. Also, there are instances where the basis of an investment may be adjusted, upwards or downwards. The simplest example would be when there is a wash sale, in which case the basis of the remaining investment may be its cost adjusted for the capital loss incurred in the sale of the investment that generated the cash needed to buy it.

How low-basis stock is acquired

The mode through which low-basis stock is accumulated is important. We will see later that it can have a significant influence on the way the investor looks at these investments and, consequently, on his or her willingness to sell the security at some future point in time. Low-basis holdings in individual portfolios arise through a number of circumstances, but three principal events typically lead to the situation: entrepreneurial success, executive success, or investment success.

Whether experienced by the current senior generation or by distant ancestors, entrepreneurial success usually will lead to the total or partial sale of the entrepreneurial venture. A partial sale of the company will take place when a privately held business is 'taken public,' with shares offered through an initial public offering, for instance. In this case, the entrepreneur and his or her family will continue to own shares in the original company, with a tax cost equal to their investment in the original venture. A total sale of the company will take place when it is sold or merged into another entity, in a transaction potentially involving some exchange of equity. In the case of an outright sale, the entrepreneur and his or her family will hold cash, and thus not have any problem with low-basis stock. In the case of a sale for stock, the entrepreneur and his or her family will be left with shares in the purchasing company, with a tax cost still equal to their investment in the original venture.

A variant on the entrepreneurial theme can be found in the case of senior executives whose compensation includes a substantial equity component. Whether made up of restricted stock or options, this equity compensation leads the executive to have accumulated substantial shareholdings in the company over time. The value of these holdings may have risen substantially above the cost at which the stock was vested or the exercise price of the options.

Although usually not leading to a single low-basis stock holding, but rather to a portfolio comprising several substantially appreciated securities, investment success can also create problems. This can occur in a variety of circumstances. The most frequent instance is the case of family wealth transferred across generations through trust vehicles. Specifically, a portfolio may own stocks that were purchased many years or decades ago, at prices substantially below currently prevailing levels. Yet it can occur in other ways, for instance in the case of passive venture capitalists who happen to invest in a particularly successful company, or in the case of the purchase in a portfolio of one or two brilliant investments that appreciate substantially over a generation or less.

Dealing with low-basis holdings

Deciding on a strategy to deal with such low-basis holdings is one of the most daunting challenges faced by individuals. This challenge has several facets, but two dominate.

Psychological issues are very important as, often, there is some history to the investment. It may be that an ancestor founded the company; it may still bear the family's name. The investment may have been acquired by a loved and revered relative. The investment may be the source of the family's fortune, and there is therefore some feeling of loyalty attached to it.

Investment issues are no less important, and they typically fall into at least two baskets. The first relates to the question of risk and return, the essence of the traditional investment problem. Am I going to be rewarded for the risk I am taking? Is there any other investment capable of providing the kind of returns I expect from this one? The second basket incorporates the inevitable question of taxes. How much will I need to pay just to sell some, or all, of this holding? How sure am I of getting the benefits that I hope to get, in exchange for the certainty associated with the initial tax-based transaction cost?

Understanding stock risk

Before delving into the emotional and tax aspects of concentrated holdings, let us step back from the problem, in order to put it in the appropriate perspective. We have seen (in Chapter 7) that investment theory teaches that the risk of any individual investment can be broken down into two components:

- *market (or systematic) risk*, which affects all securities in the same class, for instance all U.S. equities; and
- *specific risk*, which relates to each security in particular.

Visualizing the difference between market and specific risks is helped by a quotation (kindly provided to me by John W. Mitchell, U.S. Bancorp's Western Chief Economist) from a paper by Steven McNees and Geoffrey Tortell,[1] which says it all, though it applies to economic performance rather than investment risk: 'a region's economy floats on a national sea, while being buffeted by local tides and winds.' It would not be inaccurate to view specific risk through an analogous assertion: an individual stock floats on the broader market, while being buffeted by its own corporate tides and winds.

Diversification theory tells us that, if we own a sufficient number of sufficiently different individual securities, specific risk can be diversified. It is important here to place some emphasis on the term 'sufficiently different.' Indeed, it is worth remembering that a portfolio comprising 20 bank stocks, for instance, is a well diversified bank portfolio, but not necessarily a well diversified equity portfolio.

What is left after any level of specific risk diversification has taken place is known as *residual risk*.[2] Residual risk can include counterparty or regulatory risks. *Counterparty risk* exists for as long as you are still dependent upon a counterparty to complete a transaction, for example a broker, when receiving the proceeds of a sale, or a bank, in relation to the value of a hedging strategy. *Regulatory risk* exists for as long as the tax authorities can still query any transaction and reject the tax treatment that you have chosen. We will not be discussing residual risks in much detail in this chapter, but they should not be forgotten.

Visualizing equity portfolio risk

Exhibit 10.1 depicts the various levels of risk that an investor may choose to retain in an equity portfolio. It comprises two lines. The first reflects market risk, which, in this instance, is kept constant. The assumption is, therefore, that the investor has made no effort to diversify it, in the context of a balanced, or diversified portfolio, by combining several asset classes in the hypothetical portfolio, for instance by combining domestic and international stocks, or equities and bonds, or nondirectional hedge funds. The second line depicts total risk, which comprises both market and specific risk. The zone between the two lines represents specific risk.

Note that specific risk and, thus, total risk both decline substantially as we move from left to right. As the portfolio is increasingly diversified, the specific risk incurred by the investor tails off, at first rapidly, then more gradually. At the extreme right-hand side of the graph, the portfolio replicates the index, is fully diversified, and is therefore no longer exposed to specific risk. Note, however, that it is still fully exposed to the market risk.

Diversification and the 'equity holding lives' of individual investors

Exhibit 10.1 illustrates the idea that there are three essential stages to the 'equity holding life'

Exhibit 10.1

The four stages of specific stock risk

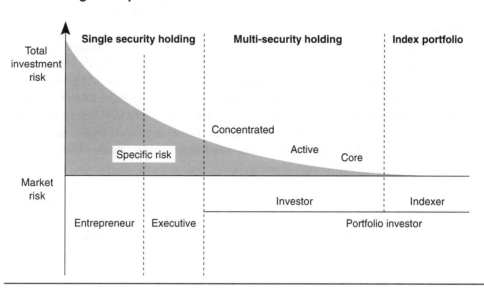

of an individual. They recall and, in fact, mirror the way in which we described the acquisition of low-basis holdings.

We start with the *entrepreneurial stage*. At the extreme left-hand end of the graph, specific risk is very high, as we are dealing both with a single security and with a company that is somewhat immature. The entrepreneur works with a new idea, develops it into a business, grows the business and, eventually and potentially, takes it public.

Once the business is public, we are dealing with the *executive stage*, where the specific risk of the company is still high, yet somewhat lower, as the business is arguably more mature than a brand new venture. The high specific risk reflects the fact that the equity holding is not diversified. Indeed, we are thinking here of an executive who still has the bulk of his or her financial wealth in that one security. Note that the executive stage encompasses both individuals who are still responsible for the management of the firm and individuals whose compensation incorporates restricted stock or options, but who do not occupy the highest positions in the company.

The next phase, the *investor stage*, moves us away from a single stock to a multisecurity portfolio. There can be no question then that each investment is held as a part of a portfolio, rather than as a means of owning a piece of a business. We saw earlier that the focus during the investor stage should shift from creating significant wealth to protecting and growing wealth.

There are two variants to the generic investor stage. The *diversified investor stage* involves a multistock portfolio that can be concentrated, actively managed or highly diversified through a core strategy. An important element of the investment strategy is to diversify specific risk, down to some acceptable level of tracking error, which is defined as the volatility of the performance of the portfolio relative to the relevant index.

The ultimate variation on this theme is the *indexing stage*, where the investor aims to replicate the risk of the relevant index and thus holds a portfolio that has virtually eliminated specific risk.

Exhibit 10.1 can help the advisor or the wealthy individual identify the appropriate equity portfolio strategy for the particular circumstances. It says, for instance, that it is perfectly normal for an entrepreneur to have the bulk of his or her wealth in that single venture. The purpose of the venture is for the entrepreneur to create wealth, and the risks associated with it are well understood. At the other end of the spectrum, it also tells us that investors should hold diversified portfolios, in the process eschewing the advice, often attributed to Warren Buffet, that individuals should own a few stocks in a few businesses that they understand well and that are managed by top-class executives.[3]

Applying the model to individual circumstances

The conceptual framework illustrated in Exhibit 10.1 is most useful when it comes to helping individuals with concentrated low-basis stock positions. We know that we will need to deal with both emotional and investment issues, and one of the important first steps must therefore be to try and get to some agreed base from which to move forward. This goal can be achieved by helping the individual, or the family, explore this stock diversification spectrum and ask themselves what kind of risk they should be taking. Let us look at each of the diversification stages in turn.

The entrepreneurial stage

As we saw earlier, no diversification is desired during the entrepreneurial stage. In fact, the investor will usually only diversify if and when selling stock in his or her company is necessary to generate the capital needed to grow the business. Venture capitalists tend to value the fact that entrepreneurs have most of their eggs in the one basket, just as many wealth managers value the fact that investment managers have substantial stakes in the strategies that they execute on behalf of their clients. The corollary of the desire by venture capitalists to see entrepreneurs financially committed is that they are usually particularly cautious when they hear that an insider is selling stock in a secondary offering. This worries them, unless there is a very good reason, because they question the entrepreneur's commitment or perceptions as to the future of the business. Meir Statman[4] explains that perception in the context of any generic transaction. He says that a transaction, when looked at in isolation, must involve a winner and a loser. Either the price of the stock goes up and the seller has experienced some opportunity loss, or it goes down and the buyer has experienced a real loss. Statman therefore suggests that prudence requires the buyer to make sure that the seller does not know something he or she (the buyer) does not know.

Entrepreneurs are not expected to want to diversify their exposure to their original great idea. Rather, they should seek maximum profit from it and would only reluctantly share in it when the alternative reduces the profit potential of the business. Entrepreneurs rarely ask themselves questions about wealth management or portfolio diversification, but when they do they should always seek advice relating to structuring the ownership of the asset. They should be looking for ways to minimize the likely transfer costs that will eventually arise as they pass their wealth onto their heirs.

The executive stage

During the executive stage, the extent to which the individual requires diversification is linked to the degree of control that he or she has over the fortunes of the company. Clearly, diversification is also dependent upon the feasibility of any sale of corporate equity, as certain executives have 'hand cuffs,' or the equity they own may only vest over time and substantially into the future.

In practice, the higher the individual is in the corporate hierarchy, the greater the appetite seems to be for specific risk. This is logical, as one can argue that there is some entrepreneurial bent still at work in the most senior executive positions. It follows that the tendency should be to seek greater diversification as one descends the management hierarchy. Ultimately, the individual would view equity ownership as only one element of compensation and not as an entrepreneurial endeavor, as proposed by Heidi Schneider and John Geer.[5] Yet, in the end, whether mostly undiversified or somewhat diversified, the ownership model remains influenced by the fact that we are still dealing with relatively concentrated positions, with higher levels of specific risk.

The investor stage

The greatest diversification challenge concerns individuals who are no longer in either the entrepreneurial or the executive stages. The fact that they no longer exercise significant control over the fortunes of the underlying company requires them to start to think in terms of that investment being essentially a financial holding.

C. Nicholas Potter, the former head of J.P. Morgan's Asset Management Group (and the individual most often credited for having turned it around in the early 1980s), once told me that he believed that 'one of the most important contributions of modern portfolio theory was to change a stock from being the same thing as a company, to becoming a set of investment characteristics.'[6] This insight is invaluable, as it recognizes that, once you no longer are in the position to direct the fortunes of a company or to access this or that asset, you are only buying the right to a dividend flow and to sell the stock to someone else at some future date.

Let me illustrate this point with an example. Recently, I was discussing this issue with a family on a day when an article in *The Wall Street Journal* mentioned a stock as being apparently cheap, as you were paying less than 'cash per share' to buy it. I did not believe the article made sense, for at least two reasons. First, singling out a significant cash reserve does not make much sense, as it is possible that the company is in fact running a negative cash flow. Thus, it may be using that cash in the next several months, without my being able, in any way, to affect it. It turns out this was a very important piece of the puzzle, as the company was a 'dot.com' and was indeed in need of further funding a few months later. Second, and more broadly, individual shareholders do not have access to single entry on the balance sheet, and thus must look at the total package, unless they have the power to remove senior management and appoint either themselves or someone who will do their bidding. It is indeed always worth remembering the legal admonition according to which you own a proportional share of the stockholders' equity of a company, and a proportional share of each asset and liability in a trust.

Focusing on the fundamentals of a company, as a proxy for it being a valuable investment, therefore makes sense only if the present value of the expected dividend flow and the likely terminal value (at which I will sell the stock) is greater than today's price. This is the essence of security analysis. Any other extrapolation effectively relies on the 'greater fool' theory, which holds that there is a greater fool (than I) who will be prepared to buy the stock from me and at a higher price, based on my current reading of the corporate fundamentals. Though arguably in keeping with the behavioral finance principles of optimism and overconfidence, this approach is fraught with danger.

I have found that getting an individual to understand the difference between an operating investment and a financial investment is a critical element of the process through which he or she eventually accepts the need to diversify a low-basis holding. At the same time, dealing with low-basis holdings requires advisors to make special efforts to understand the psychology of the individual investor.

Two cases come to mind. I have seen individuals who, though no longer in control in the underlying company, were still afforded special status. This could involve some residual honorific role or just some special recognition at annual meetings. It is important to appreciate that these will extend the direct link between the individual and the company, and require that diversification be handled in a sensitive fashion. Similarly, a public company may still bear the name of the founder, though the founder's family no longer exercises any management control. The loyalty link to one's ancestors requires sensitivity on the part of the advisor when discussing diversification.

Reducing a concentrated exposure

Once the investor has dealt with emotional issues and accepted the need to diversify some or all of the concentrated position, several options are available. Scott Welch proposes five most commonly used approaches to diversify concentrated equity positions.[7] He distinguishes between two fundamentally different sets of tools: financial strategies and charitable strategies. Charitable strategies allow an individual to diversify out of an appreciated asset through gifting. We will not discuss these here, as we already looked into gifting strategies when we reviewed multiple asset locations. Financial strategies, however, deserve a more detailed analysis: specifically, outright sales, exchange funds, completion portfolios, and hedging strategies. Outright sales are the simplest, but most investors recoil at the idea of paying the tax bill associated with them and opt for one of the more complex financial strategies.

Outright sale

The simplest and often most expensive strategy involves an outright sale of the security. Though the move will trigger the realization of an unrealized capital gain and the associated payment of capital gains tax, it is the preferred option of individuals who want to have maximum flexibility. Once the sale has been settled and the cash proceeds have been received, all residual risks (as discussed above) are eliminated, and the investor has total freedom to dispose of the proceeds of the sale as he or she wishes. Note, however, that there will typically be a lower amount of money to reinvest. If the investor is a U.S. tax resident, the net proceeds available for reinvestment would be 80% of the original amount, assuming that the tax basis in the security was zero, that it had been held it for at least one year, and that the investor is subject only to federal taxes.

Exchange funds

The classic exchange fund is created when an advisor brings together a number of individuals, each having a different concentrated position, and invites them to pool their assets. Imagine that you are an investment advisor and that you know of 50 investors, each having a position in one stock that they would like to diversify. Imagine that these 50 stocks are sufficiently different from one another that a portfolio comprising all of them would have a risk profile substantially lower than each individual stock and could, if the portfolio is constructed in the appropriate manner, be more or less similar to that of some broad market index. Note that the portfolio may hold each of these stocks in equal proportions, or may be constructed in a more complex manner, with different weightings for different companies, so that it may more closely mimic the performance of the index.

Public exchange funds

In a traditional, public exchange fund under U.S. tax law, the investors enter into a partnership for a minimum of seven years. Their portfolio will further need to comprise, at the outset, a 20% exposure to other illiquid investments, to satisfy U.S. tax requirements. Thus, they will have achieved their diversification goal, immediately and in the future, without needing to realize a capital gain at the outset. Indeed, for the first seven years the portfolio's behavior will reflect the combined performance of the original stocks, together with the returns on the illiquid investments. Depending upon the diversification within these original names and the way in which the portfolio is constructed, it may in fact mimic the return on some relevant index. At the end of the seven years, each partner may receive a proportional distribution of his or her share of the fund, that distribution now comprising that partner's proportional share of all the components of the portfolio – that is, the stocks currently in the portfolio plus the illiquid investments – rather than his or her original stock.

Note that each investor has only deferred and not eliminated the liability for capital gains tax associated with the original stock holding. Indeed, no capital gains tax has been paid as a result of entering into the partnership. However, the tax basis for the 'diversified' portfolio received upon the partnership being wound up will be the same as the tax basis of the original single stock. Diversification taxes have been deferred, but not eliminated. Yet, because the investor is now exposed to the risk of a broader basket of stocks, the specific downside risk associated with his or her low-basis holding has been effectively eliminated.

The shortcomings of exchange funds include management costs, lack of control, and inflexibility. Public exchange funds are typically costly, as the manager of the fund charges an initial fee for bringing the investors together, selecting the stocks, and deciding on their relative proportions. He or she also charges for the selection and purchase of the illiquid investment, as well as for the ongoing management of the fund.

Public exchange funds are also somewhat inflexible. Investors must accept both the fact that the fund will hold 20% of its assets in illiquid investments and the list of stocks comprising the fund. Though potential investors are shown the list of the other investments likely to be held in the fund, and are free to accept or reject the partnership, they cannot control the composition of the portfolio. They may only accept or reject the offer to join.

Public exchange funds are typically passively managed. The ongoing management of the fund principally boils down to the reinvestment of dividends. Therein lies a third, admittedly less important, shortcoming: there is usually little scope for the manager to eliminate a holding whose fundamentals have substantially deteriorated, or to buy into an interesting new opportunity.

A private exchange fund alternative

As this is being written, private exchange funds are being discussed and introduced to selected investors. However, they have yet to be tested in the broad market place and their ability to stand up to the scrutiny of the tax authorities is still unknown.

Private exchange funds are designed to address the shortcomings of public exchange funds. They usually involve a single security. The investor or investors holding that single security join forces with an external party, who purchases the same stock at current market prices and partners with the original investor or investors. Having at least one 'unrelated investor' entering into a partnership 'with a valid business purpose other than that of hedging the security' is generally thought to qualify the proposed venture as a *bona fide* private exchange fund.

The partnership then enters into a series of partial hedging, borrowing and reinvesting transactions. These transactions are designed to provide the owners of the low-basis stock with the diversification that they seek. Hedging the low-basis stock in a way that does not trigger constructive sale rules will have two benefits. First, it will create the opportunity to borrow against that stock at more advantageous terms than would be the case if it were not hedged, and without creating the additional risks associated with leverage. Second, it also helps soften the psychological blow at times associated with the sale of a low-basis stock, as the transaction is typically designed to allow the owner of the stock to retain some exposure to potential upside price movements in that stock.

Interestingly, this diversification is achieved without the constraints associated with a public exchange fund. There is no need to have a fixed exposure to illiquid investments. Further, the partners in a private exchange fund have the ability to choose, and vary over time, the investments bought with the proceeds of the borrowing. Provided the partners do not break the partnership for at least the same seven years as is the case with a public exchange fund, it is possible that the investor will have achieved his or her diversification goals in a more effective fashion.

However, the structure contains a number of residual risks, principally of a regulatory nature, as the U.S. Internal Revenue Service has not ruled on all the aspects of the transaction.

Completion portfolios

Single asset class completion portfolios

Completion portfolios can be of interest to individuals who have access to other liquid assets besides their single concentrated low-basis position. These liquid funds can come from a variety of sources, such as other financial assets that may be sold without an undue tax penalty. The concept of a completion portfolio is to allow the investor to create a portfolio that behaves like some desired index or basket, by combining the low-basis position with some or all of his or her additional liquid assets. The investor 'completes' the single security by purchasing a basket of other securities that, together with the initial stock, help reduce the overall risk of the single position and may in fact bring it closer to a reference index.

The simplest incarnation of such a strategy would be the case of an individual who has both an appreciated stock and an equal amount of cash. Let us imagine that the stock is a large bank, J.P. Morgan Chase, for instance. Let us assume finally that the investor's goal is to replicate the risk profile of the S&P 500 Index, which tracks the performance of the large-capitalization universe within the U.S. equity market. The investor could use his or her available cash to purchase a portfolio, which on its own will appear somewhat skewed. For instance, it will most certainly not include any additional exposure to other money center banks. It may in fact further eschew exposure to companies whose business is closely or even more remotely tied to interest rate movements, as it would be assumed that they have more than enough interest rate risk in their bank holding. Conceivably, they might also avoid investments in multinational companies, as the global nature of the bank's business might be deemed to provide the needed risk exposure. By contrast, they might seem to own disproportionate exposures to technology and basic industries to which the bank is not directly exposed.

The portfolio may actually be constructed and managed in at least two different ways. The simplest approach involves managing the completion portfolio through the systematic reinvestment of the dividends paid out by all stocks, thus including those paid out by the low-basis stock, in order to purchase further diversification. A more sophisticated approach involves the use of the *passive structured strategy* (discussed in Chapter 9). The manager would go beyond using dividends to generate diversification over time, and use all available opportunities to harvest the inevitable losses experienced by one or several of the stocks in the completion portfolio. These losses would be used to chip away at the concentrated holding, sheltering the capital gain realized each time any of that low-basis stock is sold.

Multi-asset class completion portfolios

Completion portfolios do not have to be constrained to the asset class to which the low-basis holding belongs, but may reach across asset or sub-asset classes. An example, appropriately modified to disguise the actual circumstances, will illustrate this point.

In the late 1980s, a large and very well known U.S. family had a substantially concentrated holding in a few health care companies that members of the family had helped build over the years. The family sought diversification, but could not accept the costs associated with unrealized capital gains. The family hired an advisor to construct and manage a portfolio of small stocks, indexed to the Russell 2000, an index produced by The Frank Russell Company that tracks the 2,000 smallest stocks in the firm's broad universe of 3,000 stocks. The manager was charged with the systematic harvesting of any loss that could be realized within the portfolio. These losses would then be used, over time, to shelter the unrealized gains in the family's low-basis legacy stocks. The portfolio was not tilted away from the drug industry.

The rationale for this strategy was that small-capitalization stocks would produce higher returns than large-capitalization equities over the long term, and would have more individual volatility. The family and its advisor thus implicitly 'credited' this outperformance against the higher cost of managing the portfolio. These higher expenses referred principally to transaction costs. The family had considered investing in large-capitalization international stocks, or even emerging market equities, but rejected these solutions for cost and risk reasons.

Knowing what we know today, and with the greater availability of selected derivative instruments, it might make sense to consider multi-asset completion portfolios. This is because they incorporate more diversified sources of risk, and thus of volatility. As we have seen earlier, the more uncorrelated volatility we can find, the greater the potential to manage the assets in a tax-efficient manner.

The major shortcomings of this strategy are twofold. First, *the strategy is ill-suited to investors who do not have a substantial pool of other financial assets alongside the low-basis holding*. In the absence of such a pool, the investor must sell some of the appreciated stock to raise the funds initially needed to diversify. An alternative would be to raise cash by leveraging the portfolio. Yet this effectively raises the portfolio's systematic risk in a fashion that may negate the diversification of the specific risk associated with the low-basis position. Some form of hedging within the scope of 'constructive sale rules' could alleviate the concern. Note that there may be some tax efficiency dimension, depending on the ability of the investor to use the interest on the debt. Having to sell some of the appreciated holding to construct a completion portfolio would usually not be viewed as tax-efficient, as taxes will be due upon the sale, in relation to the capital gains thus realized.

Second, *the diversification process typically takes time unless the low-basis position was quite a small part of the investor's wealth at the outset*. Indeed, the initial scope for diversifying the low-basis holding is directly proportional to the availability of cash to make the completion portfolio as broad as possible. Unless the investor has a substantial cash pool available, this means that, at the outset and for some time, there is little or no protection against the downside risk of the low-basis holding.

Hedging strategies

Hedging strategies have become the technique of choice for low-basis diversification. They typically comprise two distinct steps. First, the risk in the original low-basis holding is diversified, at least in the U.S. context, within the constraints of the Taxpayer Relief Act of 1997, which defined and prohibited 'constructive sales.' Mark Anson[8] suggests that a taxpayer makes a constructive sale of an appreciated financial position if the taxpayer enters into:

- a short sale of the same or substantially identical property;
- an offsetting notional principal contract with respect to the same or substantially identical property; or
- a futures or forward contract to deliver the same or substantially identical property.

Second, the investor borrows against the value of his or her portfolio, in a transaction often called 'monetization,' in that the individual effectively monetizes an otherwise illiquid position. The proceeds from this borrowing are then appropriately reinvested.

Before going any further, it is worth citing the advice of Robert Gordon,[9] who says that the most important initial decision is for the investor to choose between two fundamentally different alternatives:

- does he or she want to protect his or her gains and let profits run? or
- does he or she want to get the money out of a position without triggering a taxable event?

Gordon's advice is that in the first case the investor should hedge, while in the second he or she should monetize. This is indeed an important distinction, as the typical solution offered to investors involves a bit of both.

A pure hedging strategy involves finding a way to eliminate or reduce the downside risk associated with the stock's downward price movements, in a transaction that in many ways is akin to purchasing insurance. (Note that 'insurance' in this context is understood in a looser sense than that to which we are most accustomed. Insurance here means that the investor still accepts structural and/or counterparty risks. 'Portfolio insurance,' for example, came to grief in October 1987, because the critical assumption underpinning the strategy, the continuous pricing of physical and derivative securities, did not materialize. Similarly, in the Russian bond debacle of 1998, many investors thought they had bought a hedge, but did not expect the counterparty that had sold it to default on its obligations.) However, because most hedges appear expensive, investors often choose to accept some limit to the upside potential of their current investment.

A pure monetization strategy involves borrowing against a position and reinvesting the proceeds in the way you want. However, because most lenders will demand some security against the borrowing, and because many investors are wary about excessive portfolio leverage, many monetization strategies involve a partial hedging of the low-basis position.

Equity collars

An equity collar can be a pure hedging strategy. Using this strategy, the investor selects a combination of put and call options. (A call option is the right, but not the obligation, to purchase a security at some pre-agreed price, known as the 'strike price.' European-style contracts usually allow the purchase to take place at some precise future date; American-style options allow the purchase to take place at any time until the option matures. A put option is the right, but not the obligation, to sell a security at some pre-agreed price.) The selected combination is to provide protection at or very close to the current market price, and allow some participation in a defined amount of the upside price potential for the stock. Usually, the investor will purchase a put option, which provides the downside protection. Purchasing the put will require the payment of a 'premium,' which can be viewed as the price paid for that insurance policy. Depending upon whether the investor wishes to offset some of, all of, or even more than the price of the put, he or she will then sell a call option.

The collar can thus have one of three characteristics. First, it can *cost some money*, if the proceeds from the sale of the call option fall short of the cost of the put option. Second, it can be a '*cashless collar*,' if the proceeds from the sale of the call equal the cost of the put. Third, it can be an *income-producing collar*, if the proceeds from the sale of the call exceed the cost of the put.

The principal requirement of an equity collar is that the transaction does not run afoul of the constructive sale rule (as it is known in the U.S., but there are similar rules elsewhere). Broadly, the rule mandates that the investor must retain some ability to make or lose money. Robert Gordon believes that a 15% or more risk exposure is likely to suffice, given the fact that the example published by the Internal Revenue Service at the time the rule was introduced involved a 15% remaining risk exposure.

Monetization of the position

The investor may, however, elect to monetize the equity position on which the equity collar has been created. The collar sets a minimum value for the underlying equity position and thus may increase the collateral value of that equity from the point of view of a lender. Depending upon how the investor intends to deploy the proceeds from these borrowings, he or she may be able to borrow as much as 90% of the strike price of the put option, or as little as 50%. Usually, under U.S. tax rules, for the investor to be able to borrow more than 50%, the loan must be considered a 'nonpurpose' loan and be intended for investments in anything other than equities. In fact, the investor may still reinvest in equities and borrow more than 50%, as he or she may be able to 'margin' the securities purchased with the loan, in effect borrowing against both the original low-basis position and against the new portfolio.

Variable pre-paid forwards

Scott Welch[10] has provided the best definition of a variable pre-paid forward: 'it is essentially a forward sale of a contingent number of shares of an underlying stock, with an agreed future delivery date, in exchange for a cash advance today.' Under such an arrangement, the investor enters into a contract to deliver some or all of the underlying shares at a future date, in exchange for payment received today in cash. Welch takes this further: 'properly constructed and documented, a variable pre-paid forward does not constitute a constructive sale and is not subject to margin lending restrictions.' A variable forward contract can be viewed as an 'unbalanced collar,' a collar where the investor does not have the same number of calls and puts.

An example will help illustrate what this means. In 1998, I analyzed a variable forward contract, the TRACES on Estee Lauder stock, which were brought to the market and listed on the New York Stock Exchange by Goldman Sachs and Co. I found that the variable forward contract could be analyzed as a combination of three steps. First, the stock was sold forward, with an agreed delivery several years hence.

Second, a number of calls at US$60.875, equal to the number of shares sold, were purchased. Third, calls with a 15% higher strike price were written (the functional equivalent of a sale) on a number of shares equal to 83.3% of the underlying shares sold (note that 83.3% x 1.15 = 1).

The investor was protected against the price of the Estee Lauder stock falling below US$60.875. He or she would participate one for one in any appreciation of the stock above US$60.875 until US$73.05, and would receive only 15% of the appreciation of the stock should it rise beyond US$73.05.

Relative attractiveness of hedging transactions

The relative attractiveness of a monetized collar or a variable pre-paid forward relates to the deductibility of the interest paid on the borrowings associated with the collar.

There is little debate on the fact that the borrowing costs built into a variable pre-paid forward are capitalized. The investor will effectively be able to offset only a part of these costs, as they will help reduce the capital gain taxes due at maturity. However, with the capital gain tax rate less than 100%, a portion of that capitalized interest will indeed be paid by the investor.

By contrast, there is a debate as to the tax status of the interest paid on the borrowings associated with the equity collar. The 'straddle' rules, which apply to stocks bought after 1984, seem to mandate that the cost be capitalized, but certain advisors have come to believe that the interest expense can be offset against the income earned on the portfolio purchased with the borrowings. In such an instance, raising as it would the tax efficiency of the portfolio, an equity collar would seem the better alternative, though there is still considerable fiscal risk in this interpretation.

Summary and implications

Having looked at both the emotional and investment dimensions of the sale of low-basis stock, the conclusion still seems to be that the decision is anything but obvious or easy. Helping the investor process through the ownership risks that he or she wishes to take, and the corresponding returns that can be expected, has the potential to clarify some of the murkiness. Nevertheless, as a member of the board of a family office whose name is still directly associated with a highly prominent company traded on the New York Stock Exchange, I can testify to the fact that the decision to diversify or not to diversify is still quite a challenging one.

Though I have seen many of the possible variations on the theme, I still cannot find a simple way to predict how individuals will respond to the challenge of diversifying low-basis holdings. I do not mean that individual investors behave in a totally irrational fashion: far from it.

This is an area where the way in which Meir Statman defines behavioral finance best illustrates the issue. He says that: 'standard finance assumes that investors are rational, while behavioral finance only assumes that they are normal.'

Three case studies

Three examples illustrate the different ways in which different individuals behave. Note that, in all three cases, there are sincere and logical reasons behind each of the different behaviors.

> The co-founder of a high-technology company made the seemingly heroic decision first to step down from the company's management and then to sell out all of his shares near the stock's top market valuation. There was no personal acrimony between the two founders, but rather a fair strategic disagreement. In this instance, it seemed pretty clear that the individual had first voted with his feet and then naturally did not feel much subsequent attachment to the investment. Thus, he found it relatively easy to sell, though he did hesitate at one point when the price started to fall sharply. The main lesson, however, is that he had a systematic and orderly sale program in place, and mostly stuck with it.
>
> The widow of a successful investor found herself holding nearly 50% of her financial portfolio in one stock in the early 1990s. She could not accept the idea of diversifying the portfolio by selling that holding. It was the last investment her late husband had made and her recollection of her husband's investment prowess was that he had never made a bad investment. In this instance, it was clear that she insisted on keeping the high concentration in his memory, and that time would probably help her deal with the inherent risk. Indeed, even if her late husband was an exceptional investor, he was certainly more familiar with the company and its industry than she was. Yet she needed time to learn that she could take only those risks that she and her advisors understood well.
>
> The children of a highly successful entrepreneur were unwilling to sell the stock inherited from their father. In their view, the company was still exceptional and would continue to do as well as it had in the past. They had an instinctive trust in the remaining management, although, when questioned, they accepted that they really did not have any privileged access to information (which would have made them insiders and could have prevented them from disposing of the security if they wanted to do so). As the stock started to go down, they would look back and, in an attitude predicted by Meir Statman, they would 'view the stock's most recent high as its fair value.' In the end, the decision not to sell caused them to end up with a small fortune, having started with a much larger one.

The need for a dispassionate decision-making process

Experience suggests that the more the individual can be taken through a dispassionate and logical process, focused on why they need to hold on to a stock, and how much of it they should sell, the more they are able to start and stay on the right track. The focus is twofold. First, one must try to understand what motivates the investor and help him or her appreciate it. Second, one must be able to differentiate between making the decision to diversify and executing that decision.

Though one certainly does not want to lead the investor on an endless cycle of 'trigger points,' which rise and fall with the daily fluctuations of the market, it is worth remembering the earlier advice: individual investors need the best strategy with which they can live, not the best strategy in absolute terms. Getting an individual started on the right path is certainly more effective, in the end, than holding out for the absolute best theoretical decision, which the individual will never implement anyway.

The real and understandable difficulty that many investors have in dealing with the immediate, often psychological, pain associated with diversification makes strategies geared to reducing that pain particularly attractive. Hedging strategies that provide the potential to defer the realization of taxable capital gains and preserve some upside, should the price of the stock keep rising, seem to make the decision that much easier.

Making diversification more palatable

A final point is worth highlighting. Diversification is rarely palatable, when considered solely in a 'negative' sense. Unless the individual is clearly motivated by fear, for instance the fear of losing their wealth, the notion that a single stock is a riskier investment than a diversified portfolio is not a strongly persuasive rationale. Rather, it may be useful for individual investors or their advisors to think in terms of diversification allowing them to take advantage of opportunities that might otherwise not be available. Let me illustrate this with four simple examples.

Recently, a family had, after a long internal debate, decided to diversify some of its legacy holdings. It executed the move through a strategy that allowed it to participate in private equity investments. It had hitherto had minimal exposure to private equities, and had come to believe that venture capital and buyout investments offered important opportunities that it was not able to consider. Diversification away from the legacy stock became a means to a desirable end, rather than a negative experience.

Another family agreed to diversify one of its two legacy stocks to participate in nondirectional hedge funds, which it could not otherwise purchase, given its lack of cash. Again, the issue that the family confronted was no longer whether the risk in its portfolio would decline if it had a smaller proportion of its wealth in those legacy holdings. Rather, it was the question of how to finance a desired purchase. Should the family raise cash by leveraging its legacy holdings, or sell some of these holdings?

A third family is diversifying to start executing a broad philanthropic strategy. Note that the philanthropic nature of the move makes the diversification process easier, because it eliminates, or at least substantially reduces, adverse tax consequences. Yet the psychological issues are the same as for the other families, and they are addressed through the use of a positive motivation.

Finally, a fourth family is diversifying away from the stock of a company that has acquired the family business, in order to be able to buy some income-producing assets that will allow it to meet the income needs of selected individual members of the family. Here, the psychological issues are somewhat easier to address, as the stock being sold is not the original venture, but the equity of the group that acquired the family company. Yet I have seen families hesitate to carry out this step, when viewing solely as a diversification step, as there can be some residual loyalty to the firm that allowed them to realize the value of their wealth. The positive motivation associated with the production of income made diversification considerably more palatable.

In summary, diversifying a low-basis holding is a complex exercise, with investment, tax and estate planning, and psychological dimensions. The challenge set before the wealthy individual or the advisor is to appreciate the full extent of the problem and to work to address all dimensions as simultaneously as possible. Understanding the complex interactions between these different variables will allow progress to be made, though one should be prepared for an ultimate outcome that does not necessarily reflect the principles assumed to be optimal in investment theory. They will, however, be optimal if the solution is one with which the family can live and upon which it builds over time.

---

[1] McNees, Steven and Geoffrey Tortell, *New England Economic Review*, July-August, 1991.

[2] For a discussion of this topic, see Jacobs, Bruce I., and Kenneth N. Levy, 'Residual Risks: How Much is Too Much?,' *The Journal of Portfolio Management*, Spring 1996, pp. 10–16.

[3] For a comment on the relationship between investment performance and management quality, see Granatelli, Andy, and John D. Martin, 'Management Quality and Investment Performance,' *Financial Analysts Journal*, Vol. 40, No. 6, November/December 1984, pp. 72–74.

[4] Meir Statman, Glenn Klimek Professor of Finance at the Leavey School of Business, Santa Clara University, made the comment referenced here at the 8th Annual Family Office Forum, hosted on June 25 and 26, 2001 by the Institute for Investment Research in Chicago.

[5] See Schneider, Heidi L., and John Geer, 'Stock-based Compensation: New Opportunities, New Risks For Senior Executives,' *The Journal of Wealth Management*, Summer 2001, pp. 55–57. Both these authors are senior executives of money manager Neuberger Berman.

[6] For a discussion of 'company-ness' versus 'stock-ness,' see Clayman, Michelle, 'Excellence Revisited,' *Financial Analysts Journal*, Vol. 49, No. 3, May/June 1993, pp. 61–65.

[7] See Welch, Scott D., 'Diversifying Concentrated Holdings,' AIMR Conference Proceedings: *Investment Counseling for Private Clients III*, March 27–28, 2001, pp. 30-35 and 42-44. Scott Welch is the Director of Equity Risk Management at CMS Financial Services.

[8] See Anson, Mark J.P., 'The Impact of the Taxpayer Relief Act of 1997 on Derivatives Transactions,' *Journal of Derivatives*, Summer 1998, pp. 62–72.

[9] See Gordon, Robert M., 'Hedging Low Cost Basis Stock,' AIMR Conference Proceedings *Investment Counseling for Private Clients III*, March 27–28, 2001. Robert Gordon is the President of Twenty First Securities.

[10] See Welch, Scott, 'Was Going "Short Against The Box" Really a Perfect Hedge?,' *The Journal of Private Portfolio Management*, Winter 1999, pp. 41–50.

Planning a wealth management strategy

Chapter 11

Strategic asset allocation: moving beyond the traditional approach

Having now understood the opportunities available to the individual investor and the issues of significant concern to him or her, we are ready to move to the second phase of the wealth management process: planning. Our goal is to identify the parameters within which an individual's wealth is actually managed: we need to formulate an investment policy.

Indeed, strategic asset allocation is amply documented[1] as one of the single most important decisions that investors need to make. It would probably be an oversimplification to claim unanimity, but the general consensus is that asset allocation, which, in a tax-exempt world at least, is the backbone of the investment policy, is a *sine qua non* for the professional asset manager.

In a tax-exempt environment, developing a strategic asset allocation would eventually lead us to think in terms of a traditional optimization, using well-tested tools such as a traditional pre-tax, single-period, mean-variance optimizer. The task before us is to select the optimal mix of assets, or more specifically investment strategies, to meet the investor's objectives within his or her tolerance for risk.

Risk tolerance here would be expressed in terms of both selected initial constraints and an appropriate level of expected return volatility. A tool that generates sets of optimal portfolios at various points along the 'efficient frontier' does the job in a very creditable way. (Note that the actual location of the efficient frontier reflects the constraints that have been placed on it. It is thus not generically optimal, but optimal given these constraints.) Its inherent limitations include the fact that it ignores transaction costs and is critically dependent on the assumptions that underpin capital market forecasts.[2] Yet it is a tool that is well understood by institutional investors and can thus provide a useful base on which to build.

However, we are not dealing with a tax-exempt investor. Private wealth management requires us to go beyond the traditional discipline. Going back to the principles of tax efficiency, it is clear that thinking differently extends to the fundamental planning discipline of strategic asset allocation.

Tax considerations considerably complicate the strategic asset allocation process. It can be argued that they invalidate many of the conclusions derived through the traditional mean-variance efficient frontier approach. This is a function of the fact that the traditional analysis does not take into account all the information that it should. Using incomplete data, it produces a potentially faulty answer. While alternatives might be somewhat more complex or still incomplete, they seem preferable as they point to the real issues much more effectively.

They avoid the most significant pitfall: failing to appreciate the highly constraining limits of any traditional solution.

Flaws in the 'efficient frontier' framework

For most sophisticated investors, the efficient frontier framework is a critical element of the strategic asset allocation process. Most investors would agree that their investment goals reflect some sort of trade-off between risk and return and that a set of portfolios exist in which one cannot aim for a higher expected return without accepting a higher level of risk. The dominant role of investment policy – and its reliance on the formulation of a strategic asset allocation – is becoming increasingly accepted by individual investors.[3] Whether the formulation of a strategic asset allocation applies to a portfolio fully invested in cash or fully invested in a single, appreciated security, or anything in between, investors are using the mean-variance optimization tools associated with the efficient frontier framework to deal with the issue.

Yet that framework has at least two potential flaws in the world of individual investors. We have already looked into the first when discussing investor psychology: *individual investors do not necessarily accept return volatility as their definition of risk*. Being sensitive to the direction of volatility, as downward volatility is associated with 'loss,' they often prefer to consider downside risk as their definition of risk. Thus, one of the basic assumptions of the efficient frontier framework appears shaky. Replacing the traditional definition of risk-return volatility, with a measure of downside risk, for instance a semivariance, may not solve the problem. Indeed, Nancy Jacob argues that while semivariance-based approaches are potentially better than the original, they are still likely not to be as effective as a simple simulation.[4] Similarly, Frank Sortino and Hal Forsey caution against the difficulty associated with the calculation of 'downside deviation,' and thus discourage excessive reliance on its completeness as a risk measure.[5]

The second potential flaw is that *tax considerations considerably complicate the strategic asset allocation process and arguably invalidate conclusions derived with the traditional approach*. In many ways, the two main drawbacks of the efficient frontier framework are simply exacerbated in an after-tax context. On the one hand, the static nature of the efficient frontier framework is a significant weakness of the theory. It has been well studied, and it is clear that the final concept of risk is really second-order stochastic dominance.[6] On the other hand, transaction costs are known to pose a major challenge to the traditional theory. One can argue that taxes are a particular version of transaction costs (others might be brokerage, standard bid-ask spreads or, critically, market impact). They are known to be a problem to the model in a static sense and they give the issue a dynamic feature with which the model is not equipped to deal.

Practically, two critical assumptions underpinning the efficient frontier framework indeed no longer seem adequate when viewed from an after-tax standpoint. First, we must deal with the *cost of getting there*. It cannot normally be assumed that moving from any current portfolio to an efficient one is a cost-free transaction. There is a real cost associated with realizing any hitherto unrealized capital gains, as existing holdings must be sold to make room for more optimal ones, and this should be incorporated in the analysis. Second, we must deal with the *cost of staying there*. It cannot normally be assumed that the portfolio, once moved to the optimal asset mix, can be continuously rebalanced to that mix in a cost-free fashion. At a minimum, anticipated rebalancing costs should be considered and deducted from the long-term expected return of the optimal mix.

The cost of getting there

A critical element of the strategic asset allocation problem in an after-tax context is that one rarely starts with a portfolio whose market and book values are equal.[7] It is therefore unlikely that the returns actually achieved on a portfolio moved to an optimal mix from a position incorporating unrealized capital gains, will equal the returns expected from the optimal portfolio, computed using a weighted average of the expected returns on each of the assets within it. The investor will first need to sell some or all of the existing portfolio assets to achieve the optimal allocation, pay the appropriate taxes on any realized capital gains, and reinvest the reduced proceeds in the optimal asset mix. The expected return computed by the optimizer would therefore only apply to these reduced proceeds, and the return earned by the investor on his or her current asset base could therefore be substantially lower than expected.

That is what would happen if the tax liability associated with the portfolio transition were material. In fact, the greater the restructuring tax costs, the lower the expected returns on the original asset base. At some point, *the tax liability will be such that it does not make sense to move, meaning that the current portfolio may already be optimal from an after-tax standpoint.*

Exhibit 11.1 illustrates the potential impact of the cost of getting there on expected long-term portfolio returns. It shows the value of US$100 after 10 years in three different circumstances, based on differing initial ratios of market to book value, but assuming the same 8%

Exhibit 11.1

Impact of initial unrealized capital gains on long-term returns

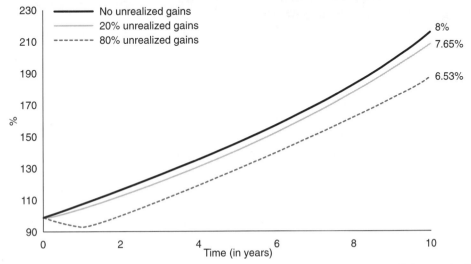

Source: Brunel, Jean L.P. 'Why should taxable investors be cautious when using traditional Efficient Frontier Too *The Journal of Private Portfolio Management*, Winter 1998, pp. 35-50

annual expected return on the 'optimal mix.' It illustrates that there is a significant difference in the average compound returns of three different portfolios with different assumptions regarding the size of unrealized gains in the starting portfolio.

One portfolio is assumed to have no initial unrealized capital gains. For the other two, unrealized capital gains are assumed to account for 20% and 80% of their respective market values. While all portfolios earn an 8% annual return *once they are invested in the assumed optimal mix*, the portfolio with a large initial unrealized gain only earns an average of 6.5% per year over the 10 years. The portfolio with no unrealized gains at the outset earns the full 8%, as it does not incur any capital gains taxes as it moves from the suboptimal to the optimal asset mix.

Adjusting for the cost of getting there

As a first step, we could agree to retain the traditional mean-variance framework, because it is so broadly accepted. We would, however, need to make an important adjustment to reflect the cost of moving to the optimal portfolio. One might consider deducting the cost of moving to the optimal asset mix from the optimal portfolio's expected return.

The following formula shows how to make that adjustment:

$$R_E = \{(1 + R_O) * \sqrt[N]{[1 - (CG_R * T_{CG}) * (1 - \frac{P_{BV}}{P_{MV}})]}\} - 1$$

where
R_E is the expected actual portfolio return
R_O is the expected optimal portfolio return
P_{MV} is the starting portfolio market value
P_{BV} is the starting portfolio book value
CG_R is the capital gain realization required by the move to the optimal asset mix
T_{CG} is the capital gains tax rate, and
N is the investment horizon, in years.

This formula simply states that the actual return earned on the portfolio after it is moved to the 'optimal mix' R_E is equal to the original expected return R_O minus the tax cost of moving to the optimal portfolio mix amortized over the investment horizon N. It illustrates the fact that the potentially large difference between R_E and R_O is dependent upon three main variables.

First, $(P_{MV} - P_{BV})$ represents the total unrealized capital gains in the starting portfolio. *The higher the unrealized gain, the higher the initial rebalancing cost and thus the higher the ultimate return penalty.*

Second, CG_R represents the capital gain realization rate required by a move from the current to the optimal asset mix. It reflects the fact that moving to the optimal portfolio may or may not require a high rate of capital gain realization. Specifically, the cost of moving to the optimal portfolio would be small if the unrealized gains are concentrated in strategies that will not need to be changed. Conversely, the cost of initial portfolio restructuring will be high if the unrealized capital gains are concentrated in the strategies that need to be sold. Thus, *the higher the required capital gain realization rate, the higher the initial rebalancing cost and thus the higher the ultimate return penalty.*

Finally, N represents the time horizon over which the initial transaction cost will have to be 'amortized.' This reflects the fact that *the longer the time period over which the initial restructuring cost can be amortized, the lower the ultimate return penalty.* Thus, a substantially expensive restructuring of the portfolio makes little sense if the time horizon over which the structure is expected to stay relevant is short, but it could be very sensible if the investor has a long time horizon.

An important caveat

While this adjustment would allow a more accurate prediction of the portfolio's real expected return, it would constitute a satisfying solution only if these three variables were incorporated in the formulation of the alternative optimal mixes in a formulaic or iterative fashion.

This is an important caveat. Indeed, once we accept the fact that the actual return on the optimal portfolio is probably less than the return calculated by the optimizer, we must ask ourselves a simple question. Might there be one or several portfolios, not located on the efficient frontier and thus considered suboptimal, which might still produce a better long-term return, once the cost of getting there is subtracted from their incomplete optimal return forecast?

For instance, going back to the example in Exhibit 11.1, we can ask two questions:

- How do we know that there was no other asset combination that would have forced less of an initial restructuring, and thus a lower capital gain recognition on the portfolio with the most unrealized gains?
- How do we know that we might not have been able to earn a higher net average return over the same period, even if these returns compound at less than the expected return of the supposedly optimal portfolio?

Assume that we find an 'optimal' portfolio with an expected return of 8%, which we translate to mean that we will earn an average of 8% per year over 10 years. Assume also, however, that the starting portfolio has substantial unrealized gains and that we must pay an amount in capital gains tax equal to 10% of its current market value. If that initial portfolio is worth US$100, we will thus be investing US$90. Applying the formula discussed earlier, one can compute that the expected return on that optimal portfolio, corrected for the cost of getting there, is 6.8%.

Now, imagine that there is another, less optimal portfolio, which has an expected return of 7.5% but requires considerably less restructuring, for instance only US$5.00. Assume that this portfolio has the same risk as the portfolio originally expected to earn 8%. We would therefore invest US$95 at that 7.5% rate of return for the next 10 years. That portfolio has an adjusted expected return of 7%.

Which of the two portfolios is optimal over this 10-year time horizon? The portfolio with an expected 7.5% return would appear less optimal than the 8% expected return portfolio to the 'raw optimizer.' Yet, once the cost of getting there is taken into consideration, the 7.5% expected return portfolio is clearly the best solution.

In short, the cost of getting there can transform an otherwise apparently optimal portfolio into a suboptimal alternative, and vice versa.

The complexity of the solution

Can we solve the problem by simply moving it from a two-dimensional context to a three-dimensional context? I have argued in the past that the efficient frontier became an efficient surface.[8] In fact, the adjustment we have just discussed clearly suggests that the problem is more complex. There may be a family of efficient surfaces *both* for each starting combination of assets *and* for each range of possible investment horizons. Indeed, the formula suggests that the speed at which the efficient surface narrows to a single line (depending upon the portfolio's ratio of market to book value) is dependent upon the investment horizon.

More importantly, however, the real weakness of that adjustment is that it ignores the costs potentially associated with the systematic and continuous rebalancing of the portfolio to the optimal asset mix.

The cost of staying there

Another critical assumption behind the efficient frontier framework is that the optimal portfolio is continuously rebalanced to the optimal asset mix. Indeed, the model calculates expected return and risk on the basis of fixed asset or investment strategy weights. Differences in the returns earned on each of the assets held in a portfolio would lead the weight of each asset to change, absent the assumption that the portfolio is continuously, or at least systematically, rebalanced.

In a normal capital market context, with nonnegative long-term average expected asset returns, portfolio rebalancing will typically require the realization of capital gains. Indeed, the exposure to an asset class or investment strategy will rise relative to another, if the return on that asset class or investment strategy is higher than that of the portfolio. An asset class whose return is lower than the portfolio average will also need to be rebalanced, but rebalancing will require additional purchases, transactions that do not trigger a tax event assuming that no short position is allowed. Note that there might be a capital gains tax payment associated with the rebalancing of an underperforming asset class or investment strategy if we are indeed allowed to go short. In that case, we would need to buy back some of our short position, and that would trigger a realized capital gain.

Working to prevent portfolio drift, rebalancing will thus require realizing capital gains, as some of the assets with the highest returns must be sold to top up the weights of assets that have underperformed the portfolio. The tax associated with these realized capital gains effectively represents the cost of staying there. This is the cost we discussed in Chapter 4, when we proposed that that one should recognize that portfolio drift is not trivial as a principle of tax efficiency.

An important insight developed in Chapter 4 is that portfolio drift causes expected portfolio risk to rise over time, since the share of the riskier asset increases as it logically outperforms the lower risk asset – as shown in Exhibit 11.2 (an expanded version of Exhibit 4.4 in

Exhibit 11.2

Expected portfolio return and risk at different period ends

	Risk (%)	*Return (%)*	*Return per unit of risk*
First year	11.6	10.0	0.86
Third year	11.8	10.0	0.85
Fifth year	12.1	10.1	0.84
10th year	12.6	10.2	0.81
20th year	13.6	10.3	0.76
50th year	16.1	10.8	0.67

Chapter 4). Note that return per unit of risk falls over time: simply allowing a portfolio to drift is not an optimal strategy.

Investors are therefore exposed to potentially negative surprises, unless their appetites for risk have also significantly increased. This has two interesting implications. On the one hand, behavioral finance, which points to the potential importance of recent experience in the perception of future likely outcomes, would suggest that investors would not necessarily mind the increase in risk on an *a priori* basis. On the other hand, investors would likely mind it when the higher risk manifests itself in the form of higher downward volatility.

This insight is central to the strategic asset allocation process. One of the most important risks to which individual investors are exposed is the decision risk, which we defined earlier as the risk of changing strategy at the point of maximum pain. The intuition is that periods of poor returns (still falling within statistically predictable norms) can lead investors who have overestimated their tolerances for risk to change their asset allocation strategies. This can have a dramatic impact on their long-term wealth, as they shift their allocations to achieve most of the negative returns and only some of the positive returns associated with the strategy.

Adjusting for the cost of staying there

The drift needs to be to adjusted in order to help investors avoid unpleasant surprises and the decision risk associated with it. Conceptually, the solution is simple: one needs to adjust the expected return of all asset classes to reflect the likely need to rebalance each asset exposure at regular intervals.

As a first cut, one might attribute a return penalty to each asset expected to earn a return higher than the expected average return of the whole portfolio. However, the problem is somewhat more complex in reality, as it has an iterative nature. Indeed, the expected return on the whole portfolio is dependent upon the expected returns on each of the assets held in the portfolio and their respective weights in the portfolio. Thus, the adjustment to the expected asset returns and the compilation of the optimal asset mix ought to be conducted simultaneously.

Practically, we simply need to assume that the average annual return on each asset is reduced by the assumed cost of selling the net increase in the exposure to that asset, which can be attributed to its earning a higher return than the portfolio's average. Mathematically, dealing with that penalty is somewhat complex. The formula could be written as follows:[9]

$$E(R_{a,i}) = R_{a,i} \pm Max \left[W_{a,i} * \left\{ \frac{(1 + R_{a,i})}{[1 + \sum\limits_{a} (W_{a,i} * R_{a,i})]} \pm 1 \right\} * CG_{Ra} * T_{CG}, 0 \right]$$

where

$E(R_{a,i})$ is the expected return on each asset potentially held in portfolio
$W_{a,i}$ is the weight of Asset A at the beginning of time period I
$R_{a,i}$ is the return on Asset A at the beginning of time period I
CG_{Ra} is the capital gain realization rate associated with rebalancing Asset A, and
T_{CG} is the capital gains tax rate.

Max in such a formula refers to the higher of two terms. Therefore, here, *Max* refers to the higher of '0' or the first term of the formula in the bracket.

The formula simply states that the adjusted expected return on any asset class or strategy is equal to one of two possible outcomes.

One possible outcome is that the adjusted return is equal to the unadjusted return, if that asset class is expected to produce a long-term return that is less than the expected return on the whole portfolio. This reflects the point that the portfolio will be systematically drifting away from that asset. Portfolio rebalancing will require the investor systematically to buy additional exposure to that asset in order to keep its weight in line with the long-term strategy. There will therefore be no need for sales that might trigger a capital gain tax liability.

The other possible outcome is that the adjusted return will be lower than the unadjusted return, if the asset class or strategy is expected to outperform the portfolio as a whole. In this case, the adjustment requires us to consider four variables:

- the weight of the asset class or strategy in the optimal portfolio mix;
- the excess return expected from the asset class relative to the return expectations for the portfolio as a whole;
- the capital gain realization rate associated with rebalancing that asset down; and
- the capital gains tax rate.

It is important to note that *the higher any of these variables is, the higher the likely rebalancing cost penalty will be*.

An important drawback

Though this approach does provide some needed adjustment, it suffers from several important drawbacks. The most important is that it does not reflect the interaction between the cost of rebalancing the portfolio, the volatility of the returns on each asset class, and the correlation between the returns in the portfolio.

We have seen earlier that investment theory applied to after-tax investments suggests that there is some value to volatility; and that the value of volatility increases when the return on

190

that asset class or investment strategy is not highly positively correlated, either to the returns on the whole portfolio, or to the returns of the other asset classes comprised in the portfolio. Thus, a better approach to the cost of rebalancing would require us to be able to think in a multiperiod environment (see below). In a single-period environment, we work with continuously compounding returns and may in fact be missing significant opportunities, possibly overstating the cost of staying there. Indeed, a highly volatile, high-return strategy would be significantly penalized in the formula shown above. Yet that strategy is just as likely to produce random capital losses, whose value to the overall portfolio might be greater than the rebalancing cost penalty we have just computed.

Summary and implications: adopting multiperiod analysis

The traditional efficient frontier analysis is really not suited to individual wealth planning. At the very least, it requires substantial modifications. Yet making these modifications resembles applying a band-aid to an open fracture.

Different assumptions, different approaches

Fundamentally, there are three key assumptions underlying the efficient frontier construct that are not really satisfied in the world of taxable individual investors.

First, though assuming transaction costs away may be acceptable where there are no tax considerations, it becomes a fundamental flaw when taxes must be integrated. As aptly suggested by Robert Jeffrey,[10] many tax-oblivious observers tend to make the erroneous assumption that individual investors always start with cash. In fact, they come to the table with a pre-existing portfolio, usually with some measure of unrealized capital gains, which create significant constraints on their ability to move. That challenge is well understood when dealing with individual security selection, but it is no less important when considering long-term strategy.

Second, the typical individual investor rarely has only one 'investment pocket.' This raises the issue of asset location (discussed in Chapter 5). In an early piece on the topic of asset location, John Shoven and Clemens Sialm[11] argued that a serious strategic asset allocation effort requires that all the relevant assets be pooled under a common strategy, and that the strategy attempt to optimize asset location as well as asset allocation. William Reichenstein[12] extended this, arguing that all assets should be placed on a common after-tax basis in order to compute a reasonable asset allocation.

I have analysed the interaction between strategic asset allocation issues, asset location issues, and the active management of asset class exposures[13]. In particular, I tested the idea of using the tax-exempt pocket of an investor's wealth as the preferred vehicle, within which tactical or rebalancing asset allocation moves could be executed. I found that there was a major interdependency between four critical factors:

- asset location;
- the relative sizes of the taxable and tax-exempt pockets;
- the size and frequency of expected cash flows relative to the size of the current wealth; and
- the after-tax risk and return trade-off.

For instance, rebalancing costs could be eliminated if periodic positive cash flows were sufficiently large to allow the rebalancing to be executed without requiring the sale of any existing holding and, thus, the realization of net capital gains. Similarly, these rebalancing costs might also be eliminated if it was possible to rebalance the portfolio strictly through transactions executed in the tax-exempt pocket.

Moving from single-period analysis to multiperiod analysis

The final drawback relates to the fact that the strategic wealth-planning problem must be conducted in a multiperiod time frame, because the lives of individual investors unfold over multiple periods. These periods can be defined in many different ways, but they are driven by at least three significant factors.

First, the portfolio structuring and rebalancing issues we just discussed give the problem its multiperiod nature. One can think of each period as the time during which the disruptions caused by differentiated asset class or strategy returns are deemed manageable. At one point, these disruptions become too significant to ignore and some rebalancing is unavoidable. Not recognizing the need for this rebalancing and its investment consequences can be very costly.

Second, looking at these issues in a multiperiod framework allows us to be much more sensible in the adjustments we might make and the conclusions we might reach.

Third, periodic cash flows also force a multiperiod analytical framework.[14] These cash flows do not need to be viewed simply as cash outflows. Human lives unfold in a sequence of saving and spending modes, and the model used to plan the management of that wealth must account for this.

Imagine the situation of a young woman whose parents have saved on her behalf to help pay the cost of university, and have given the student that capital upon her acceptance into a university. The student's cash flow sequence would therefore start with cash outflows, balanced by any inflow associated with any income that she can generate during that period. The next phase would probably be a saving phase during the early years of her working life, with goals including home purchases, retirement, and saving for the education of her own children. At some point, these savings flow might turn negative, as goals are met, and then positive again, as more goals are identified or her actual income exceeds personal spending requirements. Then, one might come to retirement and estate planning, or philanthropic gifts.

At the simplest level, then, cash flows arise from the need to meet current spending needs. In a fiduciary portfolio, these flows may be almost mandatory (when the trust document formally differentiates between income beneficiaries and remainder men). In a personal account, the same flows would be discretionary. At times, these cash flows can be considerably more involved, and may reflect a gradual transition between the operational and the financial stages of an entrepreneur's life. For instance, wealth might initially be created within one or several ventures. At some point, the entrepreneur might move part of his or her wealth into financial markets, in a process dealing with low-basis stock (see Chapter 10). Yet, particularly when an individual's business interests have involved more than one venture, that transition is rarely achieved in one fell swoop.

Consider a family that has built substantial operational wealth, involving three different industries, over the previous and current generations. At one point, the two brothers representing the current generation made the decision that they wanted to execute a radical change, shifting from wealth creation and accumulation to distributing some of that wealth through philanthropic ventures. They worked out a timetable extending to nearly 10 years, over which their various business interests would be liquidated. The planning they required, therefore, involved the ability to see these future significant cash flows from three different points of view. They obviously wanted the composition of their portfolio to reflect the nature of their operational businesses, in order to avoid doubling up on certain macroeconomic risks. They also wanted the model used by their investment consultant to be able to identify these cash flows, which would make any potential rebalancing cost considerably cheaper. Finally, they needed the investment planning carried out within the philanthropic vehicles to recognize the need for cash outflows to deal with the payments made to various charities. This family's needs could not have been met with a model or a thought process based on a single-period analytical framework.

A final element in the equation relates to the fact that individual circumstances change. At one level, this relates to the question of cash flows, but the issue is in fact more complex, involving the idea that individuals have two sources of capital. One is financial, and we all understand it relatively well. The other is probably even more important, and relates to our human capital.[15]

When advising a young investment banker, I asked her to consider the present value of her future income flows in the determination of the appropriate asset allocation. Though her current financial capital seemed large and might have justified a separate analysis, I thought that the present value of her future earnings, even if estimated conservatively and discounted at an aggressively high rate, was such that she should incorporate it in the overall process. That exercise led her to adopt a strategy with less exposure to money market instruments, as we came to the realization that she was long cash in her human capital.

Individual behavior also causes circumstances to change over time. One of the individuals we met in Chapter 1 had no difficulty with fluctuations in revenue, but found it very difficult to live with the daily fluctuations in the price of stocks. It took him time to get comfortable with the volatility of capital markets.

Predictably, moving to a multiperiod analytical framework significantly complicates the problem, principally because it creates huge matrixes, which are harder to address. Certain models have taken this multiperiod characteristic to an extreme, effectively proposing to plan over discrete numbers of years. That is not necessary. Indeed, the complexity of the problem grows exponentially with the number of periods, and there is a reasonable trade-off between perfect accuracy and manageability. That trade-off is all the more directed toward limiting the number of periods as perfect accuracy must be understood in the context of debatable assumptions and less than perfectly predictable market developments. We will turn to these issues in the next chapter, which deals with the formulation of an investment policy, using an integrated approach to wealth planning. There, investment, estate and financial planning come together in a single discipline.

---

[1] For a discussion of the preeminent role of asset allocation, see Brinson, Gary P., L. Randolf Hood, and Gilbert L. Beebower, 'Determinants of Portfolio Performance,' *Financial Analysts Journal*, Vol. 42, No. 4, July/August 1986; or Brinson, Gary P., Brian D. Singer, and Gilbert L. Beebower, 'Determinants of Portfolio Performance II: An

Update,' *Financial Analysts Journal*, Vol. 47, No. 3, May/June 1991, pp. 40–48. For a more skeptical presentation, see Ibbotson, Roger G., and Paul D. Kaplan, 'Does Asset Allocation Policy Explain 40, 90, or 100 Percent of Performance?,' *Financial Analysts Journal*, Vol. 56, No. 1, January/February 2000, pp. 26–33.

[2] For a discussion of the shortcomings of certain assumptions, see Uysal, Enis, Francis H. Trainer, Jr., and Jonathan Reiss, 'Revisiting Mean-Variance Optimization,' *The Journal of Portfolio Management*, Summer 2001, pp. 71–82.

[3] See Ellis, Charles, *Investment Policy: How to Win the Loser's Game*, second edition, Homewood, Illinois: Business One Irwin, 1993.

[4] See Jacob, Nancy L., 'After-Tax Asset Allocation: A Case Study,' *The Journal of Private Portfolio Management*, Spring 1998, pp. 55–66.

[5] See Sortino, Frank. A., and Hal J. Forsey, 'On the Use and Misuse of Downside Risk,' *The Journal of Portfolio Management*, Winter 1996, pp. 35–42; and Sortino, Frank A., and Robert Van Der Meer, 'Downside Risk,' *The Journal of Portfolio Management*, Summer 1991, pp. 27–32. See also Garcia, C.B., F.J. Gould, and Douglas C. Mitchell, 'The Historical Validity of Shortfall Estimates,' *The Journal of Portfolio Management*, Summer 1992, pp. 36–41; Johansson, Frederik, Michael J. Seiler, and Mikael Tjarnberg, 'Measuring Downside Portfolio Risk,' *The Journal of Portfolio Management*, Fall 1999, pp. 96–107; Browne, Sid, 'The Risk and Rewards of Minimizing Shortfall Probability,' *The Journal of Portfolio Management*, Summer 1999, pp. 76–85; Marmer, Harry S., and F.K. Louis Ng, 'Mean-Semivariance Analysis of Option-Based Strategies: A Total Asset Mix Perspective,' *Financial Analysts Journal*, Vol. 49, No. 3, May/June 1993, pp. 47–54; and Harlow, W. V., 'Asset Allocation in a Downside-Risk Framework,' *Financial Analysts Journal*, Vol. 47, No. 5, September/October 1991, pp. 28–40.

[6] See Jonathan Ingersoll, *Theory of Financial Decision Making*, 1987, Rowman & Littlefield Studies in Financial Economics, N.J., U.S.A., pp. 122–24.

[7] For a broad discussion of the issue, see Jacob, Nancy L., 'Taxes, Investment Strategy And Diversifying Low-Basis Stock,' *Trusts and Estates*, May 1995, pp. 8–20.

[8] See Brunel, Jean L.P., 'The Upside-Down World of Tax-Aware Investing,' *Trust and Estates*, February 1997, pp. 34–42.

[9] See Brunel, Jean L.P., 'Why Should Taxable Investors Be Cautious When Using Traditional Efficient Frontier Tools?,' *The Journal of Private Portfolio Management*, Winter 1998, pp. 35–50. Appendix I discusses the details of the derivation of the formula.

[10] See Jeffrey, Robert, 'Tax-Efficient Portfolio Management: Easier Said than Done,' *The Journal of Wealth Management*, Summer 2001, pp. 9–15.

[11] See Shoven, John, and Clemens Sialm, 'Long Run Asset Allocation for Retirement Savings,' *The Journal of Private Portfolio Management*, Summer 1998, pp. 13–26.

[12] See Reichenstein, William, 'Calculating the Asset Allocation,' *The Journal of Wealth Management*, Fall 2000, pp. 20–25.

[13] See note 9 above.

[14] See Pye, Gordon B., 'Sustainable Investment Withdrawals,' *The Journal of Portfolio Management*, Summer 2000, pp. 73–83.

[15] See Musumeci, Jim, 'Human Capital and International Diversification,' *The Journal of Private Portfolio Management*, Summer 1999, pp. 55–61. Among the references mentioned by Musumeci, three address the interactions between human capital and financial markets, directly or indirectly: Baxter, M., and U. Jermann, 'The International Diversification Puzzle is Worse Than You Think,' *American Economic Review*, March 1997, pp. 170–80; Bottazzi, L., P. Pesenti, and E. van Wincoop, 'Wages, Profits, and the International Portfolio Puzzle,' *European Economic Review*, Vol. 40, 1996, pp. 49–54; and Zarnowitz, V., and C. Boschan, 'Cyclical Indicators: An Evaluation and New Leading Indices,' *Business Conditions Digest*, May 1975.

Chapter 12

Integrated wealth planning:
investment policy

One of the ultimate goals of wealth planning is to formulate an investment policy. So far, we have looked into individual facets of the process. It is now time to bring them together.

Formulating an investment policy is not new. Charles Ellis[1] presents the asset management process as a loser's game, and draws an interesting analogy with tennis players. He says that the fundamental difference between amateurs and professionals is that amateurs lose points, while professionals win them: the asset management challenge is, in large part, about avoiding mistakes. A mathematician might reinforce that statement by reminding us of the power of compound interest as we already saw in earlier chapters: after losing 20%, a return of 25% is needed to get back to square one.

Setting an investment policy has become second nature to institutional investors, who are often driven by the need to match assets and liabilities. This also reflects the fact that they typically need to deal with a variety of governance issues, as the plan, be it insurance- or pension-related, has a supervisory structure, comprised of individuals to whom periodic reports must be provided. The managers of the plan, therefore, need to know what these board members require and be able to prepare these materials. Correspondingly, board members who have been willing to delegate certain decisions need to know how decisions are made and to have evidence that the agreed procedures are being followed.

Unfortunately, the original attempt by the asset management industry to transpose institutional investment policies to the world of individual investors was doomed from the start. It ignored the specific circumstances of individuals or families, and thus appeared artificial, onerous, and pointless to these investors whom it was supposed to help. Yet, in a case reminiscent of throwing the baby out with the bathwater, the industry wrongly argued that policy statements were neither necessary nor helpful.

Starting the process

The formulation of an investment policy is the most serious part of any consulting engagement. The process is very similar to the formulation of a flight plan in the airline industry. Without the proper flight plan, setting out expected altitude, speed, headings, and beacons, no responsible pilot would even agree to take off. The flight plan tells him or her where they are going, how they are going to get there, and what will be the intermediate targets along the way.

Similarly, investors need a plan that sets out what they are seeking to achieve, how they are planning to achieve their goals, and what intermediate targets may be needed. The latter is particularly important. It reflects the contradiction that is seemingly inherent in the very long-term nature of the wealth management process when dealing with multiple generations, on the one hand, and, on the other hand, the need to review investment performance at considerably more frequent intervals. Consider the risks. Simply focusing on long-term goals can lull investors into a sense of false security, or incite selected managers to seek open-ended long-term mandates, with little or no short-term accountability. However, the alternative is too sharp a focus on short-term performance which can play directly to the psychological tendencies of individuals to be 'momentum players.'[2]

Let us return to the airline example. The skies are crisscrossed by a number of virtual highways, which airliners follow on their way to their ultimate destinations. They do not often fly in a straight line between their take-off and landing points. Rather, they fly toward 'beacons,' which are fundamental parts of the flight plan. Thus, a pilot who is flying from London to Madrid might need to fly over Paris or Toulouse, despite the fact that neither city is on a straight line between London and Madrid. The pilot will not be concerned that the plane is not on that straight line. Indeed, for as long as the plane flies over the right beacons at the right time, the pilot will know that they are on course.

Apply the analogy to the world of investments. Imagine that an investor's goal requires him or her to be 100% invested in equities. Let us assume that this is so because the investor is seeking to grow his or her purchasing power, which means that he or she needs high, positive returns after inflation. It is reasonable to expect that equities will help the investor meet that challenge, though the example is not fully realistic, as some diversification away from equities might reduce risks without compromising returns. Yet it is highly likely that equities will periodically experience some loss in value. In fact, the statistics suggest that this will happen once every third or fourth year, on average. The investor will surely not have preserved his or her purchasing power during the year when equity prices fall. However, just like the pilot who may see the plane diverging away from a straight line, the investor should know that he or she is on course for as long as the portfolio is doing at least as well as the equity market (or markets) in which it is invested. Intermediate targets allow the investor to keep monitoring the execution of a plan, while avoiding the kind of dangerous drift that can occur if the only yardstick is either a long-term absolute return target or a short-term absolute return result.

Formulating the flight plan

A list of relevant questions (see box opposite) was developed over time to assist families seeking strategic investment advice. Their purpose is to help the investor on the road toward optimality. Personal preferences and comfort issues will be reconciled with the reality of their needs and of rational capital market expectations. The difficult task for the advisor is to help the individual discover where the appropriate trade-off points lie, given their individual circumstances, and to avoid directly or indirectly imposing the advisor's own views. The role of the advisor might be viewed as a 'moderator,' rather than as a party to the debate. In either design, the advisor should help by bringing the appropriate perspective, and correcting any misconception or factual error, but refrain from arguing any side of the debate.

Selected questions on investment policy

Investment objectives

1. List and prioritize your six most important goals (financial or otherwise).
2. Discuss time horizon issues and relate them to when and how funds will be used.
3. How will you 'justify investment success' in five, ten and 20 years?
4. What are your income needs?

Current investment portfolio

1. Current value of assets today (which assets should be included, excluded, why?).
2. Current investment position, including tax basis and constraints on change.
3. Any future expected financial inflows (earnings, inheritance, deferred compensation, etc).
4. Current and expected tax circumstances.
5. What would it take for you to feel 'unhealthy'?

Investment constraints

1. Discuss your best decision and explain (financial or otherwise).
2. Discuss your worst decision and explain (financial or otherwise).
3. Describe a situation when you changed your mind and explain.
4. Is there any preference, distaste or bias which could affect your investment program or your comfort with it (liquidity, instrument, strategy, geography, industry, philosophy, religion, social, transparency, etc.)?
5. How do you feel with respect to taxes?
6. How important is simplicity to you?
7. How much do you feel you can be influenced by others?
8. How do you deal with uncertainty? Provide examples.

Above all, the individual and his or her family must make up their own minds. To quote Charles Ellis again: 'Clients "own" the central responsibility for formulating and assuring the implementation of long-term investment policy.' Interestingly, Ellis adds:

To fulfill their responsibilities to themselves, clients need three characteristics: (1) a genuine interest in developing an understanding of their own true interests and objectives, (2) an appreciation of the fundamental nature of capital markets and investments, and (3) the discipline to work out the basic policies that will, over time, succeed in achieving their realistic investment objectives.

Setting goals

Setting goals is the easiest but also, potentially, the most dangerous part of the process. Let us first focus on the two difficulties that must be avoided. The first has to do with mistaking setting goals with setting *investment* goals. Though we do not want to mimic the institutional process by forcing ourselves back into an asset/liability framework, it is still useful to think in terms of wealth being an 'enabler.' It enables the investor to achieve goals - personal, dynastic or philanthropic - that he or she might not have been able to reach otherwise. Focusing on these broad goals is the right first step toward setting actual investment goals. Skip this general step and decision risk looms very large at some point in the future.

The second difficulty relates to the risk of remaining so 'broad' or 'general' that little progress is made beyond a desire to 'maximize returns and minimize risk.' Who would not subscribe to this goal? This is where helping the investor understand and formulate his or her own aspirations, fears, misconceptions, preferences, or, simply, uncertainty about the future comes into play. It is a very important step toward the formulation of an investment policy to appreciate that setting investment goals is rarely the real target.

In fact, the process is much easier than many make it out to be. It involves little more than listening to the wishes of the individual, and helping him or her decipher what is possible and what is not. In addition, it involves helping the individual understand the degree to which individual goals may contradict one another.

Deciphering the principal aspirations of the investor

The first three questions in our list are designed to deal with the principal aspirations of the individual. Asking about broad goals will help the investor, or his or her advisor, identify how far they need to go beyond investment issues. For instance, they will get a sense of what additional estate or financial planning might be necessary; the potential interactions with existing financial and estate plans and investment circumstances; the extent, if any, of the role of philanthropy; and the nature of potential generational issues, which may eventually require training or governance solutions. Further, asking about time horizon will help the investor eventually partition the future into relevant subperiods that might require special solutions, or identify specific events that will need to be incorporated into the overall process.

The third question was suggested to me a number of years ago by a headhunter, Richard Lanneman, and it is a good example of identifying success criteria through the right questions. Imagine that, one year after someone had been hired, I had to justify my assertion that the individual had been well worth hiring: the criteria by which the performance of the individual was measured *ex post facto* needs to be the same as those included in the original job definition. The parallel with investment policy is striking: how do I make sure that the goals that I state today are the achievements to which I will point in the future? Note, too, that we will have to bring that issue together with the psychological biases discussed in Chapter 2: overconfidence, optimism, hindsight, and overreaction to chance events. It is thus well worth taking the time to set the process at the outset, in order to frame the way in which decisions are subsequently evaluated.

Financial planning issues

The fourth question in our list concerns financial planning, as we need to make sure that the investor and any related party have access to the appropriate funds when they need them. The issue is somewhat complex, because it is entirely conceivable that the investor will need, or already has, a wide array of structures designed for estate or philanthropic planning purposes. We will therefore need to ensure that the funds required are available, whether for day-to-day expenses or to fund any form of commitment, of a philanthropic, generational planning or investment nature, from the right pocket and at the right time. Consider the worrisome consequences of being in a situation where a pocket that no longer 'belongs' to the investor has plenty of cash, while the pockets that the investor can access lack ready cash, and he or she is thus compelled to borrow or sell appreciated securities in order to raise the needed funds.

Investment philosophy

When discussing broad investment philosophy issues, individuals must also be helped along in the process and coached against making inappropriate assumptions.

There are two items for concern. The first deals with the question of the investor's beliefs with respect to the ability of managers to add value, on a tax-, risk- and fees-adjusted basis. The second relates to the question of static versus dynamic tax efficiency. We discussed both these issues earlier, but it bears repeating that there is no perfect solution for either. Nevertheless, the thoughtful advisor has a significant potential contribution to make.

Wealthy individuals are subjected to massive 'soundbiting' from many different sources. Quite often, these might be salespeople who tout a product at the expense of another, without presenting a balanced view. In other instances, these might be individual advisors or consultants who have a strong personal view, and cannot rise to the right level of intellectual honesty in order to present a balanced case to their clients. There may also be well-intentioned advisors who are so convinced that their clients cannot understand investment issues that they stick to an oversimplified view of the world. The net result is that many wealthy individuals are confused by the debate, until it is presented to them in a clear and honest fashion.

Most wealthy investors did not choose to get involved in money management, and they may or may not have had the time to develop the appropriate insights as to what is possible or not. (We looked into this issue in Chapter 7, when we discussed the need to understand capital market opportunities.) A discussion of philosophical beliefs as to the role of active money managers is a natural extension of this process.

This is a very important step, as the fact that an individual seems to support or agree with a particular philosophy does not mean that they really do. It might mean that they simply believe that there is no real other choice. They will be very surprised, and will tend to blame their advisors, if the flaw in the argument appears at some future point in time.

Take the example of the active-passive management debate. Assume that an individual investor has come to believe that active managers cannot add value, a conclusion that they may have reached as recently as a year ago, on the basis of the statistics that prevailed then. Assume that the stocks with the largest capitalizations underperform, as indeed they have since the technology bubble burst, and that mid-capitalization stocks do well. There is a good chance that active large-capitalization managers will have found it easier to outperform the market. There is an equally good chance that some newspaper or magazine will print a lead article on the topic. Finally, assume that the individual investor reads that article. How will he or she react? How much better off would the client and the advisor be, had they spent some time, early on, discussing the issue and looking into potential index biases (as discussed in Chapter 7)?

In summary, it is important to understand, as early on as possible, the key beliefs that an investor is comfortable using as the foundation of his or her investment policy. We saw earlier that there is a good chance that these beliefs will evolve over time, as the investor gains direct experience of the realities of capital markets and as comfort with certain beliefs rises, while the shadow of doubt lengthens on others. Yet, with the right process, the investor will be able to appreciate these changes in beliefs, will know how these changes should impact their strategy, and thus travel much more efficiently on the road to optimality.

Constraints

Discussion of investment philosophy often leads naturally to the question of constraints.[3] A few of these are imposed by the nature of the structures put in place by the individual or the family. For instance, one would not consider using hedge funds, which generate unrelated business income tax issues, in a charitable trust structure, as they could make the structure, if it is in the United States, lose its charitable character and make the investor lose the intended benefits. In addition, however, a number of constraints will arise from philosophical biases, or from lack of knowledge or experience of a particular asset class or strategy.

A discussion focused on constraints is also the most effective place to discuss what we might otherwise call broad risk issues. Individuals often do not respond to risk questions in a useful fashion, because they labor under a number of prejudices or challenges, which behavioral finance professionals have catalogued under headers such as cognitive biases, judgment biases, errors of preferences, regrets, and so on. Asking general questions about decision-making processes, reaction to uncertainty, or the need for coaching can help bring out the investor's real risk profile, when he or she is early in the process of discovering capital markets. This will be very helpful at the next stage, when the investor considers the strategic asset allocation that flowed from their initial definition of objectives, risk tolerance, and constraints. Usually, there will be several iterations, and this give and take is often quite constructive, as it is then that investors learn most about themselves and the real opportunities available to them.

Modeling needs

The next step in the process is to help translate the individual's goals, and constraints, into a plausible and actionable investment policy. Given a set of initial, probably somewhat rough, needs and constraints, we can identify the implications for wealth management planning through the use of a model. I do not doubt that most, if not all, of the advisor's work can be done manually, but having a model allows us to take a multitude of issues into account in a systematic and simultaneous fashion.

In the tax-exempt planning world, the tool of choice has been a single-period, pre-tax, mean-variance optimization process, the development of an 'efficient frontier': we examined its flaws in Chapter 11. Let us now identify the critical elements that we want to be able to bring to bear on the situation in order to design the 'optimal' optimizer. The ideal optimizer does not exist, of course, but there are several tools that come very close. In my view, to date they have all failed on one or other of the five criteria:

- focusing on after-tax total wealth accumulation;
- being capable of handling multiple locations;
- having a multiperiod capability;
- being able to deal with changing capital market circumstances over time; and
- being user-friendly.

After-tax wealth accumulation

Though it would seem to be a very simple requirement, focusing on after-tax return and risk is a complex endeavor. Two problems dominate: choosing the right starting point, and learning to think in after-tax terms.

What is the right starting point? Should all assets be brought to some 'parity,' in terms of the tax status of the vehicles through which they are held? Alternatively, should they be taken as they are, with pre-tax dollars located in tax-deferred vehicles considered alongside after-tax dollars in taxable locations? William Reichenstein[4] has argued that the appropriate asset allocation, in other words, the starting point, should be presented on an after-tax basis, resting on the premise that what we eventually spend are after-tax dollars and we must therefore account for our wealth in that manner.

Reichenstein further argues, and rightly, that the risk characteristics of an investment vary considerably, depending whether the investor bears the full risk of the investment or shares it with the tax authorities. Yet there are still at least two problems with this approach. First, a tax-deferred vehicle effectively allows the investor to earn a return on monies that would otherwise be paid out to the government. Second, the idea that all taxable work would best be done on a 'post-liquidation' basis is a troublesome one.

I prefer to work from an initial asset allocation through which the investor accepts mixing taxable and tax-exempt or tax-deferred structures. This forces the optimizer both to pay taxes when they are due - either annually (for taxes collected on investment returns) or periodically (when a particular tax-deferral is forced to end because a structure is wound up, or otherwise) - and to look at post-liquidation results as and when appropriate.

Next comes the question of the kind of requirements that thinking in after-tax terms imposes on the investor and his or her advisor. As we saw in Chapter 8, capital market forecasting requires a formal effort, and that effort is more complex in the world of individuals. We need to be able to predict return and risk on an after-tax and after-fee basis. This takes us into the realm of manager value added and tracking error, which are indispensable elements of any prediction made as to tax efficiency.

Multiple locations

Having established that most individuals have multiple pockets, we must be able to plan accordingly, respecting the integrity of each pocket, while capturing the efficiencies that they afford. In Chapter 5, we met Bill and Linda Burger, and discussed the extent to which their wealth management problem required them to think in terms of seven different locations. The paper I referenced there[5] looked at the impact on total portfolio expected return and risk of focusing on one, three, and seven different locations. In the case of the Burgers, a one-location outcome would focus on the whole of their wealth and thus would not reflect the fact that they can partition it into various components. The three-location outcome would reflect only their own portfolio, a foundation, and their tax-exempt retirement accounts. In other words, it would not allow them the flexibility of creating a sophisticated integrated wealth plan that brings together estate, financial and investment planning. The seven-location outcome described in Chapter 5 reflects the full extent of their integrated wealth planning. Let us now compare it to the one-location and three-location outcomes (see Exhibit 12.1). The data suggest that a careful strategic asset allocation and location analysis can produce significant increases in both expected after-tax returns and tax efficiency, without sacrificing risk. It also illustrates how a careful wealth planning effort can allow a family to achieve a multiplicity of goals, without necessarily having to suffer adverse tax consequences.

In particular, note that the returns shown in the table apply to the assets that are left after-transaction cost have been paid. Thus, the one-location and three-location returns apply to US$95 million, as the Burgers need to pay US$5 million in capital gains taxes to get to these

Exhibit 12.1

Measuring the impact of asset location (% except as shown)

	Number of asset locations		
	One	Three	Seven
Expected after-tax portfolio risk	10.9	10.9	10.9
Expected after-tax portfolio return	9.3	9.5	9.9
Expected tax efficiency	76.5	78.0	80.3
Expected probability of			
negative 12 months	18.2	17.4	15.8
negative 36 months	5.8	5.2	4.1
Diversification tax cost (US$ million)	5.0	5.0	1.135
Overall portfolio mix			
Cash and bonds	20.0	15.8	10.0
U.S. equities	35.0	39.0	42.1
Non-U.S. equities	15.0	15.3	17.9
Private equities	10.0	10.0	10.0
Nondirectional hedge funds	20.0	20.0	20.0

Source: Brunel, Jean L.P. 'Asset Location – The Critical Variable: A Case Study.' *The Journal of Wealth Management*, Summer 2001, pp. 27-43.

optimal portfolios. In the seven-location portfolio, the higher returns apply to US$98.9 million, as the Burgers need to pay only US$1.1 million in gift taxes.

Multiple periods

The next major requirement that our model must satisfy relates to the ability to deal with multiple periods. We implicitly ran into this problem when we alluded to the need to make tax payments or to deal with the termination of certain holding structures. Thus, there are numerous reasons why you must incorporate a multiperiod capability into any model, though three dominate: changes in circumstances, cash flows, and portfolio rebalancing costs.

Rare is the individual or the family who can plan for the next generation and assume that there will not be any change. At lower levels of wealth, there are certain milestones that can radically transform the nature of the wealth management problem. It is not unusual for people to alternate between saving and investment modes, as they build reserves for some major expenditure or investment and then need to replenish them. At higher levels of wealth, the same situation prevails, though the specifics are often different.

Cash flows, whether 'fiduciary' or 'discretionary,' require an ability to think in terms of multiple periods. 'Fiduciary' means that cash flows are mandated by the terms of a trust instrument or the actions of a trustee, independent or not. 'Discretionary' means that the timing and extent of these cash flows are within the control of the main decision-maker. However, certain flows, though technically discretionary, may actually be close to being compulsory, because of an income need, managers' fees, or the requirement to meet certain payment deadlines. Meeting cash flow requirements may require selling certain assets to meet obligations, thus dealing with asset allocation. Admittedly, this can be taken too far. Certain models break the future into a succession of yearly or even monthly periods. In fact (as we saw in Chapter 11), one could argue that the degree of apparent precision in such approaches is at best misleading, as the quality of the assumption set hardly justifies the extent of the detail.

As for rebalancing costs, we have already looked at this issue when discussing the need to move beyond the traditional efficient frontier analysis. Rebalancing costs require a multiperiod process to deal with what we earlier called the cost of staying there. The inherent change in the character of a balanced portfolio over time, as the better-performing assets gain in relative importance at the expense of the lower-returning strategies, cannot be ignored. Though portfolio drift can be measured in annual terms, it is much more practical to think of rebalancing events as periodic decisions: annual rebalancing would typically be required only after a period of exceptional market circumstances, where an important strategy has done particularly well or poorly, and with enough of a magnitude that its resulting portfolio weight has been altered significantly.

Changing capital market circumstances

Thinking in an after-tax context, as we have seen earlier, makes it impossible for individual investors to ignore the friction costs associated with changing the composition of the portfolio.

Typically, in a tax-oblivious mode, we need not worry about multiperiod issues and thus do not require the ability to change capital market assumptions. By contrast, in a tax-sensitive mode, we need to think in a multiperiod framework, and thus be able to vary return and risk assumptions from one period to the next, at least at the margin. This has two important dimensions:

- do we really need to worry about changing assumptions over time? and
- should the optimization process follow a single path or should there be multiple paths?

At one level, strategic asset allocation is all about forecasting the very long term, and short-term to medium-term issues should not have much of a bearing on the analysis or its outcome.[6] This is reasonable in a world in which investors have a time horizon measured in terms of 20–30 years and where they view the exercise in a very broad perspective. In that context, an asset class or strategy forecast can be assumed to remain somewhat steady over time, and short-term to medium-term variations would involve excessive tuning. Now, let us ask ourselves whether these conditions really apply to individual investors. Individual investors, thinking in a multi-period framework, will need to consider intermediate horizons. This would be the rationale for incorporating selected 'modifiers' into one's capital market forecasting process.

Arguably, the ultimate form of the art should involve a process that allows the return on each strategy or asset to vary over time, as this is the way capital markets actually behave. The Russell Realisor™ model, as discussed by Ernest Ankrim and Paul Bouchey,[7] illustrates the potential of a dynamic approach to strategic asset allocation.

How does this model differ from the norm? The contrast can be expressed as follows. Mean-variance, or single-path, optimization models work on the principle that the return assumed for each asset class or strategy is earned each and every year of the analysis. Sophisticated versions of these models allow for different returns being applied to different periods, but, within each multiyear period, the same return will be earned for each year. The asset class or strategy returns used by the Realisor are generated in a stochastic fashion, involving multiple paths, where each year encompasses a broad range of possible returns, depending upon the risk and return characteristics of each asset or strategy. It is thus possible to look at various scenarios, and to plan what future action might be needed if certain market developments occur. This makes for a highly complex model: Tim Noonan (a friend and senior executive of the Frank Russell Company) once explained that the original run of the model took 48 hours on IBM's most powerful computer in the 1980s, and even now the model may require 15 to 20 minutes to solve a problem. However, it does provide the most realistic set of circumstances.

When looking at the right model, the choice faced by the advisor or the sophisticated individual investor boils down to a simple trade-off: how much 'reality' do I gain or lose in exchange for the complexity I acquire or discard?

Applying the iterative process

Applying the process, particularly for the first iteration, requires a few simple assumptions. The simplest possible relevant set of constraints and goals should be used, together with the holding structures or locations that the investor already has in place or is contemplating at the time. The optimizer will then produce a series of optimal portfolio combinations, ranging across the full spectrum of potential outcomes. This will be the investor's efficient frontier.

Selecting a practical range of possible portfolios

Considering all possible combinations, however, may only serve to confuse all but an investor who enjoys portfolio theory and the arcane details of strategic asset allocation. Experience suggests that it is more comfortable and efficient to focus on three potential portfolios:

- the central portfolio, which is defined as the portfolio that apparently best meets the needs of the investor as one currently understands them;
- the portfolio with an expected after-tax risk 1% below the expected risk of the central portfolio; and
- the portfolio with an expected after-tax risk 1% above the expected risk of the central portfolio.

The three portfolios should be sufficiently close to allow relatively similar things to be said about the investor, while being sufficiently different for there to be a reasonable choice among them. The importance of these clauses cannot be overstated, particularly in the early iterations of the process. The investor, or his or her advisor, will be guided by the investor's reactions to the characteristics of these three variations, notably their expected risk and return. Too much difference among the portfolios will lead one to lose a sense for where the proposed current solution may be failing. Too little difference among them may mean that the actual preference of the investor is not covered by the spectrum currently considered.

Assessing the suitability of potential portfolios

The next step is to prepare a good description of these three portfolios, together with material designed to help the investor visualize what might happen if he or she should select one of them. One might typically start the conversation with a sole focus on the central portfolio. Reviewing portfolio composition, together with the transactions that would be needed should it be selected, one can identify the out-of-pocket costs that would arise, and that are usually tax-related. One might also consider the likely behavior of such a portfolio, with multiple locations anticipating selected future planned developments, over time, in order to test whether the investor's goals are indeed met and whether the ride is acceptable.

Investment education

It may become clear that some further investment education is needed. This occurs as the investor realizes the actual consequences of specific decisions. This is particularly likely when one conducts realistic scenario analyses, inviting the investor to look back at specific points in time or market circumstances, or to look at the potential shape of the portfolio many years down the road. It may become clear that the risk incurred is too high for comfort or that the investor finds out that certain cherished goals will be unachievable unless some additional risk is taken. Yet, the investor should be receptive to sharply focused education at such a time. The investor feels the need for information and it is conveyed to him or her quite naturally, rather than imparted in a seemingly academic manner, earlier in the process. Though this 'educational detour' may introduce some inefficiency in this portfolio selection phase of the process, it is well worth the efficiency gained in the educational process, which becomes less theoretical and more personalized. In the end, this reflects the need to learn both intellectually and emotionally. An example illustrates that it is important to use emotional intelligence to help individual investors at difficult points in the process.

> A movie producer had just gone through somewhat of a dry spell. After producing some wonderfully successful films, the philosophy to which he subscribed fell on hard times, and he did not seem able to produce a success. He referred to that period as his 'walk in the desert.' We were, at the time, discussing the importance of international diversification, when international assets had been doing particularly poorly. He was frustrated because he felt that he could not buy into the case emotionally, yet could not argue against it on an intellectual basis. I asked him how he had felt during his 'walk in the desert,' and whether he had considered changing his philosophy. He looked at me, smiled, and said 'Obviously not! Touché!' We had connected.

Rationalising both the intellectual and emotional ensures that the policy eventually chosen is sound, and also 'feels good.' Where a policy does not feel good, it is a virtual certainty that decision risk will rear its ugly head at some point, usually at the point of maximum pain. Education focused on the issue of the moment can be tailored to address the right concerns, impart the appropriate information, and thus help the investor avoid theory overload.

Iterations

The process is an iterative one, as it would be a very unusual case where one has effectively captured all the nuances that the investor wanted, or needed, to incorporate into the policy. Another element makes the process iterative: there often is more than one decision-maker or stakeholder, and they typically need time to reconcile their views. As one moves toward the ultimate decision, one can become more specific, going into more detail on individual asset classes or strategies. It is also a time when it is often useful to reconsider or contemplate certain structural decisions. Family partnerships, for instance, would become topical at this point, when it is visible to all that we may need to pool certain assets to avoid incurring excessive management costs or gain access to strategies or managers with high minimum portfolio sizes.

Discussing governance

Once we have adopted a strategic asset allocation, optimizing the investor's comfort/reward trade-off across multiple locations and time periods, we need to discuss the process through which these assets will be managed. This involves three broad issues.

First, we need to *specify the oversight structure*: who will be a part of it and how it will function. Though this might at first seem like corporate overkill, it does avoid many future headaches. Experience suggests that, like nature, individuals abhor a vacuum, and will make every effort to fill a vacuum if it is allowed to exist. Thus, creating a formal oversight structure, even if it means that a few people are responsible for many tasks, will ensure that the situation is clear, if and when a problem surfaces. At this time, rather than wasting time looking for a process, or, worse, solving the problem with a knee-jerk reaction, the mechanism will be in place to take the next step.

Creating an investment policy committee ahead of time, specifying who will be a member of it, and then specifying the decisions for which it will be responsible, are three very important first steps. Certain families must make these decisions in the context of also having a 'family office,' which may, or may not, comprise a chief investment officer. In such circumstances, setting out the respective roles of oversight and day-to-day management structures is paramount.

Second, we need to *formulate the investment process*, which refers in this context to the hiring and firing of managers. It is important for individuals and families to clearly state the process they plan to follow when selecting the investment managers. Pursuing a relatively informal process may create discomfort for individual family members. (We discuss manager selection in more depth in Chapter 17.)

However, setting out how individuals hire managers is still not enough. One needs to specify how they will be judged and what circumstances might lead to their termination. This is particularly important when dealing with investors who have not had a great deal of experience with targeted investment mandates. Setting out the manager review process will help you identify early pockets of potential misunderstandings.

An example illustrates the point. One family known to me was working from a long tradition of hiring external managers, yet judged its international equity managers on the basis of their performance relative to the U.S. S&P 500 Index. Not surprisingly, they kept finding themselves confusing manager insight with the nature of the opportunity really available to the international manager. In the end, almost predictably, they moved away from having international managers. Instead, they selected domestic U.S. managers, who were only really proven in the United States and who were given a global mandate on which they were never able to deliver. One of them actually did not have experience with non-U.S. stocks, and argued that owning a few multinational companies and American depositary receipts (ADRs)[8] provided the answer to the question. Thankfully, times have changed. One needs to make sure that one has addressed the issue of manager evaluation up front, before anyone becomes unhappy with a manager or the performance of an asset class.

Third, we need to *discuss the main current areas of uncertainty, and identify the circumstances in which one might consider changing the investment policy*. The point is to take the time to think of the circumstances when the investor would expect to change his or her mind. This is not to say that one should expect to be able to predict the future behavior of the investor with any certainty. Rather, taking this step will, first, bring out any nagging issue that has unwittingly been overlooked. Second, it helps differentiate ahead of time between circumstances that might justify a change and those that might not. Having this discussion at a time when there is no urgency or emotion attached to the issue makes it considerably easier to arrive at a dispassionate conclusion.

Let me illustrate this by reproducing the last section of the investment policy letter that I recently used with a family:

> Fundamentally, we believe that the overall asset or strategy allocation we have selected is the most appropriate response to our needs and constraints, given our current understanding of the structural (long-term) opportunities offered by investment markets. Though we therefore do not expect that allocation to change dramatically over any short-term time frame, four sets of circumstances could lead us to a change. We will thus review our strategy on an annual basis, focusing the review on the four possible agents of change:
>
> *New holding structures:* our current allocation is in part driven by the opportunities afforded by the structures through which the wealth is held. Any change in these structures should be expected to result in potential allocation changes.
> *Different perceptions as to our tolerance for risk:* our current allocation reflects a willingness to take equity risk, tempered by a wish not to see overly significant drops in the value of our capital over time. Greater comfort with market volatility might allow us to raise the portfolio's risk profile over time.
> *Different return needs:* our current allocation specifically trades off higher returns against a modestly aggressive risk profile. Any change in the return needs, in totality or within a particular holding structure, might require us to have to accept a higher overall risk profile and to reformulate our asset or strategy allocation.
> *New investment strategies or instruments:* our current allocation in part reflects our perception as to the opportunities currently available in the market place and our comfort with nontraditional investment strategies. New strategies or greater comfort with nontraditional investments might lead to change our current allocation.
>
> Decisions as to changes in the asset allocation process should be discussed during an investment policy committee meeting, and approved by it.

Summary and implications

Carefully formulating a well thought-out investment policy statement goes a long way toward maximizing the chances that the individual investor will achieve his or her objective and that his or her advisor will serve them well. The box overleaf sets out a number of bullet points that can serve as a guide when writing such a policy statement. Though I have seen many different formats and could not categorically argue against any one of them, I have found that the letter format I use meets with great client satisfaction. Most individuals tend to feel less threatened by a letter written in plain language than by a form, which inevitably seems daunting and intimidating. The text is drafted as a letter that the investor, or the family, writes to themselves.

Daniel Drake, one of the foremost authorities on trust history in the United States, described a trust instrument written by J.P. Morgan himself. It was exceptionally short and to the point:

Please manage the assets according to our agreed goals, distribute the income to the following beneficiaries, and upon their death pass the principal on to the following individuals.

One should expect situations where simplicity is the rule and the statement requires less than one full page plus a few generic appendices. In other instances, a large letter is appropriate as the family feels that they have been given a unique opportunity to create a business plan.[9]

Statement of investment policy

Investment objectives and constraints

- Statement of investment philosophy (what makes markets move, passive versus active – the latter driven by security selection or tax management, multiple versus single managers, specialist versus generalist mandates, etc.)
- Brief discussion of desired investment structure (holding mechanisms and their individual roles and goals, the constraints they impose, their tax implications)
- Investment horizon, for the whole portfolio and, where applicable, for all or selected structures
- Return goals or needs, for the whole portfolio and, where applicable, for all or selected structures
- Definition of risk, for the whole portfolio and, where applicable, for all or selected structures
- Specific risk tolerance levels, for the whole portfolio and, where applicable, for all or selected structures, across all assets or strategies, or specific to one or several of them
- Statement of liquidity requirements, for the whole portfolio and, where applicable, for all or selected structures (strategy implications)

Investment instruments and approaches

- List of eligible instruments, for the whole portfolio and, where applicable, for all or selected structures
- Statement of investment biases or other important subjective constraints (asset class, strategy, region, etc.)
- Specific strategy prohibitions or restrictions (alternative assets, regional limitations, leverage, currency hedging, for the whole portfolio and, where applicable, for all or selected structures, etc.)
- Comments on preferred investment execution approaches (commingled vehicles, individual portfolios, etc.), for the whole portfolio and, where applicable, for all or selected structures

Investment strategy and guidelines

- Strategic asset or strategy allocation, for the whole portfolio and, where applicable, for all or selected structures (may include additional diversification guidelines)

- Permissible deviation ranges, for the whole portfolio and, where applicable, for all or selected structures (at all times or at time of purchase)
- Specific instrument guidelines, prohibitions or restrictions (credit rating, maximum individual position, maximum share of a given issue, maximum share of average trading volume, etc.), for the whole portfolio and, where applicable, for all or selected structures
- Statement of preferences between adherence to the strategic asset or strategy allocation relative to the tax implications of periodic rebalancing
- Discussion of intended rebalancing frequency

Performance review

- Identification of the participants in the investment performance review process, their respective roles, and their reporting requirements
- Description of fiduciary process (control adherence to guidelines, etc.)
- Description of the performance review process, the data and information that are needed, and the frequency of reviews (pre-tax, after-tax or both; absolute or relative results, minimum time period for performance to be judged significant, etc.)
- Description of the decision process involved in changing managers or strategies for performance reasons

Strategic asset or strategy allocation review

- Description of the frequency of strategic asset and strategy allocation review
- Discussion of the circumstances that might require a review of the strategic asset and strategy allocation, and of the process required to make changes
- Identification of the participants in the investment performance review process, their respective roles, and their information requirements

Other potentially important considerations

- Discussion of various sources of investment risk (market or manager), and of whether and how this should be managed, continuously or in response to market cycles
- Discussion of whether certain 'factor risks' or 'exposures' are to be sought or rejected
- Discussion of policy with respect to appreciated securities (low-basis stocks, portfolio appreciation, dynamic versus static tax efficiency, etc.)

---

[1] See Ellis, Charles, *Investment Policy: How to Win the Loser's Game*, second edition, Homewood, Illinois: Business One Irwin, 1993, p. 2.

[2] See Nesbitt, Stephen L., 'Buy High, Sell Low: Timing Errors in Mutual Fund Allocations,' *The Journal of Portfolio Management*, Fall 1995, pp. 57–61.

[3] See Eichhorn, David, Francis Gupta, and Eric Stubbs, 'Using Constraints to Improve the Robustness of Asset Allocation,' *The Journal of Portfolio Management*, Spring 1998, pp. 41–48.

[4] See Reichenstein, William, 'Asset Allocation and Asset Location Decisions Revisited,' *The Journal of Wealth Management*, Summer 2001, pp. 16–26.

[5] Brunel, Jean L.P., 'Asset Location, the Critical Variable: A Case Study,' *The Journal of Wealth Management*, Summer 2001, pp. 27–43.

[6] See Goetzman, William N., and Franklin R. Edwards, 'Short-Horizon Inputs and Long-Horizon Portfolio Choices,' *The Journal of Portfolio Management*, Summer 1994, pp. 76–81.

[7] See Ankrim, Ernest M., and Paul Bouchey, 'When Diversification Hurts: The Total Portfolio Approach to Tax-Sensitive Asset Allocation,' *The Journal of Private Portfolio Management*, Summer 2000, pp. 83–88.

[8] For a discussion of the difference between buying foreign stocks or their ADRs, see Wahad, Mamoud, and Amit Khandwala, 'Why Not Diversify Internationally with ADRs?,' *The Journal of Portfolio Management*, Winter 1993, pp. 75–82. Note, however, that these authors do not address the broader issue of whether the universe of available ADRs is representative of the actual foreign security universe, in its totality or in each country. This is the most common criticism of the use of ADRs to achieve global diversification.

[9] For a discussion of the interaction between the cost of money management and its rewards and of the need to keep focused on investment policy, see Ellis, Charles D., 'Levels of the Game,' *The Journal of Portfolio Management*, Winter 2000, pp. 12–15.

Chapter 13

The market timing fallacy

Individuals are often strongly tempted to 'time the market'. This practice is often said to reflect their excessive confidence, optimism or reaction to chance events (as discussed in Chapter 2). Many authors have offered views as to the dangers associated with market timing.[1] Detractors usually make the point that asset allocation, not management value added, makes the main contribution to long-term portfolio returns.[2] On the other hand, proponents of market timing have argued that it is possible to define trading rules that are predominantly based on past price actions, or a few of their 'derivatives,' to affect a portfolio's risk/return profile in a favorable fashion.[3]

Defining market timing

Before proceeding further, it would be helpful to agree on some definition of 'market timing.' For some, timing the market encompasses any effort to change the balance of a portfolio toward or away from an asset class or strategy. For others, it covers reallocating a portfolio totally, or almost totally, out of a certain asset class or strategy when its prospects seem unattractive. For others again, it means short-term tactical trading. I view market timing as making dramatic moves toward or away from an asset class or strategy, beyond simple rebalancing or modest bets in favor of or against an asset class or strategy. Thus, any modest move that merely aims to capture real or perceived over- or undervaluation in one or another asset class or strategy, while *preserving the basic risk profile* of the portfolio, would not qualify as being based on market timing. Conversely, any move that *alters the basic risk profile* of the portfolio must be viewed as linked to market timing, whether caused by some form of panic or greed, or by some misguided view as to one's ability to predict short-term relative price trends. This definition allows us to differentiate between moderate portfolio rebalancing, reflecting a carefully calibrated and suitably humble view of the relative attractiveness or timeliness of certain markets or strategies, and wholesale changes in portfolio composition.

Experience suggests that the most common form of market timing – as we have just defined it – arises, not from the belief in it as a strategy, but as a reaction to an earlier, faulty decision. The faulty decision was to pick the wrong strategic portfolio mix. Thus, the investor starts to feel 'pain' when market developments do not fit with his or her earlier expectations, which might have been either overly optimistic or pessimistic. In this perspective, market timing can be viewed as a panic reaction by investors who have adopted too aggressive an asset allocation strategy or have not taken the time to create a long-term strategy. Alternatively, it can be viewed as a greed reaction, by investors who have adopted too conservative a strategy and, now, seeing markets seemingly running away from them, worry about missing the boat.

In order to keep things simple, let me focus on the pure panic side of the coin, recognizing that we could conduct the same analysis with greed replacing panic. Let us measure the cost associated with the temptation to time the equity market after selecting the wrong strategic asset allocation in the first place. Unable to accept the volatility inherent in too risky a strategy, we cut our equity exposure after a significant price decline. Market timing in this context can be considered as one of the factors contributing to decision risk, which we defined earlier as the risk of changing strategy at the point of maximum pain.[4]

A traditional view of market timing

When trying to demonstrate the dangers associated with market timing, people often point to the cost of missing a few good months. With long-term equity returns seemingly principally associated with a few good months, why run the risk of missing them and finding yourself with returns hardly superior to those you could have earned on cash? Implicit in the analysis is the basic assumption that it is very hard to identify exact market turning points. It would be better, on this argument, to adopt a policy of long-term systematic exposure than be tempted to decipher the mood of market participants and try to time forays into the equity market.

Exhibit 13.1 illustrates the argument. It shows the performance of the U.S. large-capitalization market, represented here by the S&P 500 Index over the past 30 years. These returns are compared to the performance of three alternatives:

- a 30-day Treasury bill, a good proxy for cash or money market investments;

Exhibit 13.1

Comparing equity and cash returns in good markets (compound data, 1969—99)

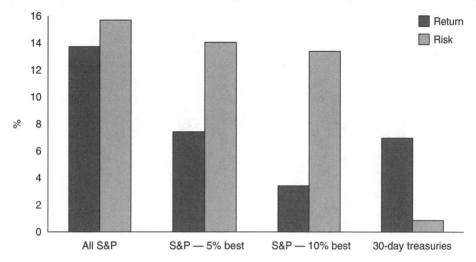

Source: Ibbotson database, author's compilation.

- the equity index minus the best 5% of all months; and
- the equity index minus the best 10% of all months.

A more accurate analysis would have simulated these last two categories, substituting the returns on U.S. Treasuries for equity returns when equity returns were particularly good (the top 5% and 10% of the full distribution of monthly returns). For the sake of simplicity, I have compounded the remaining equity returns over the shorter time periods

Exhibit 13.1 clearly suggests that missing out on the best months produces equity returns that become very close to, if not lower than cash returns, while maintaining an equity risk that is itself substantially higher than that of cash.[5]

Though the argument has been used in many occasions, it suffers from at least one critical weakness, which is illustrated in Exhibit 13.2: what happens when one misses out on the bad months, rather than the good months? In other words, what if I could just avoid the really catastrophic months and remain invested the rest of the time? To answer these questions, we can perform the same kind of analysis we just did, but in a diametrically opposite manner. Rather than excluding the best months, in order to argue that we should maintain our equity exposure through thick and thin, let us compute equity returns over the same 30-year period, but *exclude* the worst 5% and 10% monthly readings, respectively.

Predictably, Exhibit 13.2 demonstrates that average compound equity returns rise more dramatically than risk. Further, there is no point in comparing these 'enhanced' equity returns to cash, as they are not in the same range.

Gary Shilling,[6] who was one of the first to propose this argument, takes the experiment one step further. He suggests that total portfolio returns would be even better if one shorted

Exhibit 13.2

Comparing equity and cash returns in bad markets (compound data, 1969—99)

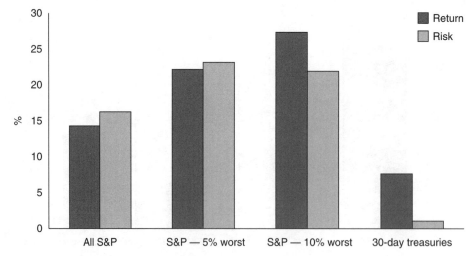

Source: Ibbotson database, author's compilation.

the market during these few bad months. Admittedly, this does not 'disprove' the case for market timing focused on a few good months, but it illustrates the dangers associated with playing with statistics. Start with a truism and you will end up with one.

A different approach

Rather than trying to argue for or against market timing *per se*, it is probably more useful to focus on something much more likely to happen in the real world. Arguing for market timing *per se* would require some initial agreement on the likely skills of any individual at predicting market developments, and some discussion of the likely persistence of such a skill over time. Returning to Mark Hulbert,[7] who came up with about as good a description of the problem as anyone has been able to offer: 'You can get run over by a truck on a highway which averages only one truck a day – especially if you panic when it arrives.' This comment related to the general proposition that one should invest the whole of one's assets, or at least a large majority of them, in equities.[8] Though the proposition certainly seems to be justified on the basis that equities provide higher returns over the long term, it often fails the test of the reality of the behavior of individual investors. Indeed, individual investors may not hold equities for the real full period. Rather, they may adopt a 100% equity investment policy based on the long-term view and then panic out of equities when the going gets tough in the short term.[9]

Let us ask ourselves, then, what would happen to an investor who either does not establish a long-term strategic asset allocation or gets greedy and adopts too high a strategic equity exposure. In this context, imagine that the investor stays with the aggressive portfolio for as long as things seem to be going well, but partially panics out of it when equity prices experience a fall that one should consider normal in market cycle terms. The question is thus whether the investor is better off with a strategy that can prove too aggressive at certain points in the cycle, or with a less aggressive strategy that can be maintained throughout a full market cycle. Clearly, our intuition is that a strategy that is not sustainable over a full market cycle will prove less rewarding, particularly on an after-tax basis.[10]

A simulation framework

Let us imagine a simple case where an investor can invest in only two assets: equities and cash. The equity returns we use are those of the S&P 500 Index during the years 1926–99, while the cash returns are those of 30-day U.S. Treasury bills. Our investor thus will tend to panic away from the equity market after a period of particularly poor equity returns, but return to the equity market when equity returns have improved. We therefore need to define two important decision points: the investor's 'panic threshold,' and his or her 'return threshold.' Initially, our investor is allowed to make decisions on a monthly basis.

The investor's portfolio is assumed to have been invested at the start of the simulation, on January 1, 1926, in the policy mix that is to be held unchanged over the full investment horizon (though, as will be discussed later, several different policy mixes can also be tested). At that time, the tax basis of the securities held in the portfolio is assumed to be the same as the market. For every month, you can observe the trailing returns on the equity portion of the portfolio and allow the investor to panic out of, or return to, equities, depending upon the relative position of these observed returns and the threshold values we assumed.

Any required transaction is executed on the basis of the month-end price of equities. Capital gains or losses are taken based on the average cost method, and assuming that they are always long-term in nature. The long-term capital gains tax rate used is set at 20% and the equity return is assumed to be of a capital nature.

For the sake of simplicity, let us assume that there is no dividend income. While this is not an accurate assumption, it should not affect our overall conclusions. Indeed, the assumption that all dividends are 'capitalized' in a tax-free fashion is applied to both managed and benchmark portfolios. Though absolute after-tax return numbers are probably overstated to some extent, the difference between managed and benchmark returns should not be unduly affected by the assumption.

Cash income is taxed at 39.6% (the current highest marginal bracket in the U.S. federal tax system). It is assumed that taxes are paid at the end of the month following the month when they are incurred. Note that this is a marginally penalizing assumption, as taxes would at most typically be due shortly after the end of the quarter in which they are accrued, so, on average, taxes are due about two months after they are accrued, rather than one month as assumed here.

Let us first consider four simple initial assumptions. First, the long-term policy asset allocation comprises 90% equities and 10% cash. Although that allocation may seem overly aggressive, think of it as the one needed to assess what happens to an investor who has mistakenly bought into the argument that equities should constitute the bulk of one's portfolio, since they produce the best returns over the long term. He or she thus elected to focus a portfolio on equities when his or her risk tolerance does not allow him or her to ride the equity rollercoaster.

Second, the 'panic threshold' is set at -20%. This means that the investor will cut back their equity exposure if equity prices fall by 20% or more from the most recent high water mark (the recent month-end closing high). One can view that level as appropriate, as it has become accepted, in the recent past at least, that we are in a bear market if prices fall 20% from the most recent peak. This allows us to be able to observe several changes in portfolio composition without having too much 'noise.' (At the same time, one could argue that this level is not sensitive enough, as people might actually start to panic before a 'bear market' has effectively been recorded. We will look into the impact of varying this level below, as we turn to a sensitivity analysis of our results when different assumptions change.)

Third, the 'return threshold' is set at +25%, reflecting the basic lack of symmetry in the distribution of returns. It effectively takes a 25% gain to get back to square one after a 20% loss. One could argue that a different number might make sense, for instance that a sharp bounce back might be enough to induce the investor back into equities. Conversely, one could also argue that the investor needs to see profits in order to regain the appropriate conviction. In the end, this assumption is 'psychologically' neutral and simply provides for the investor being prepared to return to the market when he or she sees the price levels that prevailed before the market fell sharply.

Finally, the equity variation margin is set at 60%. This level is needed to force the portfolio to move from a focus on equity to one on fixed-income instruments during difficult times. Clearly, having our investor go from a 90% to a 30% equity exposure is an aggressive move and the size of the variation will undoubtedly have a significant bearing on the costs associated with the transaction.

Let us now evaluate the impact on total portfolio returns of panicking out of the equity market. We will first look into the answer when taxes are not a part of the picture and then reconsider these conclusions after taxes are taken into consideration.

Pre-tax results

The analysis confirms the original intuition that the cost of panicking out of a strategic asset allocation can be significant. Exhibit 13.3 presents these results, showing:

- the return from both the benchmark and the managed portfolio;
- the cost of panicking, defined as the difference between those two;
- the volatility of equity markets during the period; and
- the average equity exposure of the managed portfolio during the period.

Exhibit 13.3 suggests three main observations. The first is that *panicking out of the stock market creates a significant cost to the investor, even on a pre-tax basis*. During most periods, panicking out of the market, as defined in this experiment, could be expected to cost the investor around 1% to 1.5% compound per year, relative to a naïve benchmark portfolio systematically rebalanced to the policy mix monthly.

In fact, the cost, though expressed here only in terms of 'lost return,' is even higher. The average annual return earned on the 'managed' portfolio, strategically invested 90% in equities and 10% in cash, is the same as on a portfolio passively held to a 75% equity exposure, with the 25% balance allocated to cash – at 11.1% over the period 1965–95. (Choosing this shorter period, in which the volatility of the equity market was broadly constant at around 15%, allows us to 'clean the data' to account for the impact of the crisis that began in 1929 and the subsequent sharp rebound.)

By contrast, the risk, defined as the standard deviation of returns, of our 90/10 'managed' portfolio is equivalent to the risk of a passive mix comprising an equity exposure of only 81%, with the 19% balance allocated to cash. The risk of panicking out of the equity market because of an inappropriately defined risk tolerance creates inefficiency. *The investor, in the end, is taking risk for which he or she is not compensated in the form of higher returns.*

Our second observation is that, predictably, the data also show that there is some relationship between the volatility of the equity market and the size of the panic cost. The fact that the period 1925–35 saw a benefit from a panic reaction does not invalidate this conclusion, as the period was characterized by both high volatility and, in the latter half of the period, a severe and sustained bear market.

Finally, the cost of panicking out of the equity market is not seemingly directly related to the average equity exposure of the portfolio during the period. This can be seen as a verification of the traditional proposition that missing out on even a few good months can hurt overall results in a disproportionate fashion.

Exhibit 13.3

Average cost, pre-tax, of panicking out of equities, 1925–95 (%)

	Compound returns from managed portfolio	Compound returns from benchmark portfolio	'Panic cost'	Average equity volatility	Average equity exposure
1925–35	8.6	6.0	2.6	35.4	53.0
1935–45	5.0	7.8	-2.8	22.4	36.0
1945–55	13.6	15.1	-1.5	13.4	72.0
1955–65	8.7	10.3	-1.6	11.8	85.0
1965–75	2.7	3.6	-0.9	15.8	75.0
1975–85	13.0	13.9	-0.9	14.2	87.0
1985–95	12.9	14.0	-1.1	15.0	81.0
1925–95	**9.8**	**10.6**	**-0.9**	**19.6**	**71.0**

Source: Brunel Jean L.P. 'Revisiting the Fallacy of Market-Timing in an After-Tax Context.' *The Journal of Private Portfolio Management*, Fall 1999, pp. 16-26.

After-tax results

Now, let us cut the data in a different fashion, forcing the portfolio to pay taxes each time some capital gain is incurred (see Exhibit 13.4). We will also give it credit for instances when a loss is 'harvested' and is subsequently used to shelter a capital gain.

The analysis, based on the same assumptions, confirms the intuition that panic can be even more costly on an after-tax basis. At first glance, it might seem counterintuitive that results should be so much affected by panicking when prices fall. First-level logic would indeed suggest that price falls would not only not produce a taxable event, but might in fact generate tax-loss carry-forwards that would help overall results. The reality, though, is that this intuition is only correct when the equity price falls from a level where the portfolio does not comprise unrealized gains.

A simple way to bring this point home is to consider the equity market environment in the United States in 1999. Specifically, with prices having virtually doubled over the previous three years, a 25% price decline from here would still expose most investors to a significant tax liability. Note, by contrast, that the price declines experienced by the Nasdaq in the second half of 2001 started from much lower levels, and thus exposed investors to real capital losses and tax-sheltering opportunities.

Exhibit 13.4 follows virtually the same format as figure 13.3, but incorporates the impact of taxes. It suggests that the cost of panicking out of the stock market is significantly higher once taxes are taken into considerations. Except for the 10-year period starting in January 1976, that cost averaged in excess of 2% per year. A visual inspection of the data for that exceptional period suggests that the uniqueness of the time interval may be directly related to the choice of threshold values. We will explore that in greater detail when looking into the sensitivity of our results to various assumptions.

218

Exhibit 13.4

Average cost, after tax, of panicking out of equities, 1925–95 (%)

	Compound returns from managed portfolio	Compound returns from benchmark portfolio	'Panic cost'	Average equity volatility	Difference between after-tax and pre-tax 'panic costs'
1925–35	7.4	5.8	1.6	35.4	-1.0
1935–45	4.6	7.6	-3.0	22.4	-0.2
1945–55	12.8	14.8	-2.1	13.4	-0.6
1955–65	7.0	9.8	-2.8	11.8	-1.2
1965–75	1.1	3.3	-2.1	15.8	-1.2
1975–85	12.3	13.3	-1.0	14.2	-0.1
1985–95	11.0	13.4	-2.5	15.0	-1.4
1925–95	**8.6**	**10.2**	**-1.6**	**19.6**	**-0.8**

Source: Ibbotson database, author's compilation.

As we did in the pre-tax environment, let us now look at the relationship between our managed portfolio and some passive alternative, in order to get a better sense of the full impact of panic. Our portfolio, strategically allocated 90% to equities, has the same after-tax return as one whose strategic equity exposure is only 73%, with the 27% balance allocated to cash (9.9% per year over the period 1965–95). Looking at the volatility of its returns, our definition of risk, it is however equivalent to that of a portfolio with an 83% strategic exposure to equities. Again, we can see that panic creates a substantial inefficiency, with extra risk not offset by higher returns. Returns are equivalent to those of a portfolio with a lower equity exposure (73% after-tax versus 75% pre-tax), while risks are equivalent to those of a portfolio with a higher equity exposure (83% after-tax versus 81% pre-tax).

The relationship between the volatility of the equity market and the size of the panic cost is considerably less visible and less strong than on a pre-tax basis. I suspect that this reflects the fact that more than half of the panic cost is attributable to taxes, which can be viewed as a friction cost. This is confirmed by observing that, as shown in the final column, the tax cost is not proportional to the pre-tax panic cost. This in part reflects the fact that we allow tax credits when a transaction gives rise to a net capital loss.

Sensitivity analysis

It goes without saying that any result is strongly dependent upon the assumptions built into the experiment. In the paper I referenced earlier, I tested variations on the four key variables to evaluate whether the general conclusions remained valid. The sensitivity analysis did not generate particularly surprising results. The most interesting findings relate to the behavior of panic costs on an after-tax basis, with the conclusion that taxes tend to compound the problem.

They reinforce the conviction that strategy formulation *and* execution need detailed revisiting when taxes enter the scenario.

Panic threshold

The cost of panic seems broadly to decline as the panic threshold increases, and the relationship between pre-tax and after-tax panic costs appears pretty stable. Both observations are logical.

First, the greater the panic threshold – in other words, the higher the threshold of pain – the more consistent the investor will be in staying true to the investment policy. One should, however, be careful not to infer that there is a linear relationship between the cost of panic and the panic threshold: actual outcomes are path-dependent and we do not have enough observations to be able to derive a demonstrable rule. In fact, the data show that the relationship is generally correct, but not precisely right.

Second, taxes should be seen as friction costs, dependent upon the size of the realized capital gains or losses.

Return threshold

The next logical step is to look into changes in the return threshold, which reflects the rebound required to attract an investor who has panicked out of the equity market back into the market. Three observations stand out.

First, the *panic cost moves in the same direction as the return threshold*: the lower the return threshold, the lower the panic cost. This fits with the intuition that the cost of panicking should be lower when the investor's portfolio spends the least amount of time away from the policy asset allocation. A lower return threshold will tend to bring the investor back to the policy mix faster.

Second, the data showed that there was *no obvious interaction between return threshold levels and equity market volatility.*

The third observation derives a special mention. The *relationship between pre-tax and after-tax panic costs 'deteriorates' as the return threshold gets lower.* This reflects the fact that the tax drag is broadly constant, irrespective of the return threshold level. The same tax drag will make it appear that the difference between pre-tax and after-tax observations increases as the panic cost gets lower, as the return threshold falls. For instance, when the return threshold is set at 5%, the after-tax panic cost (–1.0%) is three times higher than the pre-tax panic cost (–0.3%), but when the return threshold is set at 25%, the after-tax reading (–1.6%) is less than twice the pre-tax reading (–0.9%). This means that, when the return threshold is set low, the investor returns more quickly to the market and incurs a lower panic cost, pre-tax. However, the difference between the pre-tax and after-tax panic costs will seem higher, because the tax penalty is relatively stable and takes on a larger share of a small number.

Panic variation margin

Analyzing variations in the panic variation margin, which reflects the extent to which the investor reduces the portfolio's equity exposure, produces no surprises either. The pre-tax panic cost moves in the same direction as the panic variation margin. The smaller the move out of equities, the smaller the penalty. This conforms to the intuition that the investor is better off staying with the policy originally selected. Similarly, the relative tax cost is higher the lower the panic variation margin, but the absolute tax cost rises when the panic variation margin rises.

Neutral equity mix

Finally, evaluating the impact of changing the neutral equity mix on the cost of panicking out of the equity market demonstrated that the pre-tax panic cost is relatively constant throughout the range of the experiment. This suggests that the cost of panicking out of the equity market is principally dependent upon the extent to which one moves away from the equity market relative to the policy exposure, rather than the actual percentage change in equity exposure. Also, the after-tax panic cost does rise as the policy exposure rises, which should not be a surprise, as the tax drag must be a function of the size of the capital gains realized. These, in turn, must be a function of the size of the equity sales executed, which, itself, will be a function of the panic variation margin.

Summary and implications

The jury is still out on whether market timing does or does not make sense when one has significant insights as to short-term market direction. However, it seems clear that sharp moves into or out of a risky asset class or strategy, such as equities, are best avoided. The panic associated with having selected the wrong initial strategy is costly, both pre-tax and after-tax. The same would be true of the corresponding greed that would drive a mirror-image experiment. Thus, it seems, if anything, even more important to select the appropriate asset allocation strategy, rather than listen to the siren song of market timers, and to recognize the different pitfalls and challenges faced by investors who must be concerned with taxes.

There are three main practical conclusions, all centered on the proposition that the cost of panicking out of a strategic asset allocation is always high, particularly so for investors who must focus on long-term after-tax returns. First, *panic is costly*: panicking out of a set equity policy exposure will lead the portfolio over time to post lower returns.

Second, *panic costs should be measured in terms of both lower returns and higher risk*. One can consistently demonstrate that the managed portfolio returns are usually equivalent to those from a passive portfolio comprising a lower equity exposure than the one that experiences the same risk. This is particularly interesting, to the extent that cutting back one's equity exposure is often seen as a risk reduction measure.

Finally, it makes sense to *think of the comfort/reward trade off*: the fact that panic moves introduce some inefficiency in terms of the risk/return trade-off is one more reason to think in terms of a comfort/reward trade-off. The focus should be on adopting a strategic mix that is comfortable and minimizes the risk of panic. Further, the fact that equities are inherently more tax-efficient than fixed-income instruments – provided they are managed in a tax-sensitive manner or held passively – means that it is usually cheaper to raise the strategic risk profile of a portfolio than to lower it. Indeed, unless the change takes place soon after the strategy was put in place, the equity portion of the portfolio will likely incorporate embedded unrealized capital gains, which would trigger adverse tax consequences if some of the equity exposure is liquidated in order to reduce the portfolio's overall risk profile. By contrast, given

221

the fact that bonds generate income more than capital gains, selling bonds to add to one's equity exposure usually should not be expected to trigger significant tax liabilities.

A peripheral but very important conclusion is that taxes strike both good and bad decisions. *Every time you make a trade involving an unrealized gain, you will have to pay a tax, irrespective of whether the subsequent trade generates value added or not.* This is one more item of evidence to support the view that a taxable investor pays more for investment errors than a tax-exempt institution would. The taxable investor incurs the same opportunity and security transaction costs as the institution, but he or she may also have to incur a capital gain tax liability, which may be paid simply for the privilege of having made a bad decision.

---

[1] See, for instance, Brocato, Joe, and P.R. Chandy, 'Does Market Timing Really Work in the Real World?,' *The Journal of Portfolio Management*, Winter 1994, pp. 39–44, or their 'Market Timing Can Work in the Real World: Comment,' *The Journal of Portfolio Management*, Spring 1995, pp. 82–84. See also Vergin, Roger C., 'Market Timing Strategies: Can You Get Rich?,' *Journal of Investing*, Winter 1996, pp. 79–86.

[2] See Brinson, Gary P., L. Randolf Hood, and Gilbert L. Beebower, 'Determinants of Portfolio Performance,' *Financial Analysts Journal*, Vol. 42, No. 4, July/August 1986, or Brinson, Gary P., Brian D. Singer, and Gilbert L. Beebower, 'Determinants of Portfolio Performance II: An Update,' *Financial Analysts Journal*, Vol. 47, No. 3, May/June 1991, pp. 40–48. For a more skeptical presentation, see Ibbotson, Roger G., and Paul D. Kaplan, 'Does Asset Allocation Policy Explain 40, 90, or 100 Percent of Performance?,' *Financial Analysts Journal*, Vol. 56, No. 1, January/February 2000, pp. 26–33.

[3] See articles 55 and 56 in the Q Group, Institute for Quantitative Research in Finance, *Summary of Proceedings 1876–1982*, pp. 61–64, for digests of early presentations on the topic of market timing. These two articles suggest that it is possible in certain circumstances to generate higher returns for less risk by varying a portfolio's equity/bond mix in a tactical fashion. Interesting discussions of the topic are to be found in Trippi, Robert R., and Richard B. Harriff, 'Dynamic Asset Allocation Rules: Survey and Synthesis,' *The Journal of Portfolio Management*, Summer 1991, pp. 19–26; Wagner, Jerry, Steve Shellans, and Richard Paul, 'Market Timing Works Where it Matters Most … in the Real World,' *The Journal of Portfolio Management*, Summer 1992, pp. 86–90; Larsen, Glen A., Jr., and Gregory Wozniak, 'Market Timing Can Work in the Real World,' *The Journal of Portfolio Management*, Spring 1995, pp. 74–81; Klemkosky, Robert C., and Rakesh Bharati, 'Time-Varying Expected Returns and Asset Allocation,' *The Journal of Portfolio Management*, Summer 1995, pp. 80–88; and Wagner, Jerry C., 'Why Market Timing Works,' *Journal of Investing*, Summer 1997, pp. 78–81.

[4] See also Brunel, Jean L.P., 'A Second Look at Absolute Return Strategies,' *The Journal of Private Portfolio Management*, Spring 1998, pp. 67–78.

[5] See Chandy, P.R., and William Reichenstein. 'Market Surges and Market Timing,' *Journal of Investing*, Summer 1993, pp. 41–46; or Ferri, Michael G., and Chung-ki Min, 'Evidence that the Stock Market Overreacts and Adjusts,' *The Journal of Portfolio Management*, Spring 1996, pp. 71–76.

[6] See Shilling, Gary A., 'Market Timing: Better than a Buy-and-Hold Strategy,' *Financial Analysts Journal*, Vol. 48, No. 2, March/April 1992, pp. 46–50.

[7] Hulbert, Mark, 'Money and Investments: Which Eggs, Which Baskets?,' *Forbes*, October 23, 1995, p. 334.

[8] See Samuelson, Paul A., 'The Long Term Case for Equities,' *The Journal of Portfolio Management*, Fall 1994, pp. 15–26; Thaler, R.H., and J.P. Williamson, 'College and University Endowment Funds: Why Not 100% Equities?,' *The Journal of Portfolio Management*, Fall 1994, pp. 27–38; Asness, C.S., 'Why Not 100% Equities?,' *The Journal of Portfolio Management*, Winter 1996, pp. 29–34; Peter L. Bernstein, 'Are Stocks the Best Place to Be in the Long Run? A Contrary Opinion,' *Journal of Investing*, Winter 1996, pp. 9–12; and Bierman, Harold, Jr., 'Why Not 100% Equities? Comment,' *The Journal of Portfolio Management*, Winter 1998, pp. 70–73.

[9] See Kahneman, Daniel, and Mark W. Riepe, 'Aspect of Investor Psychology,' *The Journal of Portfolio Management*, Summer 1998, pp. 52–65.

[10] For a more detailed description, see Brunel, Jean L.P., 'Revisiting the Fallacy of Market-Timing in an After-Tax Context,' *The Journal of Private Portfolio Management*, Fall 1999, pp. 16–26.

Implementing the wealth management plan

Chapter 14

Tax-efficient portfolio management

Having looked into the first two phases of the wealth management process – understanding the investor's personal circumstances, needs, and constraints, and developing an investment plan – it is now time to focus on the third phase: implementation.

A global equity management problem

Imagine that the problem involves the management of a portfolio fully invested in global equities. One could first imagine a global equity investment process driven solely by security selection. Though we will look into tax-efficient security selection in more depth (in Chapter 15), I do not believe that it is applicable once the investment universe expands beyond a single country. Indeed, while the kind of generic process described by Roberto Apelfeld and his colleagues[1] in the context of a U.S. large-capitalization equity portfolio is conceptually applicable to a global equity environment, it is likely to prove impractical at best.

The process relies on a systematic scanning of the investment universe to allow an existing portfolio to be moved as close as possible to a target portfolio while minimizing net realized capital gains. One drawback is that it requires a large number of computations, directly related to the number of investment alternatives – here, the number of securities in the universe. However, its greatest drawback lies in the data needed to deal with the risk management part of the optimization. Each individual security is described by various risk characteristics – BARRA factors or equivalent measures of risk attributable to industry factors or selected 'common' factors. These are related to some benchmark to allow the portfolio construction process to maintain some expected tracking error level. Already complex in the context of a single market, the data needs can quickly become overwhelming when one must consider risk factors for each alternative global equity security relative to all others within a global equity universe.

The quandary created by the need to look at the whole portfolio, and the seeming impracticality of managing a truly global tax-aware equity portfolio made up of individual securities, require a different solution. It involves challenging conventional wisdom and looking at the same traditional problem from a different angle. This solution is based on the observation that portfolio returns can generally be broken down into three components:

- *the return on the strategic asset allocation*, or the normal mix of assets designed to satisfy the investor's return expectations within a set of risk parameters;
- *the return on individual security investments*, or the extent to which the investor, or a

discretionary manager, can generate value added over and above the broad market index relevant for each of the assets comprising the normal mix; and

- *the return on tactical asset allocation*, or the periodic moves made by the investor or manager to rebalance the portfolio across assets to reflect current views as to their relative attractiveness.

Each component of return depends upon and reflects individual, often independent decisions.

The traditional process can be illustrated with a simple example. Imagine that an investor needs to have a part of his or her assets dedicated to global equities. We can follow the investment process through each of the three decision axes we have just identified. The first decision will involve defining what the investor means by 'global equity': is the universe limited to developed countries or does it extend to emerging markets? Should the strategic weight of each individual countries be driven by the capitalization of its equity market or should there be another rule? For instance, reflecting the fact that the equity markets of certain countries (such as Germany) are small relative to their economies, should strategic weights be driven by relative gross domestic products?

The second set of decisions will be concerned with the goal of 'beating each country's market.' Here, the idea is to look into each country subportfolio as one, and to aim for that subportfolio to beat the relevant country index. That is normally achieved by better stock picking. However, better stock picking in fact comprises a number of implicit or explicit decisions as well. Whether intentionally or not, the portfolio manager will be making bets relative to the index, by investing away or toward certain factors, such as industry, size, growth, and value (an issue we explored in the discussion of active security selection in Chapter 9).

The final set of decisions relates to tactical country selection or currency allocation. From time to time, the portfolio manager may feel that a particular country is likely to perform better, or worse, than others, based on a variety of fundamental reasons, such as the economic cycle, the corporate profit cycle or even an equity valuation cycle. In these circumstances, the manager will typically seek to overweight or underweight the given country, relative to its strategic index weight. Similarly, the portfolio manager may have a view with respect to the relative attractiveness or unattractiveness of a given currency, and elect to act on that view by hedging the less attractive currency or increasing the portfolio's exposure to the more attractive one.

A manager may tell us that he or she does not make these decisions and simply picks stocks. Yet he or she does effectively make these bets, intentionally or not. The performance of the resulting portfolio can therefore be usefully analyzed into these decision components.

The problem with the traditional investment process

While the problem is relatively simple in a pre-tax environment, it becomes a serious challenge for a taxable investor. Indeed, though one can identify several decision axes, all but the currency hedging decisions typically involve transacting in individual securities. Let us look again at the example we have just considered and review the way in which the manager actually implements decisions two and three.

Outperforming the relevant index in a given country clearly involves buying stocks that one thinks will do better than the index and selling those that are expected to do worse. When the portfolio manager intentionally makes bets toward or away from selected risk factors, such as an industry for instance, he or she will have to purchase stocks in the attractive industry and sell those whose industries are expected to do less well than the market as a whole. This is the essence of security selection, and is a step that can be addressed with an appropriately designed tax-efficient process, such as the one discussed by Apelfeld and his colleagues.

Tilting the portfolio toward or away from a country traditionally also involves transacting in individual securities, particularly in those instances where the manager does not focus on the decision in an explicit manner and executes it implicitly. Thus, for example, moving away from the United States toward the United Kingdom will necessarily require selling U.S. equities and buying U.K. stocks.

This process has the same applicability and the same limitations when applied to multi-asset class portfolios. Imagine, for instance, that an investor's investment goals require him or her to own a balanced portfolio, hypothetically limited to bonds and equities. The investor will be faced with the same three decisions:

- selecting the appropriate breakdown between bonds and equities;
- managing the bond and equity subportfolios so that each one does better than the relevant market; and
- from time to time, modestly tilting the portfolio away from or toward equities or bonds, depending upon the relative attractiveness of each.

Once again, implementing the latter two decisions traditionally will require buying or selling individual securities.

Rethinking the problem

The challenge is to look at the portfolio management process differently, and to adopt different execution mechanisms for each of the three main decisions. We have just seen that the traditional process executes each of the main decisions through a single mechanism – buying and selling individual stocks. However, this tends to take away some of the independence of the individual decisions. Could we look at each decision and execute it independently from the others?

In an article I published in 1999,[2] I described an approach segregating the management of a physical portfolio from that of a combination of two individual derivative security strategies. The process involved the same three steps, but actually used three different execution mechanisms. Predictably, security selection relied on the traditional buying and selling of individual stocks. However, strategic asset allocation was executed through a long-term derivative contract, while tactical asset allocation and portfolio rebalancing relied on short-term derivative contracts.

Physical trades

In most countries, the tax code creates difficulties for the taxable investor who uses a traditional, physical security-driven investment process. It creates at least two quandaries. First, the investor must accept the tax classification of each investment's expected return stream. Thus, income tends to be taxed at a higher rate than capital gains, short-term capital gains tend to be taxed at a higher rate than long-term capital gains, and unrealized capital gains remain untaxed until realized. Second, an investor using physical securities typically incurs taxes first and realizes the alpha associated with a transaction later.

A simple illustration of this latter point is provided by a hypothetical country allocation decision. Assume that an investor currently has a portfolio invested 80% in the U.S. stock market and 20% outside. Now assume that the investor develops confidence in the future of Japan and decides to try to take advantage of the diverging expected return trends of the U.S. and Japanese stock markets over the past several years. The investor wants to move 4% of the portfolio from the United States to Japan. In practical terms, the investor using physical securities only will need to sell one 20th (4 divided by 80) of the assets invested in the U.S. equity market and to reinvest the proceeds in individual Japanese shares. Let us further assume that the performance of the U.S. equity market in the previous several years has resulted in the portfolio having built up significant unrealized capital gains. It is thus highly likely that the sale of U.S. stocks will lead to the realization of hitherto unrealized capital gains. As such, the investor will pay taxes first and then hope that his or her investment insights generate sufficient excess return to produce a net increment in his or her after-tax wealth. Note the difference in the certainty of both events.

Using derivative securities

Derivative security strategies may provide at least partial solutions. They may allow an investor to alter the tax treatment of selected components of return and to defer the tax consequences of an investment decision until after the alpha – or value added – has been generated (or the decision has proved unsuccessful and a loss has been booked).[3]

Let us consider the previous example in a different light, which involves allowing the investor to combine physical and derivative securities. Assume that, instead of using physical securities to execute the asset allocation trade, the investor considered using equity index futures. For the sake of simplicity, assume that 'straddle rules'[4] are not applicable in this case. The initial sale of a U.S. equity index futures contract and purchase of a Japanese equity index futures contract would both be 'opening' transactions, and would thus not give rise to a taxable event. As such, the investor can wait until the index futures trade is unwound to see whether the investment insight actually did or did not produce excess return, and to pay the taxes associated with the trade.

Note, however, that the transaction would create two new portfolio risks. First, tracking error would likely rise, as one should expect the U.S. physical security portfolio not to track perfectly with the U.S. equity index future. Although a potential source of value added, this mismatch gives rise to a new risk. Second, the portfolio would now be exposed to the risks normally associated with futures. Note, too, that any loss on that asset allocation transaction can subsequently be used either to offset future asset allocation-related gains or to increase the tax efficiency of the underlying physical security portfolios.

Physical and derivative decision sequences

Exhibit 14.1 presents a simple diagram that helps illustrate the fundamental difference between the two decision sequences, as we already saw in Chapter 1.

The exhibit helps illustrate a point to which we have come back several times in this book: *a taxable investor dealing only in physical securities can pay more than once for a mistake*. While the tax-exempt investor suffers only the cost associated with the difference in the returns of 'good' and 'bad' strategies, the taxable investor suffers that same cost *and* the bite associated with the capital gain taxes paid in the process of moving from the previous portfolio to the 'bad' strategy. Derivative instruments can allow the taxable investor to avoid that second penalty.

Exhibit 14.1

Physical and derivative decision implementation sequences

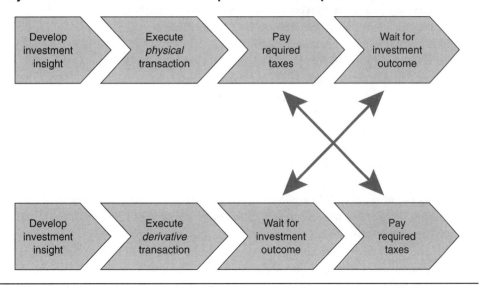

A possible solution: segregating security selection from asset allocation

Given the current impracticality of thinking globally at the individual security level, one might consider segregating security selection and asset allocation decisions, and using derivative instruments for asset allocation purposes.

Admittedly, any subdivision of the problem introduces some tax inefficiency. We know that a critical element of 'tax-awareness' is the need to think of the portfolio as a whole and thus, implicitly, to optimize all decisions simultaneously rather than sequentially. In this context, segregating security and asset allocation decisions along independent paths has the effect of preventing the investor from capturing all *ex-ante* opportunities, to the extent that physical and derivative transactions are considered independently. Note, however, that *ex-post* opportunities are captured to the extent that unrealized losses in the overlay derivative portfolio can be used to offset unrealized gains in the underlying physical portfolio. At the same time, this

229

inefficiency, if well understood and controlled, may well be a desirable trade-off given the alternative, which involves accepting one or more of three ills:

- no investment management value added (passive security selection strategies);
- possibly significant portfolio drift (no asset rebalancing); and/or
- possibly significant tax drag (tax-oblivious investment strategies).

Describing the possible strategy

The strategy we imagine here is designed for an investor whose assets are invested in a mix of U.S. large-capitalization stocks, U.S. small-capitalization stocks, and non-U.S. equities. To keep things as simple as possible, let us consider a portfolio strategically comprising 60% U.S. large-capitalization stocks, 15% U.S. small-capitalization stocks, and 25% non-U.S. equities. U.S. large-capitalization equities are represented by the S&P 500 Index, U.S. small-capitalization stocks through the Russell 2000 Index, and non-U.S. equities through the Morgan Stanley Capital International EAFE Index.

The approach comprises the same three distinct steps as the traditional process, but segregates the execution through three different mechanisms:

- *security selection through physical securities*, by investing 100% of the asset in a physical portfolio of U.S. large-capitalization stocks, managed using a tax-aware process deemed to produce pre-tax returns 225 basis points higher than those of the underlying index, with a tax efficiency[5] of 97% and a pre-tax tracking error[6] of 3.25%;
- *strategic asset allocation through a long-term index swap*, by swapping 15% of the assets out of the S&P Index into the Russell 2000 Index, and 25% of the assets out of the S&P 500 Index into the MSCI EAFE Index, the swaps being assumed to have a five-year maturity; and
- *tactical asset allocation through short-term index futures*, by using short-term index futures contracts to reflect periodical investment insights as to the relative attractiveness of individual asset classes, assuming that portfolios are rebalanced once a year.

Test design

More fully explained in the article referenced above, the testing methodology relied on comparing the simulated performance of eight different approaches, allowing us to vary assumptions and thus evaluate the relative contribution of each variable. We conducted a Monte Carlo simulation to test the impact of various asset allocation and instrument variables on portfolio returns, both pre-tax and after-tax. For after-tax returns, we considered both a pre-liquidation basis and a post-liquidation bases, to provide a full evaluation of the results.

Two specific derivative instruments

Different instruments attract different tax treatments, and there is a multitude of derivative contracts. The two we will be focusing here are publicly listed futures contracts and over-the-counter index swaps. The experiment will be considered in a U.S. tax framework, so let us briefly review their typical tax treatment.

Returns on publicly listed futures contracts generally fall under Section 1256 of the U.S. tax code and are typically taxed along a 60/40 split. That is, 60% of the return is taxed as a long-term capital gain, while 40% is taxed as a short-term capital gain. Further, in an exception to the general rule that unrealized gains are usually not taxed until realized, Section 1256 securities must be marked to market at the end of the fiscal year and tax is due at that point on any unrealized gain.

Swap returns are taxed at the short-term or long-term capital gains rate, depending on the holding period. They are not marked to market for tax purposes at the end of the fiscal year, as they are generally considered, when appropriately structured, to fall under Section 1234 of the tax code.[7]

Four principal decision variables

Conceptually, four variables could play a role in the eventual portfolio outcome and thus affect the portfolio construction and instrument selection strategies that we should consider.

The first of these variables is *security selection value added*, defined as the extent to which a manager is able to outperform a stated benchmark. We will consider circumstances where the physical commitment to a given asset class is invested in an actively managed portfolio or in a passively managed or indexed strategy, but will ignore, for the sake of simplicity, the passive structured alternative discussed in Chapter 9.

The second variable is the *tax efficiency of security selection value added*. The analysis starts with the assumption that an equity portfolio actively managed in a tax-oblivious fashion should attract a higher tax rate than one managed on a tax-aware basis. We further assume that indexed strategies would offer the highest tax efficiency, at least on a pre-liquidation basis.

The third variable is *tactical asset allocation value added*. We assume that it was possible to develop insights to generate value added with the decision, made once a year, at the beginning of the year, to raise or lower one's exposure to either or all of the three base asset classes. We calibrate a hypothetical success ratio together with a given bet size so that, over the full period, asset allocation value added averages 0.5% pre-tax per year, with a tracking error of 1%, and thus an information of 0.5. We assume that this alpha is taxed, when realized, at a 20% tax rate when executed through physical securities and at a 30% tax rate when executed through futures (though theoretically we ought to have chosen a 28% tax rate in view of the 60/40 long-term/short-term capital gains treatment afforded to futures contracts under Section 1256).

The final variable is *systematic portfolio rebalancing or drift*. We assume that investors who do not have, or do not believe in, tactical asset allocation value added must make one of two choices. They can opt to allow the portfolio to drift toward progressively higher weighting in the better performing asset; or they may systematically rebalance the portfolio to the strategic asset allocation mix once a year. We assumed the same tax treatment as above.

Eight portfolio management processes

We now have eight different approaches to managing a global equity portfolio, which we need to test in order to evaluate the anticipated benefit of an approach segregating the different decision axes and incorporating derivative instruments:

- an all-indexed physical security portfolio with drift;
- a partially active, all-physical security portfolio with drift – where the U.S. large-capitalization stocks are actively managed in a tax-aware fashion while the other stocks are indexed;
- a partially active, all-physical security portfolio, periodically rebalanced, where the asset allocation, instead of being allowed to drift, is rebalanced to the strategic norm once a year;
- an all-active, all-physical security portfolio with no tactical asset allocation alpha – where the U.S. large-capitalization stocks are managed actively in a tax-aware fashion, the other stocks are actively managed in a tax-oblivious fashion, and the portfolio's asset allocation is rebalanced to the strategic norm once a year;
- an all-active, all-physical security portfolio with tactical asset allocation alpha – same as preceding, except that asset allocation is rebalanced to a desired target reflecting a tactical asset allocation alpha once a year;
- a portfolio comprising a mix of physical and derivative securities, with drift – where all physical assets are invested in a tax-aware U.S. large-capitalization equity portfolio, strategic asset allocation is achieved through a five-year index swap, and annual actual effective asset class exposures are allowed to drift;
- a portfolio comprising a mix of physical and derivative securities, rebalanced – same as preceding, except that annual actual effective asset class exposures are rebalanced to the strategic norm once a year through index futures contracts; and
- a portfolio comprising a mix of physical and derivative securities with tactical asset allocation alpha – same as preceding, except that annual actual effective asset class exposures are rebalanced to a desired target reflecting a tactical asset allocation alpha once a year through the index futures contracts.

Test results and interpretation

The overall conclusion of the experiment was that *it seems possible to achieve a higher degree of tax efficiency – and thus to earn higher after-tax returns – when one is prepared to use a combination of physical and derivative securities*, rather than selecting strategies relying solely on physical securities. In fact, the main finding of the experiment seems to be that it is possible to preserve most of the tax efficiency gained by the use of a tax-aware security selection process applied to one of the asset classes, if the asset allocation risk profile is managed through long-dated index swaps and short-term asset allocation alpha is implemented through index future contracts.

Pre-tax return analysis

Although we are principally interested in after-tax results, it is important to evaluate the pre-tax returns across the different strategies. We know that, on a pre-tax basis, the return contributions from different decision axes can be added one to the other, so that a pre-tax analysis makes it possible to evaluate the impact of each of the various dimensions of possible value added, and thus to gain confidence in the model used in the experiment. For the integrity of the model to be established, we need to verify that the contribution of each decision follows the path that we expected, in the way we expected.

Physical-only process

Exhibit 14.2 tracks the impact of the various sources of value added in the context of a process relying solely on physical securities. We follow the portfolio as it moves from a fully indexed strategy allowed to drift over time – the all-indexed drift portfolio – to one comprising actively managed physical security exposures to all three asset classes, with tactical asset allocation insights. Only the U.S. large-capitalization stock exposure is managed in a tax-aware fashion when nonindexed. It is very encouraging to see the very close relationship between predicted and observed returns, indicating that the model does work the way it was designed to.

Introducing derivative securities into the process

Exhibit 14.3 tracks the impact of the various sources of value added in the context of a portfolio invested in a mix of physical U.S. large-capitalization stocks and derivative securities. Again, these portfolios are compared with a base comprising physical securities managed to track their respective asset class indexes, with asset weights allowed to drift in response to relative return movements. The U.S. large-capitalization stock exposure is still managed in a tax-aware fashion.

Exhibit 14.2

Simulated pre-tax returns for portfolios invested in physical securities (%)*

| | Pre-tax returns | |
	Predicted	*Observed*
Fully-indexed drift portfolio	7.965	7.965
Tax-aware LC alpha	1.360	1.366
Non-LC indexed drift portfolio	9.325	9.330
Systematic rebalancing impact	-0.020	-0.020
Non-LC indexed rebalanced portfolio	9.305	9.310
Non-tax-aware value added	0.809	0.807
Small capitalization stocks	0.302	
EAFE stocks	0.507	
All active, no TAA portfolio	10.114	10.117
TAA alpha	0.524	0.520
All active, with TAA portfolio	10.637	10.637

* Tax-aware large capitalization pre-tax alpha is equal to 1.360% (= 2.27% * 60%), while non-tax-aware non-large capitalization value added is equal to 0.809% (= [2.01% * 15%]+[2.03% * 25%]). [Note that numbers may vary marginally because of rounding, as the computer does not stop at the second or even third decimal.]

Exhibit 14.3

Simulated pre-tax returns for portfolios invested in physical and derivative securities (%)*

	Pre-tax returns	
	Predicted	*Observed*
Non-LC indexed drift portfolio	9.325	9.330
Tax-aware value added on		
Non-LC exposure	0.907	0.910
Swap costs		
Small capitalization stocks	0.105	
EAFE stocks	0.138	
Non-LC swapped drift portfolio	9.989	9.998
Systematic rebalancing impact	0.027	0.027
Non-LC swapped rebalanced portfolio	10.016	10.025
TAA alpha	0.524	0.515
Non-LC swapped with TAA portfolio	10.540	10.540

* Tax-aware value added on non-large-capitalization exposure is equal to 0.907% (= 2.27% * 40%).

Comparing these results with those in Exhibit 14.2 allows us to identify the pre-tax impact of using different mechanisms to execute different decisions. It supports the view that there is no pre-tax benefit to a hybrid strategy comprising physical and derivative securities, when compared with an alternative involving actively managed physical securities. In fact, there is a pre-tax cost. This should not cause any surprise, as it reflects the costs associated with index swaps, for which there cannot be any tax benefit in a pre-tax context.

The results shown in Exhibits 14.2 and 14.3 suggest that the model works in a pre-tax environment, as the various components of returns add reasonably well in a sequential manner, and differences, when they exist, seem minimal and insignificant. It is thus reasonable to use the same model to evaluate the after-tax impact of splitting the execution of different portfolio decisions between physical and derivative securities.

Pre-liquidation after-tax return analysis

How does taking taxes into consideration affect these results? Before going further, we should note that the analysis incorporates one minor simplifying assumption. Now that we are dealing with after-tax statistics, we cannot really break down returns into their individual after-tax components as simply as we did in the case of pre-tax returns. Taxes are paid on total portfolio return, rather than on each of the components of returns. We must therefore allow for the intrinsic inaccuracy of attributing the whole of the change in tax efficiency to the management value added – though one could argue that management activity should bear the full cost associated with the management.

Nevertheless, the results shown in Exhibits 14.4 and 14.5 make two key points. First, investment strategies implemented through actively managed physical securities can effectively prove inferior on an after-tax basis to a policy of indexing either individual security weights or asset weights, or both. Second, and conversely, an investment strategy combining tax-aware physical security selection with processes using derivative securities to execute any required shift in asset allocation seem to preserve most of the active management value added on an after-tax basis.

Physical securities only

Exhibit 14.4 traces the impact of taxation on the various sources of alpha, when the portfolio is still confined to physical securities. It points to two main conclusions. The first is not surprising, given the assumptions on which the test is based: the analysis shows that the use of a tax-aware investment strategy for U.S. large-capitalization U.S. stocks does not materially affect the portfolio's overall tax efficiency relative to an indexed alternative.

The second conclusion is that most of the expected security selection alpha is preserved on an after-tax basis. At the same time, it illustrates how little of the tax-oblivious security selection alpha assumed to accrue to the small-capitalization and non-U.S. stocks actually reaches the after-tax returns. This is understandable, as the fact of managing the assets rather than indexing them causes capital gains to be realized in these tax-oblivious portfolios, and these capital gains relate to the whole of the return on the asset class rather than just to the management value added.

Similarly, Exhibit 14.4 shows that very little of the tactical asset allocation alpha is retained on an after-tax basis if the strategy is implemented solely through physical securities. In fact, this probably overstates the amount of alpha that is retained: the drag on performance

Exhibit 14.4

Simulated after-tax returns for portfolios invested in physical securities (%)*

	Predicted tax efficiency	After-tax returns Predicted	Observed	Observed tax efficiency
Fully-indexed drift portfolio	97.5	7.766	7.710	96.8
Tax-aware LC alpha	97.0	1.319	1.304	95.5
Non-LC indexed drift portfolio		9.085	9.014	96.6
Systematic rebalancing impact		-0.11	-0.109	
Non-LC indexed rebalanced portfolio		8.976	8.904	95.6
Non-tax-aware value added		0.590	0.046	5.7
Small capitalization stocks	73.0	0.220		
EAFE stocks	73.0	0.370		
All active, no TAA portfolio		9.566	8.950	88.5
TAA alpha	80.0	0.419	0.018	3.4
All active, with TAA portfolio		9.985	8.968	84.3

* Tax-aware large-capitalization after-tax alpha is equal to 1.319% (= 97% of [2.27% * 60%]), while non-tax-aware non-large-capitalization value added is equal to 0.59% (= 73% of [2.01% * 15%]+[2.03% * 25%]). [Note that numbers may vary marginally because of rounding, as the computer does not stop at the second or even third decimal.]

is fully accounted for by the capital gains, assumed to be long-term, that are associated with cash flows into or out of each asset class. We have not assumed that this activity made the management of each portfolio even less efficient. We started with the view that the managers paid no attention to taxes, although they were allowed to take advantage at the security selection level of tax losses incurred in the asset allocation process.

It would therefore be fair to conclude that active tactical asset allocation or, even, active tax-oblivious management do not appear to be attractive strategies to a taxable investor who cannot or does not want to use derivative securities. This appears particularly relevant, considering the fact that the payment of taxes is certain, being incurred when the opening transaction is executed, while the value added that one expects to earn is uncertain, being realized, if at all, when the closing transaction is executed.

Introducing derivative securities into the process

Let us now use derivative securities to segregate execution across the different decision axes. Our portfolios now comprise a physical exposure to U.S. large capitalization stocks, managed in a tax-aware fashion, and using over-the-counter index swaps and listed index futures for asset allocation purposes, as shown in Exhibit 14.5. The results offer room for optimism to investors who believe that active management can produce value added and yet still seek to preserve as much as possible of that value added on an after-tax basis. Indeed, two points emerge.

First, the bulk of the security selection alpha is preserved on an after-tax basis. The average security selection tax efficiency of 62.1% experienced with a strategy comprising physical securities only (that is, 95.5% on tax-aware U.S. large-capitalization stock alpha and 5.7% on tax-oblivious alpha on U.S. small-capitalization stock and non-U.S. equities) rises to

---

Exhibit 14.5

Simulated after-tax returns for portfolios invested in physical and derivative securities (%)*

	Predicted tax efficiency	After-tax returns Predicted	Observed	Observed tax efficiency
Non-LC indexed drift portfolio	97.5	9.085	9.014	96.6
Tax-aware value added on				
Non-LC exposure	97.0	0.878	0.846	92.9
Swap costs				
Small capitalization stocks	100.0	0.105		
EAFE stocks	100.0	0.138		
Non-LC swapped drift portfolio		9.629	9.617	96.2
Systematic rebalancing impact		0.017	0.017	
Non-LC swapped rebalanced portfolio		9.646	9.634	96.1
TAA alpha	80.0	0.419	0.353	68.6
Non-LC swapped with TAA portfolio		10.065	9.987	94.8

* Tax-aware value added on non-large-capitalization exposure is 0.88% (= 97% of [2.266% * 40%])

92.9% when derivative securities are also used. Note that the high observed tax efficiency might be misleading, to the extent that the calculations behind the numbers assume that all the tax inefficiency associated with the active management of the portfolio is attributed to the value-added component of the investment process.

The use of derivative securities allows the manager also to retain the bulk of the tactical asset allocation alpha. This is understandable: there is no physical security penalty associated with a tactical asset allocation decision. Further, as the opening derivative transaction does not constitute a taxable event, taxes are paid only after the alpha has been generated, thus eliminating one of the most frustrating timing mismatches of an after-tax asset allocation process.

A visual inspection of the data further suggests that the fact that the non-U.S. and U.S. large-capitalization equities are not anticipated to offer significantly different asset returns over time actually provides a potential tax-sheltering opportunity. When EAFE returns exceed S&P 500 returns, then tax is paid on the gains generated by the swap. At the same time, when the reverse is true, a capital loss is available to enhance the tax efficiency of the management of the physical security portfolio or to shelter short-term asset allocation gains realized through the futures driven TAA (Tactical Asset Allocation) activity. This 'trendless volatility' may actually be a valuable portfolio asset (as observed in Chapter 4).[8] Predictably, systematic rebalancing costs fall significantly in the context of a portfolio using derivatives, from about 11 basis points with an all-physical securities portfolio (see Exhibit 14.4) to less than two basis points when derivative securities are introduced.

Post-liquidation after-tax return analysis

However, as observed in Chapter 3, the real test of a tax-efficient strategy must include both pre-liquidation and post-liquidation analyses. Focusing solely on one or the other exposes the investor to the risk of reaching the wrong conclusion.

On the one hand, too much reliance on a post-liquidation analysis can diminish the apparent benefit of tax efficiency, as it does not allow for the full compounding effect to take place. Recall that this compounding effect arises from the fact that a tax-efficient investor, by deferring the realization of taxable gains, can earn a return on monies, which would otherwise have been paid out to the government.

On the other hand, too little reliance on a post-liquidation analysis can overstate the benefit of tax efficiency, particularly when the assets may need to be sold to meet some nonfinancial goal. Indeed, the deferral of taxes associated with tax efficiency means that unrealized capital gains accumulate in the portfolio, with two important implications. First, the cost of liquidating the portfolio will ultimately be higher if the investor has followed a tax-efficient strategy. Second, the higher the ratio of unrealized gains in the portfolio, the more difficult it will likely be for a portfolio manager to produce value added through active management.

While the hierarchy of the different strategies is preserved on a post-liquidation basis, the field predictably narrows. As previewed above, an important facet of tax-awareness is that the more tax-aware a portfolio is on a pre-liquidation basis, the more likely it is that, eventually, the portfolio will comprise significant unrealized capital gains.[9] This is understandable. We have defined tax-awareness as avoiding unnecessary taxes and deferring unavoidable ones. In

Exhibit 14.6

Post-liquidation penalties for seven selected strategies (%)

	Tax efficiency		
	Pre-liquidation	*Post-liquidation*	*Post liquidation penalty*
All indexed, drift	96.8	84.4	12.8
Non-LC indexed, drift	96.6	84.8	12.3
Non-LC indexed, rebalanced	95.6	84.6	11.5
All active no TAA	88.5	81.8	7.5
All active with TAA	84.3	78.4	7.0
Non-LC swapped drift	96.2	84.8	11.8
Non-LC swapped rebalanced	96.1	84.8	11.7
Non-LC swapped with TAA	94.8	84.0	11.3

a taxable context, a significant benefit of tax-awareness resides in the fact that the portfolio is allowed to earn a return on the part of its assets representing deferred taxes, which Robert Arnott and his colleagues call an interest-free loan.[10] However, ultimately, deferred taxes must be paid, except in circumstances involving the settlement of an estate, which generally benefits from a step-up in tax basis, or when the assets are gifted to a charitable foundation, for instance.

Exhibit 14.6 shows the post-liquidation penalty associated with each strategy. In this context, the penalty is defined as the percentage of pre-liquidation returns that is given up in taxes as the portfolio is liquidated. It shows that the least tax-efficient strategy, the all-active with tactical asset allocation portfolio, has to pay the least amount of 'liquidation capital gains.' This should not be surprising, as gains have been taken all along and thus taxes have been paid all along as well. In our view, though, the most interesting and potentially useful insight is that a single-asset tax-aware physical security portfolio, complemented by derivative instrument strategies designed to produce strategic and/or tactical asset allocations, has roughly the same post-liquidation penalty as a strategy using indexed processes for each asset class with asset allocation being allowed to drift.

Risk review

Having considered the impact of the use of derivative instruments on pre-tax and after-tax returns, we must also evaluate the risks associated with the strategy. Exhibit 14.7 returns to a problem discussed in Chapter 4, and presents another illustration of the importance of portfolio drift. It shows the terminal portfolio exposure to large capitalization U.S. equities under three different sets of strategic management assumptions.

In the first case, the whole portfolio is allowed to drift, and the U.S. large-capitalization equity exposure is actively managed, while the other two equity strategies are indexed. In this design, the large-capitalization equity has the highest expected return, and the portfolio gradually drifts toward that strategy.

Exhibit 14.7

Portfolio drift with physical-only portfolios: terminal U.S. large-capitalization stock exposure

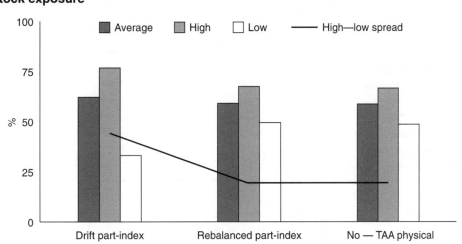

In the second case, the U.S. large-capitalization stocks are managed actively in a tax-aware fashion, while the other two strategies are indexed. The portfolio's asset allocation is rebalanced to the strategic norm once a year.

In the last case, the U.S. large-capitalization stocks are managed actively in a tax-aware fashion, while the other two strategies are also actively managed, but in a tax-oblivious fashion. The portfolio's asset allocation is rebalanced to the strategic norm once a year.

Portfolio drift and risk

Exhibit 14.7 illustrates the impact of portfolio drift, admittedly taken to an extreme. It focuses on the tails of the distribution for physical portfolios with no asset allocation alpha. (It would not make sense to consider portfolios with asset allocation alpha, as TAA insights are meant to drive the asset allocation away from the strategic mix.) The exhibit shows that the strategy allowing portfolio drift experiences a much wider dispersion between the high-end and low-end allocations to U.S. large-capitalization stocks at the end of the 10th year. In fact, the dispersion between the high-and low-end allocations for portfolios rebalanced annually reflects the drift that can accrue within a year, as asset returns range across the full spectrum of possible alternatives in a normal distribution context. By contrast, the difference between the dispersion shown for the rebalanced portfolios and the portfolio that is allowed to drift depicts the real impact of portfolio drift over a 10-year period. It stands to reason that the risk inherent in these two extreme portfolios is considerably different from the risk of the average portfolio.

This is confirmed by the data shown in Exhibit 14.8, where all strategies are considered. There, the range of fifth and 95th percentile pre-liquidation returns does not change materi-

Exhibit 14.8

Simulated pre-tax and after-tax returns for seven selected strategies (%)

	Pre-tax return	Pre-liquidation return	Post-liquidation return	Pre-liquidation range		Tax efficiency	
				5th	95th	Pre-liquidation	Post-liquidation
All indexed, drift	7.96	7.71	6.72	1.55	13.71	96.8	84.4
Non-LC indexed, drift	9.33	9.01	7.91	2.50	15.40	96.6	84.8
Non-LC indexed, rebalanced	9.31	8.90	7.88	2.51	15.26	95.6	84.6
All active no TAA	10.12	8.95	8.28	2.72	15.06	88.5	81.8
All active with TAA	10.64	8.97	8.34	2.93	14.82	84.3	78.4
Non-LC swapped drift	10.00	9.62	8.48	2.71	16.34	96.2	84.8
Non-LC swapped rebalanced	10.02	9.63	8.50	2.91	16.29	96.1	84.8
Non-LC swapped with TAA	10.54	9.99	8.86	3.08	16.68	94.8	84.0

ally when the portfolio is rebalanced, rather than being allowed to drift. In this context, we should probably not attach much significance to the narrowing of the range by 13 basis points with physical securities, or the narrowing by 25 basis points in the case of the strategy partially relying on derivative securities.

Summary and implications

The overall results of the experiment summarized in Exhibit 14.8 suggest that a strategy combining tax-aware security selection with asset allocation managed through derivative securities seems to be more tax-efficient than the other alternatives we considered. The returns shown (pre-tax, after-tax pre-liquidation, and after-tax post-liquidation) are 10-year compound averages over the 1,000 independent paths of the experiment. The pre-liquidation range of after-tax returns reflects the 10-year compound average return for the fifth and 95th percentiles of each distribution. Tax efficiency is defined as the ratio of after-tax to pre-tax average returns.

Tax-aware investors should definitely consider incorporating derivative strategies in the management of a multi-asset class portfolio. In the context of an equity portfolio invested in three asset classes, the scope offered by the use of index futures and swaps to add value seems very significant, preserving any alpha generated in any active management process.

Practically, the evidence suggests that one should:

- consider combining physical and derivative security strategies to maximize one's after-tax wealth, at least in a multi-asset class context;
- evaluate active management strategies on the basis of their ability to generate after-tax value added; and
- instead of evaluating any strategy independently, look at all strategies in a total portfolio context.

Expanding the conclusions to a balanced portfolio context

Conceptually, this experiment simply validates the idea that tax-efficient investors should look at the management of their portfolios in a different manner. Rather than focusing on the traditional decision axes and implementing all decisions through individual security transactions, they should consider alternatives. This conclusion is in fact quite consistent with the idea of constructing tax-efficient portfolios differently (discussed in Chapter 6). The portfolio might segregate security selection and asset allocation decisions, using derivative instruments to achieve the desired results, within the constraints of the tax codes of individual countries.

For instance, one could replicate the experiment with a balanced portfolio, electing to transform some of the physical equity exposure into synthetic bonds, through the use of a long-term swap. Clearly, there will be several jurisdictions where such a swap might be viewed as a 'constructive sale' and thus not be feasible, but many advisors suggest that it is still possible to design an acceptable transaction to achieve these goals.

The practical implication of the idea is to concentrate the security selection value added of the portfolio on the asset classes where it is most achievable, and to transport or add some of that value added onto assets where the value added is not achievable. Further, one can go through this analysis with after-tax value added in mind. Thus, one might elect to seek security selection alpha in the asset classes where one can both achieve some reasonable value added and where that value added can be protected after-taxes. Conversely, one can use derivative transactions to create the desired exposure to asset classes where market efficiency is such that security selection alpha is not achievable.

An important caveat: substantially increased complexity

Derivative-based strategies involve a greater degree of complexity in the management of the portfolio. First, the various indices selected for the swap or futures contracts must be sufficiently different from each other to avoid falling foul of 'straddle' tax rules. Second, any tax-aware process applied to physical securities will also typically be considerably more complex than a tax-oblivious one. Third, the 'lumpiness' of derivative contracts would make the efficient management of a portfolio with significant cash flows, such as a mutual fund, more challenging and complex. Finally, including both taxable and tax-exempt assets in the same portfolio has the potential to create another dimension of complexity.

The 'total package' nature of these strategies corresponds to the total portfolio nature of the after-tax asset management problem. At the same time, they are complex because they reflect the need for taxable investors to adopt *integrated approaches* to their asset management needs, incorporating financial planning, estate planning, and investment management into a single framework. This suggests the need for a new role: the investment management industry is still principally focused on individual product offerings, while few investors have the resources to combine different products into a single package and manage that package over time. Private investors need a wealth manager to help them through that maze (discussed in more detail in Chapter 19).

[1] See Apelfeld, Roberto, Gordon Fowler, Jr., and James Gordon, Jr., 'Tax-Aware Equity Investing,' *The Journal of Portfolio Management,*, Winter 1996, pp. 18–28.

[2] See Brunel, Jean L.P., 'A Tax-Aware Approach to the Management of a Multi-Asset Class Portfolio,' *The Journal of Private Portfolio Management*, Spring 1999, pp. 57–70.

[3] See Jacobs, Bruce I., and Kenneth N. Levy, 'Alpha Transport With Derivatives,' *The Journal of Portfolio Management,*, 25th Anniversary Issue, May 1999, pp. 55–60.

[4] For more detail, see Anson, Mark J.P., 'The Impact of the Taxpayer Relief Act of 1997 on Derivatives Transactions,' *Journal of Derivatives*, Summer 1998, pp. 62–72.

[5] Tax efficiency is defined as the ratio of after-tax to pre-tax returns. It is thus one – the portfolio's tax rate.

[6] Tracking error is defined as the volatility of the alpha. A tracking error of 3.25% associated with an alpha of 2.25% means that the portfolio's excess return will be between -1% and 5.5% two-thirds' of the time.

[7] For a discussion of the impact of the Taxpayer Relief Act of 1997 on derivatives transactions and illustrations of the complexity of the tax code, see the article referenced in note 4 above.

[8] See also Brunel, Jean L.P., 'The Upside-Down World of Tax-Aware Investing,' *Trusts and Estates*, February 1997, pp. 34–42.

[9] Jim Poterba has started to focus on the idea that the tax on unrealized capital gains should not be considered to be zero. At an AIMR Seminar in Boston in November 1998, he actually demonstrated that there is a direct interaction between the taxes associated with capital gains and the estate duties eventually payable.

[10] See Arnott, Robert D., Andrew L. Berkin, and Jia Ye, 'Loss Harvesting: What's It Worth To The Taxable Investor?,' *The Journal of Wealth Management*, Spring 2001, pp. 10–18.

Chapter 15

Tax-efficient security selection

In Chapter 14 it was shown that a tax-efficient investor should segregate the execution modes of the different axes of the investment process. In this chapter, this principle is applied to security selection. This will provide us with an opportunity to see a practical illustration of the two types of transactions we uncovered in Chapter 4: alpha-generating and alpha-enabling.

The starting point is to understand fully all the different aspects of any individual security transaction. The almost total absence of significant transaction cost in the tax-oblivious world has lulled many investors into a dangerous complacency. They have failed to analyze the real process through which an investment decision is made and executed. Though there is nothing wrong in taking the occasional short cut, it can become an important problem when the lack of a full understanding of all aspects of the process prevents the investor from thinking the transaction through in a different environment. The difference in environment is important as it involves the need to be concerned about the tax consequences of each and every move.

The fundamentals of an investment transaction

Excluding, for a short while, these cases where a portfolio holds more cash or money market instruments than desired, it is a simple truism that an investment transaction involves a two-step process. When the transaction is driven by a purchase intention, it starts with the sale of a security that one no longer considers attractive enough, and proceeds with the purchase of a security that one wants to hold in the portfolio. When the transaction is driven by a sale intention, it starts with that sale and continues with the reinvestment of the proceeds from that sale.

When I started as an investment analyst, in the early 1970s, we were explicitly taught *not* to consider both sides of any transaction. In the tax-oblivious world, the logical approach is to consider each decision on its own merits. Thus, I should not be concerned with the need to raise cash to buy a security that I believe is very attractive. Nor should I worry about the need to reinvest the cash proceeds of the sale of any security that I believe no longer belongs in the portfolio.

This logic still makes sense, as there is a risk that a decision will be corrupted when extraneous considerations are brought into the picture. The idea that one should not worry about the other leg of any decision reflects the fact that, in the tax-oblivious world, the only cost associated with a purchase or a sale relates to transaction costs. These have been brought down dramatically by substantial declines in brokerage commissions and sophisticated trading tools that minimize market impact (the extent to which the transaction causes the price of the security to move, up or down).[1] Thus, it is generally fair to assume that one can always raise sufficient cash, in an almost cost-free manner, to meet the obligation created by a purchase.

The logic is only marginally more complex when dealing with a sale. The simplest conceptual image is to assume that I can always create a 'synthetic' index with any cash in the portfolio, by buying the appropriate futures contract on the index or indexes making up the benchmark of my portfolio, which approximate the factor exposure left by the security that I just sold.

Unfortunately, this logic no longer applies when dealing with taxable portfolios. Indeed, introducing taxes into the equation makes the problem dramatically different. Just as the assumptions underpinning the traditional 'efficient frontier' wealth optimization framework no longer apply once taxes are taken into consideration (see Chapter 11), so we can no longer assume transaction costs away when dealing with individual security transactions. Though the actual commission and market costs may still be negligible, there will be real tax costs associated with any transaction, whether one is seeking to buy a security or to sell one. This creates the need for a radical change in investment decision-making. In the taxable world, individual transactions can no longer be analyzed in a vacuum. They must be considered in a total portfolio or subportfolio context. That context is best described using a three-dimensional framework, rather than a two-dimensional one, addressing return (or value added), risk (or tracking error), and tax efficiency.

An analytical framework

Before going further, let us first set out an analytical framework that I developed for a presentation to an AIMR conference[2] to look into the tax efficiency of various equity investment processes. This framework allows managers to observe their own processes or, as they recommend investments to clients, to analyze how other managers manage money. The main principle is that tax efficiency depends on the interaction of three critical variables: security selection, portfolio construction, and risk management.

Security selection

Two areas of security selection have great significance for tax efficiency: defining the investment universe and deciding how to perform investment research. We seek to understand the investment universe from which we will select investment candidates, and to formulate the research process used to select these few candidates from among the great number of stocks that we will choose to ignore.

Let us first consider the issue of the *investment universe*, which is closely related to the choice of benchmark. Imagine a case in which a manager is handling a portfolio of U.S. large-capitalization equities. The manager can think of the investment universe in one of two ways. The 'raw' approach involves deciding that all stocks in the S&P 500 Index, and maybe a few additional stocks at the periphery, are eligible for inclusion in the portfolio and are thus part of the universe. An alternative method is to screen stocks for certain characteristics that may enhance their tax efficiency. For example, holdings with long-expected investment horizons tend to be more tax-efficient, because they require less short-term turnover. This might allow the eventual return on these stocks to be taxed at the 20% long-term capital gain rate in the United States, rather than at the more expensive 40% short-term capital gain tax rate.

Choosing one or other approach will lead the manager toward different investment universes. In one case, he or she will be looking at a universe driven principally by the characteristics of the stocks included in the S&P 500 Index. The resulting investment candidates will likely not suffer from any significant bias, but tax-efficient security selection will require that the analyst adopt a research process focused on after-tax returns. In the other case, the selection of a narrower universe will lead all companies in it to display certain biases, which are effectively built into the selection criteria, but the research process may remain somewhat less focused on after-tax results and still provide tax-efficient value added.

The investment research process can also have a significant impact on the tax efficiency of security selection. Though I have not yet been able to find academic work comparing the relative benefits of doing research on a pre-tax basis versus an after-tax basis, it seems intuitively intriguing to investigate the issue. In fact, logic would suggest that tilting the research process toward identifying attractiveness from the point of view of a taxable investor makes sense. Two simple questions come to mind. First, is the research done with the purpose of forecasting expected after-tax returns, or pre-tax returns? The difference could have serious tax implications for investors. Second, is the research qualitative or quantitative? Although quantitative research has many advantages, in terms of both management costs and repeatability, one major disadvantage is that no one can make an accurate model of reality.

Portfolio construction

In this narrow context, I limit the meaning of portfolio construction to the process through which individual buy and sell decisions are made and executed. Thus, the focus is on selecting the best ideas among a series of purchase or sell candidates. (A broader definition of portfolio construction would include risk management, but, for reasons that will become clear very soon, it is important to segregate the two activities at this point.) With the exception of tax-loss harvesting, portfolio construction guidelines for tax-aware investing are not significantly different from what would be done on a pre-tax basis.

We saw earlier that the fact that most portfolios do not have significant positive cash flow during the course of a year means that buying one security usually means selling another to pay for the purchase. In a tax-oblivious portfolio, every transaction a portfolio manager makes is meant to generate alpha, in the form of either additional return or lower risk for the same return. For those who manage money on an after-tax basis, the expected alpha associated with the transaction is a function of both the excess return that is expected from the purchased stock versus the sold stock, *and* the tax cost associated with any realized capital gain on the sold stock. As a result, the threshold excess return needed to make a transaction worthwhile is inversely proportional to the amount of unrealized gain on the security that is to be sold.

To make transactions more efficient, managers can use alpha-enabling transactions (as discussed in Chapter 4). In an alpha-enabling transaction, a manager takes a loss on a security, invests in a security that is equivalent, or almost equivalent, and uses the loss generated to offset the gain on yet another transaction, thereby giving the overall transaction a reasonable expected alpha. By doing so, the manager generates an after-tax alpha, or value added, that would not exist otherwise.

Risk management

Risk management is the process through which holdings are assembled into a portfolio. Two issues in this area are important for tax management: the choice of benchmark and the role of tracking error. The former has to do with the risk/return profile sought, while the latter is related to the extent to which one is prepared to move away from the benchmark in a bid to create security selection value added.

The *choice of benchmark*, driven in part by the selection of the appropriate universe, is critical to the risk management process. Adopting a traditional index without first asking whether it will provide the best reference for a particular individual investor may well prove counterproductive.

A simple example illustrates the point. Imagine that the same investor as in the earlier example is considering a U.S. large-capitalization equity portfolio. Several choices of reference index are available. A tax-oblivious manager would likely immediately recommend either the S&P 500 or the Morgan Stanley Capital International U.S. Equity index. Yet a more careful analysis of the consequences of the choice might lead the investor toward one of two smarter alternatives. If the investor wants to focus strictly on large-capitalization stocks, a growth-titled index, such as the Russell 1000 Growth, might provide a better long-term reference, because of the inherently higher tax efficiency of growth relative to value. (The tax efficiency of mutual funds grouped in the growth category, with a record of 10 years or more and a growth bias, averaged 85.3%, compared with 81.7% for funds in the value category.) Alternatively, one might consider an index incorporating both large- and small-capitalization stocks, such as the Russell 3000, to avoid the need to rebalance between large- and small-capitalization stocks from time to time.

Now, in either of these two smarter instances, a careful selection of the benchmark can promote tax efficiency relative to a traditional yardstick. However, they may also impose different constraints, relative to industry, credit (in the case of fixed-income portfolios only), sector or other factor weights, than would be the case with a traditional index, as the narrower index comprises different factor exposures. This reflects the fact that the index incorporates certain biases, as certain tax-inefficient areas are systematically avoided. Yet, in the end, a carefully chosen benchmark can provide a substantially better long-term, after-tax return potential to a taxable investor.

The *management of tracking error* is another important element of the equation. The standard tax-oblivious practice looks at a two-dimensional trade-off, where tracking error is considered as the cost associated with the generation of value added or alpha. In the world of the taxable investor, the trade-off, as we saw earlier, comprises three dimensions, as tax efficiency must now be incorporated into the analysis. Once tax efficiency becomes part of the landscape, the trade-off becomes more complex (as we saw in Chapter 9, when we discussed a different definition of 'active management'). Yet accepting a modest increase in tracking error offset by substantially better tax efficiency may be a very wise choice for a taxable investor, who does not need to worry about the arcane style or bias differences that typically concern a tax-oblivious institutional investor.

The three-dimensional approach

Exhibit 15.1 shows a set of three axes that can be used to graph the relative positions of different equity processes, depending on the way in which they score on each of the three dimensions of the analytical framework: security selection, risk management, and portfolio construction.

Note that the range of value on each axis does not extend from zero to infinity, but from tax-oblivious to tax-sensitive. At one end of the spectrum, we find a tax-oblivious manager, with a portfolio represented by a point at the origin where all three axes intersect. By definition, he or she does not take taxes into consideration when making any of the three decisions. By contrast, at the other end of the spectrum we have the hypothetical ideal tax-sensitive manager, represented by a point with coordinates near the end of each axis. He or she takes taxes fully into account in every single decision.

Though I believe that only one solution is optimal, one can think of three different approaches to tax-efficient security selection:

- minimizing the tax drag associated with tax-oblivious investment decisions;

Exhibit 15.1

A three-dimensional approach to assessing tax efficiency

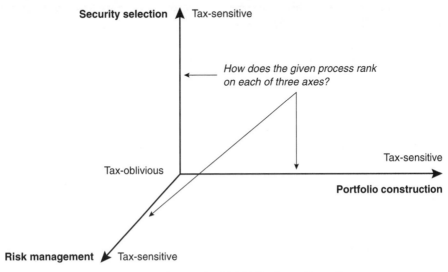

Source: Brunel, Jean L.P. 'Tax-Aware Equity Investing,' AIMR Conference Proceedings. *Investment Counseling for Private Clients II,* November 9-10, 1999, pp 50-57

- incorporating taxes into an otherwise standard tax-oblivious investment decision- making process; or
- creating a custom tax-efficient investment process.

Let us look into each approach in turn.

Minimizing the tax drag associated with tax-oblivious investment decisions

This first step toward tax efficiency involves an approach that I call the 'traditional tax-managed process.' The approach, which has been adopted by a substantial number of mutual funds, boils down to two major process steps: lot accounting and year-end loss harvesting.

Lot accounting

Most tax jurisdictions allow managers to select the approach they want to use to account for the different lots comprising their portfolios. Many tax-oblivious managers have traditionally used the average cost accounting (ACA) method, because their investment accounting systems did not provide for lot identification. Thus, the book value of any share of stock held in their portfolio is calculated by computing the average cost of all the different purchases comprising the holding. Other approaches are feasible, however, and a sensible approach to tax lot identification can help minimize net capital gain realization.

Jeffrey Mink[3] suggests that: 'one way to minimize realized gains is to sell from the tax lot with the highest purchase price. This is the "highest in, first out" (HIFO) strategy.' Mink found that HIFO outperforms ACA by one to 93 basis points each year, depending upon the age of the portfolio. (We will come back to this point in more detail in Chapter 18).

In fact, since Mink wrote his article many managers have moved to a new approach, dubbed 'HIFO+.' This approach differentiates between both tax cost associated with each lot and the age of the lot, ensuring that the lot selection process minimizes taxes more fully, owing to the lower tax rates applied to long-term capital gains.

Year-end loss harvesting

Though it has proven quite difficult to convince traditional portfolio managers that it makes sense to harvest losses, the practice of year-end loss harvesting has been around for many years. Traditionally, portfolio managers would look at their portfolios with an eye sensitized to taxes in the last few weeks of the fiscal year. Starting in early December, U.S. portfolio managers – together with colleagues in other countries, who might perform the same task at different times, reflecting different fiscal year-ends – would identify positions they held at a cost lower than the current market value and sell them to realize a loss. This approach has been adopted by many managers seeking solely to minimize the tax drag on their portfolios. Though this approach is arguably better than doing nothing, the process is grossly incomplete. As has been pointed out by Robert Arnott (already quoted in Chapter 5):

Exhibit 15.2

Minimizing the tax drag associated with tax-oblivious investment decisions

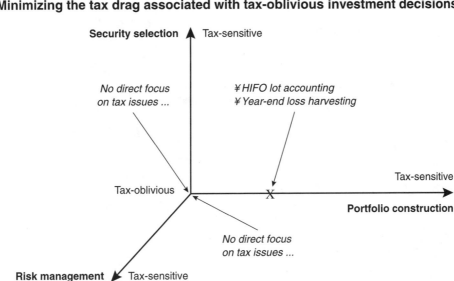

Source: Brunel, Jean L.P. 'Tax-Aware Equity Investing,' AIMR Conference Proceedings.
Investment Counseling for Private Clients II, November 9-10, 1999, pp 50-57

The *so-called* tax-sensitive investment manager, who engages in loss harvesting only once at the end of the fiscal year, has probably seen numerous loss-harvesting opportunities appear and disappear in the course of the year.

In other words, merely aiming to minimize the tax drag on the portfolio is only a limited first step, adopted by managers who wish to appear sensitive to taxes while disrupting their traditional investment processes to the minimum possible extent. Exhibit 15.2 characterizes the process, using our three-dimensional analytical framework.

Incorporating taxes in a standard tax-oblivious investment process

In this case, managers are willing to accept some disruption to their traditional, tax-oblivious investment processes, but the degree to which they tolerate these changes varies. A few accept only minimal disruptions, while, at the other end of the spectrum, others stop barely short of optimal tax efficiency. These modified processes essentially come in three different variations, which we discuss here in order of increasing sophistication and likely contribution to tax efficiency: goal-based tax efficiency, screen-based tax efficiency and systematic tax efficiency.

Goal-based tax efficiency

In this design, the portfolio manager imposes dramatic but subjective limits on the investment

---

Exhibit 15.3

Goal-based tax efficiency

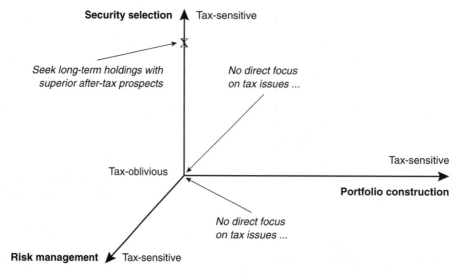

Source: Brunel, Jean L.P. 'Tax-Aware Equity Investing,' AIMR Conference Proceedings.
Investment Counseling for Private Clients II, November 9-10, 1999, pp 50-57

---

universe from which he or she plans to select securities. The choice is focused on stocks for which the expected holding period is very long or the expected return is extremely high.

For example, a manager I know focuses on the emerging leaders of an industry, which he defines as the firms that are taking market share away from the industry's established players. He expects that the emerging leader stocks will double, triple, or quadruple in value. On a normal day, his portfolio consists of 10–30 stocks. These positions are investments that the manager has made for the very long term. He has very sharp selection criteria, but they are all subjective. He does not follow complex portfolio construction techniques. Individual stocks are often equally weighted, although conviction can play a role in allowing a stock to drift higher as a proportion of the portfolio, or in building positions from a smaller starting weight.

In this design, a manager would effectively ignore broad tax-efficient portfolio construction approaches, the tax implications associated with selling securities, and even the potential to harvest losses. Such a manager would likely have loose risk management, if any, because he or she would probably not feel that the portfolio is tied to any real benchmark or reference index. Rather, they would concentrate entirely on seeking stocks with long-term potential. Exhibit 15.3 describes that process in terms of our three analytical axes.

Note that this approach can be very close to the process used by certain 'directional hedge fund' managers. Directional, here, means that the portfolio is exposed to market risk, which the manager does not seek to hedge. Thus, it follows that certain hedge funds can be tax-efficient, at least within the confines of this limited definition of tax efficiency.

250

Screen-based tax efficiency

In this case, the search for tax efficiency is first still based on a narrowing of the broad investment universe, but the process is often more quantitative and may incorporate additional steps.

For example, a large institution developed a process initially based on four screens, depicting long-term historical earnings growth, medium-term forecast earnings growth, current and prospective profitability, and market valuation. For each of these conceptual screens, the firm developed an appropriate set of objective criteria, sourced from standard databases and processed internally, to reflect industry and other factor exposures for which the manager wanted to adjust. Each stock in the firm's large-capitalization equity universe was ranked relative to all others on the basis of its scores on the four screens. These individual screen scores were then aggregated, with appropriate weights assigned to each screen. The manager would then consider the stocks in the top 20% of the ranked universe and apply qualitative research and portfolio construction processes to them.

The goal of a screen-based investment process is thus not necessarily to select stocks through a purely quantitative analysis, but to focus the qualitative part of the process on stocks that possess attributes that the manager believes will help the portfolio generate superior after-tax investment returns. Also, as contrasted with the goal-based tax efficiency process, the manager is not selecting the stocks on the single basis of an investment theme. Thus, a screen-based portfolio construction process often also has buy and sell disciplines that focus on a net positive after-tax alpha, and may also use HIFO accounting and systematic loss harvesting, although this is not always the case. The main weakness of the approach still

Exhibit 15.4

Screen-based tax efficiency

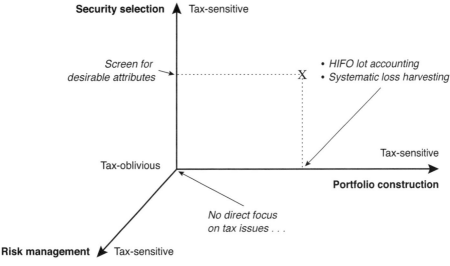

Source: Brunel, Jean L.P. 'Tax-Aware Equity Investing,' AIMR Conference Proceedings.
Investment Counseling for Private Clients II, November 9-10, 1999, pp 50-57

Exhibit 15.5

Systematic tax efficiency

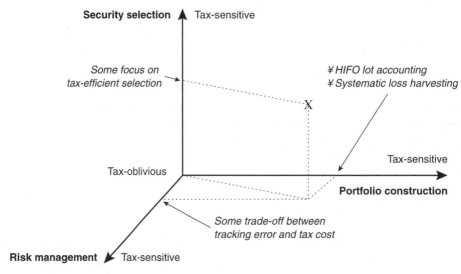

Source: Brunel, Jean L.P. 'Tax-Aware Equity Investing,' AIMR Conference Proceedings. *Investment Counseling for Private Clients II,* November 9-10, 1999, pp 50-57

relates to the lack of a tax-efficient risk management dimension to the process: typically, a screen-based process has no specific focus on the interaction between tracking error and tax efficiency. Exhibit 15.4 shows the process in our three-dimensional framework.

Systematic tax efficiency

Though arguably still not optimal, systematic tax efficiency is very close to the state of the art as this is written. There are several possible approaches to systematic tax efficiency, but they all share one common feature: tax efficiency enters into the equation in one fashion or another in each of the three dimensions of the investment process, down to the level of each individual portfolio.

Let me illustrate the two steps that usually characterize a systematic tax-efficient process. First, one constructs tax-sensitive target portfolios. These typically combine qualitative and quantitative disciplines. For instance, Manager A uses quantitative, tax-oblivious investment research and combines it with the qualitative insights of tax-sensitive portfolio managers. Manager B uses a screen-based investment process to arrive at the target portfolio, combining quantitative screens to promote tax efficiency and qualitative portfolio construction. Second, one uses a formal risk-management model to move each individual portfolio as close to the target as possible, given each account's current position, tax circumstances, and investor constraints.

Systematic tax efficiency provides important benefits in that it considers all three dimensions of the investment process. Yet it still lacks a real integration, to the extent that

Exhibit 15.6

Integrated tax efficiency

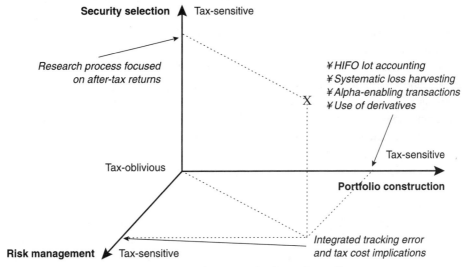

Source: Brunel, Jean L.P. 'Tax-Aware Equity Investing,' AIMR Conference Proceedings.
Investment Counseling for Private Clients II, November 9-10, 1999, pp 50-57

it does not incorporate all the techniques that are now or will soon become available to portfolio managers. Exhibit 15.5 describes systematic tax efficiency in terms of these three variables.

Creating a custom tax-efficient investment process

It can only be a matter of time before managers are forced to practice 'integrated tax efficiency.' The concept is described in Exhibit 15.6, in more theoretical than practical terms, though we can begin to guess at the critical innovation still ahead of us.

Security selection

Though the current practice is for formal research to be effectively tax-oblivious, one can imagine that the growth in the volume of assets managed on behalf of taxable investors may motivate certain firms to ask their analysts to refocus on tax-awareness. This may be done in at least one of two ways.

The first would simply involve inviting analysts to focus on the longer-term prospects of the companies they follow and downplay the short-term trends that tax-exempt investors typically emphasize. More complex, but still conceptually reasonable, would be a process geared to equating prices and long-term, after-tax returns. Some variant on the traditional dividend discount model might allow analysts to evaluate the trade-off between capital gains and dividends, or short-term and long-term prospects.

Portfolio construction

In addition to the simple tools currently available, one could imagine at least three additional features that would promote tax efficiency. First, a systematic use of portfolio optimizers[4] should help capture more investment opportunities, whether related to new purchase ideas or to intelligent loss harvesting. Second, a careful integration of single derivative securities should allow portfolio managers to minimize the risk associated with stocks that they should not sell for a while for tax reasons. Third, a systematic use of multiple security derivative instruments should help manage more effectively all the appropriate factor exposures, such as industry in a single country portfolio or currency, or country and industry in a multi-country portfolio.

Imagine, for example, that a difficult market environment has brought most of the stocks in a given industry down as a block. A manager may be able to produce higher after-tax returns through the simultaneous use of standard loss harvesting and either call options on those stocks that he or she did not hold (to avoid tangling with the 'wash sale' rules), or exchange-traded baskets.

Risk management

Risk management will likely evolve along two different axes. First, there will be a need to optimize the target to which individual portfolios are managed. This will involve the need to evaluate with greater care the extent to which the manager is effectively compensated for the risk that he or she takes in a bid to generate higher after-tax returns. One could imagine a risk model using formal estimates of after-tax returns for each security in the universe to accomplish this task.

Second, there will remain the need to manage the risk associated with each individual investor portfolio. The challenge faced by any tax-aware portfolio manager is to translate as much of his or her insights into each client portfolio as feasible, given the client's current position, tax circumstances, and investment preferences or constraints.

A compelling case for integrated tax efficiency

Work by Roberto Apelfeld and two colleagues[5] suggests an interesting observation that illustrates the need to follow an integrated approach to tax-efficient portfolio management. Apelfeld and his colleagues used a sophisticated portfolio optimizer to evaluate the potential benefits of tax-efficient portfolio management. More to the point, they compared the potential benefits of portfolio tilts, such as the traditional value or growth approaches, together with momentum and a J.P. Morgan proprietary stock valuation model. They found that:

> among the BARRA strategies, the value-oriented stock selection measures display a distinct edge over the momentum-based ones. In fact, the book/price strategy produces the highest returns at every level of risk, while the success strategy generally produces the lowest.

This is interesting, as we know that a typical value portfolio, managed in a tax-unaware manner, will normally produce returns that are less tax-efficient than a similarly managed growth portfolio. The need for total process integration is found in their explanation of the phenomenon:

This result makes sense in light of the fact that the tax-aware optimization process has a measure of momentum investing built into it: Winners are held, while losers end up being sold for their tax losses. A momentum-based alpha ends up being somewhat redundant in this context, while the value-based alpha acts as a complement to the portfolio construction procedure.

Going back to the partial tax-efficient processes discussed earlier, it stands to reason that focusing on tax efficiency in one aspect of the investment process, while ignoring it in the others, exposes the investor to the risk of losing some or all of the edge that he or she thought had been built in. A similar risk is not present when the investment process is created with after-tax return and risk measures in mind from the start.

Fixed-income issues

Tax-efficient security selection is certainly not limited to the world of equity portfolios. The issue is equally important in the fixed-income arena, as Guy Davidson[6] has acutely observed:

> For individual investors … tax considerations are important because value can be added after-tax over time, through active management, without appreciably changing the risk of the portfolio.

Davidson discusses the value of tax management in municipal and high-yield corporate bond portfolios, and proposes two critical conclusions. First, 'the objectives of municipal tax management are to harvest losses and insure your client is compensated when gains are realized.' Second, 'tax management for taxable bonds (bonds whose income is subject to federal tax) takes advantage of the difference between the income and capital gains tax rates for individuals, and the timing of tax payments.' Let us consider each of these conclusions in turn.

Municipal bond management

An essentially U.S. creature, a municipal bond offers tax-exempt income. Certain bonds offer a triple exemption, to the extent that their interest is exempt from city, state and federal taxes; others offer only partial exemptions, as they may or may not be exempt from state and city taxes.[7] In either case, however, they retain a typical capital gain treatment when sold at prices higher than their tax bases. Therein lies the focus of the portfolio manager. Any yield swap – selling a bond to buy another one with a higher yield – must reflect the tax consequences associated with a potential capital gain if the bond being sold is held with an unrealized capital gain. Yet, just as was the case earlier when we were looking into equities, bonds can also be sold at a loss, thus providing opportunities to shelter gains elsewhere in the portfolio.

Davidson investigates the value of harvesting losses with a Monte Carlo simulation, assuming that changes in interest rates were normally distributed. For each maturity, he began with current interest rate levels and randomly generated 6,000 different interest rate scenarios for one year later, based on the historical yield volatility of each maturity. These scenarios allowed him to compute changes in yield and thus price changes. He used a constant maturity bond as a proxy for the change in value of a laddered portfolio with a constant maturity. If the

Exhibit 15.7

The value of harvesting municipal bond losses (%)

Short-term gains rate:	39.6		Short-term gains rate:	20.0
Long-term gains rate:	20.0		Long-term gains rate:	20.0

	Annualized over holding period				Annualized over holding period		
Maturity	One-year horizon	Five-year horizon	10-year horizon	Maturity	One-year horizon	Five-year horizon	10-year horizon
Two years	0.21	0.16	0.15	Two years	0.11	0.09	0.08
Five years	0.45	0.34	0.31	Five years	0.22	0.18	0.17
10 years	0.77	0.56	0.52	10 years	0.39	0.31	0.29
20 years	1.28	0.92	0.87	20 years	0.63	0.50	0.47

	Value by year				Value by year		
Loss in	First year	Fifth year	10th year	Loss in	First year	Fifth year	10th year
Two years	0.21	0.11	0.09	Two years	0.11	0.07	0.05
Five years	0.45	0.22	0.18	Five years	0.22	0.14	0.12
10 years	0.77	0.35	0.28	10 years	0.39	0.22	0.18
20 years	1.28	0.57	0.47	20 years	0.63	0.36	0.30

Source: Davidson III, R.B.

price fell over the year, he realized the loss and credited the account with the benefit of using a short-term loss. If a gain or no change in price occurred, he assumed the bond was held.

Exhibit 15.7, sourced from Davidson's work, shows both the annualized value of tax management for three investment horizons and the value of realizing losses in that year. Capital gains tax rates of 39.6% and 20% are used in the left-hand side of the table; Davidson assumed that the investor had sufficient short-term and long-term gains to offset the losses in the year in which they were realized. The same numbers are generated on the right-hand side of the table, assuming that all losses offset long-term gains.

The numbers in the table represent the value of losses realized across all the scenarios. Davidson explains:

> For example, in the first year, the value of harvesting losses for a five-year security is 45 basis points, or about a half of a percent, using a 39.6% short-term capital gains rate. This means the average value of realizing losses over that period was 90 basis points. Only half of the observations are losses – the other half were gains. So, while the average loss is worth 90 basis points, half of the observations have zero losses. The expected value of harvesting losses is 45 basis points in this scenario.

Davidson then points to three interesting observations. First, loss harvesting is increasingly valuable as the maturity of the bond lengthens. This reflects the increased price volatility associated with rising duration (or maturity). Thus, the principle we saw earlier, that volatility has value in the tax-aware investment world, is illustrated here, as average losses increase with maturity. Also, as one would expect, the value of harvesting losses in municipals is strongly impacted by the client's tax rate. Using losses to offset long-term gains has half the benefit of sheltering short-term gains.

Second, the longer the investment horizon, the less important tax management becomes. This effectively reflects the 'portfolio freeze' that we discussed earlier. As time passes, the proportion of bonds held with an unrealized gain increases, as bonds roll down the yield curve. At the same time, because the volatility of bond prices is considerably lower than the volatility observed in the equity market, the time it takes for the portfolio to tend to freeze is correspondingly reduced.

Third, as Davidson explains:

> transaction costs also need to be addressed, because they reduce the benefit of realizing losses. In the municipal market, the most significant determinant of transaction cost is transaction size. For example, the typical bid/ask spread for a $1 million trade is 0.25%. Transaction costs for lots of $50,000 to $100,000 average about 1.25%.

This is a very important insight, as it tends to suggest that most taxable investors would do well to think twice before asking for individually managed municipal bond portfolios. It would often be more beneficial for them to use municipal bond mutual funds, which can provide similar benefits with lower transaction costs and higher liquidity.

Corporate and high-yield bond management

Unlike municipal bond management, taxable bond management involves realizing both losses and gains. A strategy of realizing long-term gains and harvesting short-term losses can increase the after-tax return of taxable bond portfolios for individual investors. This strategy assumes that the individual's income tax rate is greater than their long-term capital gains rate.

Using a simulation similar to the one developed for municipal bonds, Davidson analyzed the benefit associated with tax management in the context of a taxable bond portfolio. He used high-yield bonds because they offer high pre-tax income and are volatile securities, which increases the potential for tax management. He observed that there is a significant benefit to harvesting losses there as well. In particular, he notes that 'by selling and paying a tax, the portfolio manager increased the after-tax return to the client.' This reflects the fact that the investor 'paid tax on future income today at 20% rather than hold[ing] the bond and pay[ing] 39.6% over time.' Thus, according to Davidson:

> assuming that an individual is subject to the top federal income tax bracket and consistently has short-term gains, a high turnover strategy of realizing short-term losses and long-term gains is very profitable.

Exhibit 15.8 shows the annual expected value of this tax strategy, assuming an income tax rate of 39.6%, a capital gains tax rate of 20%, and an annual yield volatility of 30%.

Exhibit 15.8

The value of tax management in high-yield bond portfolios (%)

Maturity	Total value of tax management	Value due to harvesting loss	Value due to realizing gain	Value due to yield used
Two years	0.38	0.06	0.32	7.74
Five years	1.01	0.29	0.72	8.40
10 years	1.94	0.93	1.01	9.26

Note that, because Davidson assumed that short-term losses are realized on the 364th day and that gains are taken on the 366th day, the portfolio turns over completely each year. Consequently, there is no need to progress through time: the expected value of tax trading high-yield bonds is consistent over time. Further, though transaction costs are usually modest when dealing in large lots, they tend to rise dramatically as the size of the transaction decreases. This gives further support to the idea that taxable individuals should consider the use of mutual funds, with all their inherent weaknesses, rather than aim for individual bond portfolios.

Davidson also discusses the portions of this tax-management activity attributable to harvesting losses and realizing gains, as is also shown in Exhibit 15.8.

The value of harvesting short-term losses is a function of the time value of money. While the client is able to use the loss to shelter a short-term gain today, the client will be earning higher income on the new bond going forward. The portion that is due to realizing long-term gains comes from paying today a 20% tax on future income rather than holding the bond and paying 39.6% over time.

However, Davidson also notes that:

the merits of paying taxes today to avoid taxes in the future … are limited, for two reasons:

First, paying taxes today reduces the money at work in the market. At some point, the present value of paying income taxes in the future is less than paying capital gains taxes today.

Second, paying taxes today rather than delaying assumes a high level of certainty about both the tax code and the client's taxes in the future. For both of these reasons, the strategy of realizing losses is most appropriate for short- to intermediate-term taxable bonds.

Summary and implications

Tax-efficient security selection is one area where a lot of progress is needed, as too many taxable portfolios seem currently managed in ways that should be called almost tax-oblivious. Tax efficiency appears to be an after-thought, still limited to minor process changes and year-end loss harvesting. The potential to use systematic tax-loss harvesting to add value is (as we saw in Chapter 9) such that, at the very least, its use should be broadly applied across the board, to include both equity and fixed-income securities.

Fortunately, it is also one of the areas where I would expect private asset managers to score the greatest gains in the next several years, for three major reasons. First, investors will begin to demand it. It does not take a very long memory to recall the time when the performance of mutual funds was reported only on a pre-tax basis. Times have changed and only a fool would think that tax efficiency is a fad. Progress will be assured, and even accelerated, because of the work being done by regulatory agencies and professional organizations to foster meaningful performance computation, as well as the work being done by consultants and related service providers to process that additional information, to help investors select the best managers.

Second, improving the tax efficiency of security selection can be done without requiring a dramatic shift away from the sequential optimization, building block or 'individual silo' processes that have been the norm in the institutional world. Though we will not necessarily find the integrated tax efficiency I would view as optimal, substantial progress can be achieved without totally upsetting the apple cart.

Third, tax-efficient security selection requires a great deal of computing power to be practical. J.P. Morgan's Private Bank introduced a revolutionary tax-aware equity investment process in the Fall of 1994. As the chief investment officer at the time, I participated in what we came to call the 'idiot testing phase,' during which individual portfolio managers competed with the computer to verify that the transactions recommended by the optimizer made sense. While it took approximately two minutes for the computer to scan all possible alternatives and arrive at a recommendation for any portfolio, the time it took us was measured in hours. Thus, having access to the high-speed compiling capabilities of modern computers provides a very real boost to portfolio managers who want to execute tax-efficient processes in each of their individual client portfolios.

In the end, however, tax-efficient security selection is only one of the dimensions of the problem. It needs to be combined with all other aspects of wealth management to provide each client with the most tax-efficient solution to his or her specific problem.

---

[1] For insights on trading costs, see Stoll, Hans R., 'Equity Trading Costs In-The-Large,' *The Journal of Portfolio Management*, Summer 1993, pp. 41–50; Wagner, Wayne H., and Evan Schulman, 'Passive Trading: Point and Counterpoint,' *The Journal of Portfolio Management*, Spring 1994, pp. 25–29; and Treynor, Jack L., 'The Invisible Cost of Trading,' *The Journal of Portfolio Management*, Fall 1994, pp. 71–78.

[2] See Brunel, Jean L.P., 'Tax-Aware Equity Investing,' AIMR Conference Proceedings: *Investment Counseling for Private Clients* II, November 9–10, 1999, pp. 50–57.

[3] See Mink, Jeffrey L., 'Tax-Adjusted Equity Benchmarks,' *The Journal of Private Portfolio Management*, Winter 1998, pp. 45–55.

[4] For important caveats on this issue, see Rohweder, Herold C., 'Implementing Stock Selection Ideas: Does Tracking Error Optimization Do Any Good?,' *The Journal of Portfolio Management*, Spring 1998, pp. 49–59.

[5] See Apelfeld, Roberto, Gordon Fowler, Jr., and James Gordon, Jr., 'Tax-Aware Equity Investing,' *The Journal of Portfolio Management*, Winter 1996, pp. 18–28.

[6] See Davidson, R.B., 'The Value of Tax Management for Bond Portfolios,' *The Journal of Private Portfolio Management*, Spring 1999, pp. 49–56.

[7] See Murphy, Austin, 'An Empirical Investigation into the Components of Long-Term Municipal Bond Yields,' *The Journal of Private Portfolio Management*, Spring 1998, pp. 27–36.

Chapter 16

Style diversification: an impossible challenge?

This chapter considers an example of the philosophical change required when moving from a tax-oblivious to a tax-sensitive approach. Chapter 4 established the need to challenge conventional wisdom and to keep a focus on the whole portfolio. It also previewed the idea that work by David Stein[1] is directly germane to the question that needs to be addressed here: when constructing an equity portfolio, does it make sense to think in terms of investment styles?

In a tax-oblivious world, the answer to the question is 'yes.' Differentiating among various styles is one of the most frequently used and soundest portfolio diversification tools. There is a mountain of evidence[2] pointing to the potential offered by differentiating between growth or value styles, not only within the large-capitalization universe, but also in the medium- or small-capitalization areas as well. Though the correlation between the returns of these various sub-universes is still high, given that the market, or systematic, component of risk is substantially common to all, one can identify well-defined cycles among the various styles that, over time, provide a valid diversification axis.[3]

Taxable investors are often also advised to diversify their portfolios among large-capitalization equities by value or large-capitalization equities by growth, because institutional investors do. Yet doing so is questionable, particularly when one asks how that approach fits with the need to focus on the total portfolio.

The traditional pre-tax case

Let us look at moving from a broadly diversified portfolio to an approach using at least two sub-portfolios, each focused on a specific style. For this approach to make sense, one has to share one or both of two beliefs. The first of these beliefs relates to *style timing*. Proponents argue that there are long cycles during which growth or value is in or out of favor, and that these allow the astute investor to emphasize one at the expense of the other.[4] It is indeed possible to argue that one can outperform a passive 50/50 mix of both styles if able to predict which of the two styles will do best. The second belief is based on the view that the *more managers specialize, the more likely they are to produce excess returns*. Does this still hold when taxes are taken into consideration? To what extent are either or both of these beliefs reasonable?

What follows is a summary of the principal conclusions of an article published in 2000.[5] Details of the methodology I used can be found in the article. Its principal attribute was that it was based on a 'modified perfect forecasting simulation framework' that I first developed working with officers of the Government of Singapore Investment Company, as a means of testing the abilities of individual managers. I then successfully adapted the idea to circumstances where uncertainty needs to be injected into an experiment. Unfortunately, for our analysis to produce statistically meaningful results we need to rely on a simulation, rather than a review of actual market returns. This reflects the fact that historical observations would not provide a large enough number of data points, and would not offer sufficient flexibility to test a variety of potential circumstances, to lend some generality to the findings. The modified perfect forecast process allows actual data to be used and yet injects a measure of uncertainty, in order to replicate real-life situations.

In this instance, the uncertainty relates to the fact that a manager will not typically allocate across different styles perfectly, or add value in a totally predictable fashion. Rather, he or she will make these decisions with varying degrees of success.

For example, imagine that an investor wants to evaluate the results of a market timing strategy, where the only variable concerns the relative proportion of the portfolio allocated to growth or value. A possible approach might involve developing a valuation tool to determine when value is cheap relative to growth and vice versa. Then one could construct an allocation equation varying the relative allocation to each style depending upon the extent to which one style is cheap or expensive. This would certainly reflect the way in which such a decision might be made in practice. However, it suffers from a very important flaw: it eats up a lot of data. The valuation process would have to be calibrated from history, using data to determine relative value parameters. The valuation process thus calibrated would then have to be tested on data from a different period of history to satisfy the basic principles of statistical rigor. One would be able to use only some of the available data for testing purposes, with the balance serving only to calibrate the model.

An alternative is to assume that the manager can only be perfectly right or perfectly wrong each time he or she makes a decision. Over time, we can vary the success of each manager, by varying the probability characterizing each individual decision. For instance, a manager who makes the perfectly right decision 60% of the time and the perfectly wrong decision the other 40% would be said to have a 60% probability of success. This unfortunately takes away some of the texture of individual decisions, as it introduces a binary nature to a process that would typically have a number of possible variations. Yet it does allow us to model the uncertainty of the outcomes of the decisions made by managers, and to use market data to describe the relative performance of each decision.

Style timing

Let us first test whether it is reasonable to expect a manager to be able to add value by allocating across different styles. Our goal is to mimic the performance of a portfolio allocated between the two distinct styles, and then compare the performance of that portfolio to two benchmarks: first, a naively rebalanced portfolio split evenly (50/50) between the two styles; and, second, the Russell 1000 index, which blends both styles.

Assumptions

Let us first agree upon three main assumptions. First, all transactions occur at the end of the period, based on end-market values. Second, taxes are calculated using a 20% rate, assuming that the investor is a U.S. taxpayer and that all capital gains are of a long-term nature; and realized capital gains are based on the average cost-accounting method – we do not keep track of individual lots. Third, taxes are paid at the beginning of the next period, so the periodic starting portfolio value is equal to the ending portfolio value minus the tax cost incurred in the previous period. Note that the model allows net capital losses to be carried forward and assumes that they are invested at the portfolio's overall rate of return for the period during which they are carried.

The same assumptions are used to deal with the managed portfolio, where there is an active allocation process between styles, and the naïve portfolio, where the two styles are systematically rebalanced to a 50/50 mix at the end of each period.

To keep the simulation as simple as possible, we do not take into consideration the taxes that might arise other than from the realization of capital gains associated with the rebalancing process, such as taxes on dividend income, or on the net capital gain realization arising from the management of the value and growth subportfolios.

Note that the analysis probably overestimates the after-tax returns of both benchmarks. These indexes are reweighted on an annual basis and, according to David Stein, should be expected themselves to bear some taxation as companies leave the index and others enter it. We estimate drag somewhere between 0.5% and 1%, but do not incorporate that estimate into the analysis, to keep things simple. Such simplicity should not prejudice our results, because we do not focus on individual index or strategy returns, but rather on the difference between the returns of individual strategies or indexes. For that assumption to be acceptable, one must simply accept that the tax efficiency of a two-style portfolio will not be dramatically different from that of a style-neutral portfolio.

Style timing potential – pre-tax analysis

The first step is to verify that allocating between the Russell 1000 Growth and Russell 1000 Value indexes with perfect foresight would have produced better results than investing either in the Russell 1000 Index or in an equally weighted and monthly rebalanced index of the Russell 1000 Growth and Russell 1000 Value indexes. We consider four different alternatives: at the beginning of each month, the manager decides to invest 100%, 75%, 60% or 55% of the portfolio in the best performing index, with the balance in the other. We do not take into account any transaction cost associated with the rebalancing of the portfolio at the end of each month. Exhibit 16.1 shows the results of this analysis, which, though highly predictable, are interesting.

First, during the 20 years under review there was no significant return advantage to either style bias, though there were periods during which either style produced significant excess returns. The single most important difference between the two style-based strategies, as represented by the Russell 1000 style indexes, was that growth produced much more volatile returns than value. Indeed, during the period 1979–99, returns for growth and value styles were virtually identical, at 18.1% and 18.0%, respectively. Interestingly, the volatility of value returns, at 14.2%, was considerably lower than the volatility of growth returns, at 17.3%, but they were still highly correlated (0.91), underscoring the importance of market over style risk.

Second, there was, however, significant scope to add value by emphasizing one or other style, and the value added was broadly proportional to the size of the bet made in favor of one or other strategy. This reflects both the sustained cycles of under- and outperformance by either index, and periodic volatility capture related to short-term under- and outperformance. In particular, there was a significant potential alpha even if the size of the bet was quite small (5% in favor of the best-performing asset).

Thus, though there is theoretical room for substantial value added, which is

Exhibit 16.1

Style allocation with perfect foresight, 1979–99 (%)

	Average rolling 12-month returns	Volatility of returns
Russell 1000 Index	18.1	15.3
Russell 1000 Growth	18.1	17.3
Russell 1000 Value	18.0	14.2
Fixed 50/50 mix	18.1	15.3
100/0 allocation	29.8	16.4
75/25 allocation	23.8	15.7
60/40 allocation	20.3	15.4
55/45 allocation	19.2	15.3

Source: Brunel, Jean L.P. 'Active Style Diversification in an After-Tax Context: An Impossible Challenge?' *The Journal of Private Portfolio Management*, Spring 2000, pp. 41-50.

an important element of the case for style timing, we need to take the analysis further, to verify that there is room, in conditions similar to the real world, to allocate across styles successfully. In reality, no manager is able, consistently and over 20 years, to demonstrate perfect foresight on a monthly basis. The question then becomes the following: how right should a manager be when making the allocation decision for there to remain significant value added potential? Our revised perfect forecasting simulation process allows us to replicate the behavior of a portfolio manager who systematically attempts to time the value versus growth bias on a monthly basis, and to see the value added associated with varying degrees of forecasting ability.

Nevertheless, one could argue, that our portfolio construction process is too simplistic. An unvarying bet size assumes a constant conviction level in every bet. In reality, we know that portfolio managers will make larger bets when they perceive the strategy to be to their advantage (higher confidence level) and vice versa. One could construct a more complex and more intellectually satisfying experiment by introducing some measure of variation in the bet size. This could be done using an equation such as:

$$Bet = \chi * \{[E(R_G) - E(R_V)] - \lambda * (\sigma^2[E(R_G) - E(R_V)])\}$$

where

χ is the aggressiveness factor,
$E(R_G)$ is the expected return from growth style,
$E(R_V)$ is the expected return from value style,
λ is the risk aversion coefficient, and
σ^2 is the variance notation.

263

Such an approach would further help deal with the issue of the alternative offered to a manager: adding value by moving along the efficient frontier, as opposed to moving the frontier straight up as he or she attempts to outperform it. In the end, we elected to accept the imperfection associated with our methodology for the sake of simplicity, but we would encourage any reader to conduct the experiment in an improved fashion to verify whether our results still hold.

Returning to our simplified experiment, our evaluation recognizes two different variables:

- *investment success*, defined as the probability given to the manager that he or she will make the right decision; and
- *bet size*, defined as the extent to which the manager is allowed to stray away from the benchmark 50/50 allocation to growth and value styles

Exhibit 16.2 presents the results of the experiment, where the manager is measured against both the Russell 1000 Index, and an equally weighted and monthly-rebalanced index of the Russell 1000 Growth and Russell 1000 Value indexes. One could argue that our rebalancing to a 50/50 weighting of both style indexes on a monthly basis provides false information, as the Russell indexes are in fact rebalanced annually: we may be setting too high a benchmark for our experiment. In fact, the rationale behind our decision was to correct for another inherent weakness in the experiment. As we did not factor in the annual index rebalancing costs in the Russell 1000 index, we felt that forcing our portfolios to be compared with an index that had to bear rebalancing costs was a preferable assumption. A comparison of Exhibits 16.2 and 16.3 bears this out. On a pre-tax basis, the rebalanced 50/50 index and the Russell 1000 index produce roughly the same returns. On an after-tax basis, however, the Russell 1000 index materially outperforms the Rebalanced 50/50 index. It would be fair to assume that some of

Exhibit 16.2

Value added and tracking error with monthly style allocation, under various assumptions (%)

| | *Probability of success* | | | | | |
| | *55%* | | *60%* | | *65%* | |
Bet size	*Alpha*	*Volatility*	*Alpha*	*Volatility*	*Alpha*	*Volatility*
Versus 50/50						
5%	2.50	2.43	2.77	2.46	2.98	2.51
15%	3.11	2.47	3.95	2.55	4.56	2.66
25%	3.72	2.85	5.14	2.95	6.17	3.05
Versus Russell 1000						
5%	2.48	2.42	2.76	2.46	2.96	2.51
15%	3.09	2.47	3.94	2.55	4.55	2.66
25%	3.71	2.84	5.12	2.94	6.15	3.04

Source: Brunel, Jean L.P. 'Active Style Diversification in an After-Tax Context: An Impossible Challenge?' *The Journal of Private Portfolio Management*, Spring 2000, pp. 41-50.

that outperformance may be accounted for by the fact that our Russell 1000 index is 'allowed' to be rebalanced freely once a year, while the Rebalanced 50/50 index actually bears monthly rebalancing costs. Assuming that the whole of that outperformance relates to annual rebalancing costs would place those costs right in the middle of our estimate of 0.5% to 1%, based on David Stein's work.

The exhibit also presents both the value added associated with each set of assumptions and the volatility of that value added. We considered only three levels of investment success: that is, we looked at managers who are 'right' 55%, 60%, and 65% of the time. This choice is dictated by two simple observations. First, there would be little point evaluating the performance of a manager who is not right more often than he or she is wrong. We would find that there is no potential for value added, but I am not sure how insightful that conclusion would be. Second, there would also be little point evaluating the performance of a manager who is right more than 65% of the time. We noted earlier the view attributed to Sir John Templeton, that no manager could be right more often than 65% over any sustained period of time.

Exhibit 16.2 verifies that the scope for value added through variations in style allocations is significant, even when one assumes a relatively modest level of investment success, for instance when the manager is right 55% of the time. These results overstate the case to the extent that they involve monthly decisions and yet ignore transaction costs. However, they seem to validate the belief that some alpha, or value added, can be earned, and that active style allocation might make sense, at least on a pre-tax basis.

Style timing potential – after-tax analysis

How much of that pre-tax alpha remains when taxes are taken into consideration? Exhibit 16.3 shows the results of the same experiment with taxes paid every time the style allocation is modified, using the same format as Exhibit 16.2 to allow direct comparisons. It shows that, contrary to the outcome of the pre-tax analysis, there seems to be very little scope for monthly style allocation adding value on an after-tax basis.

The only circumstance where we are able to see a minor positive after-tax value added is when the managed portfolio is built assuming somewhat exceptional manager insight, at a success level of 65%, and also assuming large bets, as compared with a portfolio of the two style indexes systematically rebalanced to 50/50 on a monthly basis. Using more realistic assumptions, such as a success level of 55%, leads the managed portfolio always to underperform either benchmark. Again, remember that the analysis probably over-estimates the after-tax returns of both benchmarks. These indexes are reweighted on an annual basis and therefore should be expected themselves to bear some taxation as companies leave the index and others enter it.

There is another interesting difference between the pre-tax and after-tax results: the expected value added or subtracted (as the case may be) is more influenced by the probability of success than by the size of the bet; by contrast, the tracking error is more influenced by the size of the bet than by the probability of success. This is different from the results of the pre-tax experiment, but still seems logical. I suspect that it may well be related to the timing of the tax bite. A taxable investor will typically first pay taxes and then see the results of the invest-

Exhibit 16.3

After-tax value added and tracking error with monthly style allocation, under various assumptions

| Bet size | Probability of success | | | | | |
| | 55% | | 60% | | 65% | |
	Alpha	Volatility	Alpha	Volatility	Alpha	Volatility
Versus 50/50						
5%	-1.80	1.07	-1.57	1.09	-1.40	1.01
15%	-1.83	2.09	-1.16	2.11	-0.66	1.98
25%	-1.50	2.83	-0.41	2.87	*0.42*	2.67
Versus Russell 1000						
5%	-2.50	1.14	-2.27	1.16	-2.10	1.09
15%	-2.52	2.13	-1.86	2.15	-1.36	2.02
25%	-2.19	2.85	-1.10	2.89	-0.28	2.69

Source: Brunel, Jean L.P. 'Active Style Diversification in an After-Tax Context: An Impossible Challenge?' *The Journal of Private Portfolio Management*, Spring 2000, pp. 41-50.

ment bet. Thus, the higher the assumed investment success, the lower the impact of unnecessary taxes, defined as taxes incurred to rebalance the portfolio in an unfortunate direction.

Finally, let us look into the difference between the return of the managed portfolio in relation to the overall and therefore blended index on the one hand, and, on the other, a portfolio of style indexes, therefore comprising a value index and a growth index. It appears that it can be explained by the cost associated with rebalancing the portfolio of style indexes to 50/50 on a monthly basis. During the period under review, the 50/50 portfolio returned 17.3% pre-tax and 16.6% after-taxes. This is the same difference of approximately 70 basis points, found in Exhibit 16.3, between the observed alphas of the managed portfolio versus the Russell 1000 Index and the 50/50 portfolio of Russell 1000 style indexes, for all three levels of postulated investment success.

During the period under review, there was little significant benefit to systematic portfolio rebalancing to a style-neutral 50/50 portfolio. While the systematically rebalanced portfolio produced an average annual pre-tax return of 18.1% with a 15.3% volatility, a portfolio allowed to drift would have produced an average annual pre-tax return of 18.0% with a 15.2% volatility. Both differences fall well within rounding errors.

Annual rather than monthly decisions

With portfolio rebalancing assumed to take place monthly, one could fairly question whether the apparently high tax cost could be related to overly frequent portfolio rebalancing. To deal with this issue, let us repeat the process with one change: rather than allowing for monthly portfolio rebalancing between value and growth styles, let us allow for these decisions to be made yearly. We can then calculate both pre-tax and after-tax value added and tracking error.

Exhibit 16.4

Pre-tax and after-tax value added and tracking error with yearly style allocation, under various assumptions

| | *Probability of success* | | | | | |
| | *55%* | | *60%* | | *65%* | |
Bet size versus 50/50	*Alpha*	*Volatility*	*Alpha*	*Volatility*	*Alpha*	*Volatility*
Pre-tax						
5%	0.41	0.50	0.50	0.47	0.55	0.44
15%	0.78	1.45	1.03	1.34	1.18	1.24
25%	1.15	2.43	1.56	2.24	1.81	2.08
After-tax						
5%	-0.37	0.76	-0.32	0.72	-0.32	0.71
15%	-0.69	2.00	-0.51	1.84	-0.44	1.77
25%	-0.72	3.11	-0.40	2.87	-0.24	2.73

Source: Brunel, Jean L.P. 'Active Style Diversification in an After-Tax Context: An Impossible Challenge?' *The Journal of Private Portfolio Management*, Spring 2000, pp. 41-50.

The results of this test are presented in Exhibit 16.4, and suggest that our earlier findings are still valid: it is very hard for a 'non-exceptional style allocator' to preserve any significant value added after taxes are taken into consideration.

The pre-tax results follow the pattern that we expected, though the magnitude of the potential alpha and its tracking error is reduced. This probably reflects the fact that our monthly rebalancing strategy captured both style outperformance cycles and short-term volatility across styles. The after-tax results also follow the anticipated pattern, though the smaller number of individual observations seems to create some statistical 'noise.' That noise leads to individual observations appearing at times surprising, not in absolute terms, but rather relative to others. The fact that the worse after-tax alpha is obtained at the 15% bet size level for both 60% and 65% probabilities illustrates the phenomenon. In any case, it seems reasonable to conclude that, after-tax, the potential to produce value added by attempting to time styles is limited at best.

Why style timing does not work in after-tax conditions

Why is it that so much pre-tax potential value added disappears when taxes are introduced into the equation? Conceptually, style timing, by definition, requires periodic reallocation between two subportfolios, each of which is dedicated to a particular style. Assuming that reallocation decisions are based on relative value and that the capital market line is positively sloped, moving from one style to the other will require realizing a capital gain. This will occur when one needs to sell a part of the exposure to the better performing style and reinvest the net proceeds in the other. The greater the bet size in favor of any asset, the higher the likely tax-related rebalancing cost. Recall the point discussed in Chapter 14: when dealing with physical instruments, one will need to pay the taxes associated with the sale part of the trade before you know whether the trade was insightful or not. In other words, style timing does not work because, at least some of the time, one will pay a capital gains tax for the privilege of making an unfortunate decision.

Specialist versus generalist analysis

Let us now turn to the other decision axis: does it make sense to appoint style specialist managers rather than select a blended approach to the management of an equity portfolio?

The simulation we use for this test is a very close relative of the one used to analyze market timing. The most important change is the need to add one other simulation in the original model to account for the randomness associated with manager value added. Here, the value added we need to consider relates to the management process within a given style: how much better should we assume a specialist manager would be relative to a generalist?

Let us use the original simulation tool, freezing the style allocation to 50/50 and forcing multi-style portfolios to be rebalanced to 50/50 at the end of each period, which, in this experiment, was a month.

Value added and style bias – pre-tax analysis

The Morningstar Principia Pro mutual fund database allows us to perform a simple analysis to evaluate the validity of the belief that specialized managers will generate higher value added than generalists. Let us consider five- and 10-year return and risk data for funds clas-

Exhibit 16.5

Style bias and relative performance

	10-year data			Five-year data		
	Return (%)	Risk (%)	Return/risk	Return (%)	Risk (%)	Return/risk
Morningstar categories						
Large blend (892 funds)	15.3	16.0	0.96	16.0	22.1	0.73
Large growth (503 funds)	17.4	19.1	0.91	20.3	23.2	0.87
Large value (537 funds)	15.3	14.7	1.04	15.6	20.2	0.77
Russell 1000 Indexes						
Aggregate	18.3	13.4	1.37	24.4	14.0	1.75
Growth	19.9	14.9	1.33	27.1	15.5	1.74
Value	16.5	12.5	1.32	21.6	13.1	1.65
Active/passive difference						
Large blend	-3.0		-0.41	-8.4		-1.02
Large growth	-2.5		-0.42	-6.8		-0.87
Large value	-1.3		-0.28	-6.0		-0.88

Source: Brunel, Jean L.P. 'Active Style Diversification in an After-Tax Context: An Impossible Challenge?' *The Journal of Private Portfolio Management*, Spring 2000, pp. 41-50.

sified under one of three Morningstar categories: large blend, large growth and large value. These categories refer to the U.S. equity market, and apply to the large-capitalization segment of the market. They classify managers according to the style biases found in their portfolios. We can compare these results with the five- and 10-year average return, volatility of return (risk), and return per unit of risk of the Russell 1000 indexes, themselves classified under the same three categories.

Exhibit 16.5 presents the results of this simple analysis, which seems to suggest that the average manager in the universe has performed dismally relative to the indexes.

However dismally managers have done relative to the index, the point of the analysis is to focus on the relative performance of the generalist vesus specialist managers. The results shown in Exhibit 16.5 suggest that managers with a clear style bias do tend to outperform those focusing on the market as a whole. This seems to be true over both periods. The return per unit of risk statistics points in the same general direction.

After-tax analysis – manager tax efficiency

Intuitively, one might expect a specialist manager alpha differential to be less negatively impacted by taxes than was the case when considering a style timing process. Indeed, while it will be necessary to rebalance the portfolio periodically to avoid style drift, the size of the moves may well be small enough to allow the investor to retain some return advantage. One might well be prepared to accept style drift, given the observation that there seems to be little advantage to either relative to the other.

Let us now investigate the relative attractiveness of a style-specialist approach versus an alternative involving granting a manager a generalist mandate. We need to evaluate the extent to which the additional value added by specialist (style-focused) managers relative to generalist managers would be sufficient to offset the inherent tax-inefficiency of holding two distinct subportfolios, which need at least some rebalancing to avoid style drift. We constructed another simulation that allowed us to test the excess after-tax returns available to a portfolio of specialist managers relative to a portfolio solely managed by a generalist manager. Having assumed three different potential levels of value added for both specialist and generalist managers, we generated expected returns for all three types of managers (specialist value, specialist growth, and generalist), based on the same period as in the earlier market timing experiment.

Comparing the after-tax results of the two alternatives, we can assess the excess return and tracking error associated with a specialist manager strategy relative to one involving the use of a single style-neutral manager. The first, style-neutral portfolio was represented by a combination of the returns on the Russell 1000 and the value added generated by the style-neutral manager. The second, specialist portfolio was represented by a 50/50 mix (rebalanced monthly) of a growth manager (Russell 1000 Growth + growth manager alpha) and a value manager (Russell 1000 Value + value manager alpha). Let us assume that taxes were paid at the rate of 20% on the capital gains realized on monthly portfolio rebalancing.

Note that we did not worry about taxes on investment returns. While this may appear surprising at first, the logic behind the assumption is the following. First, the bulk of the experiment is concerned with index funds. Thus, one can make the heroic assumption that they

Exhibit 16.6

Comparing specialist strategies to generalist strategies (%)

Excess return of specialist strategy				*Tracking of error of excess return*			
	Generalist alpha				*Generalist tracking error*		
Specialist alpha	*1.0*	*2.0*	*3.0*	*Special tracking error*	*1.5*	*3.0*	*4.5*
2.0	0.24	-1.26	-2.69	3.0	2.94	3.80	5.85
3.0	1.30	-0.08	-0.99	4.5	3.91	4.82	6.39
4.0	1.88	0.73	-0.04	6.0	5.28	5.88	7.35

Source: Brunel, Jean L.P. 'Active Style Diversification in an After-Tax Context: An Impossible Challenge?' *The Journal of Private Portfolio Management*, Spring 2000, pp. 41-50.

generate little by way of net capital gains taxes and that dividend yields are small enough not to make a significant difference. We appreciate that this argument is not as strong as it may appear, given the turnover inherent in the Russell indexes, but this should apply equally to all three indexes (stock style classification drift aside) and thus not bias results based on comparisons among them. Further, even in the managed part of the experiment, one might argue that taxes may not be sufficiently different across the three styles to matter. Indeed, though it may well be that the growth manager will have a more tax-efficient investment process than the generalist manager, it will also be true that the value manager will likely be the least tax-efficient. Thus, we implicitly assumed that there would not be any significant difference between the tax efficiency of the generalist portfolio and that of the combined specialist portfolios. This deserves further analysis, though it would significantly complicate the experiment.

Exhibit 16.6 displays the results of the analysis, showing the level of excess return achieved by a specialist strategy relative to one that relies on a generalist. For instance, the data suggest that a specialist strategy, employing two specialist managers, one focused on growth and the other focused on value, would add 0.24% to a generalist strategy, if we assume that the generalist can earn a 1% value added, while both specialists can earn 2% (the number in the top left-hand corner of the exhibit). Similarly, the data suggest that the tracking error of that excess return will be 2.94%, if the tracking errors of the generalist and the specialists are 1.5% and 3.0%, respectively.

The data seem to tell us that a specialist strategy portfolio, or, in other words, a multistyle, multimanager portfolio, is likely to outperform a generalist manager only in instances where the value added of the specialist manager is *substantially* higher than that of a generalist manager. Further, in all instances, the tracking error of that specialist outperformance seems to be very large in relation to the potential excess return. The information ratio associated with the specialist outperformance is substantially higher than the level that would typically be considered meaningful when assessing the performance of a single diversified equity manager relative to a benchmark index.

Though essentially not surprising, this conclusion is important as it sets out clearly the nature of the choice that an individual investor must make. Opting for a specialist strategy requires the investor to have a strong conviction that specialist managers will generate substantially higher value added than a generalist. Specifically, Exhibit 16.6 would tell me that the decision to select a specialist strategy requires me to be convinced that my specialist managers will beat a generalist by at least 2% to 3% per year, over time. The evidence provided by the Morningstar database suggest that this is an extremely tough hurdle, as substantially less than 5% of all managers could conceivably make such a claim.

Therefore, a generalist approach is much more likely to provide satisfactory returns over time, and is much more consistent with the tax efficiency admonition to focus on the whole portfolio and make decisions that are as broad as feasible.

An important caveat

This experiment suffers from at least one potential important flaw. Our analysis does not assume that operational steps could be taken within the multistyle portfolio to minimize the impact of taxes. We have seen that it is possible to raise the tax efficiency of a portfolio by careful administration of lots, for example (see Chapter 15). Thus, in this instance, one could assume that the multimanager portfolio is viewed, operationally, as a single portfolio of securities, with each style manager having management access to only a portion of the total, but with the custodian processing transactions being able to select securities from any part of the portfolio. This might create opportunities to bypass markets when securities are crossed from one subportfolio to the other, or to select tax lots in a fashion such that net realized gains are minimized.

At the same time, this experiment also does not take into consideration one potential pitfall associated with multimanager strategies within a single asset class: wash sales. Technically, an individual stock does not fully migrate from one Russell universe to another, as the new methodology introduced by the firm involves attributing some weight to value or growth characteristics for each security in the index as and when appropriate. Yet a given stock can shift from being 60% growth and 40% value, for instance, to 40% growth and 60% value. At some point, the risk thus exists that a stock would shift from the investment universe selected by a growth manager to that of a value manager, or vice versa. Given the likelihood that individual securities might thus migrate from one universe to another, it is at least conceivable that a stock sold at a loss by a growth manager, for instance, might be bought within the prescribed two-month period by a value manager. This carries significant and cumbersome administrative and tax implications.

Summary and implications

It should by now be reasonably clear that there is much less, if any, potential for a taxable investor to benefit from a strategy based on selecting several managers, each with a different style, relative to the alternative of having one single multistyle portfolio. The data show that, while a case can be made for such an approach on a pre-tax basis, the case crumbles once we start looking at after-tax results.

In fact, timing growth and value investing on an after-tax basis offers little convincing potential for adding value. Intuitively, this is probably because returns on the two styles are highly correlated. While a tax-exempt investor could benefit from the relative value opportunities within the highly correlated distribution, a taxable investor is penalized by the significant tax costs associated with the first leg of any trade, which may or may not produce the expected benefit when it is unwound. It might be interesting to create a separate experiment, using artificial or synthetic data with a lower correlation, to test whether this intuition is correct. At the same time, however, these experiments are not meant to suggest that it is practical to manage an overall portfolio across all asset classes and strategies in one single whole.

A possible tax-sensitive alternative

One might use the insights gained in Chapter 14 to design a strategy aimed at capturing the greater value added that specialist managers can demonstrably earn, *and* to maintain portfolio tax efficiency, even in the face of possible style timing attempts. The key is to refrain from the Pavlovian response learned in the institutional world and to segregate the execution of each decision. In practice, one might consider a combination of two or three simple steps.

Assuming that one does not seek to time styles, but simply looks for the potential value added of a style-specialist portfolio, one would take the following two steps. One would appoint a style-specialist manager to handle the physical part of the portfolio. For instance, one might appoint a large-capitalization growth manager who would be tasked with providing tax-efficient security selection value added, measured against a growth benchmark. Assuming that one does not want such a large style bet, one could then enter into over-the-counter swap contracts to hedge half, or some other fraction, of that portfolio's market value out of the growth style into a value style. The portfolio would thus reflect the style blend of the broader market, and yet benefit from the ability to earn higher expected returns from a specialist manager.

Tax-aware optimization processes will often have a measure of momentum investing built into them, as winners are held, while losers end up being sold for their tax losses. Thus, a momentum-based alpha ends up being somewhat redundant in this context, while the value-based alpha acts as a complement to the portfolio construction procedure (this is the argument proposed by Apelfeld and his two colleagues,[6] as discussed in Chapter 15). If one is sensitive to this point, one could select a value manager and partially hedge out of value into growth.

The investor who seeks to be more aggressive and hopes to benefit from style timing can add a third step. He or she can use appropriately defined derivative contracts to vary the proportion of the effective portfolio exposure to growth or value, or any other style variable that makes sense.

In summary, the main insight discussed in this chapter is that investors ought to question their instincts, which often tend to push them into adopting, without further analysis, practices or policies that they see being used in a tax-exempt environment.

---

[1] See Stein, David, presentation at AIMR Conference: Investment Counseling for Private Clients III: *Integrated Wealth Management, Taxes, Estate Planning, and Wealth Transfer*,' Atlanta, GA, March 27–28 2001, Session IV: The Trade-Offs between Tax Efficiency and Tracking Error.

[2] For an early discussion of the role of 'management style' as an important adjunct to the definition of an asset class, see Sharpe, William F., 'Asset Allocation: Management Style and Performance Measurement,' *The Journal of*

Portfolio Management, Winter 1992, pp. 7–19; and Lebaron, Dean, 'A Universal Model of Equity Styles,' *The Journal of Portfolio Management,* Fall 1994, pp. 85–88. For deeper insights into equity styles, see Cogin, Daniel T., and Frank J. Fabozzi, *The Handbook of Equity Style Management,* Mew Hope, PA: Frank J. Fabozzi Associates, 1995. See also Christopherson, Jon A., 'Equity Style Classification,' *The Journal of Portfolio Management,* Spring 1995, pp. 32–43; Trzcinka, Charles A., 'Equity Style Classification: Comment,' *The Journal of Portfolio Management,* Spring 1995, pp. 44–46; Gallo, John G., and Larry J. Lockwood. 'Benefits of Proper Style Classification of Equity Portfolio Managers,' *The Journal of Portfolio Management,* Spring 1997, pp. 47–56; and Bauman, W. Scott, and Robert E. Miller, 'Investor Expectations and the Performance of Value Stocks versus Growth Stocks,' *The Journal of Portfolio Management,* Spring 1997, pp. 57–68.

[3] See Asness, Clifford S., Jacques A. Friedman, Robert J. Krail, and John M. Liew, 'Style Timing: Value versus Growth,' *The Journal of Portfolio Management,* Spring 2000, pp. 50–60. For an application of this idea in the U.K., see Lewis, Mario, and Manolis Liokadis, 'The Profitability of Style Rotation Strategies in the United Kingdom,' *The Journal of Portfolio Management,* Fall 1999, pp. 73–86.

[4] See Kuberek, Robert C., 'Using Style Factors to Differentiate Equity Performance over Short Horizons,' *The Journal of Portfolio Management,* Spring 1998, pp. 33–40. Though the author does not advocate style market timing, his work is interesting and germane to the extent that he questions whether style factors exist as short-term risk factors. The study focuses on the metrics for individual styles, analyzing their impact on short-term performance and their mutual correlations. Note that we are sidestepping the issue of whether 'growth' and 'value' can be easily and consistently defined. For an early discussion of the topic, with respect to growth, see Peters, Donald J., 'Valuing a Growth Stock,' *The Journal of Portfolio Management,* Spring 1991, pp. 49–51.

[5] See Brunel, Jean L.P. 'Active Style Diversification in an After-Tax Context: An Impossible Challenge?,' *The Journal of Private Portfolio Management,* Spring 2000, pp. 41–50.

[6] See Apelfeld, Roberto, Gordon Fowler, Jr. and James Gordon, Jr. 'Tax-Aware Equity Investing.' *The Journal of Portfolio Management,* Winter 1996, pp. 18–28.

Chapter 17

Manager selection and managing multimanager stables

Having spent the bulk of my investment manager career within a single multiproduct and multi-faceted institution, I come to the multimanager debate with the conviction of the recent convert. I simply do not believe that any asset management firm, however great, can reasonably support the claim that it has a broad enough and good enough product line to be able to serve all the needs of an individual investor. The breadth of the array of possible products and strategies, and their complexity, the need to manage business risk and compensate portfolio managers competitively, and the entrepreneurial spirit needed to succeed in certain strategies all militate in favor of an 'open architecture' that allows an investor to deal with more than one asset manager.

The institutional model

There is nothing inherently new in the fact that investors rely on more than one manager. Institutional investors have followed the practice for decades, in most countries, seeking both the 'best of breed' and 'diversification of manager risk.' There is a story that illustrates the move from a single-manager to a multimanager mode, and back, in the institutional world. Industry gossip often dates the onset of multimanager stables to the time when the internal manager of the ATT pension fund could no longer cope with the challenges brought about by the multiplicity of possible stocks available to him. The same gossip claims that the trend toward manager consolidation started when the ATT pension fund found that it had more managers than it had had individual stocks 20 to 30 years earlier.

Whether true or fabricated, the story does provide a believable image of the process toward open architecture in the institutional world. Egged on by consultants who artfully developed a multiplicity of labels to describe different investment styles, as well as a multiplicity of analytical tools to evaluate their relative performance, attractiveness, and usefulness in a total portfolio context, institutional investors naturally moved away from the single manager approach that was the norm in the 1950s.[1] Admittedly, the investment problem had become considerably more complex, as pension funds in the United States, for instance, moved away from a principally fixed-income strategy to one that incorporated many of the new opportunities that became available. These included, first, the move toward equities, then the specialization between large-capitalization and small-capitalization stocks, the trend toward the internationalization of the investment world in the 1970s, and, finally, over the past 20 years or so, a multitude of highly focused and specialized traditional and nontradi-

274

tional strategies, such as real estate, hedge funds, private equities, emerging markets, and extended fixed-income securities.

The challenge associated with a manager stable growing too large is nothing more than the predictable consequence of the trend, but it can be particularly painful in the world of taxable investors. In Chapter 4, we discussed the difference between two alternative approaches to portfolio optimization. We contrasted the 'sequential optimization' used by institutional investors to the 'simultaneous optimization' that should be the preferred choice of taxable individuals. This dichotomy is also relevant to the topic at hand. Excessive manager diversification does not necessarily have dramatic consequences in the institutional world, because sequential optimization makes sense there. The cost of excessive manager diversification in this context can therefore only be measured in terms of missing out on some of the available economies of scale, such as lower management fees, or in terms of the increased administrative burden, which grows more quickly than the number of managers.

The taxable investor problem

The same cannot be said in the world of the taxable investor. Sequential optimization no longer works and simultaneous optimization requires that the decision to add another manager be weighed against the anticipated benefits. The total portfolio focus required of the taxable individual investor suggests the need for a new role,[2] similar to that of the coach of a sports team, whose function is threefold:

- to assemble the players needed for the particular game;
- to develop the skills or plays required to win, given the specific conditions and the players available; and
- to monitor the execution of these plays during the game, and to use periods of time between games to improve players and plays.

Applied to the world of the taxable individual investor, the critical function played by this coach is to coordinate the activities of each of the managers. This coordination takes on many dimensions, but the most important relates to the management of overall portfolio tax efficiency. This requires ensuring that each manager makes optimum use of the opportunities arising within the whole portfolio to shelter capital gains that any manager may need to realize. It therefore stands to reason that the larger the number of managers in a stable, the more complex the coordination of their respective activities will be. Yet excessive manager diversification does happen in the individual world.

A few years ago, I met a family whose wealth approximated US$2 billion. Though it had been expertly advised with respect to manager selection, and its investment performance had been commendable on a pre-tax basis, the family found itself with more than 100 managers, and some family members wondered whether this was really necessary. A close analysis of the composition of the manager stable revealed three major problems. First, the family ran significant risks of wash sales, as several managers had comparable mandates. Second, it paid higher management fees than necessary, as certain subportfolios were not large enough to qualify for the lowest fees. Finally, its investment program had substantial unnecessary complexity, as the definition of certain mandates was so narrow as to make periodic rebalancing almost nightmarish, because of the migration of individual investments across strategies as a result of normal market developments (as discussed in Chapter 9).

Manager research

Manager research can at times be mistaken for a simple assessment of a given manager's performance. This is one of the biggest mistakes that an individual can make, as the main issue is to determine the skill of a manager and thus his or her ability to perform in a competitive manner prospectively. My mentor, the late Nick Potter, once told me:

> We must lead our clients and prospects to trust that the performance we have achieved in the past tells them something favorable about our ability to be better than our competition in the future.

As always, he was right, encompassing in a simple sentence the whole of the issue. Historical performance is one of the dimensions of the problem, but often by far not the most important one. In fact, many of the best manager analysts argue that the role of historical performance[3] in the assessment process is limited to excluding managers who have not proven that they could produce competitive results. I will add that it also helps raise many of the questions that one will eventually want to ask managers as one gets to know them better.

Historical performance assessment

Assessing historical performance can be tricky because of at least two important considerations. First, one must understand the fact that it takes quite a long period of time to eliminate the randomness of managers' outperformance or underperformance cycles. (We implicitly caught a first glimpse of this in Chapter 9, when we compared the respective records of active and passive management.) Second, one must be able to distinguish between insight and bias, and adjust for the difference.

The importance of selecting a long-enough assessment horizon

The first major hurdle faced by a performance analyst is to ensure that the time horizon he or she considers is long enough to take care of the pure random fluctuations in manager performance.[4] In the mid-1980s, a group of analysts conducted an experiment that demonstrated that predictable random fluctuations in manager performance can substantially upset any attempt at ranking them. Further, they showed that it could take a very long time for the impact of such fluctuations to dissipate.

I was unfortunately unable to trace the original article discussing the experiment, but I did manage to replicate it, at least in spirit, if not with the same specific assumptions and conclusions. The results of this replication show that it can take as many as 30 years before managers are in the right performance order.

Let me explain how the experiment was conducted. It comprises three simple steps. First, a group of 100 *hypothetical* managers is broken down into five subgroups, each of which is given a set margin of outperformance relative to an index. Thus, we will have a reference, with certain managers preordained to outperform the index by a substantial margin, others to do so with a smaller margin, and others to underperform. Each group's preset margin of outperformance, together with the expected volatility of this outperformance, is shown in Exhibit 17.1. For instance, managers in group A are preordained to outperform the index by 4% per year, with a 4% tracking error, while managers in group E are preordained to underperform the same index by the same 4%, also with a 4% tracking error.

Assuming that each manager's distribution of returns is normal, we then generate five sets of random numbers to describe the expected performance of each manager over each of the 30 years for which we carry on the simulation. The relative returns of all managers are then compounded and the managers ranked for each of the 30 rolling periods (one year, two years, and so on up to 30 years.)

We can then compare the observed rank of each manager, based on the preordained expected alpha. For instance, managers assigned to group A should be ranked in the top 20, managers belonging to group B between 21 and 40, and so on. A manager is deemed to be ranked accurately if his or her rank is in the right preordained cluster, and incorrectly if not. We do not worry about the rank of a manager within a group: a manager from group A ranked among the top 20 is 'good,' but we do not differentiate among or even identify the 20 managers in group A. The percentage of managers accurately ranked is then noted. The results are shown in Exhibit 17.2.

The data shown in Exhibit 17.2 suggest that one should be very cautious when evaluating short-term manager performance. A caveat is, however, in order. The experiment comprises a limited number of paths and therefore contains a significant margin of error. This explains, for instance, the fact that the number of managers appropriately classified in the first year is not 50%, which it should be. Nevertheless, we are still close to 50%, and the increase in the proportion of managers found in the right group seems to follow the rules of a normal distribution: one would expect to find two-thirds of the distribution within one standard deviation of the mean, 95% within two standard deviations, and 99% within three. These patterns are encouraging, and suggest that the experiment is still probably statistically valid. However, note

Exhibit 17.1

Expected relative performance of 100 hypothetical managers (%)

Manager group	Expected alpha	Expected tracking error
A	4	4
B	2	2
C	0	1
D	-2	2
E	-4	4

Exhibit 17.2

Manager ranking accuracy (%)

Number of years	Proportion of managers accurately classified
One	48
Three	76
Five	84
10	92
20	96
25	96
30	100

that the volatility of the expected manager alpha that we assumed is, if anything, generous to managers, as most would be very happy with an information ratio (the ratio of value added to its own volatility) of one. Rather than interpreting the data too literally, one should simply conclude that it is best to avoid any judgment based on a return history shorter than five years, or possibly even 10 years.

Insight versus bias

Let me now turn to the issue of insight versus bias and illustrate it with an example.

> In the mid-1990s, a client asked me for my opinion of a study that he had just completed on the performance of selected managers of equities in Europe, Australia, and the Far East (EAFE, the developed world other than North America). He was surprised by the outcome of his study, as the best managers, in terms of pre-tax returns relative to the index, were also those with the lowest risk, measured in terms of the volatility of returns. This seemed an odd conclusion, until we realized that we were looking at one half of the problem. The Japanese equity market peaked late in December 1989 and fell almost in a straight line in subsequent years. The index, which comprised a very heavy exposure to Japan in early 1990, experienced significant volatility downward, while those managers who were successful, because they did not have as large a Japanese equity exposure as the index, experienced much less of it. The other half of the problem was that the data did not tell us anything about whether the managers who avoided Japan did so through unusual insight, or as a result of a structural bias against that country.
>
> A more appropriate analysis involved looking at a 10-year period centered on the onset of the fall, rather than the past five years of this same period. Japan had been by far the best performer among the larger EAFE markets from 1985 to 1989. Eliminating the implicit structural reward given to managers who had a bias against Japan, the new analysis leveled the playing field and provided the answer to the riddle. Many of the managers with the best record during the early 1990s had been among the worst in the preceding five years, as their relative performance was indeed the result of a structural bias, rather than brilliant judgment as to the unattractiveness of Japan in the early 1990s.

This suggests that analysis of historical performance must be sure to distinguish between a successful insight that generated superior investment results and the random confluence of a manager's bias toward or against a particular investment theme that, coincidentally, proved successful merely because that bias happened to play out in the right direction.[5]

Evaluating the investment process and manager skills

The very limitations of historical performance assessment demonstrate that it is critical to go beyond a simple quantitative analysis of a manager's track record,[6] even when it includes a focus on the consistency of the manager's performance over time.[7] In the end, the fundamental question one is trying to answer is: to what extent is the track record I am considering relevant and significant enough to be useful to predict future performance? Admittedly then only focusing on hedge fund managers, Mark Anson[8] phrases the problem particularly well:

Most investors prefer a well-defined investment process that describes how an investment manager makes its investments. The articulation and documentation of the process can be just as important as the investment results generated by the process.

The main insight, in my view, is simply to consider three fundamental questions.

- what decisions does the manager say he or she makes?
- how does the manager say he or she is making these decisions? and
- how does the manager manage risks?

Additionally, one should evaluate the human capital available to the manager.

What investment decisions are made?

Let me first focus on the issue of the decisions that a manager says he or she makes. Imagine that you are looking at the record of a global equity manager, and assume that this record is outstanding. Having asked the manager what decision he makes, let us assume that he has told us that he is a basic stock picker who is not very concerned with country, industry or currency issues. Now, imagine that we perform a simple performance attribution analysis, allocating actual performance along currency, country, industry and stock selection lines. One of two situations will likely develop. On the one hand, it is possible that the analysis will confirm that the real value added produced by the manager is mostly attributable to individual stock selection, with the other possible decision axes marginal at best. On the other hand, it is conceivable that the analysis of the manager's record suggests that his real value added boils down to a few great currency, country or industry calls, but that his actual stock picking prowess cannot be verified.

Which one of the two outcomes would make you more comfortable? An example illustrates how important this issue is. In the late 1970s, a major U.S. pension fund had hired J.P. Morgan and another manager to handle the non-U.S. equity portion of its portfolio. The other manager had been given a relatively free mandate, based on the manager's strong record on making macro decisions, such as country or industry selection. J.P. Morgan had been appointed to manage a core portfolio, the value added of which was expected to be driven by individual security selection and with a risk profile expected to track closer to the Morgan Stanley Capital International EAFE Index than the other manager's. Also, correspondingly, J.P. Morgan's portfolio was expected to produce lower returns than the other manager's. This diversification strategy made great sense, as it combined two different approaches and thus diversified manager risk quite effectively.

A couple of years into the mandate, J.P. Morgan had produced substantially better returns than the other manager. Worried that J.P. Morgan was not being faithful to its mandate, the client analyzed the results. Thankfully for J.P. Morgan, the portfolio's risk relative to the index had indeed been relatively low, the exceptional returns reflecting exceptional security selection success during the period.

The example makes two points, one directly, the other indirectly. First, it is critical to be able to confirm that the manager does make the decisions he or she says he will make when he or she is appointed. Second, and often counterintuitively for many individual investors, *exceptionally good performance should raise a red flag, just as exceptionally poor performance should*. Manager results should track expectations, in terms of both expected return and volatility, and if they do not, there may well be something amiss. The individual investor should thank his or her lucky stars when a management problem comes out through great performance, but be just as ruthlessly bent on finding out why expectations are exceeded as he or she would be if there had been a significant performance shortfall.

A postscript to the example also illustrates that the client was quite smart. The other manager, who had not done very well for that relatively short period of time, was not terminated. The firm went on to produce highly commendable returns, justifying the client's original choice.

How are investment decisions made?

Analysing how decisions are made is probably the most difficult part of the process, because it calls upon both mechanical and human elements. The mechanical elements include the resources that are brought to bear and the sequence in which they come into the process. The human elements have to do with the judgments that must be made, both in the development of initial investment insights and in making each specific decision. Basically, the decision sequence explicitly or implicitly comprises the same five steps:

- developing an investment idea or thesis;
- analyzing the fundamental validity of the investment idea;
- assessing the attractiveness of the investment idea;
- evaluating the fit of the investment idea in the context of the current portfolio; and
- deciding upon the transaction needed to incorporate the idea in the current portfolio.

Each step requires a specific process that should be explainable in a way that makes sense. For instance, one can think of three potential sources of investment ideas:

- external recommendation, for example by a brokerage firm;
- systematic internal screening of a set investment universe, using fixed or changing criteria, in a quantitative or qualitative manner; or
- the 'light bulb' that suddenly comes on.

Manager research analysts will often prefer idea generation processes that seem to have a repeatable character to those that rely on the occasional brain wave. The role of the analyst is not so much to make judgments on the validity of the process used by the manager as to verify that the process is sensible and that the appropriate resources are dedicated to its success.

Risk management

The notions of risk and risk management are both central to the investment process, though at times it is hard for individual investors to appreciate them. In an institutional context, risk is easier to appreciate, because it is defined in objective terms (see Chapter 2). In the world of the individual investor, whether taxable or tax-exempt, risk is defined in multiple fashions, and can at times become very nebulous. The ultimate form of fuzziness arises when one looks at decisions after the fact, the picture perfect illustration of the use of hindsight.

Understanding the risks associated with the investment process is still a critical activity, and one must appreciate that risk exists as soon as *there is the potential for things to come out in a way that differs from expectations*. This means that risk can manifest itself when one has a bad surprise, which would be a circumstance where there would be little doubt that risk was present. It also means that risk can appear when one has a good surprise, which does not always raise the same kind of red flag as a disappointment would.

The investment process can comprise a wide variety of risks, but five seem to dominate. Before discussing them, it is worth focusing on a fundamental aspect of the activity of an investment manager. Whether stated explicitly or not, *any investor assumes that he or she knows something that others do not*. In the final analysis, relative performance must be a zero sum game. If I buy a stock or a bond, I must be thinking that the stock or the bond will do better than alternatives in the same market. Conversely, if I sell a bond or a stock, it must mean that I expect some alternative to do better. Buyers and sellers thus have opposite views on the particular instruments that they are trading. Admittedly, one could argue that the process is considerably more complex in real life, principally because there are more than two actors in the play. In the end, however, the statement holds that the multiple actors must disagree on a particular investment when they are on opposite sides of any transaction. This helps us appreciate the five different forms of investment process risk.

Strategy risk

Strategy risk is associated with the belief that underpins the activity of the manager. Going back to the premise we set out earlier, that an investor must assume that he or she knows something that others do not, one quickly appreciates that this knowledge can have two different dimensions. First, it may relate to information legally acquired: I am therefore explicitly excluding any form of insider advantage. Second, it may arise because of a belief in a theme or the behavior of markets, in which others may not believe or of which they may not be aware. For instance, value investors will tend to buy cheap net assets, while growth investors will often prefer long-term growth prospects. Arbitrageurs believe that differences in the price of certain securities arise because of market inefficiencies, while others will eschew the leverage often necessary to execute the strategy. Finally, market timers believe that they can foresee major market turning points, while trend followers believe that the trend is their friend.

This would be a good time for the analyst to look into the use of portfolio leverage, and the limits placed on it. In general, one would expect traditional managers to make no use of leverage, except for unusual operational purposes, such as difference in settlement dates or exceptional cash flows, while nontraditional or hedge managers may need leverage to post the returns they want to generate.

Valuation risk

Valuation risk is a close cousin of strategy risk, and yet differs from it materially. Strategy risk involves beliefs, while valuation risk relates to the process through which value is determined, often based on some form of model. Model risk must be very carefully assessed, particularly when managers state that their investment processes rely on quantitative tools. There are many ways in which a model can produce the wrong answer.

First, the model can be based on the *wrong thesis,* in which case we would be dealing with strategy rather than valuation risk. The portfolio insurance meltdown of October 1987 is a good example of such a risk. Investors had assumed that prices move in a continuous fashion in both physical and derivative markets. They thought that they could always hedge a move in one market through a transaction in the other, and were surprised when prices gapped down, making it impossible for dynamic hedges to be kept in place.

Second, the model may have been *poorly tested*: this arises when managers fail to abide by the main principles of statistics. The most important consideration is that the uncertainty associated with real-life operations must have been present in the back-testing environment. Usually, this means that the period during which the model is tested should be different from the period during which the model is calibrated. I would add that this is one of the points in the manager research process when I like to focus on 'data mining,' a term that describes the tendency certain managers have to torture the historical data until some form of relationship can be elicited.[9]

Third, the model may have been *incompletely tested*: this often occurs when one fails to appreciate that the distribution of investment returns is usually not really normal. The tails of the distributions may be fatter than expected (a phenomenon called 'kurtosis' by statisticians), which means that exceptional events may occur more frequently than anticipated.[10] The Long Term Capital Management crisis of 1998 is an example of such a problem, although the trigger was not really a faulty model. The problem was with the assumption, inherent in the model, that the firm could keep borrowing until the exceptional event reverted to the norm.

Portfolio construction risk

Portfolio construction risk is linked to the way in which the relative sizes of individual investments are controlled. One can imagine two simple examples to illustrate the issue.

First, one can think in term of risk relative to a benchmark. In the world of fixed-income investments, one might want to evaluate the maximum deviation one might accept relative to the interest rate sensitivity or duration of the benchmark, or the extent to which the average or specific credit of the portfolio may deviate from that of the index. In an equity portfolio, one might look into industry or, more broadly, factor bets.

Second, one can think in terms of the extent to which a specific investment may be allowed to influence the overall results of the portfolio. This is often called concentration risk.

Execution risk

Execution risk covers most of the internal administrative controls that a manager puts in place. Though it is true that many of the risks associated with the execution of a strategy do not directly affect an investor client, they are still critical to the evaluation of the manager. They do not affect clients directly, as a manager would typically be expected to compensate a client for mistakes, such as breach of guidelines, faulty trade execution or unintended leverage arising from a mismatch of settlement dates. Yet this is an important risk, because one must ensure that the manager carries the appropriate insurance to cover the risk, or has sufficient capital to be able to compensate clients without having to declare bankruptcy.

Counterparty risk

Counterparty risk is a close cousin of execution risk, but takes on a particularly important dimension when derivative trades are a standard part of the investment process. Counterparty risk arises in one of two circumstances.

First, each time a trade is executed there is the implicit assumption that the counterparty will deliver the security or the proceeds of a sale as and when expected. Again, this kind of risk is more relevant to the manager's business than to the performance of a client portfolio, as a manager is typically expected to cover his or her clients for failed trades.

Second, most over-the-counter trades explicitly rely on the assumption that the counterparty will be able to meet its obligations when required. The Russian ruble crisis of 1998 is a good example of counterparty risk gone very bad. Many managers had hedged the ruble exposure associated with investments in Russian bonds or equities. They found themselves uncovered when the Russian counterparty defaulted on its obligation.

Human capital evaluation

Evaluation of the human capital at the disposal of the manager brings up a variety of issues:

- are the resources adequate, given the scope of the business?
- how experienced are the individuals who contribute to the investment process?
- what are their respective reputations, professionally and as to their character?
- are they compensated well enough to ensure that they will remain in the job for the foreseeable future? and
- how is the manager providing for the development of its human capital, from training to continuing education?

Two quotations from David Swensen[11] illustrate the importance of the qualitative part of this evaluation. First, 'nothing matters more than working with high-quality partners.' Second: 'Integrity tops the list of qualifications. Aside from the powerful fact that moral behavior defines a fundamentally important standard, acting in an ethical manner represents a pragmatic means of improving the probability of investment success. Choosing external advisors of high integrity reduces the gap between the actions of the advisors and the interests of an institutional fund.'

Manager evaluation: summary

In the end, manager evaluation requires the analyst to obtain both factual and judgmental insights. The factual part of the process can typically be provided by inviting manager candidates to complete a 'request for proposal' (RFP), containing a large number of questions. One such RFP is reproduced in the box below. It was designed for nontraditional investment managers (hedge funds and private equity managers), a category chosen principally because it requires the most comprehensive effort. It is broken down into three general areas of inquiry: the firm, its investment activity and investment results. While phrases such as 'k1s', 'wash sales' or 'ADV Part II' indicate that our sample RFP was formulated in the U.S. context, it is easy to adapt it for application to other contexts.

The judgmental part of the process usually requires both a number of interviews with the manager, and sufficient industry experience to be able to place answers and data in the appropriate perspective. One of the most critical elements of the research process is for the analyst to maintain continuous contact with the manager he or she follows, in order to ensure that the information is most current and that he or she can get a sense of the dynamics at work within the manager.

Example of a request for proposal (RFP)
The firm

1. The firm
- When was it founded? By whom? Why?
- Experience of principals and their tenure with the firm.
- Any financial partners? If yes, their roles and responsibilities.
- Any affiliation? If yes, scope and nature of agreements.
- How many offices and respective roles?
- Plans for the future.
- How principals handle their own assets.

2. Its structure
- Ownership: how much is owned by employees, how far employee ownership is spread.
- Organizational structure.
- Roles.
- Mission statement.

3. Its fiduciary and legal policies, and standing
- How much fiduciary liability insurance?
- How much errors and omission insurance?
- Registration of principals and employees: is the firm or its employees a CPO, CTA or RIA? What registration has been done with CFTC? Can you provide an ADV Part II if available?
- Any current litigation? If yes, please explain.
- Any judgments against the firm and its principals? If yes, please explain.
- Trading policies for individual securities.
- Trading and rebate policies for commingled products.

4. Its target markets
- Individual or institutions?
- Onshore or offshore?
- Principal desired client attributes.
- Average desired account size – please provide mean and median.
- Average actual account size – please provide mean and median.

5. Its product line

- Product range.
- Delivery process: individual accounts, commingled vehicles, other.
- Servicing process: nature, frequency and extent of reporting, access to investment specialists, other.
- Willingness to work on a consulting basis.
- Fee philosophy – discuss fee process when using sub-advisors.
- Specific fee schedules for all products discussed herein – please provide different schedules for onshore and offshore activities if applicable and relevant.
- Is there a high water mark or preferred return provision? If yes, please discuss procedure.

6. Its personnel

- Total number of employees.
- Biographies for as many individuals as possible.
- Investment professionals (fundamental analysts, quantitative analysts, macroeconomists, portfolio managers, other): respective experience levels, whether they are principals, tenure with the firm.
- Support staff (numbers and roles): respective experience levels, whether they are principals, tenure with the firm.
- Staff turnover by category: how has it changed over the past five years and what was done to deal with any issue? Please provide details as to the names and positions of individuals who left during the past five years.

7. Employee compensation

- Compensation philosophy.
- Principal components of compensation package.
- Role of equity ownership.
- Other issues.

8. Administrative issues

- Middle and back office functions:
    - tenure of current personnel;
    - turnover in the past three years;
    - any operational problem in the past three years;
    - what performance information is available monthly?
    - when did you mail your k1s in each of the past three years?
- Systems used, their origin, and their maintenance – any change, recent or planned?
- Securities and/or fund pricing methodology.
- Custody relationship(s).
- Internal and external audit procedures.

9. Risk management
- Risk management process.
- Major perceived risk factors.
- Segregation of duties.
- Derivatives policy.
- Leverage policy.
- Portfolio review policy.

10. Assets under management
- Total assets.
- Assets per major strategy.
- Assets per type of account – individual account, commingled vehicle, other.
- Assets per geographical location of client – onshore United States, onshore other, offshore.
- Assets per type of client – institution, individual, other.
- Assets per account size – less than US$1 million, US$1–5 million, US$5–10 million, US$10–25 million, US$25–100 million, more than US$100 million.
- Number of clients gained and lost for each strategy in each of the past three years.
- How much of the firm's assets under management are beneficially owned by the principals and how much by individuals associated with the principal – please provide definition of 'associated'.

11. General terms
- Minimum account size – segregated account, commingled vehicle, other – per major strategy and per type of account – individual account, commingled vehicle, other.
- Auditors.
- Legal counsel.
- Prime broker(s) (if applicable).
- AIMR-compliant?

12. Other
- Any additional comment with respect to the firm as a whole.

Investment activity

1. Investment philosophy
- Have your critical beliefs changed in the past several years? If yes, why?
- Is maximizing tax efficiency important? If no, why?
- How do you view diversification and how does that translate in practice in the portfolios you manage?
- How do you approach the issue of the optimal size of the firm?
- Has the firm ever stopped accepting new mandates? If yes, why?

2. Investment process

- Focus
  - Individual managers: please describe in specific detail the principal features of each strategy you employ.
  - Private equity managers: do you invest in all phases of the capital-raising process or specialize in certain phases? Why?
  - Multimanager managers: what do you view as your value added?
  - All: do you have structural industry or sector preferences?
- Sources of insights
  - Internal or external.
  - If internal, describe research capabilities, focus, and resources dedicated to the activity.
  - If external, describe sources, their persistence, and their compensation, as well as vetting procedures.
  - Research process: for multimanager managers, please provide a sample manager questionnaire.
- Access
  - Do you believe you have privileged access to managers? If yes, please provide example and rationale.
  - For private equity managers in particular, discuss the number of deals you saw, reviewed and eventually selected in each of the past three years, discussing both numbers and dollar amounts.
- Investment decision-making
  - Who is involved? Who has the final say?
  - How often do you review portfolio composition?
  - Describe a recent purchase, focusing on buy criteria.
  - Describe a recent sale, focusing on sell criteria.
  - What was your best decision in the past three years? Why?
  - What was your worst decision in the past three years? Why?
- Capacity
  - How much do you believe you could manage if the only constraint was your ability to execute your strategy?
  - What can be done to create additional capacity?
  - Describe steps taken to enhance tax efficiency.
  - Operational capacity: lot accounting, other.
  - Investment capacity: portfolio construction rules, systematic loss harvesting, use of derivatives, other.
  - Other capacity: limits on redemptions, other.
  - How do you control for wash sales?
- Risk management
  - How do you measure portfolio risk?
  - How often is it done?

- How do you control portfolio risk?
- How frequently is it reviewed?
- What do you view as the greatest risk in your investment approach?
- What do you view as the greatest risk in your current portfolios?

• Portfolio construction – individual strategies: please provide as many sets of answers as the number of strategies you offer.
  - How many positions do you normally own? Please provide a breakdown between long and short positions. If you use options, please include the notional value in this calculation. Is that typical?
  - Describe the current market exposure (% long and % short) of a typical portfolio. How has that ranged in the past three years?
  - Diversification/concentration: how much of a typical portfolio is accounted for by the five largest positions? How much by the 10 largest positions?
  - Do you currently use leverage? If yes, how much? Please provide a range for each of the past three years.
  - Use of derivatives.
  - Do you hedge currency exposure?

• Portfolio construction – multimanager portfolios: please provide as many sets of answers as the number of strategies you offer.
  - How many managers do you currently own? Is that typical?
  - What drives your manager decision process: bottom up, top down, combination, other (please specify)?
  - Describe the current market exposure (% long and % short) of a typical portfolio. How has that ranged in the past three years?
  - Diversification/concentration: how much of a typical portfolio is accounted for by the five largest positions? How much by the 10 largest positions? Is there a limit to the acceptable exposure to any single manager? If yes, what?
  - Do you currently use leverage outside positions held by managers? If yes, how much? Please provide a range for each of the past three years.
  - Do you have guidelines for maximum total portfolio leverage? If yes, how do you monitor leverage within the portfolios of underlying managers?
  - Use of derivatives (if any) outside the positions held by managers.
  - Do you hedge currency exposure outside the positions held by managers?
  - Information flows between your managers and yourself.

• Trading
  - For individually managed strategies: How do you trade? What is your commission policy? Do you hold core positions versus short-term trading? Who does the trading?
  - For multimanager portfolios: How do you structure your relationship with the underlying managers? Do you accept fee rebates, 12b(1) or shareholder servicing fees?

> **Investment performance**
>
> **1. Portfolio composites**
> - Do you use portfolio composites? If yes, how are they created?
> - How much of the assets you manage do they cover?
>
> **2. Returns**
> - Please provide the following for each strategy:
>   - pre-tax returns for each of the past five years – discuss the basis for those returns (fund, composite, representative account, other).
>   - after-tax returns for each of the past five years – state assumptions.
>   - comparison of these returns to an appropriate benchmark or benchmarks – explain which and why.

Building and administering a manager stable

This issue calls to mind the principles discussed in earlier chapters dealing with multiple asset location (Chapter 5), the construction of a tax-efficient portfolio (Chapter 6), and the formulation of an investment policy (Chapter 12). When thinking of the problem of building and managing a stable of managers,[12] I usually focus on three principal questions:

- what are the investment strategies that I need to achieve my investment goals?
- what opportunity do I have to manage manager risk with the multiple locations through which I hold my or my family's wealth? and
- how do I optimize the ongoing tax efficiency of my overall portfolio?

Selecting the appropriate investment strategies

Taxable investors should avoid defining individual investment strategies in too much detail (see Chapters 9 and 16). In particular, the migration of individual securities across the line separating value and growth can cause undue portfolio rebalancing costs when the investor selects a different mandate for each style. Just as it makes sense to consider styles in as broad a scope as possible, so as broad a perspective as possible should be applied when considering such issues as small-capitalization versus mid-capitalization versus large-capitalization stocks, or geographical mandates when dealing with foreign securities. The selection of investment strategies within the tax-efficient part of the portfolio will also probably be most effective when individual mandates are as broad as reasonable. By contrast, the strategies comprising the tax-oblivious part of the portfolio can be as specific as one wants, provided one does not drift too far into such a high level of manager diversity as to create administrative problems.

Thus, the general principles governing the selection of investment strategies stable are threefold:

- minimize the total number of strategies to keep the management challenge – defined in terms of both administrative simplicity and tax efficiency coordination – as simple as possible;
- divide the universe of potential strategies between those strategies that lend themselves to tax efficiency and those that do not to minimize the risk of selecting a tax-inefficient variant of a strategy that could be tax-efficient; and
- aim to diversify only those strategies that entail significant strategic or manager risks,[13] recognizing that diversification brings greater administrative and coordinating complexity.

For example, a family with a total wealth of US$100 million designed a strategy aimed to generate real (inflation-adjusted) returns of 4–6% while minimizing the risk that the value of the portfolio would fall over any rolling five-year period. Though philosophically prepared to accept the proposition that traditional managers can produce after-tax, after-fee value added, the family was very interested in active tax management, which seemed to provide a useful shelter to the tax-inefficient strategies that its members also felt they needed to consider. The solution the family selected comprised three different axes.

First, the 20% of the portfolio allocated to fixed-income securities was evenly split between two municipal bond strategies, both of which are highly tax-efficient. While 10% was focused on the investment grade sector of the market, the other 10% was committed to high-yield securities.

Second, the 45% allocated to equities was also split two ways. The 5% allocated to emerging markets was to be managed by an active traditional manager, while the remaining 40% was committed to a single global equity portfolio, comprising both small- and large-capitalization stocks, managed in a passive structured manner to provide both tax efficiency within the subportfolio, and the opportunity to shelter the tax-inefficient returns earned on hedge funds and emerging market equities.

Finally, the 35% allocated to nontraditional strategies was placed in a more complex structure. Within this 35%, 15% was committed over five years to five private equity programs, each managed by a 'fund of funds' manager, reflecting the need to maintain appropriate manager, stage and strategy diversification, and to deal with time diversification issues as well. Another 10% was committed to two different semidirectional hedge fund managers, one using a multimanager structure applied to hedged equities, the other using four distinct semidirectional strategies: one focused on Japan, another on global interest sensitive equities, the third on technology, and the fourth on health care. This ensured appropriate manager and strategy risk diversification. The remaining 15% was allocated to three nondirectional hedge fund managers, two using multimanager structures and the third being a single manager using four different strategies: risk arbitrage, index arbitrage, hedged distressed, and event-driven. In all, the family chose a very limited number of traditional strategies (four in all), while getting substantial diversification in the nontraditional side of their portfolio, where it may have as many as 50 or 60 strategies or managers.

Using asset location to handle manager risk

In the example we just considered, we assumed that there was only one significant pocket through which the family held its wealth. Thus, overall tax efficiency considerations mandated that the large bulk of the family's traditional equity exposure be managed in a single subportfolio, providing 'hyper' tax efficiency. In reality, most families hold their wealth through multiple pockets, thus providing additional opportunities, when needed, to deal with manager diversification issues.[14]

Assume, for instance, that, instead of one pocket, we have two, with everything else unchanged. The fact that we have two pockets now allows us to consider using two different managers for the traditional, developed equity portfolio. This can be done in one of several ways, but one example will make the point. Let me go back to our family and assume that it is prepared to pay for active security selection on some of the non-U.S. stock portfolio and on the small-capitalization part of its U.S. equity assets. By contrast, it might still think that the tax-sheltering benefit potentially associated with a passive structured mandate in the U.S. large-capitalization equity universe is too attractive to reject. It would then need to draw a clear distinction between the tax-efficient and tax-inefficient parts of its portfolio, and allocate the strategies to the appropriate pockets.

For instance, the family might place the structured mandate in the same pocket as the hedge funds to shelter the returns earned on the most tax-inefficient strategies with the hyper tax efficiency of a passive structured mandate. Alternatively, the family might combine the tax-efficient municipal fixed-income and private equity mandates with the less tax-efficient actively managed non-U.S. large-capitalization and U.S. small-capitalization subportfolios. In this instance, having both passive structured and active mandates potentially invested in the same broad markets, would not be a problem with respect to wash sales, provided the strategies are held in appropriately different pockets.

Optimizing the ongoing tax efficiency of the whole portfolio

Having the right overall strategy, and a set of well defined and appropriately mandated individual subportfolios, are only two of the three conditions governing the management of taxable wealth. The third relates to the need to coordinate the activities of each subportfolio in such a way that total portfolio tax efficiency is maximized, while allowing each manager enough space to deliver on whatever promises have been made.

Coordinating overall portfolio activity does not have a direct equivalent in the world of tax-exempt institutional investing. We saw earlier that the analogy of a coach works well to describe the role of this coordinator. One aspect not mentioned then was the need for the coordinator to have access to the information he or she needs to do the job. This is where the administrative duties of keeping records and processing transactions come in.

It is the master custodian or master trustee (the difference in terms depending upon the legal structure of the various pockets) who provides overall transaction-processing, trade-settlement, cash-management and record-keeping services. Typically accessible through electronic means, the reports that this coordinator provides allow the investor, his or her manager, and/or his or her family office to look at the whole portfolio across the multiple manager mandates. Each manager is expected to custody the assets with the master custodian. Whenever a transaction is executed, the manager informs the master custodian, who is in charge of settling the trade, and thus also the handling all cash and security movements. With all assets held in one place, the investor can request a variety of reports. Certain reports will be created for each mandate, so that the performance of each manager can be appropriately assessed. Others will reflect asset class, strategy or total portfolio pictures, and thus ignore the artificial distinctions between managers. Armed with these reports, and with access to the information and data behind them, the coordinator can identify all opportunities to maximize the tax efficiency of the overall portfolio. He or she is not captive to the need to assemble the whole through selected building blocks. Rather, he or she can view the whole edifice and instruct each manager accordingly.

Summary and implications

Selecting managers and managing a multi-manager stable are complex and yet also deceptively simple enterprises. They are complex, because many of our own biases tend to lead us in the wrong direction and because manager evaluation is a serious task. Biases such as overconfidence, optimism, overreaction to chance events, improper framing of decisions, or hindsight, together with years of accumulated, but at times irrelevant, institutional experience tend to motivate us toward the construction of overly specialized and complex stables, and the making of overly short-term commitments to strategies or managers. As we saw earlier, individual investors need to view the relationship established with each manager differently[15] and in a long-term context. Only in that context will it make sense for each manager to accept the disruption that may arise within his or her mandate, for the greater good of the overall endeavor. In fact, this is a requirement to ensure that each manager proactively makes suggestions to the investor, or his or her advisor, that might negatively affect the mandate for which the manager is responsible.

At the same time, selecting managers and managing a multimanager stable can be viewed as deceptively simple enterprises once a few simple rules are taken into consideration. They involve both important things to do and things to avoid:

- manager evaluation should be conducted in an appropriately long time frame;
- manager evaluation should be focused on process and individuals to maximize the chances of identifying real talent, and of differentiating between bias and insight;
- manager evaluation should incorporate close attention to the five sources of risk (discussed above);
- the number of individual strategies should be managed with an eye both to desirable diversification and to the need for overall portfolio coordination;
- manager stables should be kept as small as practical to maximize fee leverage and administrative simplicity; and
- a specific overall coordination role must be specified to ensure that the practical necessity of having a 'building block' approach is not allowed to detract from the need to focus on the total portfolio focus.

[1] See Horvitz, Jeffrey, 'Asset Classes and Asset Allocation: Problems of Classification,' *The Journal of Private Portfolio Management*, Spring 2000, pp. 27–32.

[2] See Brunel, Jean L.P., 'The Upside-Down World of Tax-Aware Investing,' *Trusts and Estates*, February 1997, pp. 34–42.

[3] For a discussion of the limitations of historical performance as a predictor of future returns, see Kahn, Ronald N., and Andrew Rudd, 'Does Historical Performance Predict Future Performance?,' *Financial Analysts Journal*, Vol. 51, November/December 1995, pp. 43–52.

[4] See Bauman, W. Scott, and Robert E. Miller, 'Can Managed Portfolio Performance Be Predicted?,' *The Journal of Portfolio Management*, Summer 1994, pp. 31–40; or Bauman, W. Scott, and Robert E. Miller, 'Portfolio Performance Rankings in Stock Market Cycles,' *Financial Analysts Journal*, Vol. 51, No. 2, March/April 1995, pp. 79–87. For a discussion of the role of luck in manager performance, see Beckers, Stan, 'Manager Skill and Investment Performance: How Strong is the Link?,' *The Journal of Portfolio Management*, Summer 1997, pp. 9–23.

[5] For a discussion of potential adjustments to the evaluation process to get better insights into managers' skills, see Ferson, Wayne E., and Vincent A. Warther, 'Evaluating Fund Performance in a Dynamic Market,' *Financial Analysts Journal*, Vol. 52, No. 6, November/December 1996, pp. 20–28. For a more technical discussion on tests that can be performed to ensure that 'observed results are due to a real effect or reside within the realm of noise,' see Kritzman, Mark, 'What Practitioners Need to Know … About Hypothesis Testing?,' *Financial Analysts Journal*, Vol. 50, No. 4, July/August 1994, pp. 18–22.

[6] See Goetzman, William N., and Roger G. Ibbotson, 'Do Winners Repeat?,' *The Journal of Portfolio Management*, Winter 1994, pp. 9–18.

[7] See Stewart, Scott D., 'Is Consistency of Performance a Good Measure of Manager Skill?,' *The Journal of Portfolio Management*, Spring 1998, pp. 22–32.

[8] See Anson, Mark. 'Selecting a Hedge Fund Manager,' *The Journal of Wealth Management*, Winter 2000, pp. 45–52.

[9] See Markowitz, Harry M., and Gan Lin Xu, 'Data Mining Corrections,' *The Journal of Portfolio Management*, Fall 1994, pp. 60–70.

[10] See Lucas, Andre, and Pieter Klaasen, 'Extreme Returns, Downside Risk, and Optimal Asset Allocation,' *The Journal of Portfolio Management*, Fall 1998, pp. 71–80.

[11] See Swensen, David F., *Pioneering Portfolio Management – An Unconventional Approach to Institutional Investment*, New York: The Free Press, 2000.

[12] For a discussion of this issue in a tax-oblivious context, see Waring, Barton, Duane Whitney, John Pirone, and Charles Castille, 'Optimizing Manager Structure and Budgeting Manager Risk,' *The Journal of Portfolio Management*, Spring 2000, pp. 90–104. See also Baieri, Gary T., and Peng Chen, 'Choosing Managers and Funds,' *The Journal of Portfolio Management*, Winter 2000, pp. 47–53.

[13] See Billingsley, Randall S., and Don M. Chance, 'Benefits and Limitations of Diversification Among Commodity Trading Advisors,' *The Journal of Portfolio Management*, Fall 1996, pp. 65–80.

[14] For a discussion of manager diversification with a single equity style, see Fant, L. Franklin, and Edward S. O'Neal, 'Do You Need More than One Manager for A Given Equity Style?,' *The Journal of Portfolio Management*, Summer 1999, pp. 68–75.

[15] For a discussion of the need to move beyond the conventional to improve the scope for excess manager returns, see Thomas, Lee R., 'Active Management,' *The Journal of Portfolio Management*, Winter 2000, pp. 25–32.

The supervising and monitoring process

Chapter 18

Computing and assessing after-tax returns

Supervising the execution of the wealth management plan is the last phase of the wealth management process, but it is by no means the least important. Predictably, it revolves around the measurement and assessment of the performance both of the total portfolio, and of each of its component parts. It shares a number of the attributes of the manager selection and management processes discussed in Chapter 17, but it also involves at least two unique challenges.

First, we are now in charge of the *computation* of the after-tax returns that we have actually achieved. In an article to which I have referred before,[1] I looked into the issue of measuring investment performance and concluded that:

> Unlike the rather simple presentation of performance for tax-exempt investors, which follows commonly agreed definitions and calculations, after-tax performance can be measured in a number of different – and equally valid – ways. Each depends upon whether (a) the portfolio is to be considered on its own or as a part of a broader wealth total; (b) performance is to be measured before or after liquidation costs; (c) there were significant cash flows, and, if so, whether they were into or out of the portfolio; and (d) what inception date is selected.

The second challenge concerns the need for *assessment* of performance, that is, for comparisons to some external benchmark, enabling us to answer a simple question: is the return good, bad or indifferent? The answer to that question will allow us to decide whether we should be satisfied or dissatisfied with the results obtained. As I noted in the same article:

> Ultimately, there are a virtually limitless number of defensible after-tax return computations for an index and thus for relevant benchmarks. It would seem only fair to subject the benchmark to the same constraints as those used in the management of the portfolio – such as cash flows, market-to-book ratio limits, external portfolio circumstances (losses or gains realized outside of the portfolio, for instance) or liquidation horizon. As these constraints affect the way in which the portfolio is managed, they should also be imposed on the benchmark against which the performance is assessed. This, needless to say, is no simple matter.

Performance measurement and assessment questions are important, because answering them will eventually drive decisions as to whether to stay the course or change manager in the broad plan. A normal and serious process in the tax-exempt world, this becomes even more important in the context of taxable investors, because of the need to maintain loyal and long-term relationships. David Swensen[2] phrases the issue quite well, though he considers it in the context of institutional investment mandates:

Loyalty plays an important part in investment management relationships, allowing longer-term thinking to dominate decision-making. ... Loyalty flows both ways. Investors owe external advisors the opportunity to pursue investment activities within a reasonable time frame. Firing a poorly performing manager simply to remove an embarrassing line item from an annual report fails to meet the test of reasonableness. Similarly, an investment advisor abandoning reliable partners simply to pursue a lower-cost source of capital follows a shortsighted strategy.

AIMR performance presentation standards

Before going further, it is worth setting out the presentation principles on which there is some agreement in the industry. I am referring here to the after-tax performance presentation standards promulgated by the Association for Investment Management and Research (AIMR). These standards are often referred to simply as AIMR-PPS[TM].[3]

AIMR understood very well the problem at hand and its report includes the following telling admonition to readers:

Professionals evaluating taxable managers should realize that after-tax performance analysis is both a science and an art. The '*scientific*' aspects are manifested in the discrete requirements and details, while the '*artisan*' aspects recognize that cash flows, substantial unrealized capital gains, and composite definitions can have a significant impact on after-tax results.

AIMR standards, which are focused on the question of reporting after-tax returns, broadly impose three requirements:

- each portfolio should be considered as a single entity, with 'portfolio' being defined from the point of view of the firm that reports the returns, rather than from the point of view of the investor. In this context, it is probably preferable to call them subportfolios;
- the impact of taxes should be entirely considered and applied within that subportfolio, which specifically excludes the potential to work toward total portfolio tax efficiency; and
- the performance of the subportfolio should be measured on a pre-liquidation basis only.

These standards are very reasonable in the context of reporting performance through the creation and management of composites. The composites group accounts with comparable circumstances and mandates, and allow investors and their advisors to review the record of several managers on some equal footing. This is much more satisfying than the alternative, which would involve considering only one or two representative portfolios, as the selection of these portfolios would expose investors to the risk of not seeing the whole picture.

Exhibit 18.1 shows a sample performance report included in the Report of the After-Tax Subcommittee of the AIMR-PPS Implementation Committee. It is standard practice for such a report to be accompanied by a statement that:

XYZ investment firm has prepared and presented this report in compliance with the Performance Presentation Standards of the Association for Investment Management and Research (AIMR-

PPS™), the North American version of the Global Investment Performance Standards (GIPS™). AIMR has not been involved with the preparation or review of this report.

One should also note, in passing, that AIMR is not the only organization that proposes performance-reporting standards. In the United States, the Securities and Exchange Commission is charged with regulating mutual funds, while the Commodity Futures Trading Commission oversees hedge funds. Similarly, the Financial Services Authority in the United Kingdom and the COB in France are responsible for oversight activities, including issues related to performance reporting.[4]

All such standards have at least one very important limitation: they are not very useful for the investor who wants to be able to consider total portfolio issues. In fairness, one should note that the AIMR-PPS report does address a number of the issues that need to be resolved when dealing with total portfolio issues. For instance, the report indicates that this equation can be modified to include an adjustment term that removes the effect of client-initiated gain realizations. The adjustment term credits the manager for taxes that were not at his discretion. By reducing the tax payments, the adjustment factor should always have the effect of raising

Exhibit 18.1

Sample AIMR-PPS-compliant presentation for an after-tax composite, 1996–2000 (% except as shown)

	1996	1997	1998	1999	2000
Required if claiming compliance with					
AIMR-PPS and showing after-tax performance					
After-tax total return	21.99	31.03	25.02	22.02	-6.17
After-tax composite dispersion	3.10	5.10	3.70	3.20	2.4
Before-tax total return	24.31	34.02	27.33	24.03	-8.44
Before-tax benchmark total return	22.95	33.35	28.58	21.04	-9.01
Before-tax total return	24.31	34.02	27.33	24.03	-8.44
Proportion of unrealized capital gains to overall assets	9	25	37	43	19
Composite assets as proportion of assets managed to the same strategy	75	78	81	79	82
Dollar-weighted highest applicable anticipated tax rate	44.2	44.3	44.5	44.1	43.9
Portfolios (number)	26	32	38	45	48
Total assets at end of period (US$ million)	165	235	344	445	420
Proportion of firm's assets	33	36	39	43	37
Firm's total assets (US$ million)	500	653	882	1,035	1,135
Recommended					
After-tax return adjusted for nondiscretionary capital gains	21.99	31.07	25.25	24.12	-5.99
After-tax benchmark return	21.78	32.05	27.78	20.21	-9.37

Source: Report of the After-Tax Subcommittee of the AIMR-PPS Implementation Committee

the measured after-tax return. Nevertheless, in a world where the 'open architecture' of multimanager stables has become the rule rather than the exception, the challenge for individual investors remains the same: he or she needs the ability to analyze the total picture at least as much as the ability to make judgments about selected portions of it.

Measuring after-tax performance

It is worth considering a few examples that illustrate the nature of the problem.[5] This will eventually help us formulate the principal aspects of a possible solution.

Formulating the problem

In the article referenced earlier, I proposed a simple set of three examples that illustrate the main issues associated with the computation of after-tax returns. They are shown in Exhibit 18.2.

In all three scenarios, we start with a common set of assumptions: the portfolio has a beginning market value of US$10 million; it is invested in a strategy that should produce a pre-tax return of 10%; the average tax rate of the investor is 35%; and all gains made during the year are realized. This last condition is not critical to the experiment, but is included here simply to make the mathematics of the calculation of return more transparent and thus easier to follow. In real life, the problem would be somewhat more complex, but the concept we are investigating would remain unchanged.

In scenario A, the portfolio simply earns the 'normal' return assigned to the strategy, the 10% we postulated at the outset. It is fully taxed on these returns, we do not need to worry about unrealized capital gains at the outset, and we cannot benefit from the tax-sheltering potential provided by some external tax loss.

In scenario B, the starting portfolio is saddled with a substantial unrealized gain, which constrains its ability to earn the normal return associated with the strategy. This can be seen as an illustration of the 'cost of getting there' (see Chapter 11). We assume that the portfolio earns only half of the return available from the selected strategy, as management is constrained by the low tax basis of its current holdings. Performance is not only worse on a pre-liquidation basis, but becomes extremely poor when we look at it on a post-liquidation basis, because the annual return is made to absorb the full brunt of hitherto unrealized capital gains.

In scenario C, the portfolio suffers from the same challenging initial conditions as in scenario B, but it is no longer considered in

Exhibit 18.2

Computing after-tax returns for three scenarios

	A	B	C
Values (US$ million)			
Beginning tax basis	10	5	5
External tax loss	0	0	5
Beginning market value	10	10	10
Ending market value	11	10.5	11
Returns (%)			
Pre-tax	10.0	5.0	10.0
Pre-liquidation after-tax	6.5	3.25	6.5
Post-liquidation after-tax	6.5	-14.25	6.5

Source: Author's compilation from Jean L.P. Brunel, CFA 'The Upside-Down World of Tax-Aware Investing', *Trust and Estates*, February 1997, pp. 34-42.

isolation. In a total portfolio context, the subportfolio is allowed to benefit from the tax-sheltering potential provided by some external tax loss. Effectively, this external tax loss neutralizes the impact of the cost of getting there, as the tax basis of the portfolio is effectively brought back to market. The portfolio can earn the same return as in scenario A, as the external loss eliminates the tax management constraints.

These somewhat naïve examples show how critical it is to select the appropriate computation method. More specifically, they illustrate the limitation of any approach that, explicitly or implicitly, excludes circumstances beyond a given subportfolio.

The theoretical solution

Lee Price was intimately involved in the formulation of AIMR-PPS, chairing the subcommittee on after-tax performance reporting. He recently proposed[6] a simple set of two formulae that summarize the more detailed requirements contained in the AIMR's report:

- after-tax return = pre-tax return − tax burden
- tax burden =[(realized gains x capital gains tax rate) + (income x income tax rate)]/[beginning market value + weighted cash flows].

Though sensible, these formulae suffer from an important flaw, which was not lost on David Stein,[7] who observed that applying them might not be straightforward. More specifically, he argued that:

> While it is straightforward to determine the fair market value of a portfolio of marketable securities, the notion of 'value' is less obvious for a portfolio with a tax liability.

The question of after-tax portfolio valuation

As with the constraints imposed by the portfolio's starting conditions, the challenge set before the performance analyst is to decide on the factors that he or she will incorporate into the computation and those that will be excluded. The current standard practice is to create a conceptual dichotomy between pre-liquidation and post-liquidation performance measurement approaches, and to sidestep the vexing question of these starting conditions altogether.

Chapter 3, introducing tax efficiency and its basic tenets, briefly looked at an idea proposed by Jim Poterba,[8] who noted that it was conceptually wrong to follow the tax code and assume that unrealized capital gains are not taxed. Indeed, though the tax rate on unrealized capital gains *appears* to be zero: 'capital gains that are not realized in one period are carried forward to future periods, creating "contingent future tax liabilities" for the investor.'

The insight that both Stein and Poterba offer is subtle. Though one cannot debate the fact that unrealized capital gains may not be taxed in the current period, that is, until they are realized, they will eventually be taxed, unless one assumes that the portfolio is transferred through an estate or a charitable gift. The conceptual framework that Poterba presents for evaluating the actual tax rate that one should apply to unrealized gains is similar to the one that Stein proposes for calculating after-tax returns. In both cases, one must deal with the expected present value of the taxes that an investor may pay in the future on a gain that accrues today.

A methodology for computing a full-cost evaluation

David Stein has devised a process to compute a 'full cost equivalent' portfolio value. As he explains: 'this is essentially the present value of the portfolio under assumptions on horizon, investment return, tax rates, and turnover.' Stein's methodology allows one to step away from the quandary of having to decide between pre-liquidation and post-liquidation valuation. Using the concept of present value allows the analyst to recoup the market value of the portfolio with the taxes that, soon or at some assumed later date, will fall due on any unrealized capital gain, effectively incorporating the insight initially offered by Poterba.

Imagine that you are offered the opportunity to own one of two portfolios. One has a market value of US$100, with a cost basis of US$50, while the other has a market value of US$95, with a cost basis of US$90. How would you compare them and decide which one is more valuable?

One option is to consider the traditional pre-liquidation approach. Effectively, assuming away the deferred tax liability, we would be overstating the true value of the portfolio, as any time we sell a security, we will need first to pay taxes on the thus realized capital gain, reducing the market value of the portfolio.

At the other extreme, we could consider the traditional post-liquidation approach. Effectively assuming that all taxes are paid today, we will be understating the true value of the portfolio. Indeed, any security we keep and hold will earn a return based on its current market value. This is the equivalent of Robert Arnott's 'interest-free loan from the government.'[9]

Stein's process elegantly solves the problem. He needs to make assumptions as to future returns on the portfolio for some given time horizon, dividend received, and the capital gains realized in each of the individual years until one reaches the end of the time horizon. Then, he can compute the final after-tax value of the portfolio. Let me summarize here two tables that Stein presents, which clearly show the usefulness of his methodology. He assumes that the market in which each portfolio is invested will return 10% per year, including a 3% dividend rate. The tax rate is 28% on capital gains and 40% on the dividends, and 5% of the capital gains are realized each year, over 20 years.

The table in Exhibit 18.3 helps us create a full-cost equivalent for a portfolio the market value of which today is US$100 with a US$50 cost basis. If an investor received a cash payment of US$100 today, that cash would grow to US$425.31 at the end of 20 years, on the basis of the assumptions set out earlier. Thus, given that the US$100 portfolio with a US$50 cost basis will grow to only US$398.80 at the end of the same 20 years the full-cost equivalent for the portfolio would be US$93.77 (US$100 x [398.80/425.31]). Stein indicates that performing the same computation on the portfolio worth US$95 today, with a US$90 tax basis, would yield a full-cost equivalent of US$94.40. Stein concludes that the second portfolio, with a current market value of US$95 and a tax basis of US$90, as compared with the portfolio with a current market value of US$100 and a tax basis of US$50, is slightly preferable, but this conclusion is sensitive to the numerical values specified. That is, changes in the return expectation, the tax rates, and the realization rate will change this evaluation.

Exhibit 18.3

Examples of full-cost evaluation (US$)

	Portfolio with high unrealized gains		Portfolio with no unrealized gains	
	First year	20th year	First year	20th year
Starting market value	100.00	430.97	100.00	453.05
Starting cost basis	50.00	210.79	100.00	243.32
Ending market value				
before taxes and dividends	107.00	461.14	107.00	484.76
Dividends	3.00	12.93	3.00	13.59
Unrealized gains	57.00	250.35	7.00	241.44
Realized gains	2.85	12.52	0.35	12.07
Taxes paid	2.00	8.68	1.30	8.82
Reinvestment	3.85	16.77	2.05	16.85
Ending cost basis	53.85	227.56	102.05	260.17
Ending value	108.00	465.39	108.70	489.53
Liquidation value		398.80		425.31

Source: Stein, David M. 'Measuring and Evaluating Portfolio Performance After Taxes.' *The Journal of Portfolio Management*, Winter 1998, pp. 117-124.

Stein's methodology allows us to arrive at the relative value of two portfolios with different starting conditions and ending market values, and thus, eventually, at sensible after-tax return computations. However, one will probably continue to see after-tax returns computed in a much simpler fashion for quite some time. It is therefore worth keeping in mind that the numbers on which we may be basing significant decisions are somewhat flawed. The solution I prefer at this point simply involves calculating several variants of the portfolio's after-tax returns, using each of them to tell me about the insights that it can reveal and avoiding drawing any conclusion on a single computation basis alone.

Assessing performance

The complexity of the performance assessment process arises from the fact that it must involve some form of comparison, in an environment where approximations used in the computation of either portfolio or benchmark returns can substantially distort either of them. Most people tend to think in terms of market benchmarks, the returns of the capital market universe in which the portfolio was invested: for instance, an equity market index for an equity portfolio, or a bond market index for a fixed-income portfolio. Yet this is much too narrow a perspective in which to consider the question. One can think of at least three dimensions to the problem:

- how did the returns earned compare with expectations?
- how did they compare with the opportunities actually available in the marketplace? and
- how did they compare with what the universe of managers actually obtained?

The tax-exempt solution

In the article already referenced, David Stein helps us observe that the problem is well known in the tax-exempt world of institutional investors.

> There are well-established methods for evaluating portfolio performance on a pretax basis (see, e.g. Grinold and Kahn [1995][10]). The investor observes the stream of investment returns over time and evaluates the performance of the portfolio manager via a set of summary measures, often making comparisons with a benchmark. A major focus is on adjustments for risk, in terms either of total standard deviation or [of] tracking error.

Note that risk adjustment can be rudimentary or quite complex, depending on whether it is focused on simple measures of volatility or on more sophisticated variables.[11]

The choice of benchmark and universe is not straightforward

Though the steps through which one should proceed are well known, John Bowen and Meir Statman[12] suggest that there is still a significant challenge, as the appropriate adjustments are not always performed. In particular, they illustrate the problem with a discussion of the issue associated with the selection of a relevant competitive universe, looking into the way in which mutual funds are rated and showing apparent inconsistencies in these ratings. The crux of their argument, which is one of the fundamental insights we need to explore, is that the universe within which a fund is placed must be appropriately selected. The argument can be expanded to state that the universe within which any portfolio is located for comparative purposes, or the benchmark against which it is compared, must be appropriately selected.

An example from Bowen and Statman's article illustrates the point:

> The Vanguard Index 500 fund was awarded an A because its 24.3% return placed it among the top 20% funds in the growth and income category. The Vanguard Index Small Company fund got a D because its 24.6% return placed it in the 20% group just a notch above last in the small-company growth category. Clearly benchmarks matter a great deal.

Bowen and Statman analyze the apparent inconsistency of having two index funds score in so different a manner and conclude that they were not placed in the appropriate universe:

> The A rating of the Vanguard Index 500 fund is, therefore, too much evidence in favor of index funds to be true. Rather, the A rating of the Vanguard Index 500 fund is an indication that the fund is not matched properly to its growth and income peer group.

> Similarly, and even more dramatically, the D rating of the Vanguard Index Small Company fund is not an indication of the superiority of managed funds over index funds, but an indication that the Vanguard Index Small Company fund is not matched properly to its small-company peer group.

In the end, however, the challenge we have just uncovered is relatively simple to address in

304

the tax-oblivious, or pre-tax, world. The message is that we need to be very careful when comparing the return of any portfolio with any benchmark. We must go beyond a cursory analysis of the portfolio or strategy and ensure that we are not comparing apples with oranges. (This is a conceptual equivalent of the discussion in Chapter 17, concerning the need for a long-enough evaluation period.)

After-tax performance assessment

Introduce taxes into the equation and the challenge becomes considerably more complex. We have just observed that the complexity of calculating after-tax returns boils down to two main observations:

- there can be more than one after-tax return for any given portfolio, depending upon the way in which one chooses to compute that return and the assumptions underpinning the computation; and
- the after-tax return on any portfolio is therefore critically dependent upon circumstances that may well be unique to that portfolio.

Note that the tax efficiency of a given portfolio or subportfolio is a function of several individual factors, which can be broadly grouped into two categories:[13] those that are under the control of the manager and those that are not. Understanding the nature of these constraints will help us appreciate the challenges we face as we develop comparative measures, or benchmarks, against which we will assess these returns.

Factors over which the manager has control

These are typically governed by the manager's strategy and investment process. The two most

---

Exhibit 18.4

After-tax equity returns assuming 40% income tax and 28% capital gains tax rates (%)

Return from:

	Appreciation	4.0	5.0	6.0	7.0	8.0	9.0	10.0
	Dividends	6.0	5.0	4.0	3.0	2.0	1.0	0.0
	Total	10.0	10.0	10.0	10.0	10.0	10.0	10.0
Proportion	5	7.5	7.9	8.3	8.7	9.1	9.5	9.9
of	10	7.5	7.9	8.2	8.6	9.0	9.3	9.7
capital	20	7.4	7.7	8.1	8.4	8.8	9.1	9.4
gains	40	7.2	7.4	7.7	8.0	8.3	8.6	8.9
realized	60	6.9	7.2	7.4	7.6	7.9	8.1	8.3
each	80	6.7	6.9	7.1	7.2	7.4	7.6	7.8
year	100	6.5	6.6	6.7	6.8	7.0	7.1	7.2

important ones are the split between income and capital gains in the strategy's expected return and the rate at which capital gains are realized.

Exhibit 18.4 illustrates the impact on after-tax returns of variations in either the split between dividends and capital appreciation, or the rate at which capital gains are realized each year. It illustrates the interactions between these two variables. Practically, it shows that there are at least four ways of earning 7.4% after-tax returns, investing in a strategy that produces 10% pre-tax returns.

The combination of higher or lower dividend tilt with higher or lower capital gain realization rate drives the observed portfolio tax efficiency. You can earn 7.4% after-tax if dividends account for 60% of your pre-tax return and if the portfolio has a 20% rate of capital gains realization, which is broadly similar to turnover, assuming that the manager does not use alpha-enabling transactions. Alternatively, you can earn 7.4% after-tax, if dividends and capital gains contribute to total return in equal proportions (50% each), and if the rate of capital gain realization rises to 40%. You can also earn 7.4% after-tax, if dividends only account for 40% of total return, and capital gains thus account for 60%, and if the rate of capital gain realization is 60%. Finally, you can still get the same result, if capital gains represent 80% of total return – in a portfolio therefore tilted against dividends – and if the rate at which these capital gains are realized is 80%.

These factors are almost entirely within the control of the manager. Indeed, the manager has the opportunity both to select a portfolio tilt away from or toward dividends, or indeed interest income, in which case he or she might be buying equity-like convertible bonds, *and* to manage the rate at which he or she chooses to realize capital gains.

However, though the interaction between the rate of capital gains realization and the amount of unrealized gains in the starting portfolio is under the control of the manager, it can substantially affect the ability of the manager to implement his or her strategy (as we saw in Exhibit 18.2). As the manager effectively controls these factors, there is seemingly no compelling need to adjust the benchmark, the problem being reduced to the choice of an appropriately representative measure.

Factors beyond the control of the manager

There are a number of factors that can have a major impact on the performance of the portfolio and escape the manager's control. Broadly, they are external to the portfolio, when portfolio is narrowly defined, and yet crucial to the overall circumstances of each investor. They fall into two general categories: cash flows into or out of the portfolio; and overall portfolio tax circumstances.

Cash flows into or out of the portfolio should be expected to have a significant impact on its tax efficiency. Positive cash flows provide managers with an opportunity to rebalance the portfolio away from unattractive or overly concentrated positions, without necessarily realizing capital gains. Indeed, the incoming monies can be used to add to positions that have become too small. By increasing the overall size of the portfolio, they naturally diminish the weight of positions left unchanged. Conversely, negative cash flows, or flows out of the portfolio, can be highly disruptive to tax efficiency, unless one assumes an environment in which prices are falling, in which case, there is less scope for unrealized gains to remain in the portfolio, and where selling current holdings does not need to generate a capital gain. Yet, in most circumstances, with prices rising over time, the requirement for a manager to meet a request for cash will force him or her to liquidate some of the portfolio. This will require him either to generate a fair proportion of capital gains, or to accept that the portfolio shifts away from its desired composition, by selling only those assets that may not have substantially appreciated. Therefore, cash flows out of the portfolio are all the more disruptive to overall portfolio tax efficiency when:

- the portfolio comprises unrealized gains at the outset;
- market prices are rising sharply;
- the manager needs to remain close to some risk benchmark; and
- the cash flows themselves are large in relation to total portfolio size.

The converse would be true in the case of cash flows into the portfolio.

Other external circumstances can be equally important to the tax efficiency of the portfolio. In certain instances, an external development will lead the portfolio to experience cash flows, as the overall wealth of the investor is rebalanced among different strategies. Let us go back to the examples in Exhibit 18.1. Though there may, or may not, be any related cash flow, the ability to take advantage of some tax loss outside the given subportfolio has the potential to make its tax efficiency look very poor, when considered in a vacuum, though it may have been exactly what the investor needed.

Imagine a case where an investor has two subportfolios, of equal size, invested in two different markets. Imagine that one portfolio experiences an increase in market value, while the other sees a decline. Finally, for the sake of simplicity, imagine that the appreciation experienced by the one subportfolio is equal, dollar for dollar, to the fall registered in the other. The careful tax-efficient investor might well invite the manager with the unrealized capital losses to realize them, so that the manager with the unrealized capital gains can use the shelter. Using this shelter would reduce the risk that the portfolio rising in value might freeze or be otherwise constrained by substantial unrealized gains.

Now, imagine that we have made these 'smart' tax-efficient decisions and yet look at each of the two subportfolios in isolation. The portfolio falling in price will appear to have a high level of tax efficiency, which should not be surprising, as there are no taxes on negative returns. At the same time, the portfolio whose assets are rising in value may appear to have a poor level of tax efficiency, as all of the gains are realized, and therefore taxed, possibly at the short-term capital gains tax rate. Yet, when considered from the point of view of the investor, and thus from a total portfolio standpoint, the tax efficiency of the investment process would have been very high, as losses are used to offset gains, which are taken to refresh the tax basis of the overall portfolio.

In practice, specific portfolio circumstances can thus have a significant impact on tax efficiency and thus on the observed after-tax returns. However, it seems much more practical to keep the portfolio return computation as simple as possible, and to reflect unusual or individual portfolio circumstances in the benchmark with which these returns are compared.

After-tax performance benchmarking

AIMR offers a great introduction to the problem:

> At the outset, one must recognize that benchmarks for after-tax reporting need to strike a balance between simplicity and flexibility for application in a wide range of contexts. True after-tax performance depends on the investor's sequence of investment flows. After-tax returns depend on when the cost basis was established and how the cash flows evolve. Two portfolios that have precisely the same current holdings will have different after-tax returns if they were initiated at different points in time and if they had different cost bases or cash flows. It is therefore impossible to envision a precise after-tax benchmark return each period that is applicable to all portfolios, even if they are managed the same. This is an important conceptual issue, since before-tax benchmarks are not subject to adjustments for tax basis and cash flows.

What is needed is a different approach that customizes the analysis of performance for each investor. Understandably, AIMR, in the Report of the After-Tax Subcommittee of the AIMR-PPS Implementation Committee suggests that:

> A good after-tax benchmark will have all of the properties of a good before-tax benchmark, plus one more important property: it will reflect the tax status and actions of the client.

AIMR suggests two broad approaches to constructing after-tax benchmarks:

> The first tries to develop and report an after-tax version of standard benchmark indices. Such after-tax returns would be easy to use, since practitioners could simply look them up in a table. Using such indices requires strong (and, for some taxable clients, potentially inappropriate) assumptions about the investor's returns and cash flows.

> The second approach, which involves the development of a 'shadow benchmark portfolio,' abandons the goal of a single benchmark return that can fit all situations. Instead, it develops a benchmark return that is tailored to the manager's style and the individual investor's cash flows and cost basis and tax rates. This approach allows for more complex modeling of the investor's returns and flows. However, it is probably not useful for a composite because of the difficulty in creating a shadow portfolio covering multiple client portfolios at once.

Further, AIMR notes that: 'these two approaches to benchmark computation can be complementary, and in many cases both approaches will be useful.'

Developing an after-tax version of a pre-tax benchmark

Jeffrey Minck and David Stein have both focused on the problem in the context of the U.S. equity market. Stein was first with his methodology, which is described in the article referenced above. Having observed that the ideal benchmark would be 'an indexed portfolio with the same cash flows as the investor,' his first intuition was to consider using the return sequence of an S&P 500 indexed mutual fund, appropriately adjusted for taxes on dividends and capital gains. He quickly appreciated that this is problematic, because mutual funds have cash flow patterns different from those that an investor would incur. In good markets, they will tend to have positive cash flows, which allows the manager to experience less of an increase in the ratio of unrealized capital gains in his or her fund than an individual investor would. The converse is also true in poor markets.

Stein therefore proceeded along a different path, computing the returns of an index portfolio by making 'a stock-by-stock simulation using historical price returns, dividends, and S&P 500 constituent weights.' The portfolio is appropriately adjusted over time because of changes to the index, as new stocks are added and others are removed, and corporate actions, such as mergers. This calculation allows Stein to produce a set of S&P benchmark returns with one very important property: there is no such thing as a single return for any year. As has traditionally been the case in the world of private equities, Stein effectively has to use the concept of 'vintage year.'[14] Indeed, the performance of a portfolio in any given year is critically dependent upon the amount of unrealized gains in it at the onset of that year. The size of these unrealized gains is in turn directly dependent upon the year in which the portfolio was funded, which we call its vintage year. Thus, there are as many after-tax returns for any given year as there are possible vintage years in which to fund a portfolio.

Given the complexity of this analysis, Stein notes that simplifications can yield close approximations. For instance, he suggests that, 'by treating an investment in the S&P 500 as a single security and using the actual S&P 500 turnover level each month,' one can estimate how the cost basis and the value of the benchmark change over time.

Jeffrey Minck[15] took the issue even further, noting that the concept of tax-efficient management applied to investor portfolios should also be applied to indexes when computing benchmark performance. He first considered the issue of the changes in the index caused by corporate actions. He noted that they should be evaluated individually, and afforded the actual tax treatment to which each would be entitled, given the nature of each transaction, rather than an overall approximation. For instance, he suggested applying a different tax treatment to the different components of a tender offer, with cash payments being taxed and share exchanges being tax-exempt. Comparing his approach with Stein's, he states that: 'the differences between our after-tax returns range from −29 to 34 basis points and approximate the size of the effects of the unique tax treatment of corporate actions.'

Minck then turned to the issue of tax lot accounting versus average cost accounting. Specifically, he compared the 'highest in, first out' (HIFO) strategy with the simple average cost accounting (ACA) approach. He noted that:

> The outperformance of HIFO over ACA ranges from 1 to 93 basis points of annual after-tax returns. Not surprisingly, the degree of outperformance generally increases as the portfolio ages, because, with an older portfolio, HIFO has more lots among which to choose.

Once the benchmark has been appropriately estimated, the performance assessment process is ready to start in earnest, with a number of adjustments required to cover individual investor circumstances, such as cash flows, imbedded gains, individual tax rates. Minck notes that:

Dealing with constraints on the level of unrealized gains in a portfolio is considerably more difficult and can have a dramatic effect on after-tax returns. Many investors restrict the level of unrealized gains in their portfolio by mandating either a maximum market-to-book ratio or some rate of gain realization. If the managed account faces these constraints, so too should the after-tax benchmark.

Minck conducted an experiment in which he imposed a constraint on a portfolio assumed funded in 1985. Exhibit 18.5 presents the results, which show that the imposition of such a constraint can markedly affect after-tax returns. The constraint Minck imposed was that the book-to-market ratio of the portfolio must not fall below 0.8, meaning that unrealized gains should not rise above 25% of the market value of the portfolio.

Minck advocates a stock-by-stock replication of the index that minimizes the forced realization of gains and includes the unique taxation of corporate actions. Stein would probably generally agree, though I suspect that he would accept some form of minor error in the computation, for the sake of simplicity.

An alternative approach

Looking for an alternative approach to performance benchmarking, I came up with the idea of mimicking the practice of the private equity world, which formally uses the vintage year approach to assess performance.[16] The performance of all private equity funds created in any given year is combined in one notional composite and tracked over time. At the end of any given performance period, a number of reference performance indexes are available, one for each vintage year, very much as we saw earlier in the work of either Stein or Minck.

As noted in the referenced article, two main factors support the idea that the vintage year

Exhibit 18.5

Annual after-tax returns, 1988–97, with and without a 0.8 constraint on the book-to-market ratio of a portfolio purchased in 1985 (% except where shown)

	Without constraint	*With constraint*	*Difference (basis points)*
1988	14.70	15.04	-34
1989	29.73	29.07	66
1990	-4.16	-4.43	27
1991	29.22	25.44	378
1992	6.63	5.73	90
1993	8.75	8.24	151
1994	0.04	-0.32	36
1995	35.94	29.22	672
1996	21.51	16.54	497
1997	32.02	26.91	511

Source: Mink, Jeffrey L. 'Tax-Adjusted Equity Benchmarks.' *The Journal of Private Portfolio Management*, Winter 1998, pp. 45-55

approach is particularly well suited to the world of tax-efficient investing. First, a tax-aware investment manager will vary the structure of a portfolio to reflect any 'legacy' issue within the portfolio. The likelihood that a manager will sell a stock to purchase another will then depend upon any unrealized gain in the sale candidate. Therefore, the more appreciated a portfolio, the more likely it must be that the manager will be constrained. Second, as asset prices tend to rise over time, the older the portfolio, the more likely it will have constraining unrealized capital gains. Assuming that unrealized capital gains are driven by overall market movements, comparing a portfolio with other portfolios of the same vintage seems to make sense.

However, a true vintage year approach might prove complex to implement in practice. Unlike private equity portfolios which ultimately mature and are fully distributed, portfolios comprising publicly quoted securities potentially live on forever. Over time, one could end up with cumbersome data that would add only limited practical value.

Two other issues militate in favor of a simpler approach. First, individual portfolio circumstances may not be captured in the context of vintage portfolio comparisons. For instance, substantial cash flows may produce significant changes in the proportion of unrealized gains to the portfolio's total market value. The ratio of the portfolio's market to book value can fluctuate in ways that are not related to overall market movements. Second, the average annual return on a typical portfolio in any given year may not be sufficiently high for the market-to-book ratio to vary significantly between two consecutive vintage years.

Instead of grouping portfolios according to the year in which they were funded, one might consider grouping them according to their market-to-book ratios at the onset of the management period. This management period might be assumed to start on the date a portfolio is funded or when a manager is entrusted with a new mandate. One could determine a few ranges of sufficiently close market-to-book ratios, for instance, less than 1, between 1.0 and 1.2, between 1.2 and 2.5, and so on. Then, irrespective of when the portfolio was funded or the mandate granted, portfolios would be assigned to the appropriate group and a benchmark return would be computed for the relevant index, burdened with the same arbitrary ratio of unrealized gains. This would potentially reduce considerably the number of alternative benchmarks and provide our industry with the solution to this vexing problem. The issue of substantial interim cash flows could be handled by defining a threshold above which a cash flow requires a portfolio to be reclassified.

One could imagine these indexes being published on both pre-tax and after-tax bases. Any after-tax computation would have to incorporate some standard tax rate assumption. From that point on, managers could offer pre-tax and after-tax comparisons, proposing, for instance, pre-tax portfolio returns relative to the appropriate composite, and portfolio tax efficiency relative to the composite. Harmonizing overall tax rate assumptions and allowing everything else to vary could enable managers to produce performance reports that are relatively automated but still offer meaningful insights into after-tax performance assessment.

Summary and implications

Serious after-tax performance analysis is still in its infancy, as the industry struggles between the obvious need and the challenges that addressing this need creates. Irrespective of the way in which one eventually elects to compute after-tax returns and benchmark them, the admonitions stated in Chapter 17 remain valid:

- any performance assessment must be based on a period long enough to account for the random variations in manager performance; and
- the process by which performance is assessed must ensure that one can distinguish between insight and bias.

Performance assessment is the same as ongoing manager selection. The questions one should put to an existing manager are the same as those that one would put to a new manager candidate.

[1] Brunel, Jean L.P., 'The Upside-Down World of Tax-Aware Investing,' *Trust and Estates*, February 1997, pp. 34–42

[2] Swensen, David F., *Pioneering Portfolio Management – An Unconventional Approach to Institutional Investment*, New York: The Free Press, 2000.

[3] Association for Investment Management Research Performance Presentation Standards (AIMR-PPS), Report of the Subcommittee on Taxable Portfolios, Charlottesville, VA, July 1994, pp. 10–13.

[4] For a U.S.-centered discussion of the appropriate standard to apply to hedge funds in particular, see Anson, Mark J.P., 'Performance Presentation Standards: Which Rules Apply When?,' *Financial Analysts Journal*, Vol. 57, No. 2, March/April 2001, pp. 53–61.

[5] For an early discussion of the problem, in the context of nuclear decommissioning trusts, see Rogers, Douglas S., 'After-Tax Equity Returns for Non-Qualified Nuclear Decommissioning Trusts,' *Financial Analysts Journal*, Vol. 48, No. 4, July/August 1992, pp. 70–73.

[6] Lee Price presented these formulae at the AIMR Seminar Investment Counseling for Private Clients III, '*Integrated Wealth Management: Investment Management, Taxes, Estate Planning and Wealth Transfer*,' Session V: 'After-Tax Benchmarks and Performance Reporting for Taxable Accounts,' Atlanta, GA, March 27, 2001.

[7] Stein, David M., 'Measuring and Evaluating Portfolio Performance After Taxes,' *The Journal of Portfolio Management*, Winter 1998, pp. 117–24.

[8] See Poterba, James M., 'Unrealized Capital Gains and the Measurement of After-Tax Portfolio Performance,' *The Journal of Private Portfolio Management*, Spring 1999, pp. 23–34. Dr. Poterba is a professor at the Massachusetts Institute of Technology.

[9] See Arnott, Robert D., Andrew L. Berkin, and Jia Ye, 'Loss Harvesting: What's It Worth To The Taxable Investor?,' *The Journal of Wealth Management*, Spring 2001, pp. 10–18

[10] Grinold, R.C., and R.N. Kahn, *Active Portfolio Management*, Burr Ridge, IL: Richard D. Irwin, Inc., 1995

[11] For an example of one such adjustment, see Obosco, Angelo, 'Style/Risk-Adjusted Performance,' *The Journal of Portfolio Management*, Spring 1999 pp. 65–68; or Ankrim, Ernest, 'Risk-Adjusted Performance Attribution,' Financial Analysts Journal, Vol. 48, No. 2, March/April 1992, pp. 75–82.

[12] See Bowen, John J., and Meir Statman, 'Performance Games,' *The Journal of Portfolio Management*, Winter 1997, pp. 8–15. See also Melnikoff, Meyer, 'Investment Performance Analysis for Investors,' *The Journal of Portfolio Management*, Fall 1998, pp. 95–107.

[13] For another discussion of these factors, see Poterba, James M., 'After-Tax Performance Evaluation,' AIMR Conference Proceedings. Investment Counseling for Private Clients II, November 9–10, 1999, pp. 58–67.

[14] For a discussion of the weakness of this approach and of a potential alternative, see Nesbitt, Stephen L., and Hal W. Reynolds, 'Benchmarks for Private Market Investments,' *The Journal of Portfolio Management*, Summer 1997, pp. 85–90.

[15] See Minck, Jeffrey L., 'Tax-Adjusted Equity Benchmarks,' *The Journal of Private Portfolio Management*, Winter 1998, pp. 45–55.

[16] See Brunel, Jean L.P., 'An Approach to After-Tax Performance Benchmarking,' *The Journal of Wealth Management*, Winter 2000, pp. 61–67.

Conclusion

Conclusion

From portfolio manager to wealth manager

So far, we have uncovered and discussed the main concerns that a careful taxable investor and his or her advisor will typically want to address to ensure that his or her wealth is managed in an optimal fashion. We have illustrated the differences between the wealth management process and an institutional asset management endeavor. The influence of taxes forces us to rethink the Pavlovian reactions we have all acquired. They set before the investor a daunting challenge: to be prepared to turn down proposals that are ostensibly designed to apply standard or marginally altered tax-oblivious practices to his or her circumstances. We also described the importance of behavioral factors. When confronted with the management of our financial affairs, we are normal, although not always rational.

A final proposition is that the central role afforded to the portfolio manager in the tax-exempt institutional world cannot be transposed to the world of the taxable individual investor. Let us examine the central role of the portfolio manager in an institutional framework and ask ourselves how that function must change to meet the true needs of taxable individual investors.

The central role of the institutional portfolio or mutual fund manager

Though many asset management firms would rightly argue that the whole team, not solely the portfolio manager, is responsible for performance, the role of the portfolio manager is central. A number of people contribute greatly to the process. Plan sponsors or other clients also play critical roles, as they set the fund's investment policy and hire the appropriate managers, thus creating the demand that individual firms seek to meet through original product design and professional excellence. Investment analysts, particularly those who work for asset managers – the 'buy side' – also play a central role in the development of those investment insights, without which there can be no investment performance. Even further, individuals working in the mid- and back-offices also contribute significantly to the process, whether they are traders, account administrators or transaction processing specialists.

However, the people who most often share the limelight with the star 'sell side' analysts or market strategists are the fund or portfolio managers. Their mission is to construct portfolios and report on their performance on a periodic basis. They select the themes and securities that are reflected in their clients' portfolios, and thus find themselves in the front line for both praise and criticism. In a world characterized by what we called sequential optimization, this is reasonable and should not cause surprise. After all, the plan sponsor or other institutional client feels responsible for having selected the appropriate strategies, turned to the asset management industry for these strategies to be executed, and expected value added to be generated.

The performance of portfolio managers is posted on a frequent basis, at least daily in the case of mutual fund managers. It can readily be compared either with a highly specialized market benchmark or with a group of their peers. Yesterday's heroes can find themselves today's fools when they have not been nimble enough, or simply when their style has become unfashionable. Though they should think of helping their clients with broad asset management issues, and many feel a desire to do so, institutional portfolio managers are often solely focused on generating investment alpha.

In fact, the industry has been evolving toward a dichotomy in the roles of what we used to call portfolio managers. A number of individuals are emerging as 'client portfolio managers': their roles involve packaging the firm's investment alpha in their institutional clients' separate portfolios, and reporting to these clients on a frequent basis. A smaller group of individuals have evolved into 'alpha portfolio managers,' whose role is almost solely dedicated to investment issues. The idea behind this change is often that the skills involved in the successful management of portfolios are quite different from those required to be a solid relationship manager. In a world where institutional clients still have difficulty accepting a pure relationship manager, the idea of having investment-trained individuals playing the role of relationship manager seems natural.

Very often, the portfolio managers assigned to individual clients belong to the client portfolio manager category. Many institutions catering to both institutional and private clienteles reserve their best investors, intentionally or not, for their institutional clients and ask others to deal with private clients, even though, in many cases, the private client asset management business is more profitable than its institutional counterpart. Thankfully, a few firms have been working hard to fight this tendency. They realize that allowing private clients to be served by self-perceived second-class citizens is a sure way to kill the business, leading traditional asset managers to lose market share. For instance, we have seen substantial growth in brokerage-based and boutique asset management, two forms of competition that have been taking market share away from the traditionally well established trust banks. Yet only a few institutions have responded to the need to redefine the role of the portfolio manager serving individual clients.

A new role: wealth manager

In the preceding pages, we have identified at least three fundamentally different needs that individual investors have and that the industry now must find a way to serve:
- individuals require a different kind of relationship management process, as they need help traveling on the road to optimality;
- taxable individuals must be concerned with long-term after-tax wealth accumulation – and in the right 'pockets' – rather than periodic pre-tax returns; and
- they must be concerned with the total portfolio picture, rather than a piece of it.

These require a different set of skills on the part of the portfolio manager and effectively contribute to the need for a new emphasis, away from the traditional portfolio manager and toward what I like to call the wealth manager.

Traveling the road to optimality

Along with the need to worry about taxes, this is the most important element of the wealth

316

management conundrum. Individual investors usually do not decide to become wealth managers; they morph into the role as a result of some life-changing event that finds them having to deal with wealth. Depending upon the mode through which this wealth was accumulated, the change can be more or less gradual.

The heir to a family fortune may have had more time to get acquainted with, and educated on, the issues associated with wealth management. He or she may also have less need for sophisticated estate and financial planning, as, presumably, some of that work will have been carried out by previous generations. By contrast, the newly liquid entrepreneur or senior executive will often not have given more than a very cursory consideration to the issue of managing his or her wealth. Their time will have been devoted to creating the wealth, and, if anything, to setting out on the road to financial and estate planning. In either case, individuals now needing to manage some wealth may not start with all the tools and knowledge they need. Rather, they must acquire them on the job.

This places an unusual burden on their wealth managers, who must develop a different relationship management model. First of all, managers must resist the temptation to pander to investors. The job is to help them on their journey, and the reward will come in the form of a long-term relationship. Trying to gain more business or to save the relationship over the short term often will lead to the wrong outcome for the family. One could argue that this is a variant on the agency risk noted in the Introduction.

We saw earlier the example of a family whose deceased patriarch had accumulated a substantial fortune, having helped found a high-tech company. The wealth of the family was still chiefly in the form of that single low-basis stock when he died, and his wife and children were finding it very hard to come to terms with the idea of diversifying the portfolio. They found all sorts of excuses to justify holding on to that stock, as its price fell by almost 75% over two years. The family's two advisors, in my view, clearly did not do their jobs. The case for diversifying away from the single holding was clear-cut.

Helping an individual investor travel on the road to optimality also requires the wealth manager to serve as a trusted professional advisor and educator. He or she must be firmly grounded in the details of the profession and share those insights in a careful fashion with the investor. This can be counter-intuitive, as it involves placing intellectual honesty ahead of any short-term business benefit.

The need for a broader set of skills

The successful wealth manager must be able to improvise to help his or her clients deal with the issues at hand. Therein lies an important and exciting difference between the world of the individual investor and the institutional world. With the science or even the art of private wealth management still a work in progress, there is ample room for creativity. Consider Statman's behavioral portfolio pyramid,[1] reproduced in Exhibit 19.1, which aligns individual goals with specific subportfolios.

Behavioral portfolios are constructed not as a whole but layer by layer, where each layer is associated with a goal and is filled with securities that correspond to that goal. Covariance between assets is overlooked. This is an approach that makes a great deal of sense, applicable, for instance, to individuals who need to divide their wealth between an income replacement portfolio and a growth portfolio.

We can combine the behavioral portfolio approach with Gregory Friedman's hierarchy of objectives,[2] which sets out three broad categories of personal, dynastic and philanthropic objectives, and argues that one of these categories must be the residual risk-taker. This framework allows the families of investors to articulate their goals by creating a fourth category of objectives, the others: an insurance against a future decision by the members of one particular family to change their minds. The framework would be particularly well suited to families whose members were fortunate enough that the size of their wealth was more than enough to cover relatively modest current personal needs. Even after parceling out some of the total to cover the first three goals, there would be money left over to be allocated at a future date, as they move toward discovering what the future would bring and what opportunity capital markets offered. Exhibit 19.2 illustrates a possible outcome.

Essential, therefore, is the need for the wealth manager to bring together at least three different sets of skills: investment planning, understanding of family wealth planning issues, and behavioral finance or, more broadly, psychology.

Considering the impact of taxes

The impact of taxes is not only critical, but strikes in at least two different areas: investment returns and wealth transfers. This imposes a new burden on the wealth manager that traditional portfolio managers do not often need to consider. Portfolios are normally spread over several locations, creating both investment and administrative issues. The wealth manager must adopt an integrated approach to investment, estate and financial planning. This can become quite complex, when dealing with multiple locations and thus, often, multiple ownerships of the assets in the whole portfolio.

Take this example. A family was discussing the role of family partnerships. Recall that family partnerships are vehicles that can be used to pool the assets of individual owners of the wealth, providing them access to strategies, to which they may not have access because of minimum account size or portfolio concentration issues. Often, families will create selected asset class partnerships, to allow all members to participate in all strategies, even if their own individual objectives and asset allocations differ. The manager of the family office mentioned that the family had received advice from one of its lawyers to the effect that the family would be better off focusing on a single partnership, comprising multiple asset classes. This would improve the chances that the family might benefit from gifting discounts as it transferred assets across individual owners.

The legal counselor was absolutely right to argue that certain single asset class partnerships would probably not qualify for much of a gifting discount, given the highly liquid nature of the assets they contain and despite the minority position that might be gifted. The pure investment advice that there should be as many partnerships as there were asset classes was also fundamentally sound, when considered within the narrow investment framework.

Yet both were only partially right. A single partnership would not allow the different pockets to follow appropriately differentiated strategies. Too many partnerships would not allow the family to capitalize on all wealth transfer opportunities.

Exhibit 19.1

Behavioral portfolio

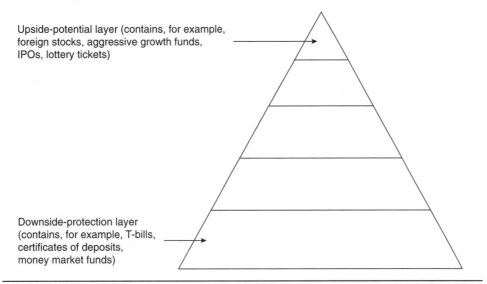

Upside-potential layer (contains, for example, foreign stocks, aggressive growth funds, IPOs, lottery tickets)

Downside-protection layer (contains, for example, T-bills, certificates of deposits, money market funds)

Integrated wealth management demands that the wealth manager consider all relevant angles and provide advice that optimizes the opportunity from both investment and estate viewpoints. Liquidity issues also require a financial planning perspective.

Tax issues are not static, but rather dynamic. This has a number of interesting implications for wealth managers, who are called upon to review structures and investment strategies. Two different ideas illustrate the point.

The potential provided by transactions with defective trusts is very significant. Recall that the assets are transferred from the point of view of estate taxes, but not with respect to income taxes. This allows the grantor of the trust, for instance, to manage both the extent of the gifts that are made over time and to react to unanticipated capital market developments. It behooves wealth managers to be fully conversant with these strategies and tools to help their clients capitalize on all reasonable opportunities.

Taxes can also provide unique opportunities to be creative. Working with one client, we discovered the potential to locate unrelated strategies within the same holding vehicle and, in the process, to create unexpected tax efficiencies, taking advantage of the U.S. tax law that classifies income under both passive and active categories. Pooling in the same structure an investment that generates systematic passive but not necessarily real losses – depreciation, for instance – and another that generates substantial realized passive capital gains, can shelter the latter in a very effective fashion. The wealth manager should set the goal to scan for potential strategies on a continuous basis to help the client benefit from maximum tax efficiency.

Understanding the need to focus on taxes highlights at least two additional skills, which our wealth manager must now have. First, he or she must have a solid grounding in estate planning and fiduciary management. Clearly, one does not expect a wealth manager to replace

Exhibit 19.2

Resulting portfolio

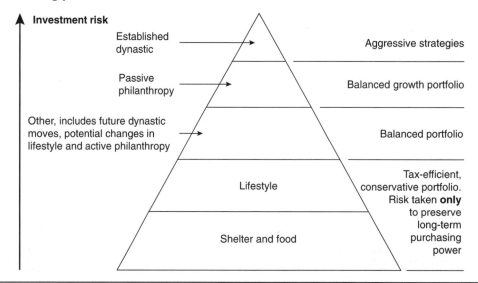

an estate lawyer: this is often prohibited by regulatory considerations and would at any rate be counterproductive. At the same time, a wealth manager needs to be sufficiently conversant with the issues in order that he or she can integrate the estate planning solutions into a broader plan. Critically, the wealth manager must understand and explain the interactions between any estate planning solution and the current investment plan, on the one hand, and the new or lost opportunities it creates, on the other.

Second, a wealth planner must have a solid understanding of current taxation considerations. Again, we do not anticipate that he or she would replace the investor's trusted tax accountant. Yet the wealth advisor must be able to understand the implications of changes in tax laws, and to integrate the various opportunities afforded by the country's tax code to optimize the portfolio's after-tax performance.

Focusing on the whole portfolio

The wealth manager must focus on the whole portfolio, though this will likely prove the most challenging task to professionals schooled in the institutional world of increasingly sharp specialization. In the preceding pages, we have encountered at least five different instances where thinking of the portfolio as a whole required both a significant change in attitude on the part of the wealth manager, and novel solutions or approaches.

Adopting a different portfolio construction model

Taxable investors are better served by a portfolio structure that emphasizes the extremes of the tax efficiency and portfolio activity ranges. A 'barbell portfolio,' comprising some exposure to tax-efficient and 'hyper' tax-efficient strategies, on the one hand, and to tax-inefficient, high-value-added strategies, on the other hand, will often produce better returns than the traditional alternative. This forces the wealth manager to become more conversant with nontraditional strategies, such as hedge funds or concentrated portfolios, and with tax-efficient approaches, such as passive or passive structured processes.

Playing a new role: total portfolio coordinator

The need for a portfolio coordinator arises on many levels. At the most basic level, the portfolio coordinator can help the managers responsible for individual mandates work together to the benefit of the investor, for instance by avoiding the most obvious mistakes or missed opportunities, such as wash sales, or the use of the most appropriate tax lot, even if it is technically held by another manager. More sophisticated is the need for the portfolio coordinator to ensure that systematically harvested losses are used in the way that is most beneficial to the total portfolio. Finally, moving beyond the pure investment dimension, the portfolio coordinator can use charitable gifting processes to manage down the unrealized capital gains found in the portfolio. This is achieved by systematically gifting the most appreciated assets, even if it means that the portfolio that owns that asset and wishes to retain exposure to it must repurchase it in the market.

Abandoning the traditional style distinctions

Though intuitively attractive to the tax-exempt investor, traditional style distinctions tend to lead the investor in the wrong direction. Breaking the portfolio into overly small individual pockets can expose the investor to unnecessary friction costs as sub-indexes are rebalanced, at which point a manager tracking these sub-indexes would in turn rebalance their portfolios. This would likely result in cross-selling within the whole portfolio, creating tax liabilities with no real net change in total portfolio position. Similarly, the traditional tendency to diversify managers must be resisted, as the undeniable diversification benefits may be substantially outweighed by the tax inefficiencies thus created.

Discovering a potentially greater use for derivative securities

Disassociating the various portfolio decision axes is, in my view, both one of the most complex and one of the most promising strategies. It is complex, as it requires a level of financial engineering to which many managers are not yet accustomed. Just as one found plenty of opportunities to learn the hard way when derivatives first appeared in the world of tax-exempt investing, there is a need for managers to force themselves through the full thought process. In the words of the late Robert Engel (Treasurer of J.P. Morgan in the 1970s), they need to remember that it is extremely difficult to 'unscramble the eggs'. Yet it is also among the most promising strategies, as it provides the scope for really different approaches to tax-efficient portfolio management. These approaches, though customized to the needs of taxable individual investors, can capitalize on some of the work still ongoing within the tax-oblivious world, thus providing multiple opportunities to leverage insights across multiple client end markets for asset management firms.

Using different performance measurement requirements

Finally, we have seen that calculating an after-tax return on a narrow segment of a total portfolio, without real consideration for the whole, can at best provide incomplete information and at worst lead to misleading conclusions.

Stepping away from the detail of the portfolio

The knowledge of investment issues that our wealth manager needs is dramatically different from the traditional baggage of a portfolio manager. We have not devoted much space here to such issues as individual stock selection or investment research. In my view, we have now arrived at the biggest change the asset management industry will need to manage.

Wealth managers are true investors, but they are rarely detail-oriented individual sub-portfolio managers. They should be positioned as standing above the traditional portfolio manager, not hierarchically but chronologically. It should not be a problem that they rarely are called upon to generate detailed investment insights. These insights matter little, as their role is much more important: it involves translating detailed insights into actionable strategies that make sense in the individual context of each client's circumstances.

The more a portfolio manager is able to step away from the investment rationale of a particular piece of raw investment insight, the more he or she is able to do the right thing for the portfolio. The analogy of an Impressionist painting may help: the closer one is to the picture, the less able one is to see and appreciate it, but move away from it and it reveals itself in its full beauty.

In summary

Our successful wealth manager is thus

- a strong investor;
- someone with a solid understanding of tax accounting, as well as financial and estate planning issues; and
- a trusted advisor who appreciates the specifics of each client's psychology and the tenets of behavioral finance.

His or her investment skills encompass the full spectrum from planning to execution. He or she understands and has the ability to explain a wide array of investment strategies, encompassing both traditional and nontraditional approaches, to deal with physical as well as derivative transactions, and to judge other investment managers.

Tax-efficient wealth management is, in my view, the new frontier in the asset management industry. It has the potential to create as much change in the landscape as the advent of modern portfolio theory did to the institutional investment management world. The industry is changing, with the inevitable implication that the needs of individual investors will be better served tomorrow than they are today.

---

[1] See Statman, Meir, 'Behavioral Finance: Past Battles, Future Engagements,' *Financial Analysts Journal*, Vol. 55, No. 6, November/December 1999, pp. 18–28.

[2] See Friedman, Gregory R., 'Philanthropy in Estate Planning,' AIMR Conference Proceedings – Continuing Education, *Investment Counseling for Private Clients* III, March 27–28, 2001, pp. 65–72.

Bibliography

Albrecht, Steven. 'Changes in the Private Wealth Marketplace.' *The Journal of Wealth Management*, Fall 2000, pp. 59-67.

Alletzhauser, Al. *The House of Nomura*, Bloomsbury, Great Britain, 1990, pp. 144-145.

Ambachtsheer, Keith P. 'Active Management that Adds Value: Reality or Illusion?' *The Journal of Portfolio Management*, Fall 1994, pp. 89-93.

Ankrim, Ernest. 'Risk-Adjusted Performance Attribution.' *Financial Analysts Journal*, Vol. 48, No. 2, March/April 1992, pp. 75-82.

Ankrim, Ernest M., and Paul Bouchey. 'When Diversification Hurts: The Total Portfolio Approach to Tax-Sensitive Asset Allocation.' *The Journal of Private Portfolio Management*, Summer 2000, pp. 83-88.

Anson, Mark J.P. 'The Impact of the Taxpayer Relief Act of 1997 on Derivatives Transactions.' *The Journal of Derivatives*, Summer 1998, pp. 62-72.

Anson, Mark J.P. 'Maximizing Utility with Commodity Futures Diversification.' *The Journal of Portfolio Management*, Summer 1999, pp. 86-94.

Anson, Mark J.P. 'Selecting a Hedge Fund Manager.' *The Journal of Private Portfolio Management*, Winter 2000, pp. 45-52.

Anson, Mark J.P. 'Performance Presentation Standards: Which Rules Apply When?' *Financial Analysts Journal*, Vol. 57, No. 2, March/April 2001, pp. 53-61.

Apelfeld, Roberto, Gordon Fowler, Jr., and James Gordon, Jr. 'Tax-Aware Equity Investing.' *The Journal of Portfolio Management*, Winter 1996, pp. 18-28.

Apelfeld, Roberto, Michael Granito, and Akis Psarris. 'Active Management of Taxable Assets: A Dynamic Analysis of Manager Alpha.' *The Journal of Financial Engineering*, Vol.5, No. 2 (1997) pp. 117-146.

Apelfeld, Roberto, and Jean L.P. Brunel, CFA. 'Asset Allocation for Private Investors.' *The Journal of Private Portfolio Management,* Spring 1998, pp. 37-54.

Appelbach, Jr., Richard O. 'The Capital Gains Tax Penalty?' *The Journal of Portfolio Management*, Summer 1995, pp. 80-88.

Arnott, Robert D., Andrew L. Berkin, and Jia Ye. 'How Well have Taxable Investors Been Served in the 1980s and 1990s?' *The Journal of Portfolio Management*, Summer 2000, pp. 84-94.

Arnott, Robert D., Andrew L. Berkin and Jia Ye. 'Loss Harvesting: What's it Worth to the Taxable Investor?' *The Journal of Wealth Management*, Spring 2001, pp. 10-18.

Arnott, Robert D. and Robert H. Jeffrey. 'Is Your Alpha Big Enough to Cover its Taxes?' *The Journal of Portfolio Management*, Spring 1993, pp. 15-25.

Asness, C.S. 'Why not 100% Equities?' *The Journal of Portfolio Management*, Winter 1996, pp. 29-34.

Asness, Clifford S., Jacques A. Friedman, Robert J. Krail, and John M. Liew. 'Style Timing: Value versus Growth.' *The Journal of Portfolio Management*, Spring 2000, pp. 50-60.

Bibliography

Association for Investment Management Research Performance Presentation Standards (AIMR-PPS). *Report of the Subcommittee on Taxable Portfolios,* Charlottesville, VA. (July 1994), pp. 10-13.

AIMR – Invitation to Comment. *Redrafting the After-Tax Provisions of the AIMR-PPS Standards,* 5/23/2001.

Baieri, Gary T. and Peng Chen. 'Choosing Managers and Funds.' *The Journal of Portfolio Management,* Winter 2000, pp. 47-53.

Bailey, Jeffery V. 'Are Manager Universes Acceptable Performance Benchmarks?' *The Journal of Portfolio Management,* Spring 1992, pp. 9-13.

Barber, Brad M., and Terrance Odean. 'The Courage of Misguided Convictions.' *Financial Analysts Journal,* Vol. 55, No. 6, November/December 1999, pp. 41-55.

Bauman W. Scott and Robert E. Miller. 'Can Managed Portfolio Performance be Predicted?' *The Journal of Portfolio Management,* Summer 1994, pp. 31-40.

Bauman, W. Scott and Robert E. Miller. 'Portfolio Performance Rankings in Stock Market Cycles.' *Financial Analysts Journal,* Vol. 51, No. 2, March/April 1995, pp.79-87.

Bauman, W. Scott, Robert E. Miller. 'Investor Expectations and the Performance of Value Stocks versus Growth Stocks, *The Journal of Portfolio Management,* Spring 1997, pp. 57-68.

Bauman, Scott W., C. Mitchell Conove, and Robert E. Miller. 'Investor Overreaction in International Stock Markets.' *The Journal of Portfolio Management,* Summer 1999, pp. 102-111.

Baxter, M. and U. Jermann. 'The International Diversification Puzzle is Worse than You Think.' *American Economic Review,* March 1997, pp. 170-180.

Beckers, Stan. 'Manager Skill and Investment Performance: How Strong is the Link?' *The Journal of Portfolio Management,* Summer 1997, pp. 9-23.

Bernatzi, Shlomo, and Richard H. Thaler. 'Myopic Loss Aversion and the Equity Premium Puzzle.' *Quarterly Journal of Economics,* February 1995, pp. 73-92.

Bernstein, Peter L. *Capital Ideas,* The Free Press, a Division of McMillan, Inc. New York. 1992.

Bernstein, Peter L. *Against The Gods, the Remarkable Story of Risk,* John Wiley & Sons, Inc. 1996, pp. 69-70.

Bernstein, Peter L. 'Are Stocks the Best Place to be in the Long Run? A Contrary Opinion.' *The Journal of Investing,* Winter 1996, pp. 9-12.

Bierman Jr., Harold. 'Bubbles, Theory, and Market Timing.' *The Journal of Portfolio Management,* Fall 1995, pp. 54-56.

Bierman, Jr., Harold. 'A Utility Approach to the Portfolio Allocation Decision and the Investment Horizon.' *The Journal of Portfolio Management,* Fall 1998, pp. 81-87.

Bierman, Harold, Jr. 'Why not 100% Equities?: Comment.' *The Journal of Portfolio Management,* Winter 1998, pp.70-73.

Billingsley, Randall S., and Don M. Chance. 'Benefits and Limitations of Diversification Among Commodity Trading Advisors.' *The Journal of Portfolio Management,* Fall 1996, pp. 65-80.

Blazzard, Norse and Robert Stone. 'Offshore Variable Insurance Products.' *The Journal of Private Portfolio Management,* Winter 1999, pp. 37-40.

Bogle, John C. 'Selecting Equity Mutual Funds.' *The Journal of Portfolio Management,* Winter 1992, pp. 94-100.

Bogle, John C. 'Mutual Funds: Parallaxes and Taxes.' Speech to the Association for Investment Management and Research. November 12, 1997.

Bottazzi, L., P. Pesenti, and E. van Wincoop. 'Wages, Profits and the International Portfolio Puzzle.' *European Economic Review,* Vol. 40 (1996), pp. 49-54.

Bowen, John J., and Meir Statman. 'Performance Games.' *The Journal of Portfolio Management,* Winter 1997, pp. 8-15.

Brinson, Gary P., L. Randolf Hood, and Gilbert L. Beebower. 'Determinants of Portfolio Performance.' *Financial Analysts Journal,* Vol. 42, No. 4, July/August 1986.

Brinson, Brinson, Gary P., Brian D. Singer, and Gilbert L. Beebower. 'Determinants of Portfolio Performance II: An Update.' *Financial Analysts Journal,* Vol. 47, No. 3, May/June 1991, pp. 40-48.

Brocato, Joe, and P.R. Chandy. 'Does Market Timing Really Work in the Real World?' *The Journal of Portfolio Management*, Winter 1994, pp.39-44.

Brocato, Joe, and P.R. Chandy. 'Market Timing Can Work in the Real World: Comment.' *The Journal of Portfolio Management*, Spring 1995, pp.82-84.

Browne, Sid. 'The Risk and Rewards of Minimizing Shortfall Probability.' *The Journal of Portfolio Management*, Summer 1999, pp. 76-85.

Brunel, Jean L.P. 'The Upside-Down World of Tax-Aware Investing.' *Trust and Estates*, February 1997, pp. 34-42.

Brunel, Jean L.P. 'A Second Look at Absolute Return Strategies.' *The Journal of Private Portfolio Management*, Spring 1998, pp. 67-78.

Brunel, Jean L.P. 'Why should Taxable Investors be Cautious when using Traditional Efficient Frontier Tools?' *The Journal of Private Portfolio Management*, Winter 1998, pp. 35-50.

Brunel, Jean L.P. 'A Tax-Aware Approach to the Management of a Multi-Asset Class Portfolio.' *The Journal of Private Portfolio Management*, Spring 1999, pp. 57-70.

Brunel, Jean L.P. 'The Role of Alternative Assets in Tax-Efficient Portfolio Construction.' *The Journal of Private Portfolio Management*, Summer 1999, pp. 9-26.

Brunel, Jean L.P. 'Revisiting the Fallacy of Market-Timing in an After-Tax Context.' *The Journal of Private Portfolio Management*, Fall 1999, pp. 16-26.

Brunel, Jean L.P. 'Tax-Aware Equity Investing.' AIMR Conference Proceedings. *Investment Counseling for Private Clients II*, November 9-10, 1999, pp. 50-57.

Brunel, Jean L.P. 'Active Style Diversification in an After-Tax Context: An Impossible Challenge? *The Journal of Private Portfolio Management*, Spring 2000, pp. 41-50.

Brunel, Jean L.P. 'An Approach to After-Tax Performance Benchmarking.' *The Journal of Wealth Management*, Winter 2000, pp. 61-67.

Brunel, Jean L.P. 'Asset Location – The Critical Variable: A Case Study.' *The Journal of Wealth Management*, Summer 2001, pp. 27-43.

Brunel, Jean L.P. 'A Tax-Efficient Portfolio Construction Model.' *The Journal of Wealth Management,* Fall 2001, pp.43-50.

Brush, John S. 'Comparisons and Combinations of Long and Long/Short Strategies.' *Financial Analysts Journal*, Vol. 53, No. 3, May/June 1997, pp.81-89.

Budge, G. Scott. 'The Psychology of Investments: An Overview of Emerging Insights.' *The Journal of Wealth Management*, Summer 2000, pp. 39-52.

Buetow, Gerald W. and Hal Ratner. 'The Dangers in Using Return Based Style Analysis in Asset Allocation.' *The Journal of Wealth Management*, Fall 2000, pp. 26-38.

Buetow, Jr., Gerald W., Robert R. Johnson, and David E. Runkle. 'The Inconsistency of Return-Based Style Analysis.' *The Journal of Portfolio Management*, Spring 2000, pp. 61-77.

Butler, Kirt C., and Dale L. Domian. 'Risk, Diversification, and the Investment Horizon.' *The Journal of Portfolio Management*, Spring 1991, pp. 41-48.

Caliendo, Frank, W. Cris Lewis and Tyler J. Bowles. 'New Findings on Strategic IRA Investing.' *The Journal of Wealth Management*, Spring 2001, pp. 49.53.

325

Camerer, Colin F. 'Prospect Theory in the Wild – Evidence from the Field.' *Choices, Value, and Frames*, Daniel Kahneman and Amos Tversky, eds., Russell Sage Foundation, Cambridge University Press, 2000, pp. 288-300.

Camerer, Colin F., and Dan Lovallo. 'Overconfidence and Excess Entry – An Experimental Approach.' Choices, Value, and Frames, Daniel Kahneman and Amos Tversky, eds., Russell Sage Foundation, Cambridge University Press, 2000, pp. 414-423.

Cattanach, Katherine A., Mary Frances Kelley, and Gail Marmorstein Sweeney. 'Hidden Treasure: A Look Into Private Equity's History, Future, and Lure.' *The Journal of Private Portfolio Management*, Summer 1999, pp. 27-34.

Chandy, P.R., and William Reichenstein. 'Market Surges and Market Timing.' *The Journal of Investing*, Summer 1993, pp.41-46.

Christopherson, Jon A. 'Equity Style Classification.' *The Journal of Portfolio Management*, Spring 1995, pp. 32-43.

Christopherson, Jon A., and Andrew L. Turner. 'Volatility and Predictability of Manager Alpha.' *The Journal of Portfolio Management*, Fall 1991, pp. 5-12.

Chopra, Vijay K., and William T. Ziemba. 'The Effect of Errors in Means, Variances, and Covariances on Optimal Portfolio Choice.' *The Journal of Portfolio Management*, Winter 1993, pp. 6-11.

Clarke, Roger G., Scott Krase, and Meir Staman. 'Tracking Errors, Regret, and Tactical Asset Allocation.' The *Journal of Portfolio Management*, Spring 1994, pp. 16-24.

Clarke, Roger G., and Meir Statman. 'The DJIA Crossed 652,230.' *The Journal of Portfolio Management*, Winter 2000, pp. 89-94.

Clayman, Michelle. 'Excellence Revisited.' *Financial Analysts Journal*, Vol. 49, No. 3, May/June 1993, pp. 61-65.

Cogin, Daniel T., and Frank J. Fabozzi. *The Handbook of Equity Style Management*, Mew Hope, PA: Frank J. Fabozzi Associates, 1995.

Cohen, James R., Jeffrey S. Bortnick and Nancy L. Jacob. 'Tax-Efficient Investing Using Private Placement Variable Life Insurance and Annuities.' *The Journal of Private Portfolio Management*, Winter 1999, pp. 27-36.

Constantinides, G.M. 'Optimal Stock Trading with Personal Taxes.' *Journal of Financial Economics*, (13) (1984), pp. 65-89.

Daniel, Kent, and Sheridan Titman. 'Market Efficiency in an Irrational World.' *Financial Analysts Journal*, Vol. 55, No. 6, November/December 1999, pp. 28-40.

Davidson III, R.B. 'The Value of Tax Management for Bond Portfolios.' *The Journal of Private Portfolio Management*, Spring 1999, pp. 49-56.

Dickson, J.M., J.B. Shoven, and C. Sialm. 'Tax Externalities of Equity Mutual Funds.' *National Tax Journal*, 53, 3.2 (2000), pp. 607-628.

Edwards, Franklin R., and Mustafa Onur Caglayan. 'Hedge Fund and Commodity Fund Investments in Bull and Bear Markets.' *The Journal of Portfolio Management*, Summer 2001, pp. 97-108.

Eichhorn, David, Francis Gupta and Eric Stubbs. 'Using Constraints to Improve the Robustness of Asset Allocation.' *The Journal of Portfolio Management*, Spring 1998, pp. 41-48.

Eller, M.B. 'Federal Taxation of Wealth Transfers, 1992-1995.' *Statistics of Income Bulletin*, Winter 1996-1997, pp. 8-63.

Ellis, Charles *Investment Policy: How to Win the Loser's Game*, Second edition. Business One Irwin, Homewood, Illinois, 1993.

Ellis, Charles D. 'Levels of the Game.' *The Journal of Portfolio Management*, Winter 2000, pp. 12-15.

Etzioni, Ethan S. 'Indexing can be Beat.' *The Journal of Portfolio Management*, Fall 1992, pp. 24-26.

Ewing, Terzah, and Jeff Bailey. 'Dashed Futures: How a Trading Firm's Founders were Blindsided by Bombshell.' *The Wall Street Journal,* February 18, 1999.

Ezra, D. Don. 'Asset Allocation by Surplus Optimization.' *Financial Analysts Journal*, Vol.47, No.1, January/February 1991, pp. 51-57.

Fant, L. Franklin, and Edward S. O'Neal. 'Do You Need More than One Manager for A Given Equity Style?' *The Journal of Portfolio Management*, Summer 1999, pp. 68-75.

Fender, William E., and Brian P. Cunningham. 'What's the Chance of That Happening?' *The Journal of Private Portfolio Management*, Winter 1999, pp. 51-56.

Fergusson, Robert. 'On Crashes.' *Financial Analysts Journal*, Vol.45, No.2, March/April 1989, pp. 42-52.

Fergusson, Robert and Yusif Simaan. 'Portfolio Composition and the Investment Horizon Revisited.' *The Journal of Portfolio Management*, Summer 1996, pp. 62-67.

Ferri, Michael G., and Chung-ki Min. 'Evidence that the Stock Market Overreacts and Adjusts.' *The Journal of Portfolio Management*, Spring 1996, pp. 71-76.

Ferson, Wayne E., and Vincent A. Warther. 'Evaluating Fund Performance in a Dynamic Market.' *Financial Analysts Journal*, Vol. 52, No.6, November/December 1996, pp. 20-28.

Finnerty, John D., and Dean Lestikow. 'The Behavior of Equity and Debt Risk Premiums.' *The Journal of Portfolio Management,* Summer 1993, pp. 73-82, together with comment and reply in the Summer 1994 issue of the same publication.

Fisher, Kenneth L., and Meir Statman. 'The Mean-Variance Optimization Puzzle: Security Portfolios and Food Portfolios.' *Financial Analysts Journal*, Vol. 53, No. 4, July/August 1997, pp. 41-50.

Friedman, Gregory R. 'Philanthropy in Estate Planning.' AIMR Conference Proceedings – Continuing Education. *Investment Counseling for Private Clients III*, March 27-28, 2001, pp. 65-72.

Froot, Kenneth A. 'Hedging Portfolios with Real Assets.' *The Journal of Portfolio Management*, Summer 1995, pp. 60-77.

Gallo, John G., and Larry J. Lockwood. 'Benefits of Proper Style Classification of Equity Portfolio Managers.' *The Journal of Portfolio Management*, Spring 1997, pp. 47-56.

Garcia, C.B., F.J. Gould, and Douglas C. Mitchell. 'The Historical Validity of Shortfall Estimates.' *The Journal of Portfolio Management*, Summer 1992, pp. 36-41.

Giles, Lionel M.A. *Sun Tzu on The Art of War: The Oldest Military Treatise in the World,* First published in 1910.

Gilovich, Tom, Robert Vallone, and Amos Tversky. 'The Hot Hand in Basketball: On the Misperception of Random Sequences.' *Cognitive Psychology*, 1985, pp. 295-314.

Goetzman, William N. and Franklin R. Edwards. 'Short-Horizon Inputs and Long-Horizon Portfolio Choices.' *The Journal of Portfolio Management*, Summer 1994, pp. 76-81.

Goetzman, William N., and Roger G. Ibbotson. 'Do Winners Repeat?' *The Journal of Portfolio Management*, Winter 1994, pp. 9-18.

Goodwin, Thomas H. 'The Information Ratio.' *Financial Analysts Journal*, Vol. 54, No. 4, July/August 1998, pp. 34-43.

Gordon, Robert N. 'Hedging Low Cost Basis Stock.' AIMR Conference Proceedings: *Investment Counseling for Private Clients III*, March 27-28, 2001, pp. 39-44

Gordon, Robert N., and Jan Rosen. 'The Benefits and Methods of Harvesting Your Losses, and Not Just at Year-End.' *The Journal of Wealth Management,* Fall 2001, pp.60-63

Granatelli, Andy, and John D. Martin. 'Management Quality and Investment Performance.' *Financial Analysts Journal*, Vol. 40, No.6, November/December 1984, pp. 72-74.

327

Gray, William S. 'Historical Returns, Inflation and Future Return Expectations.' *Financial Analysts Journal*, Vol. 49, No. 4, July/August 1993, pp.35-45.

Granito, Michael R. 'Bond Portfolio Immunization.' Lexington Books D.C. Heath and Company, Lexington Massachusetts, Toronto, Canada. 1984.

Greer, Robert J. 'What is an Asset Class Anyway?' *The Journal of Portfolio Management*, Winter 1997, pp.86-91.

Grerend, William J. *Fundamentals of Hedge Fund Investing – A Professional Investor's Guide*, McGraw-Hill, 1998.

Grinold, Richard C., and Mark Stuckelman. 'The Value Added/Turnover Frontier.' *The Journal of Portfolio Management*, Summer 1993, pp. 8-17.

Grinold, R.C., and R.N. Kahn. *Active Portfolio Management*. Burr Ridge, IL. Richard D. Irwin, Inc., 1995.

Gross, Leroy. *The Art of Selling Intangibles: How to Make Your Million ($) by Investing Other People's Money*, New York: New York Institute of Finance, 1982.

Gunthorpe, Deborah, and Haim Levy. 'Portfolio Composition and the Investment Horizon.' *Financial Analysts Journal*, January-February 1994, pp. 51-56.

Gupta, Francis, Robertus Prajogi, and Eric Stubbs. 'The Information Ratio and Performance.' *The Journal of Portfolio Management*, Fall 1999, pp. 33-39.

Gurney, Kathleen. *Your Money Personality*, Doubleday, New York 1988.

Hammond, Dennis. R. 'Cloudy Days and Sunny Days.' *The Journal of Investing*, Spring 1995, pp. 82-83.

Hansson, Björn, and Mattias Persson. 'Time Diversification and Estimation Risk.' *Financial Analysts Journal*, Vol.56, No. 5, September/October 2000, pp. 55-62.

Harlow III, W. V. 'Asset Allocation in a Downside-Risk Framework.' *Financial Analysts Journal*, Vol. 47, No. 5, September/October 1991, pp. 28-40.

Haugen, Robert A., and Nardin L. Baker. 'The Efficient Market Inefficiency of Capitalization Weighted Stock Portfolios.' *The Journal of Portfolio Management*, Spring 1991, pp. 35-40.

Healey, Thomas J., and Donald J. Hardy. *Financial Analysts Journal*, Vol. 53, No.4, July/August 1997, pp. 58-65.

Hill, Joanne M., and Humza Naviwala. 'Synthetic and Enhanced Index Strategies Using Futures on U.S. Indexes.' *The Journal of Portfolio Management*, 25th Anniversary Issue, May 1999, pp. 61-74.

Hirschey, Mark. 'How Much is a Tulip Worth?' *Financial Analysts Journal*, Vol.54, No.4, July/August 1998, pp. 11-17.

Holton, Glyn A. 'Transient Effects in Taxable Equity Investment.' *Financial Analysts Journal*, Vol. 49, No.3, May/June 1994, pp. 70-75.

Hopewell, L. 'Decision Making Under Uncertainty: A Wake Up Call for the Financial Planning Profession.' *Journal of Financial Planning*, 10(5)(1997), pp. 84-91.

Horvitz, Jeffrey. 'Asset Classes and Asset Allocation: Problems of Classification.' *The Journal of Private Portfolio Management*, Spring 2000, pp. 27-32.

Hughes, James E. Jr. 'Modern Portfolio Theory, Estate Taxes, and Investor Allocation.' *The Journal of Private Portfolio Management*. Spring 1998, pp.8-12.

Hughes, James E., Jr. *Family Wealth: Keeping it in the Family*, Princeton Junction, NJ: NetWrx, 1997, pp. 61-66.

Hulbert, Mark. 'Money and Investments: Which Eggs, Which Baskets?' *Forbes*, October 23, 1995, p.334.

Ibbotson, Roger G., and Paul D. Kaplan. 'Does Asset Allocation Policy Explain 40, 90, or 100 Percent of Performance?' *Financial Analysts Journal*, Vol. 56, No. 1, January/February 2000, pp. 26-33.

Ikenberry, David, Richard Schockley and Kent Womak. 'Why Active Fund Managers often Underperform the S&P 500: The Impact of Size and Skewness.' *The Journal of Private Portfolio Management*, Spring 1998, pp. 13-26.

328

Ingersoll, Jonathan E. *Theory of Financial Decision Making*, Rowman & Littlefield, Studies in Financial Economics, NJ, 1987, pp. 122-124.

Jacob, Nancy L. 'Taxes, Investment Strategy and Diversifying Low-Basis Stock.' *Trusts and Estates*, May 1995, pp. 8-20.

Jacob, Nancy L. 'After-Tax Asset Allocation: A Case Study.' *The Journal of Private Portfolio Management*, Spring 1998, pp. 55-66.

Jacobs, Bruce I., and Kenneth N. Levy. 'Long/Short Equity Investing.' *The Journal of Portfolio Management*, Fall 1993, pp. 52-63.

Jacobs, Bruce I., and Kenneth N. Levy. '20 Myths About Long-Short.' *Financial Analysts Journal*, Vol. 52, No. 5, September/October 1996, pp. 81-85.

Jacobs, Bruce I., and Kenneth N. Levy. 'Alpha Transport With Derivatives.' *The Journal of Portfolio Management*, 25th Anniversary Issue, May 1999, pp. 55-60.

Jeffrey, Robert. 'Tax-Efficient Portfolio Management: Easier Said than Done.' *The Journal of Wealth Management*, Summer 2001, pp. 9-15.

Johansson, Frederik, Michael J. Seiler, and Mikael Tjarnberg. 'Measuring Downside Portfolio Risk.' *The Journal of Portfolio Management*, Fall 1999, pp. 96-107.

Johnson, Eric J., John Hershey, Jacqueline Meszaros, and Howard Kunreuther. 'Framing, Probability Distortions, and Insurance Decisions.' *Choices, Value, and Frames*, Daniel Kahneman and Amos Tversky, eds., Russell Sage Foundation, Cambridge University Press, 2000, pp. 224-240.

Jones, C.P. and J.W. Wilson. 'Probabilities Associated with Common Stock Returns.' *The Journal of Portfolio Management*, Fall 1995, pp.21-32.

Jones, C.P. and J.W. Wilson. 'The Incidence and Impact of Losses from Stocks and Bonds.' *The Journal of Private Portfolio Management*, Summer 1998, pp.31-40.

Kahn, Ronald N., and Andrew Rudd. 'Does Historical Performance Predict Future Performance?' *Financial Analysts Journal*, Vol.51 November/December 1995, pp.43-52.

Kahneman, Daniel, and Amos Tversky. 'Advances in Prospect Theory: Cumulative Representation of Uncertainty.' *Journal of Risk and Uncertainty*, (1992), pp.297-323.

Kahneman, Daniel, and Mark W. Riepe. 'Aspects of Investor Psychology.' *The Journal of Portfolio Management*, Summer 1998, pp. 52-65.

Kahneman, Daniel, and Amos Tversky. 'Conflict Resolution – A Cognitive Perspective.' *Choices, Value, and Frames*, Daniel Kahneman and Amos Tversky, eds., Russell Sage Foundation, Cambridge University Press, 2000, pp. 473-487.

Kahneman, Daniel, and Amos Tversky. 'Prospect Theory – An Analysis of Decision under Risk.' *Choices, Value, and Frames*, Daniel Kahneman and Amos Tversky, eds., Russell Sage Foundation, Cambridge University Press, 2000, pp. 17-43.

Kallberg, Jarl G., and William T. Ziemba. 'Mis-Specification in Portfolio Selection Problems.' G. Bamberg and K. Spremann, eds., *Risk and Capital: Lecture Notes in Economics and Mathematical Systems*, New York: Springer-Verlag, 1984.

Klemkosky, Robert C., and Rakesh Bharati. 'Time-Varying Expected Returns and Asset Allocation.' *The Journal of Portfolio Management*, Summer 1995, pp. 80-88.

Kritzman, Mark. 'What Practitioners Need to Know … About Optimization?' *Financial Analysts Journal*, Vol. 48, No. 5, September/October 1992, pp. 10-13.

Kritzman, Mark. 'What Practitioners Need to Know … About Time Diversification?' *Financial Analyst Journal*, Vol. 50, No. 1, January-February 1994, pp. 14-19.

Kritzman, Mark. 'What Practitioners Need to Know … About Hypothesis Testing?' *Financial Analysts Journal*, Vol. 50, No. 4, July/August 1994, pp.18-22.

Kuberek, Robert C. 'Using Style Factors to Differentiate Equity Performance over Short Horizons.' *The Journal of Portfolio Management*, Spring 1998, pp. 33-40.

Kuhn, Thomas S. 'The Structure of Scientific Revolutions, Second Edition, Enlarged,' O. Neurath, R. Carnap, and C. Morris, eds., Foundation of the Unity of Science, Vol. 2. Chicago: University of Chicago Press, 1970.

Larsen, Glen A. Jr., and Bruce G. Resnick. 'Empirical Insights on Indexing.' *The Journal of Portfolio Management*, Fall 1998, pp. 51-60.

Larsen, Glen A., Jr., and Gregory Wozniak. ' Market Timing Can Work in the Real World.' *The Journal of Portfolio Management*, Spring 1995, pp.74-81.

Lebaron, Dean. 'A Universal Model of Equity Styles.' *The Journal of Portfolio Management*, Fall 1994, pp. 85-88.

Lederman, Jess, and Robert A. Klein, eds., *Hedge Funds – Investment and Portfolio Strategies for the Institutional Investor*, Irwin, 1995.

Lederman, Jess, and Robert A. Klein, eds. *Market Neutral – State-of-the-Art Strategies for Every Market Environment*, Irwin, 1996.

Levy, Haim. 'The CAPM and the Investment Horizon.' *The Journal of Portfolio Management*, Vol. 7, 2 (1980), pp. 32-40.

Levy, Haim. 'The CAPM and the Investment Horizon: Reply.' *The Journal of Portfolio Management*, Vol. 9, 1 (1982), pp. 66-68.

Levy, Haim. 'Measuring Risk and Performance over Alternative Investment Horizons.' *Financial Analysts Journal*, Vol. 40, 2, (1984), pp. 61-68.

Levy, Haim, and P.A. Samuelson. 'The Capital Asset Pricing Model with Diverse Holding Periods.' *Management Science*, 38 (1992) pp. 1529-1542.

Levy, Haim, and Deborah Gunthorpe. 'Optimal Investment Proportions in Senior Securities and Equities under Alternative Holding Periods.' *The Journal of Portfolio Management*, Summer 1993, pp.30-36.

Levy, Haim, and Yishay Spector. 'Cross-Asset versus Time Diversification.' *The Journal of Portfolio Management*, Spring 1996, pp. 24-35.

Levy, Haim, and Allon Cohen. 'On the Risk of Stocks in the Long Run: Revisited.' *The Journal of Portfolio Management*, Spring 1998, pp. 60-69.

Lewis, Mario, and Manolis Liokadis. 'The Profitability of Style Rotation Strategies in the United Kingdom.' *The Journal of Portfolio Management*, Fall 1999, pp. 73-86.

Liang, Brian. 'Hedge Fund Performance: 1990-1999.' *Financial Analysts Journal*, Vol. 57, No. 1, January/February 2001, pp. 11-19.

Lopes, Lola. 'Between Hope and Fear: The Psychology of Risk.' *Advances in Experimental Social Psychology*, 1985, pp. 255-295.

Lucas, Andre, and Pieter Klaasen. 'Extreme Returns, Downside Risk, and Optimal Asset Allocation.' *The Journal of Portfolio Management*, Fall 1998, pp. 71-80.

Macklin, Lawrence J. 'Wealth Management through Dynasty Trusts.' *The Journal of Wealth Management,* Spring 2001, pp. 43-48.

Manning, Jerome A. *Estate Planning – How to Preserve Your Estate for Your Loved Ones?* Practicing Law Institute, New York, 1992.

Manzke, Sandra L. 'Private Placement Life Insurance.' *The Journal of Private Portfolio Management*, Summer 1999, pp. 45-48.

Marmer, Harry S., and F.K. Louis Ng. 'Mean-Semivariance Analysis of Option-Based Strategies: A Total Asset Mix Perspective.' *Financial Analysts Journal*, Vol. 49, No. 3, May/June 1993, pp. 47-54.

Markowitz, Harry M., and Gan Lin Xu. 'Data Mining Corrections.' *The Journal of Portfolio Management*, Fall 1994, pp. 60-70.

McCabe, Bernard J. 'Monte Carlo Analysis of the Impact of Portfolio Volatility on After-Tax Wealth.' *The Journal of Private Portfolio Management*, Winter 1998, pp. 22-34.

McCabe, Bernard J. 'Analytic Approximation of the Probability that a Portfolio Survives Forever.' *The Journal of Private Portfolio Management*, Spring 1999, pp. 43-48.

McFall Lamm, R. Jr. and Tanya E. Ghaleb-Harter. 'Do Hedge Funds Belong in Taxable Portfolios?' *The Journal of Wealth Management*, Summer 2001, pp. 58-73.

Meehan, James P., Daihyun Yoo, and H. Gifford Fong. 'Asset Allocation in a Taxable Environment: The Case of Nuclear Decommissioning Trusts.' *Financial Analysts Journal*, Vol. 49, No. 6, November/December 1993, pp. 67-73.

Melnikoff, Meyer. 'Investment Performance Analysis for Investors.' *The Journal of Portfolio Management*, Fall 1998, pp. 95-107.

Merrill, Craig, and Steven Thorley. 'Time Diversification: Perspectives from Option Pricing Theory.' *Financial Analysts Journal*, Vol. 52, No. 3, May/June 1996, pp.13-19.

Meyers, Darryl L. 'Asset Location: Client Goals and Objectives.' AIMR Conference Proceedings: *Investment Counseling for Private Clients III*, March 27-28 2001, pp. 11-17.

Meyers, Darryl L. 'Volatility and Mortality Risk Considerations in Estate Planning.' *The Journal of Wealth Management*, Fall 2000, pp. 52-58.

Michaud, Richard O., 'The Markowitz Optimization Enigma: Is 'Optimized' Optimal?' *Financial Analyst Journal* Vol. 45, No. 1, January/February 1989: 31-42.

Michaud, Richard O. 'Are Long-Short Equity Strategies Superior?' *Financial Analysts Journal*, Vol. 49, No. 6, November/December 1993, pp. 44-49.

Miller, Ross, and Evan Schulman. 'Money Illusion Revisited.' *The Journal of Portfolio Management*, Spring 1999, pp. 45-54.

Miller, Todd, and Timothy S. Meckel. 'Beating Index Funds with Derivatives.' *The Journal of Portfolio Management*, 25th Anniversary Issue, May 1999, pp 75-87.

Mink, Jeffrey L. 'Tax-Adjusted Equity Benchmarks.' *The Journal of Private Portfolio Management*, Winter 1998, pp. 45-55.

Minor, Dylan B. 'Beware of Index Fund Fundamentalists.' *The Journal of Portfolio Management*, Summer 2001, pp. 45-50.

Murphy, Austin. 'An Empirical Investigation into the Components of Long-Term Municipal Bond Yields.' *The Journal of Private Portfolio Management*, Spring 1998, pp. 27-36

Musumeci, Jim. 'Comment: Statistics Never Lie.' *The Journal of Portfolio Management*, Winter 1994, pp. 81-83.

Musumeci, Jim. 'Human Capital and International Diversification.' The *Journal of Private Portfolio Management*, Summer 1999, pp. 55-61.

Nagy, Robert A., and Robert W. Obenberger. 'Factors Influencing Individual Investor Behavior.' *Financial Analysts Journal*, Vol. 50, No. 4, July/August 1994, pp. 63-68.

Nesbitt, Stephen L. 'Buy High, Sell Low: Timing Errors in Mutual Fund Allocations.' *The Journal of Portfolio Management*, Fall 1995, pp. 57-61.

Nesbitt, Stephen L., and Hal W. Reynolds. 'Benchmarks for Private Market Investments.' *The Journal of Portfolio Management*, Summer 1997, pp. 85-90.

Obosco, Angelo. 'Style/Risk-Adjusted Performance.' *The Journal of Portfolio Management*, Spring 1999, pp. 65-68.

Olsen, Robert A. 'Behavioral Finance and its Implications for Stock-Price Volatility.' *Financial Analysts Journal*, Vol. 54, No. 2, March/April 1998, pp. 10-19.

Olsen, Robert A. 'Investment Risk: The Experts' Perspectives.' *Financial Analysts Journal*, Vol. 53, No. 2, March/April 1997, pp. 62-66.

Paulson, Bruce L., and Gregory Owens. 'The Economics of Charitable Remainder Trusts and Related Asset Management Issues.' *The Journal of Wealth Management*, Winter 2000, pp. 33-38.

Peters, Donald J. 'Valuing a Growth Stock.' *The Journal of Portfolio Management*, Spring 1991, pp. 49-51.

Poterba, James M. 'Estate Tax Avoidance by High Net Worth Households: Why are there so Few Tax-Free Gifts?' *The Journal of Private Portfolio Management*, Summer 1998, pp. 1-10.

Poterba, James M. 'Unrealized Capital Gains and the Measurement of After-Tax Portfolio Performance.' *The Journal of Private Portfolio Management*, Spring 1999, pp. 23-34.

Poterba, James M. 'After-Tax Performance Evaluation.' AIMR Conference Proceedings. *Investment Counseling for Private Clients II*, November 9-10, 1999, pp. 58-67.

Price, Lee N. 'Taxable Benchmarks: The Complexity Increases.' AIMR Conference Proceedings: *Investment Counseling for Private Clients III*, March 27, 2001, pp. 54-64.

Pye, Gordon B. 'Sustainable Investment Withdrawals.' *The Journal of Portfolio Management*, Summer 2000, pp. 73-83.

Quinlin, Thomas. 'Private Foundations: An Old Tool for the New Millennium.' The 8th Annual Family Office Forum, organized by the Institute for International Research, June 25-26, 2001, Chicago, IL.

Raiffa, Howard. *Decision Analysis*, Reading. MA: Addison-Wesley, 1968.

Reichenstein, William. 'Savings Vehicles and the Taxation of Individual Investors.' *The Journal of Private Portfolio Management*, Winter 1999, pp. 15-26.

Reichenstein, William. 'After-Tax Wealth and Returns Across Savings Vehicles.' *The Journal of Private Portfolio Management*, Spring 2000, pp. 9-19.

Reichenstein, William. 'Frequently Asked Questions Related to Savings Vehicles.' *The Journal of Private Portfolio Management*, Summer 2000, pp. 66-82.

Reichenstein, William. 'Calculating the Asset Allocation.' *The Journal of Wealth Management*, Fall 2000, pp. 20-25.

Reichenstein, William. 'Asset Allocation and Asset Location Decisions Revisited.' *The Journal of Wealth Management*, Summer 2001, pp. 16-26.

Reichenstein, William and Steven P. Rich. 'The Market Risk Premium and Long-Term Stock Returns.' *The Journal of Portfolio Management*, Summer 1993, pp. 63-72.

Riley, William B., and K. Victor Chow. 'Asset Allocation and Individual Risk Aversion.' *Financial Analysts Journal*, Vol. 48, No. 6, November/December 1992, pp. 32-37.

Rohweder, Herold C. 'Implementing Stock Selection Ideas: Does Tracking Error Optimization Do Any Good?' *The Journal of Portfolio Management*, Spring 1998, pp. 49-59.

Rogers, Douglas A. 'Tax-Aware Equity Manager Allocation: A Practitioner's Perspective.' *The Journal of Wealth Management,* Winter 2001, pp.39-45

Rogers, Douglas S. 'After-Tax Equity Returns for Non-Qualified Nuclear Decommissioning Trusts.' *Financial Analysts Journal*, Vol. 48, No. 4, July/August 1992, pp. 70-73

Rom, Brian M. 'The Psychology of Money: Its Impact on Individual Risk Tolerance and Portfolio Selection.' *The Journal of Wealth Management*, Fall 2000, pp. 15-19.

Rozeff, Michael S. 'Lump-Sum Investing versus Dollar-Averaging.' *The Journal of Portfolio Management*, Winter 1994, pp.45-50.

332

Russo, Edward, and Paul Shoemaker. *Decision Traps*, New York: Simon & Shuster, 1989.

Samuelson, Paul A. 'The Judgment of Economic Science on Rational Portfolio Management: Indexing, Timing and Long-Horizon Effects.' *The Journal of Portfolio Management*, Fall 1989, pp. 4-12.

Samuelson, Paul A. 'Asset Allocation can be Dangerous to Your Health.' *The Journal of Portfolio Management*, Spring 1990, pp. 5-8.

Samuelson, Paul A. 'The Long Term Case for Equities.' *The Journal of Portfolio Management*, Fall 1994, pp. 15-26.

Scherer, Bernhard. 'Cost Averaging – Fact or Myth?' *The Journal of Private Portfolio Management*, Winter 1998, pp. 18-21.

Schiereck, Dirk, Werner De Bondt, and Martin Weber. 'Contrarian and Momentum Strategies in Germany.' *Financial Analysts Journal*, Vol. 55, No. 6, November/December 1999, pp. 104-116.

Schneider, Heidi L. and John Geer. 'Stock-based Compensation: New Opportunities, New Risks for Senior Executives.' *The Journal of Wealth Management*, Summer 2001, pp. 55-57.

Shafir Eldar, Peter Diamond, and Amos Tvesky. 'Money Illusion.' *Choices, Values, and Frames*, Daniel Kahneman and Amos Tversky, eds., Russell Sage Foundation, Cambridge University Press, 2000, pp. 335-355

Sharpe, Marc J. 'Constructing the Optimal Hedge Fund of Funds.' *The Journal of Private Portfolio Management*, Summer 1999, pp. 35-44.

Sharpe, William F. 'Asset Allocation: Management Style and Performance Measurement.' *The Journal of Portfolio Management*. Winter 1992, pp. 7-19.

Sharpe, William F. 'The Sharpe Ratio.' *The Journal of Portfolio Management*, Fall 1994, pp. 49-59.

Shefrin, Hersh. 'Irrational Exuberance and Option Smiles.' *Financial Analysts Journal*, Vol. 55, No. 6, November/December 1999, pp. 91-103.

Shefrin, Hersh. 'Recent Developments in Behavioral Finance.' *The Journal of Private Portfolio Management*, Summer 2000, pp. 25-37.

Shefrin, Hersh, and Meir Statman. 'The Disposition to Sell Winners Too Early and Ride Losers Too Long: Theory and Evidence.' *Journal of Finance*, 40 (1985), pp. 770-790.

Shilling, Gary A. 'Market Timing: Better than a Buy-and-Hold Strategy.' *Financial Analysts Journal*, Vol. 48, No. 2, March/April 1992, pp. 46-50.

Shoven, John B. *The Location and Allocation of Assets in Pension and Conventional Savings Accounts*, Working Paper 493, Center for Economic Policy Research, Stanford University, March 1998

Shoven, John B. and Clemens Sialm. 'Long Run Asset Allocation for Retirement Savings.' *The Journal of Private Portfolio Management*, Summer 1998, pp. 13-26.

Shoven, John B., and Clemens Sialm. 'The Dow Jones Industrial Average: The Impact of Fixing Its Flaws.' *The Journal of Wealth Management*, Winter 2000, pp. 9-18.

Shula, Ravi, and Charles Trzcinka. 'Research on Risk and Return: Can Measures of Risk Explain Anything?' *The Journal of Portfolio Management*, Spring 1991, pp. 15-21.

Siegel, Jeremy J. 'The Shrinking Equity Premium.' *The Journal of Portfolio Management*, Fall 1999, pp. 10-17.

Siegel, Laurence B., and David Montgomery. 'Stocks, Bonds, and Bills after Taxes and Inflation.' *The Journal of Portfolio Management*, Winter 1995, pp. 17-25.

Simon De Laplace, Pierre. 'Concerning Probability.' *The Journal of Portfolio Management*, Fall 1994, pp. 8-14.

Sorensen, Eric H., Keith L. Miller, and Vele Samak. 'Allocating Between Active and Passive Management.' *Financial Analysts Journal*, Vol.54, No.5, September/October 1998, pp. 18-31.

Sortino, Frank A., and Robert Van Der Meer. 'Downside Risk.' *The Journal of Portfolio Management*, Summer 1991, pp. 27-32.

Sortino, Frank. A., and Hal J. Forsey, 'On the Use and Misuse of Downside Risk', *The Journal of Portfolio Management*, Winter 1996, pp. 35-42.

Spitzer, John J., and Sandeep Singh. 'Optimizing Retirement Savings.' *The Journal of Wealth Management*, Winter 2000, pp. 30-44.

Statman, Meir. 'A Behavioral Framework for Dollar-Cost Averaging.' *The Journal of Portfolio Management*, Fall 1995, pp. 70-79.

Statman, Meir. 'Behavioral Finance: Past Battles, Future Engagements.' *Financial Analyst Journal*, Vol. 55, No. 6, November/December 1999, pp. 18-28.

Stein, David M. 'Measuring and Evaluating Portfolio Performance After Taxes.' *The Journal of Portfolio Management*, Winter 1998, pp.117-124.

Stein, David M., and Premkumar Narasimhan. 'Of Passive and Active Equity Portfolios in the Presence of Taxes.' *The Journal of Private Portfolio Management*, Fall 1999, pp. 55-63.

Stein, David M. 'Equity Portfolio Tracking Risk in the Presence of Taxes.' AIMR Conference Proceedings: *Investment Counseling for Private Clients III*, March 27-28, 2001, pp. 45-53.

Stein, David M. 'Equity Portfolio Structure and Design in the Presence of Taxes.' *The Journal of Wealth Management*, Fall 2001, pp. 37-42.

Stewart, Scott D. 'Is Consistency of Performance a Good Measure of Manager Skill?' *The Journal of Portfolio Management*, Spring 1998, pp. 22-32.

Stoll, Hans R. 'Equity Trading Costs In-The-Large.' *The Journal of Portfolio Management*, Summer 1993, pp. 41-50.

Strongin, Steven, Melanie Petsch, and Greg Sharenow. 'Beating Benchmarks.' *The Journal of Portfolio Management*, Summer 2000 pp. 11-28.

Sun Tsu. *The Art of War,* edited and with a Foreword by James Clavel. Delacorte Press, Bantam Doubleday Dell, NY, 1983.

Swensen, David F. *Pioneering Portfolio Management – An Unconventional Approach to Institutional Investment*, The Free Press, New York, NY, 2000.

Thaler, Richard H., and Werner F.M. De Bondt, *Advances in Behavioral Finance*, The Russell Sage Foundation, Cambridge University Press, 1994.

Thaler, Richard H. 'Mental Accounting Matters.' *Choices, Value, and Frames*, Daniel Kahneman and Amos Tversky, eds., Russell Sage Foundation, Cambridge University Press, 2000, pp. 241-268.

Thaler, R.H., and J.P. Williamson. 'College and University Endowment Funds: Why Not 100% Equities?' *The Journal of Portfolio Management*, Fall 1994, pp. 27-38.

Thomas, Lee R III. 'Active Management.' *The Journal of Portfolio Management*, Winter 2000, pp. 25-32.

Thompson, Patricia M. 'Family Limited Partnerships: Pros and Cons.' AIMR Conference Proceedings: *Investment Counseling for Private Clients III*, pp. 84-93

Thorley, Steven R. 'The Time-Diversification Controversy.' *Financial Analysts Journal*, Vol.51, No. 3, May/June 1995, pp. 67-75.

Treynor, Jack L. 'The Invisible Cost of Trading.' *The Journal of Portfolio Management*, Fall 1994, pp. 71-78.

Treynor, Jack L. 'Bulls, Bears, and Market Bubbles.' *Financial Analysts Journal*, Vol. 54, No. 2, March/April 1998, pp. 69-74.

Trippi, Robert R., and Richard B. Harriff. 'Dynamic Asset Allocation Rules: Survey and Synthesis.' *The Journal of Portfolio Management*, Summer 1991, pp.19-26.

Trzcinka, Charles A. 'Equity Style Classification: Comment.' *The Journal of Portfolio Management*, Spring 1995, pp. 44-46.

Uysal, Enis, Francis H. Trainer, Jr., and Jonathan Reiss, 'Revisiting Mean-Variance Optimization.' *The Journal of Portfolio Management*, Summer 2001, pp. 71-82.

Vergin, Roger C. 'Market Timing Strategies: Can You Get Rich?' *The Journal of Investing*, Winter 1996, pp.79-86.

Wagner, Jerry C. 'Why Market Timing Works.' *The Journal of Investing*, Summer 1997, pp.78-81.

Wagner, Jerry, Steve Shellans, and Richard Paul. ' Market Timing Works Where it Matters Most ... in the Real World.' *The Journal of Portfolio Management*, Summer 1992, pp.86-90.

Wagner, Wayne H., and Evan Schulman. 'Passive Trading: Point and Counterpoint.' *The Journal of Portfolio Management*, Spring 1994, pp. 25-29.

Wahad, Mamoud, and Amit Khandwala. 'Why Not Diversify Internationally with ADR's?' *The Journal of Portfolio Management*, Winter 1993, pp. 75-82.

Waring, Barton, Duane Whitney, John Pirone, and Charles Castille. 'Optimizing Manager Structure and Budgeting Manager Risk.' *The Journal of Portfolio Management*, Spring 2000, pp. 90-104.

Welch, Scott D. 'Was Going "Short-Against-The-Box" Really a Perfect Hedge?' *The Journal of Private Portfolio Management*, Winter 1999, pp. 41-50.

Welch, Scott D. 'Diversifying Concentrated Holdings.' AIMR Conference Proceedings: *Investment Counseling for Private Clients III*, March 27-28 2001, pp. 30-35 and 42-44.

Wilson, Jack W., and Charles P. Jones. 'Long-Term Returns and Risk for Bonds.' *The Journal of Portfolio Management*, Spring 1997, pp. 15-28.

Yamaguchi, Katsumari. 'Estimating the Equity Risk Premium from Downside Probability.' *The Journal of Portfolio Management*, Summer 1994, pp. 17-27.

Zarnowitz, V. and C. Boschan. 'Cyclical Indicators: An Evaluation and New Leading Indices.' *Business Conditions Digest*, May 1975.

Zeikel, Arthur. 'Memorandum to My Daughter.' *Financial Analysts Journal*, Vol.51, No. 2, March/April 1995, pp. 7-8.